Sean Landers
Kunsthalle Zürich

jrp|ringier

Table of Contents

This monograph was first published to accompany the exhibition
SEAN LANDERS, *at the Kunsthalle Zürich, August 28–October 31, 2004*

PUBLICATION

Editor
Beatrix Ruf, Kunsthalle Zürich
Design
Gavillet & Rust
Assistance
Fabian Monod
Typeface
Genath
Editing
Beatrice Steiner
Translations
Gudrun Meier *(English-German)*
Jeanne Haunschild *(German-English)*
Proofreading
Clare Manchester *(English)*
Doris Senn *(German)*
Color Separation
Andreas Hönigl
Print
Ringier Print, Ostrawa

First edition: 2004
Second printing: 2008

ISBN 978-3-905829-87-7

Published by
JRP|Ringier
Letzigraben 134
CH–8047 Zurich
T +41 (0)43 311 27 50
F +41 (0)43 311 27 51
E info@jrp-ringier.com
www.jrp-ringier.com

Distribution:

Switzerland
Buch 2000, AVA, www.ava.ch

France
Les Presses du réel, www.lespresses-dureel.com

Germany and Austria
Vice Versa Vertrieb, www.vice-versa-vertrieb.de

UK and other European countries
Cornerhouse Publications, www.cornerhouse.org/books

USA, Canada, and Australasia
D.A.P./Distributed Art Publishers, www.artbook.com

EXHIBITION

Exhibition
Sean Landers
Beatrix Ruf
Assistance
Beatrice Steiner
Samuel Leuenberger
Alfonso Negri
Technical Support
Attila Panczel
Dany Boller

Kunsthalle Zürich
Limmatstrasse 270
CH–8005 Zurich
T +41 (0)44 272 15 15
F +41 (0)44 272 18 88
E info@kunsthallezurich.ch
www.kunsthallezurich.ch

ACKNOWLEDGEMENTS

Friedrich Petzel Gallery, New York
Andrea Rosen Gallery, New York

Kunsthalle Zürich thanks:

the generous lenders of the exhibition:
Gottfried Graf von Bismarck
Collection of Nasher Museum of Art at Duke University
Mathias van Daele
Yvonne Force Inc.
greengrassi, London
Sammlung Hoffmann
Art & Public–Cabinet PH, Geneva
Pierre Huber
Sean Landers
Peter Lecoutere & Annemarie Leloup
Dominique Levy & Dorothy Berwin, New York
Collection C. Lienart de Jeude, Brussels
Collection of Doreen Remen & Steven M. Weiner
Sammlung Ringier
Andrea Rosen Gallery, New York
Gian Enzo Sperone, New York
and those who wished not to be mentioned.

For support and assistance thanks to:
Andrea Rosen Gallery, New York
greengrassi, London
Alex Farquharson
Caoimhín Mac Giolla Leíth
Marina Bassano
Jordan Bastien
Sarah Cohen
Mimi Dusselier
André Gordts
Cornelia Grassi
Ariane Grigoteit
Jeanne Haunschild
Felix Lehner
Gudrun Meier
Michael Münch
Michelle Reyes
Renee Reyes
Andrea Rosen
Rahel Blättler
Dany Boller
Corina Enzler
Basil Kobert
Boris Knorpp
Flavio Morganti
Sandra Porchet
Nina Weber

Präsidialdepartement der Stadt Zürich
Stiftung Kunsthalle Zürich

Kultur-Stiftung der Deutschen Bank

Introduction

BEATRIX RUF

Since the early 90s, the work of Sean Landers has been one of the most fascinating and repeatedly irritating projects in contemporary art. The polar opposites of tormented self-doubt and endless self-aggrandizement run like a thread through the artist's work along with a number of symbols of failure used by the subject as a strategy to preserve himself from impending failure. Sean Landers undertakes this project as an artist. He can do anything (write, paint, sculpt, perform, shoot videos, write reviews) and has doubts about it all. Even doubting he does with virtuosity.

With text and video works that appear masked as conceptual art in the early 90s, he introduced into this art genre the inadequacy and taboo of the subject and the emotionality of the artist. Radical soul-baring, an emotional quarrel with his own and others' estimations, private and professional longings and torments all run through his works. He is known as the artist who – with confessional and stream-of-consciousness texts such as ART, LIFE AND GOD (1990) and [SIC] (1993), with text art and cartoons, such as FOR THE LOVE OF NOTHING (1994), with video works that filmed him or a monkey in his studio, and with 'unfinished' sculptures – presents himself as an artist who is failing with his art, his life, and his relationships. This is conceptual art about the art system with its protagonists and institutions, but is distinguished from Conceptualism's rational rules and procedures by human, emotional, and intimate disclosures.

Over the course of the past fifteen years Landers' work has repeatedly surprised his audience by the artistic production of new styles and a dabbler's input. With a formal vocabulary and a history of art motifs, he has managed to come up with a multi-faceted undertaking that revolves around the contradictions and the odyssey of human feelings, around the constructions of the subject between historical reassurance and today's incertitude, around self-aggrandizement and self-debasement, around the general human tragedy of the identity-seeking subject and naturally, and above all, around making art. Sean Landers' work is provocative in a grandiose way with contradictions and false trails. The mimicry of anti-heroic artistic existence is always also the deconstruction of the same; in his confessional writings and diverse exposures the subject is always also the object of the artist and thereby the fictionalization of his persona.

Landers' performances of the authentic bring up to date the tradition of the great 'idiots' from the history of culture and art. Jean-Yves Jouannais in his publication L'IDIOTIE – ART, VIE, POLITIQUE pointed out the difference between the 'primal idiot' who disappears in his work and the 'cunning idiot' who evades disappearance: "[...] two antithetic positions for the modern artist stand out: the one [...] with an earnest and suicidal connotation, the work as a ritual form of self-sacrifice [...] the unspoilt idiocy of Kafka, Mallarmé, Valéry, and Flaubert [...] whose works are characterized by a peculiar idiocy and self-sufficiency, are a form of suicide" and, as an opposing position, authenticity as cleverness, as cunning idiocy, such as Magritte's 'vache' period, the work of Kippenberger, Roman Signer, or Erik Satie.[1] Sean Landers' idiocy is that of cunning or idiocy as symbolic protection.

The voyeuristic access to the authentic person and to the authentic production of the artist has been shaken up several times in his works. The video ANYONE'S ORGASM (1992) turns out to be a mad trip into the private life of the artist because of the irritating codes that affect the medium: video art? Performance? Sculpture? Painting? Or what? The videos REMISSIONEM PECCATORUM (1994) and ITALIAN HIGH RENAISSANCE AND BAROQUE SCULPTURE (1993) remind us of the endurance performances of the 70s, yet Landers mimes the postures of famous classical sculptures, he fractures and counteracts iconic real time and, with iconic artistic virtuosity, the claim of video art's authenticity.

Landers has us (and himself) step into countless authenticity traps; again and again he stands before us naked in such a way that lets any kind of voyeuristic satisfaction fizzle, transforming it into a

1 Jean-Yves Jouannais: "Der Un-Untergeher," extracts from *L'idiotie – art, vie, politique*, Beaux-Arts magazine/livre, Paris, 2003; transl. by Stefan Zweifel in "Kunst & Idiotie. Eine Typologie des Vergesens. Flaubert – Kant – Warhol – Hölderlin – Dostojevsky," *ProLitteris Gazzetta*, Zurich, 2004, p 81.

shame that arises from the thought, or rather, the judgment of the shame of the 'idiots' or the exposed. Rapid categorization or assessment of Sean Landers' work often backfires when trying to analyze his work and concurrently becomes a 'déjà vu' experience.

Pablo Picasso (the resourceful craftsman-artist) and Marcel Duchamp (the resourceful conceptual artist) are the great genealogical lines along which Sean Landers develops a work that – behind the mask of the idiot and standup comic – successively penetrates the whole of art history as an arena for his own identity and his own production.

All the prototypes of the subject/artist-subject as idiots and art as idiocy have come up in his work: the 'idiot savant' of the 20th century with Landers-specific self-divestments that drive authenticity into absurdity; the 'singerie' that is introduced in the 18th century as a topic for the doubtful, aping and manipulative role of the artist and of art in I'M A CLOWN IN A WORLD OF CHIMPS (1994) or SINGERIE: LE PEINTRE (1995), SPACE-APE ON MARS (1997), and so on. Since the 19th century, the clown with his changing appearances, has played an allegory role of failure and gaucherie and a grandiose masquerade of the self (in Joyce, Miller, Mallarmé, Baudelaire, Toulouse-Lautrec, Picasso, Rouault, Beckmann, Klee, Nauman, Scholte, Borofsky, Rondinone, Cattelan, to name only a few...). And then naturally Sean Landers' personal ancestral portraits of the great artists and their works: Hogarth, Picasso, Matisse, Picabia, Michelangelo, Bernini, Ernst, Duchamp, De Chirico, Magritte (his 'période vache'), Dalí, Braque, Beckmann, which enter the artist's works as pastiches (in the late 90s) or are present as ghosts or masks of themselves: GHOST 1 (ERNST) or ELF (BRAQUE), both from 2003, among others.

With Sean Landers, a listing of his heroes and forerunners and references to art history can hardly be inflated enough, since he is always just set to pull the next masterpiece out of his hat. In the present that is full of the referentiality and collective conventions of reception, to create one's own picture with pictures available to the world is his goal and thereby make it as an artist – self-doubt and self-abasement or no, relativizing authenticity and fictionalization – with an independent, form-in-progress subject.

Sean Landers' last body of work took the 'genealogy' of his art cosmos one step further: his newest pictures are landscapes with pastiches of his own confessions. They are a kind of painterly, polished visual poetry that contaminates the genre of sublime landscape painting and, at the same time, refers to his earlier texts and text art (for example, 36 HOURS, 1995) as ghosts and, in so doing, once again parodies authenticity as a criterion for perceiving his art.

The first monographic exhibition in an institution and the first monographic catalogue on the work of Sean Landers has been realized only thanks to the magnificent support of countless people. We thank the Andrea Rosen Gallery in New York for their help in organizing the loans and in seeking out the artist's widely dispersed works; in particular we acknowledge Andrea Rosen, Jordan Bastien, Sarah Cohen, Michelle Reyes and Renee Reyes. Cornelia Grassi of greengrassi in London also supported the project in many ways. Caoimhín Mac Giolla Leíth used his long friendship with Sean Landers and knowledge of his work to contribute to the in-depth conversation with the artist and bring the hours of interview into a readable form. Alex Farquharson's enlightening analysis of Sean Landers' oeuvre provides us with new ways of reading his work, positioning it within the art history of his time. For the translations and editing of the texts we thank Gudrun Meier and Jeanne Haunschild. Gilles Gavillet as graphic designer and Lionel Bovier as publishing director overseen the production of the catalogue in all its details.

We owe Beatrice Steiner and the team at the Kunsthalle Zürich all our gratitude for their untiring commitment to the exhibition and catalogue. Through its sponsorship, the Kultur-Stiftung der Deutschen Bank has enabled us to carry out this large project that the Kunsthalle Zürich on its own would, financially, not have been capable of.

Above all, our thanks go out to Sean Landers – for his work and for the enthusiastic energy with which he has assisted every aspect of this project.

Einführung

BEATRIX RUF

Seit den frühen neunziger Jahren gehört das Werk Sean Landers' zu den faszinierenden und immer wieder von Neuem irritierenden künstlerischen Projekten der zeitgenössischen Kunst.

Wie ein roter Faden zieht sich das Gegensatzpaar quälender Selbstzweifel/heillose Selbstüberschätzung durch das Werk des Künstlers und mit ihm eine Vielzahl an Masken des Scheiterns als Strategie des Subjektes, sich vor dem unausweichlichen Versagen zu bewahren.

Sean Landers unternimmt dieses Projekt als Künstler. Er kann alles (Schreiben, Malen, Plastiken machen, Performer sein, Videos drehen, Kritiken verfassen), und er zweifelt an allem. Und auch das tut er mit Virtuosität.

Anfang der neunziger Jahre führte er mit Text- und Videoarbeiten, die in der Maske der Konzeptkunst auftreten, die Fehlstelle und das Tabu des Subjektes und der Emotionalität des Künstlers in dieses Kunstgenre ein. Radikale Selbstentblössung, das emotionale Hadern mit Selbst- und Fremdeinschätzungen, private und professionelle Sehnsüchte und Qualen durchziehen seine Arbeiten. Er gilt als der Künstler, der sich mit Selbstbekenner- und Stream-of-Consciousness-Texten präsentiert wie u.a. ART, LIFE AND GOD (1990) oder [SIC] (1993), mit Textbildern und Cartoons, z.B. FOR THE LOVE OF NOTHING (1994), mit Videoarbeiten, die mit ihm oder einem Affen in seinem Studio gedreht sind, und mit ‚unfertigen' Skulpturen, die ihn als ein an der Kunst, seinem Leben und seinen Beziehungen scheiternden Künstler zeigen. Er macht Konzeptkunst über das Kunstsystem mit seinen Protagonisten und Institutionen, die sich von den rationalen Regeln und Vorgehensweisen der Konzeptkunst mit menschlichen, emotionalen, intimen Mitteilungen unterscheidet.

Im Verlaufe seiner künstlerischen Arbeit der letzten fünfzehn Jahre hat er sein Publikum immer wieder mit neuen Stilen und Winkelschmieden seiner künstlerischen Produktion überrascht und mit dem Formenvokabular und der Motivgeschichte der Kunst ein facettenreiches Unternehmen angestellt, das um die Widersprüche und Irrfahrten der Gefühle des Menschen, um die Konstruktionen des Subjekts zwischen historischer Rückversicherung und zeitgenössischer Verunsicherung, um Selbstüberschätzung und Selbsterniedrigung und um die allgemein menschliche Tragik des sich in Formation befindlichen Subjektes – und selbstverständlich vor allem um das Kunstmachen – kreist.

Sean Landers' künstlerisches Werk irritiert auf grandiose Weise mit Widersprüchen und Fehlleitungen: Das Mimikry antiheroischer Künstlerschaft ist immer auch die Dekonstruktion desselben; in seinen Bekennerschriften und diversen ‚Nacktheiten' ist das Subjekt, das sich äussert, immer auch das Objekt des Künstlers und damit die Fiktionalisierung der gleichen Person.

Landers' ‚Performances' des Authentischen führen die Tradition der grossen ‚Iditiotien' der Kultur- und Kunstgeschichte in die Gegenwart. Jean-Yves Jouannais hat in seiner Publikation L'IDIOTIE – ART, VIE, POLITIQUE auf den Unterschied des ‚ursprünglichen Idioten', der in seinem Werk verschwindet, und dem ‚listigen Idioten', der dem Verschwinden entgeht, hingewiesen: „... [es] zeichnen sich zwei antithetische Haltungen für den modernen Künstler ab: zum einen [...], voll Ernst und suizidärem Beigeschmack, das Werk als rituelle Form der Selbstaufopferung; [...] die urtümliche Idiotie bei Kafka, Mallarmé, Valéry und Flaubert, [...] deren Werke von einer eigentümlichen Idiotie und Eigenständigkeit gezeichnet sind [...], eine Form des Selbstmords", und als gegenteilige Haltung die Authentizität als List, als listige Idiotie, wie etwa die „‚Kuhbild-Periode' von Magritte, das Werk von Kippenberger, Roman Signer" oder Erik Satie.[1] Sean Landers' ‚Idiotie' ist die Idiotie der List, ist Idiotie als symbolischer Schutz.

Der Zugang zur authentischen Person und zum authentischen Schaffen des Künstlers ist in seinen Arbeiten mehrfach gebrochen. Das Video ANYONE'S ORGASM (1992) entpuppt sich als wahnsinniger Trip in das Privatleben des Künstlers angesichts irritierender Codes, die das verwendete

1
Jean-Yves Jouannais: „Der Un-Untergeher", Auszüge aus *L'idiotie – art, vie, politique*, Beaux-Arts magazine/livres, Paris 2003; übersetzt von Stefan Zweifel in: „Kunst & Idiotie. Eine Typologie des Vergessens. Flaubert – Kant – Warhol – Hölderlin – Dostojewski", *ProLitteris Gazzetta*, Zürich 2004, S. 81

Medium betreffen: Videokunst?, Performancekunst?, Skulptur?, Malerei? oder was nun? Die Videos REMISSIONEM PECCATORUM (1994) und ITALIAN HIGH RENAISSANCE AND BAROQUE SCULPTURE (1993) erinnern an die Endurance-Performances der siebziger Jahre, doch Landers mimt Haltungen bekannter klassischer Skulpturen, bricht und konterkariert damit die ikonische Realzeit und den Anspruch des Authentischen dieser Videokunstform mit Ikonen künstlerischer Virtuosität.

Landers lässt uns und sich in zahlreiche Authentizitätsfallen treten, er steht uns immer wieder in einer Art und Weise ‚nackt' gegenüber, die jede Art von voyeuristischer Befriedigung scheitern lässt und diese in eine Scham wandelt, die sich beim Gedanken oder vielmehr der Beurteilung der Scham des ‚Idioten' oder Entblössten einstellt – Eigentore in vorschnellen Kategorien und Einschätzungen schiessen ist eine wiederkehrende Erfahrung mit dem Werk Sean Landers'.

Pablo Picasso (der genialische Handwerker-Künstler) und Marcel Duchamp (der genialische Konzeptkünstler) sind die grossen Genealogielinien, entlang derer Sean Landers sich ein Werk erarbeitet, das sukzessive in der Maske des ‚Idioten' und ‚Stand-up Comedian' die gesamte Kunstgeschichte als Feld der eigenen Identität und des eigenständigen Schaffens durchdringt.

Sämtliche Prototypen des Subjektes/Künstlersubjektes als ‚Idioten' und der Kunst als ‚Idiotie' sind inzwischen in seinem Werk zum Einsatz gekommen: Der ‚idiot savant' des 20. Jahrhunderts mit Landers-spezifischen, die Authentizität ad absurdum führenden Selbstentäusserungen; die ‚Singerie', die im 18. Jahrhundert als Topos für die zweifelhafte, nachäffende, manipulierbare Rolle des Künstlers und der Kunst eingeführt wurde – I'M A CLOWN IN A WORLD OF CHIMPS (1994) oder SINGERIE: LE PEINTRE (1995), SPACE-APE ON MARS (1997) u. a.; der Clown in den wechselnden Erscheinungen, in denen er seit dem 19. Jahrhundert in der Kunst und Kulturgeschichte als allegorisches Bild des Scheiternden und Tollpatschigen und als grandiose Maskierung des Selbst eine Rolle gespielt hat (u. a. bei Joyce, Miller, Mallarmé, Baudelaire, Toulouse-Lautrec, Picasso, Rouault, Beckmann, Klee, Nauman, Scholte, Borofsky, Rondinone, Cattelan, um nur einige zu nennen...). Und dann natürlich Sean Landers' persönliche Ahnengalerie der grossen Künstler und ihrer Werke: Hogarth, Picasso, Matisse (seine ‚idiotische' Phase, die ‚période vache'), Picabia, Michelangelo, Bernini; Ernst, Duchamp, De Chirico, Magritte, Dalí, Braque, Beckmann, die als Pasticcios in den Werken des Künstlers Eingang finden (Arbeiten der späten neunziger Jahre) oder als Geister oder Masken ihrer selbst nun in den Bildern präsent sind – GHOST 1 (ERNST) (2003) oder ELF (BRAQUE) (2003) u. v. a.

Bei Sean Landers kann eine Aufzählung der ‚Helden' und ‚Vorbilder' und seiner Referenzen in der Kunstgeschichte nicht ausufernd genug sein, da er immer wieder sein ‚Meisterstück' kreiert: in einer Gegenwart, die voller Referentialität und kollektiven Konventionen der Rezeption ist, ein eigenständiges ‚Bild' mit den vorhandenen Bildern der Welt zu schaffen und damit – Selbstzweifel und Selbsterniedrigung hin oder her, Authentizität und Fiktionalisierung relativierend – bei einem eigenständig, sich in Formation befindlichen Subjekt und also Künstler ankommt.

Sean Landers' letzte Werkgruppe führt die ‚Genealogie' seines Kunstkosmos konsequent weiter: Seine neuesten Bilder sind Landschaften mit Versatzstücken seiner eigenen Bekenntnisse. Sie sind eine Art malerisch ausgefeilte Visuelle Poesie, die das Genre erhabener Landschaftsmalerei kontaminieren und zugleich seine frühen Texte und Textbilder (36 HOURS, 1995) als ‚Geister' referieren – und damit das Authentische als Wahrnehmungskriterium seiner Kunst erneut persiflieren.

Die erste monographische Ausstellung in einer Institution und dieser erste monographische Katalog zum Werk von Sean Landers konnten nur dank der grossen Unterstützung zahlreicher Personen realisiert werden. Wir danken der Andrea Rosen Gallery, New York, für die Mithilfe in der Organisation der Leihgaben und dem Auffinden der weit verstreuten Werke des Künstlers, insbesondere Andrea Rosen, Jordan Bastien, Sarah Cohen, Michelle Reyes und Renee Reyes. Cornelia Grassi, greengrassi, London, unterstützte das Projekt in vielfältiger Weise. Caoimhín Mac Giolla Leith hat seine langjährige Freundschaft mit Sean Landers und seine Kennerschaft des Werkes des Künstlers in das ausführliche Gespräch mit dem Künstler eingebracht und die gigantischen Transkripte der langen Interviewstunden in lesbare Form gebracht. Alex Farquharsons erhellende Analyse von Sean Landers Werk schafft neue Lesarten und positioniert es in der Kunstgeschichte seiner Zeit. Die Übersetzungen der Texte verdanken wir Gudrun Meier und Jeanne Haunschild. Gilles Gavillet als graphischer Gestalter und Lionel Bovier als Verlagsleiter haben den Katalog in gedruckter Form für das Publikum auf den Weg gebracht.

Beatrice Steiner und dem Team der Kunsthalle Zürich gebührt aller Dank für den unermüdlichen Einsatz für die Ausstellung und den Katalog. Die Kultur-Stiftung der Deutschen Bank ermöglichte mit ihrer Unterstützung ein grosses Projekt, das die Kunsthalle Zürich nicht ohne zusätzlichen finanziellen Beistand hätte durchführen können.

Vor allem aber geht unser Dank an Sean Landers – für sein Werk und für die begeisternde Energie, mit der er jeden Aspekt dieses Projektes realisiert hat.

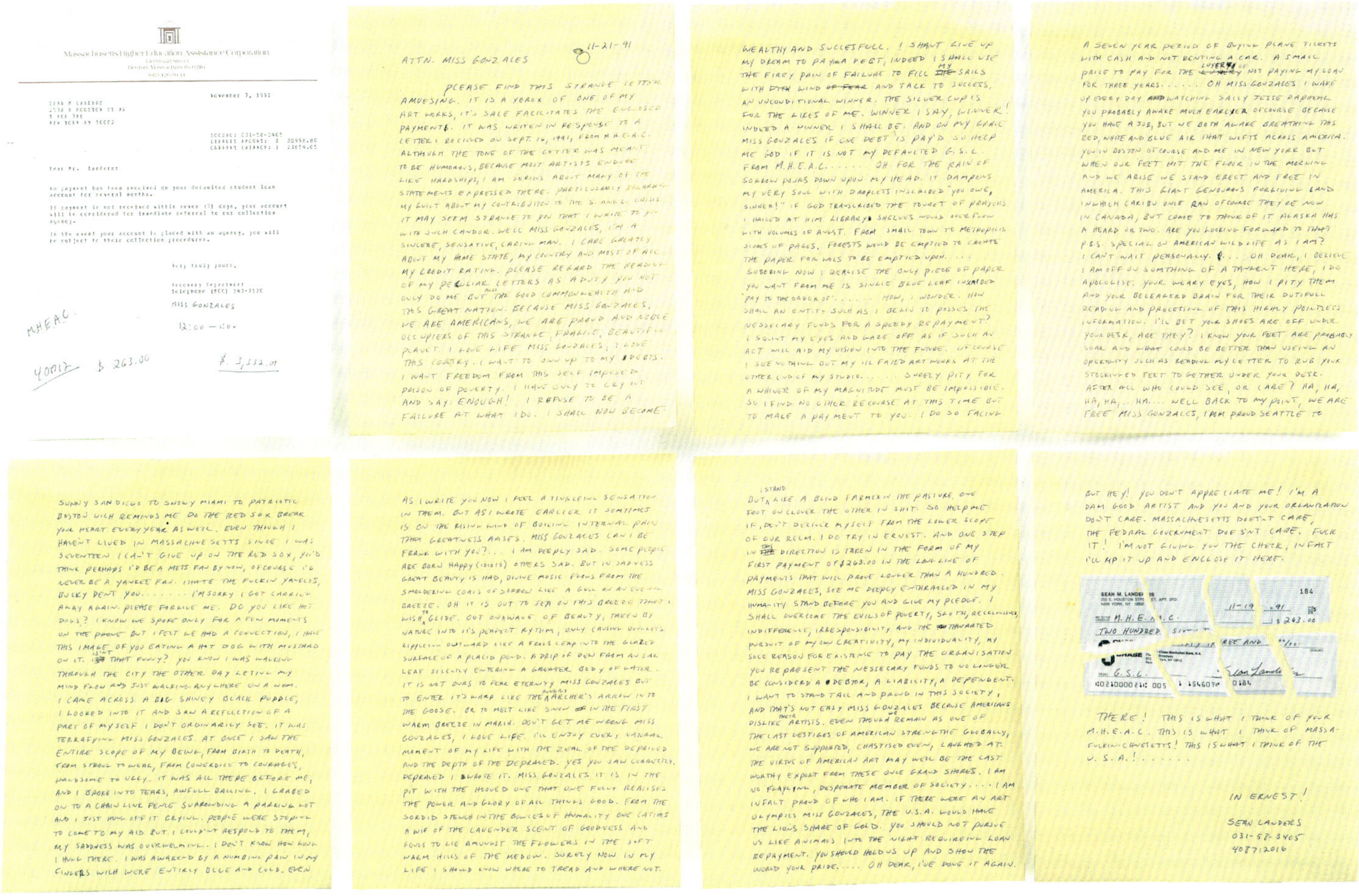

ATTN. MISS GONZALES, 1991
Ink on paper
8 leaves, each 27.94 × 21.59 cm

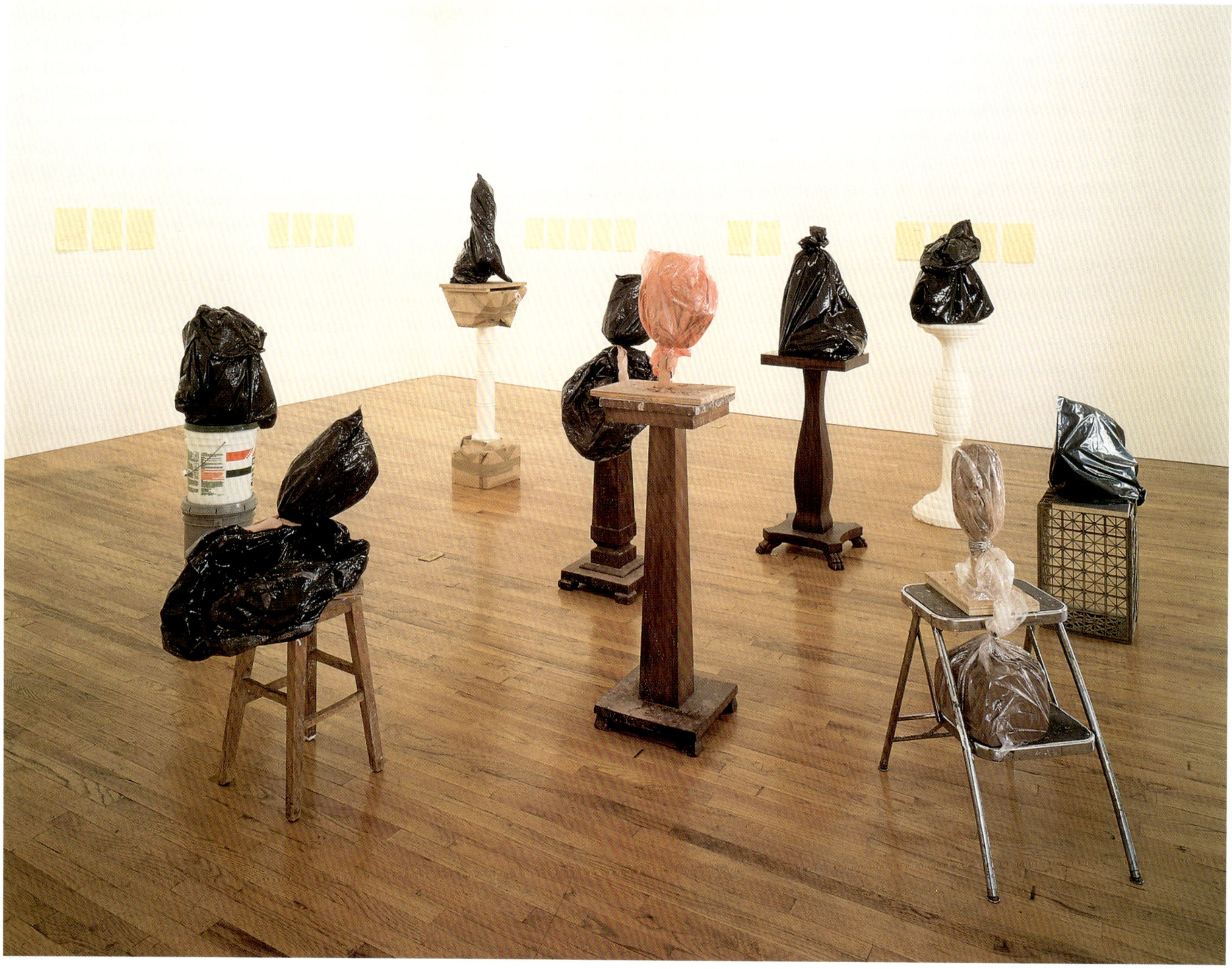

Installation view
Postmasters Gallery, New York, 1990

From the ART, LIFE AND GOD series
Drawings from various dimensions
Ink on paper
Each leaf 27.94 × 21.59 cm
Sculptures of various dimensions
Wet clay, plastic, wire, metal and wood

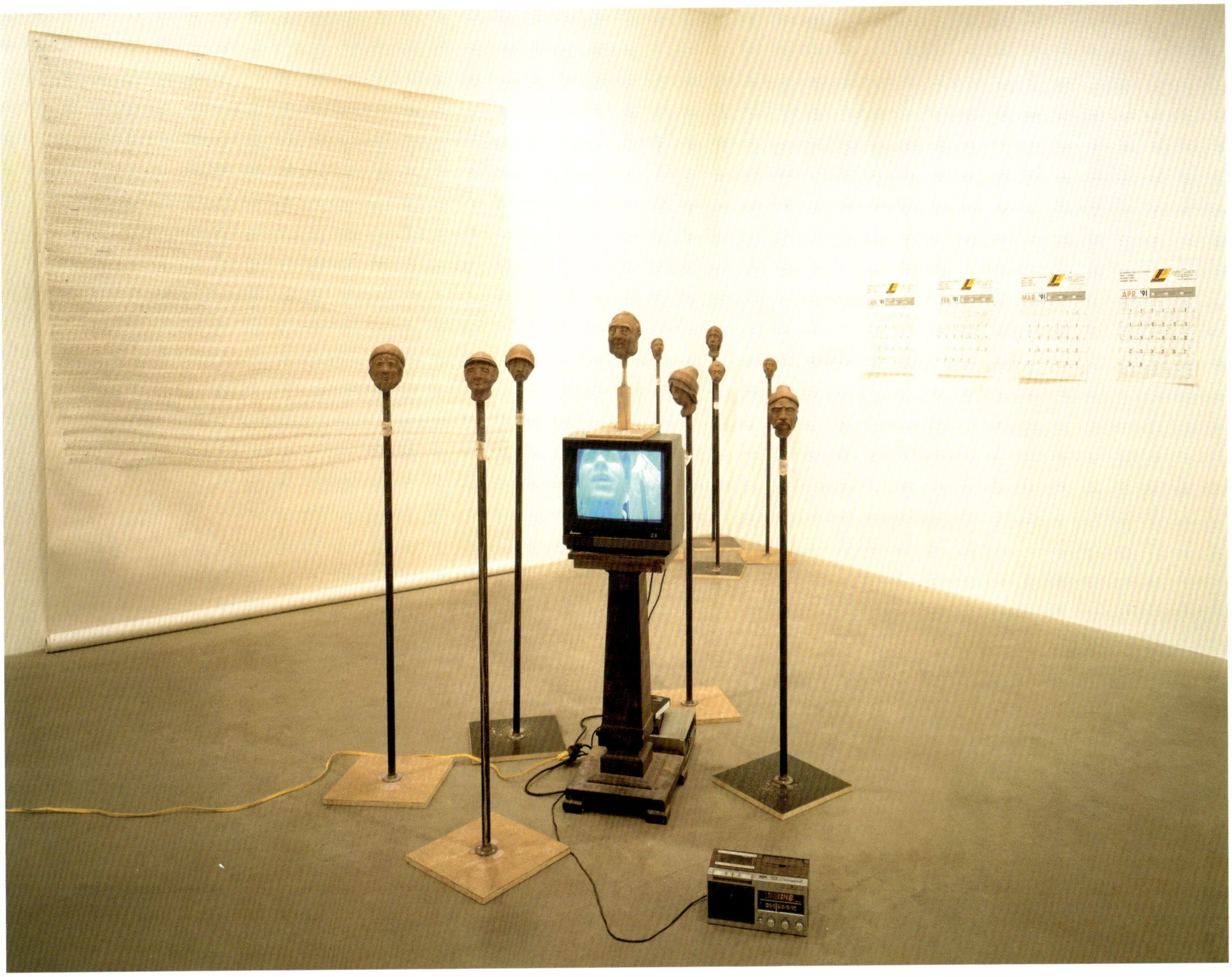

Installation view
Andrea Rosen Gallery, New York, 1992

Left to right:
ANYONE'S ORGASM, 1991
Ink on paper
304.8 × 274.32 cm

CALENDAR PAGES FROM 1991, 1991
Ink on paper
12 leaves, each 59.1 × 40.64 cm

Sculptures of various dimensions
Wet clay, aluminum, steel and wood

ANYONE'S ORGASM, 1992
Videotape
60 min.

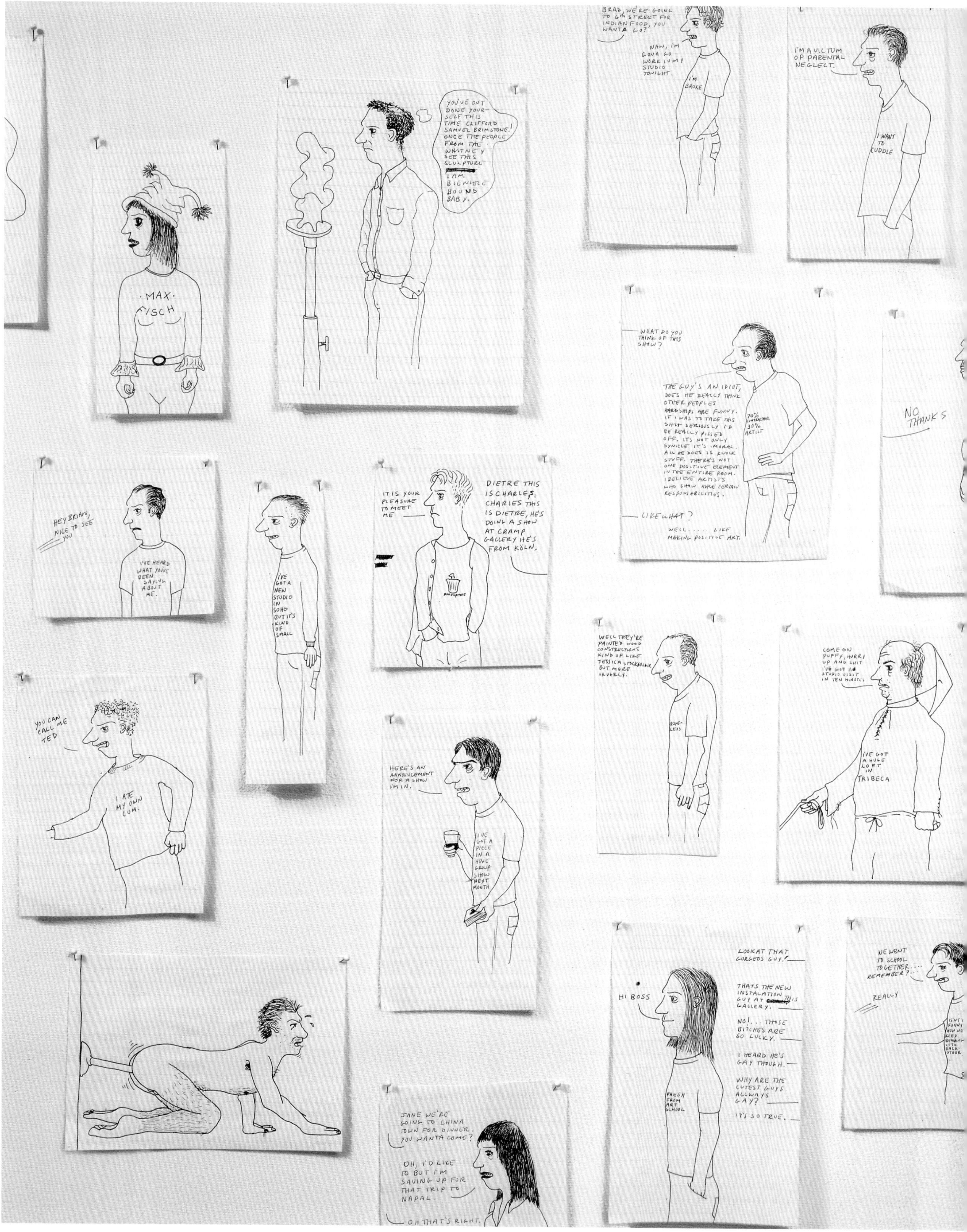

MAX FISCH
YOU'VE OUT DONE YOUR-SELF THIS TIME CLIFFORD SAMUEL BRIMSTONE! ONCE THE PEOPLE FROM THE WHITNEY SEE THIS SCULPTURE [redacted] I AM BIENNIELE BOUND BABY.
BRAD, WE'RE GOING TO 6th STREET FOR INDIAN FOOD, YOU WANTA GO?
NAW, I'M GONNA GO WORK IN MY STUDIO TONIGHT.
I'M BROKE
I'M A VICTUM OF PARENTAL NEGLECT.
I WANT TO CUDDLE
WHAT DO YOU THINK OF THIS SHOW?
THE GUY'S AN IDIOT, DOES HE REALLY THINK OTHER PEOPLES HARDSHIPS ARE FUNNY. IF I WAS TO TAKE THIS SHIT SERIOUSLY I'D BE REALLY PISSED OFF. IT'S NOT ONLY SYNICLE IT'S IMORAL. ALL HE DOES IS KNOCK STUFF. THERE'S NOT ONE POSITIVE ELEMENT IN THE ENTIRE ROOM. I BELIEVE ARTISTS WHO SHOW HAVE CERTAIN RESPONSABILITIES.
70% CONTRACTOR 30% ARTIST
LIKE WHAT?
WELL..... LIKE MAKING POSITIVE ART.
NO THANKS
HEY BRIAN, NICE TO SEE YOU
I'VE HEARD WHAT YOU'VE BEEN SAYING ABOUT ME.
I'VE GOT A NEW STUDIO IN SOHO BUT IT'S KIND OF SMALL
IT IS YOUR PLEASURE TO MEET ME
[redacted]
DIETRE THIS IS CHARLES, CHARLES THIS IS DIETRE, HE'S DOING A SHOW AT CRAMP GALLERY HE'S FROM KÖLN.
WELL THEY'RE PAINTED WOOD CONSTRUCTIONS KIND OF LIKE JESSICA STOCKHOLDER BUT MORE ORDERLY.
HOPE-LESS
COME ON PUFFY, HURRY UP AND SHIT I'VE GOT A STUDIO VISIT IN TEN MINUTES
I'VE GOT A HUGE LOFT IN TRIBECA
YOU CAN CALL ME TED
I ATE MY OWN CUM.
HERE'S AN ANNOUNCEMENT FOR A SHOW I'M IN.
I'VE GOT A PIECE IN A HUGE GROUP SHOW NEXT MONTH
LOOKAT THAT GORGEOS GUY.
HI BOSS
THATS THE NEW INSTALATION GUY AT [redacted] THIS GALLERY.
NO!... THOSE BITCHES ARE SO LUCKY.
I HEARD HE'S GAY THOUGH.
WHY ARE THE CUTEST GUYS ALLWAYS GAY?
IT'S SO TRUE.
FRESH FROM ART SCHOOL
WE WENT TO SCHOOL TOGETHER... REMEMBER?
REALLY
JANE WE'RE GOING TO CHINA TOWN FOR DINNER. YOU WANTA COME?
OH, I'D LIKE TO BUT I'M SAVING UP FOR THAT TRIP TO NAPAL.
OH THAT'S RIGHT.

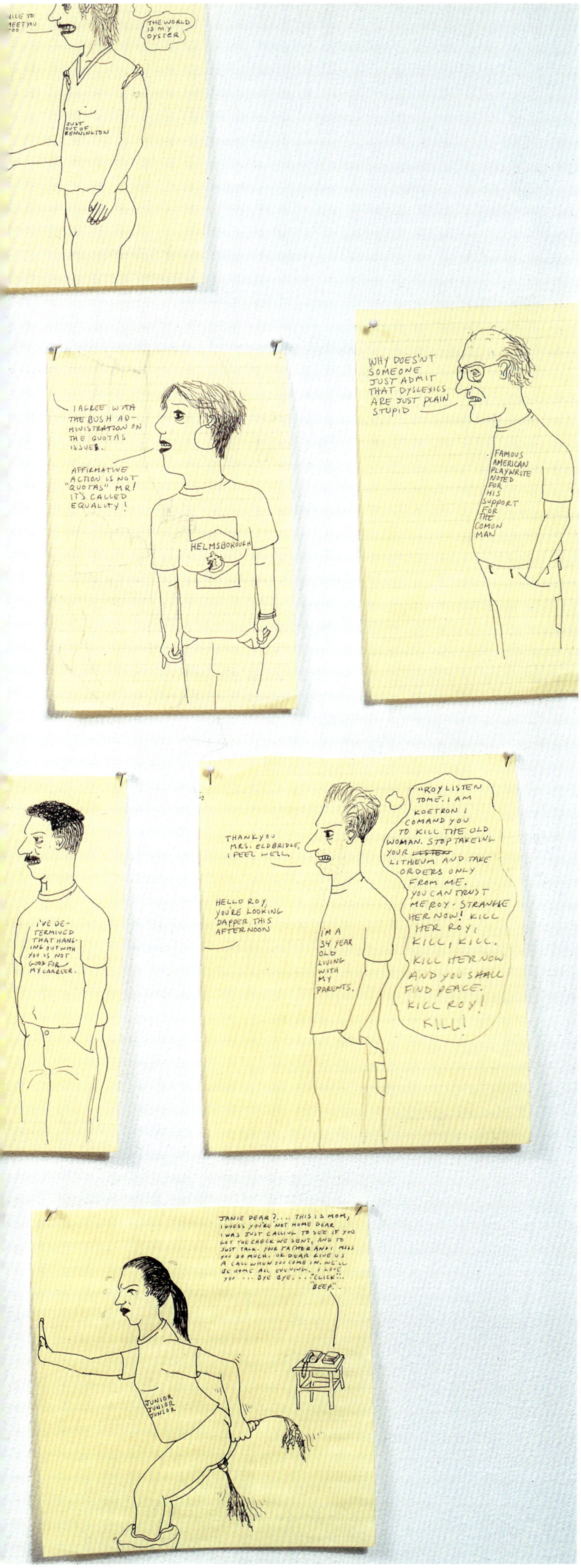

CARTOON installation, 1992
Ink on paper
Various dimensions

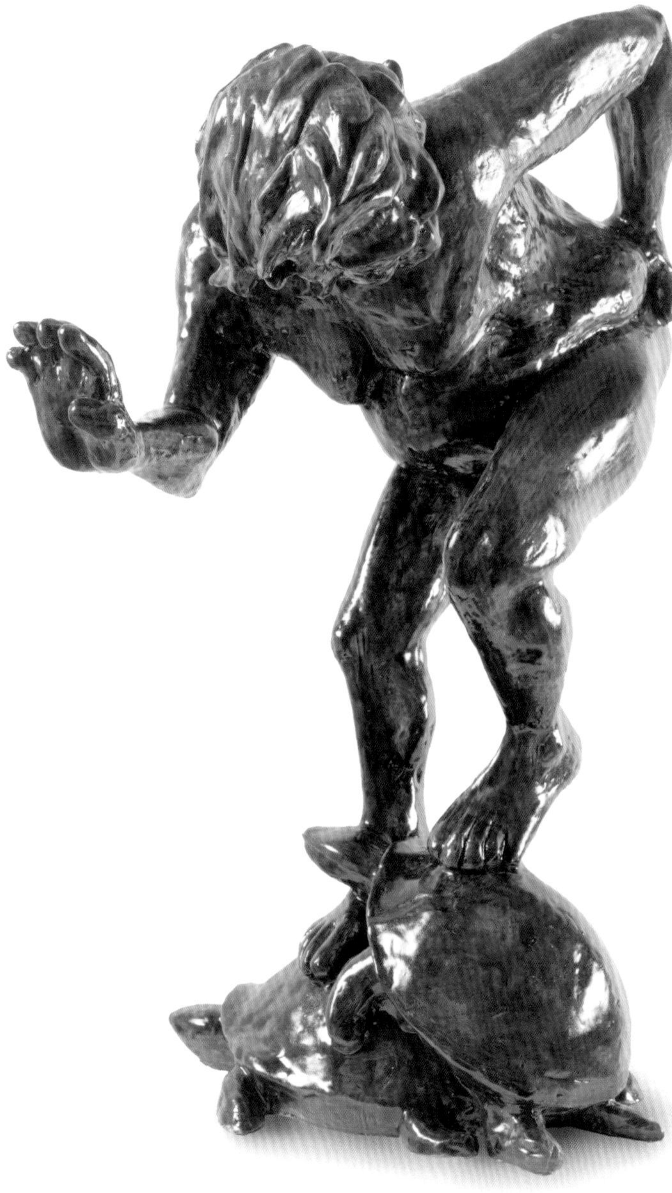

DANNY BOY OF DINGLE, 1993
Terracotta and green glaze
63.5 × 38.1 × 38.1 cm

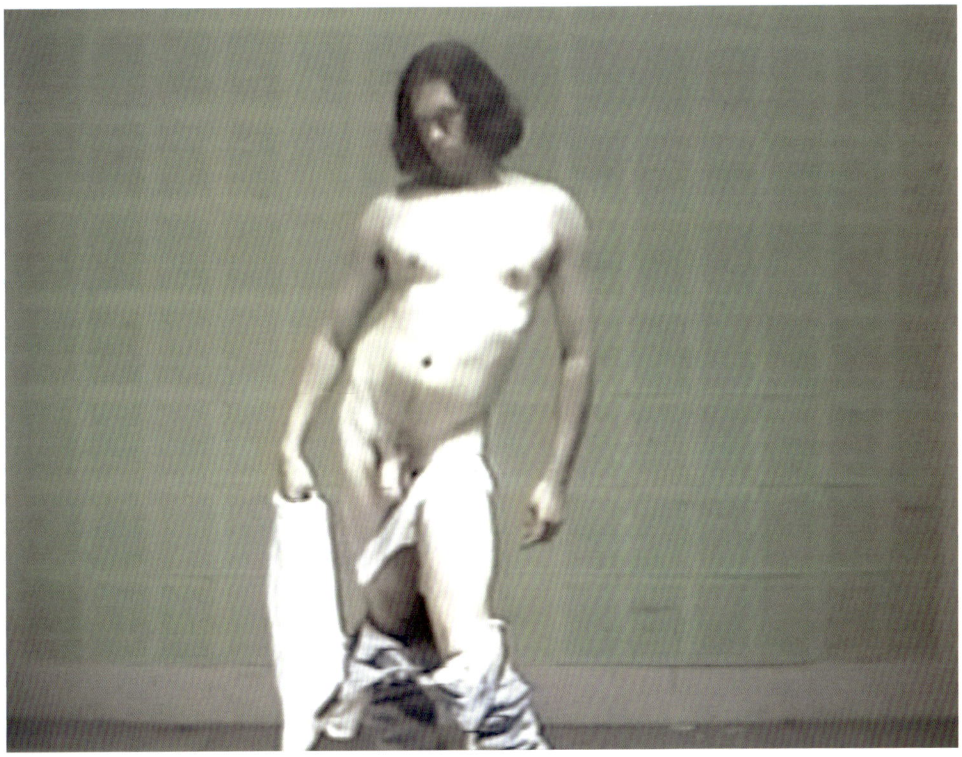

ITALIAN HIGH RENAISSANCE AND BAROQUE SCULPTURE, 1993
Videotape
45 min.

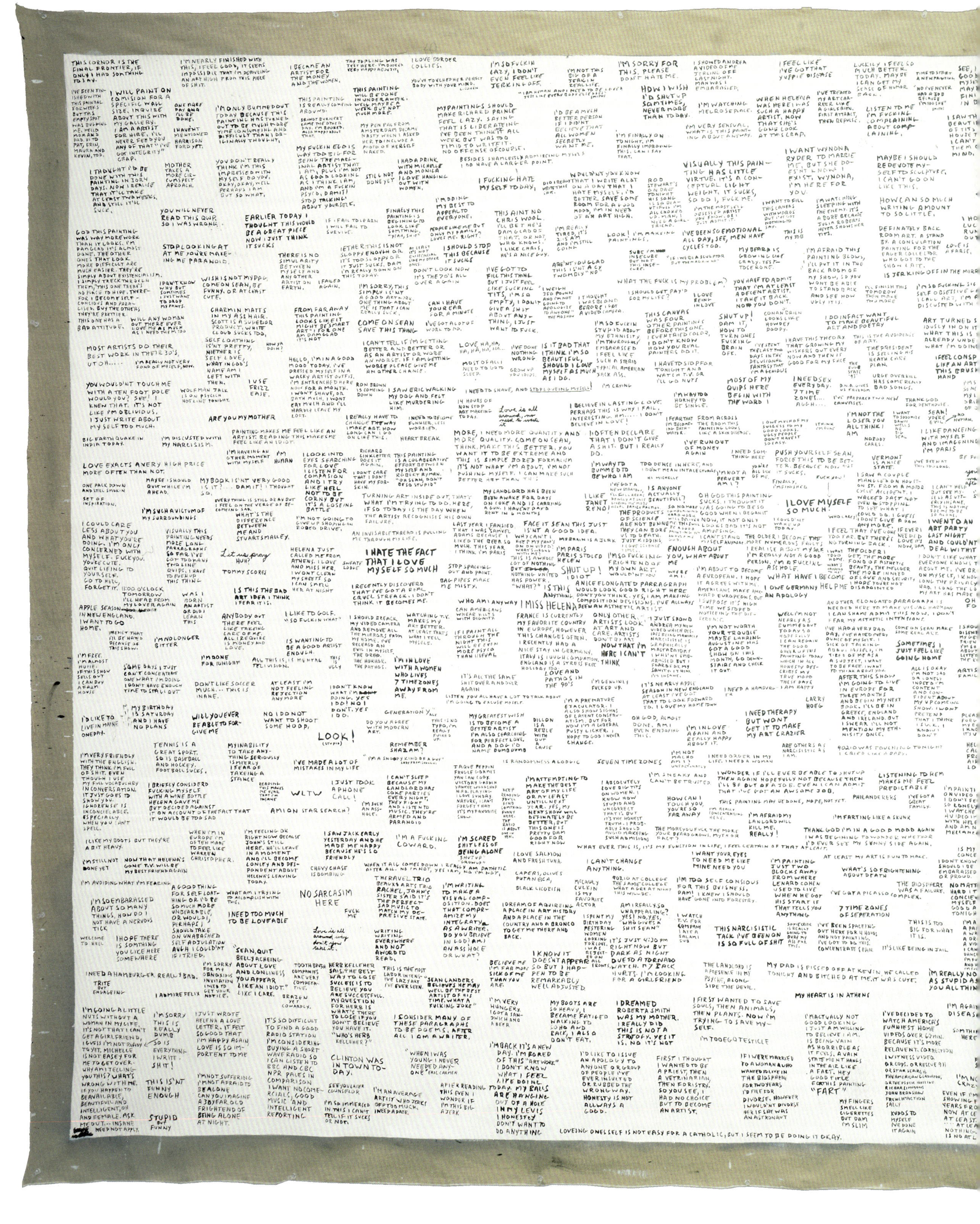
I HATE THE FACT THAT I LOVE MYSELF SO MUCH
I MISS HELEN
I LOVE MYSELF SO MUCH
SHUT UP! IDIOT
LOOK!
MY HEART IS IN ATHENS
LOVEING ONES SELF IS NOT EASY FOR A CATHOLIC, BUT I SEEM TO BE DOING IT OKAY.

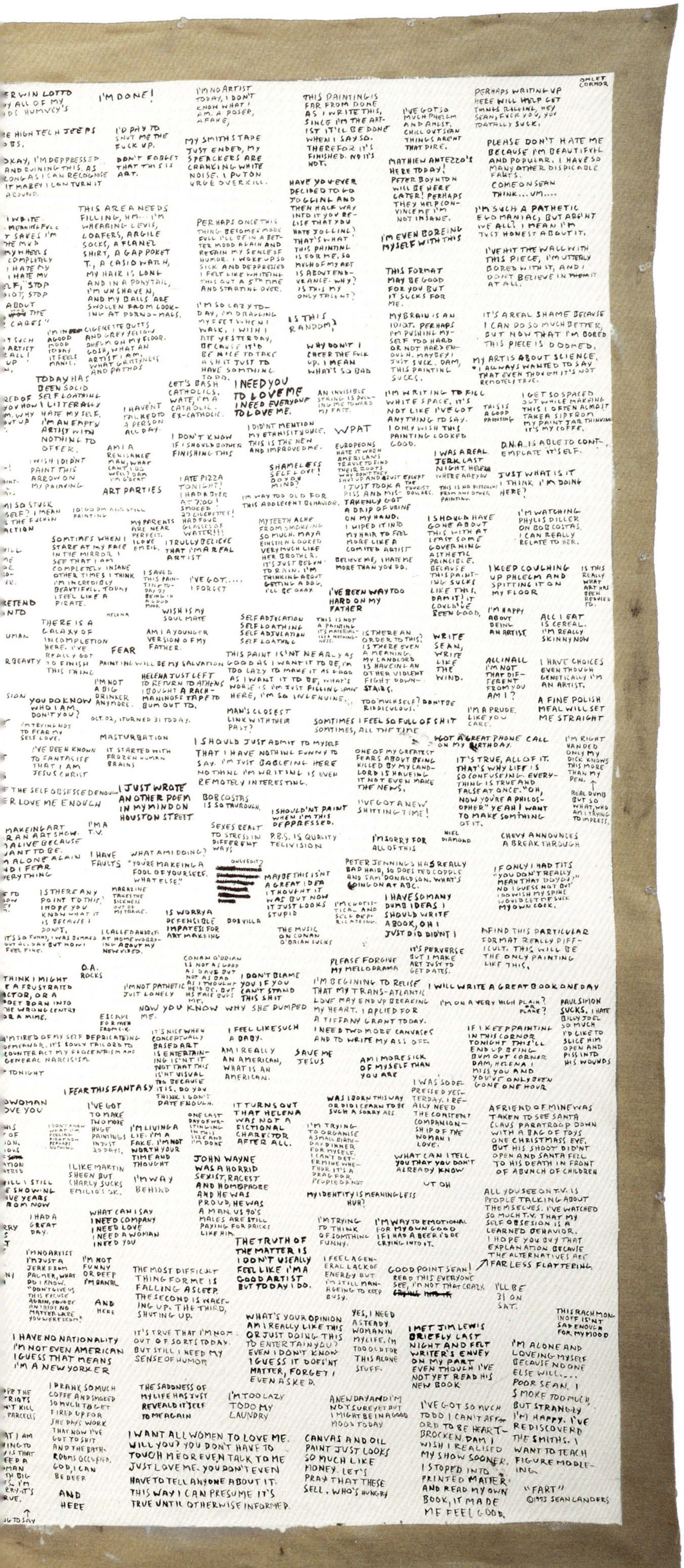

Pages 18–19
SELF-SOMETHING, 1994
Oil on linen
274.32 × 426.72 cm

FART, 1993
Oil on linen
213.36 × 285.75 cm

HEY, STUPID, SHUT UP!!
WHAT AN ASSHOLE!
ENOUGH!
NOW WHAT?
MILLIGAN

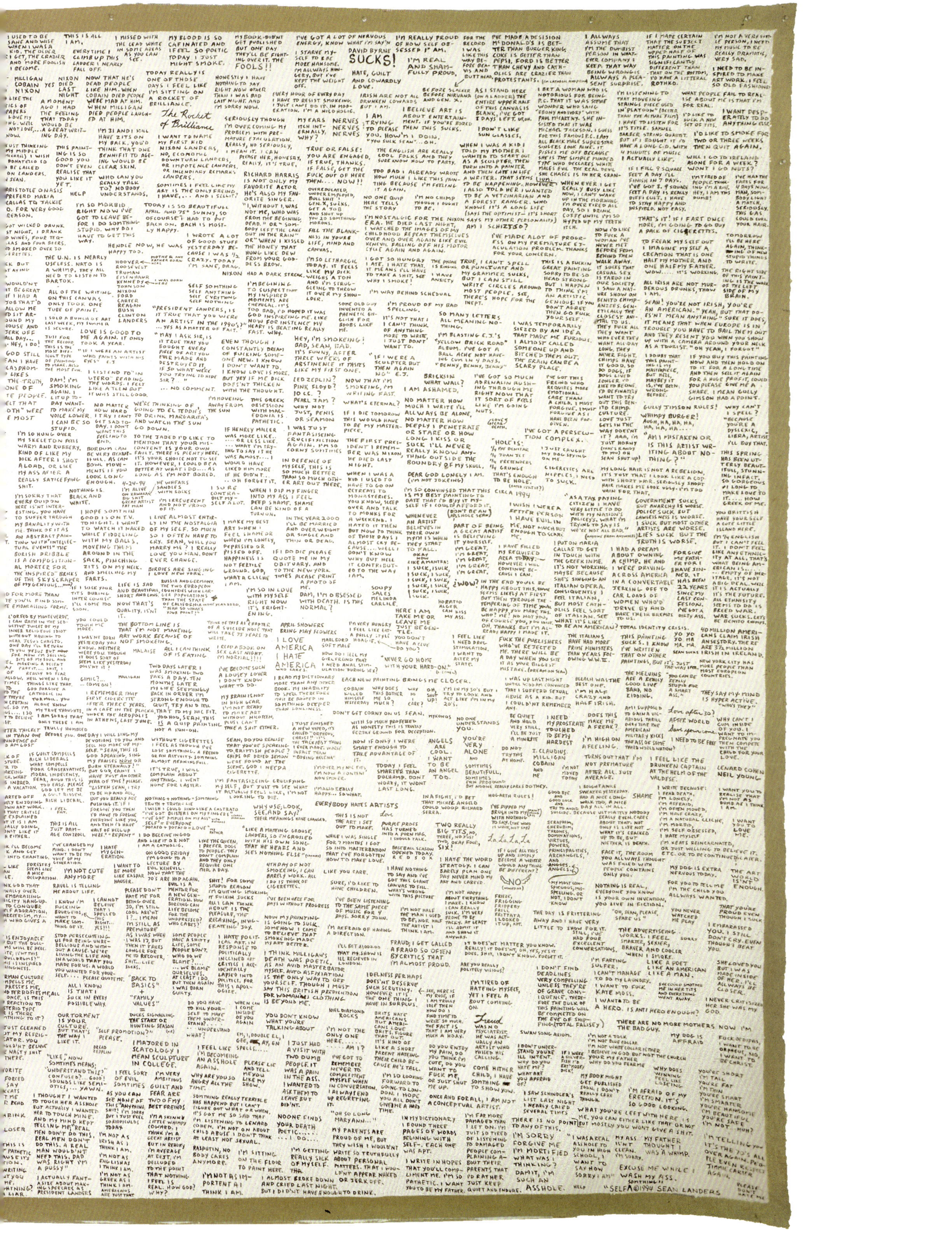

SUCKS!
The Rocket of Brilliance
"SELFA"©1994 SEAN LANDERS

"FOR THE LOVE OF NOTHING" ©1994 SEAN LANDERS

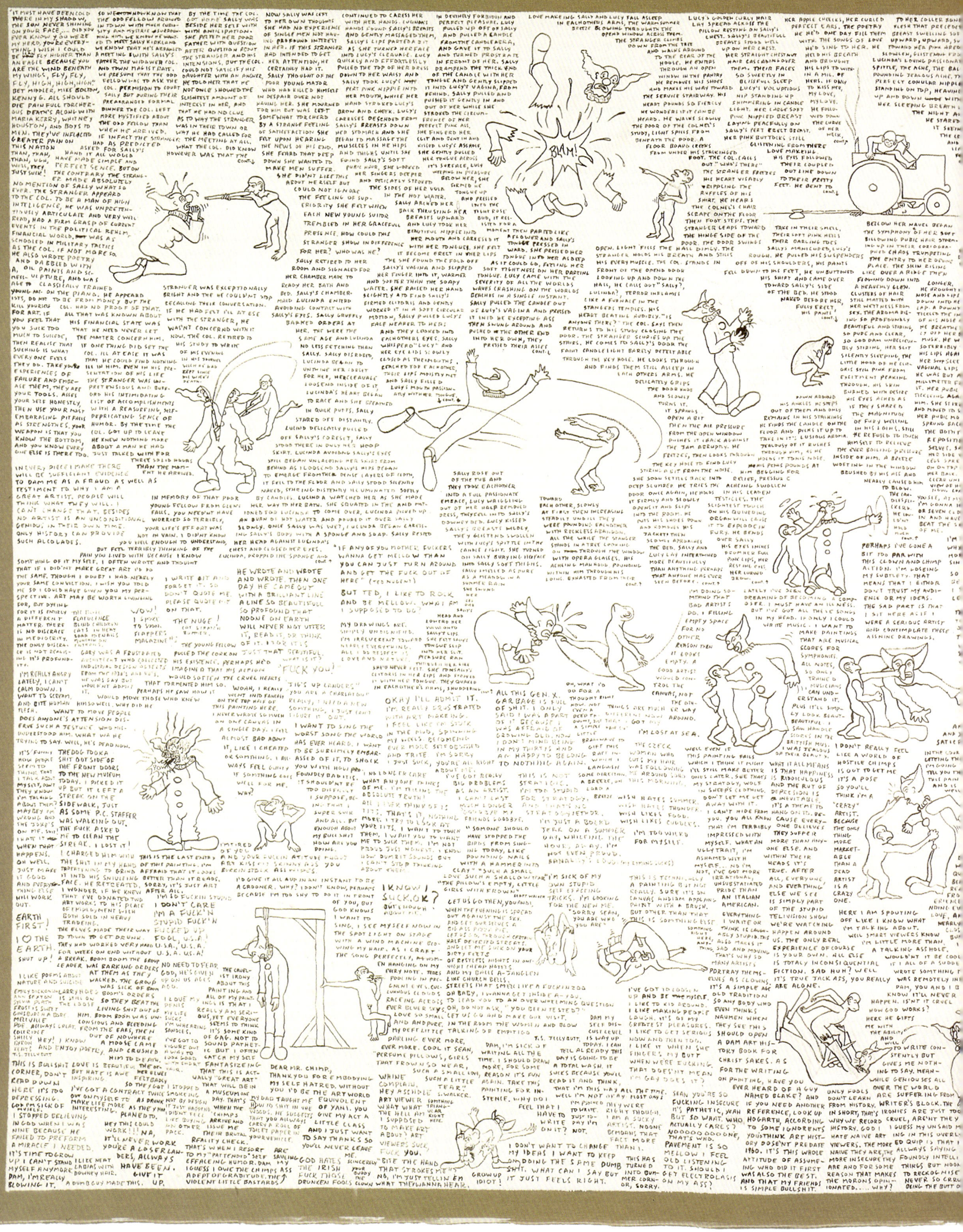

BLAM!
"IF ANY OF YOU MOTHER FUCKERS WANNA GET MELLOW THAN YOU CAN JUST TURN AROUND AND GET THE FUCK OUT OF HERE" (TED NUGENT)
BUT TED, I LIKE TO ROCK AND BE MELLOW. WHAT AM I SUPPOSED TO DO?
"FUCK YOU!"
I KNOW, SUCK, OK?
EARTH FIRST!
I ♡ THE EARTH.
SHUT UP!

Pages 20 – 21
FOR THE LOVE
OF NOTHING, 1994
Oil on linen
274.32 × 426.72 cm

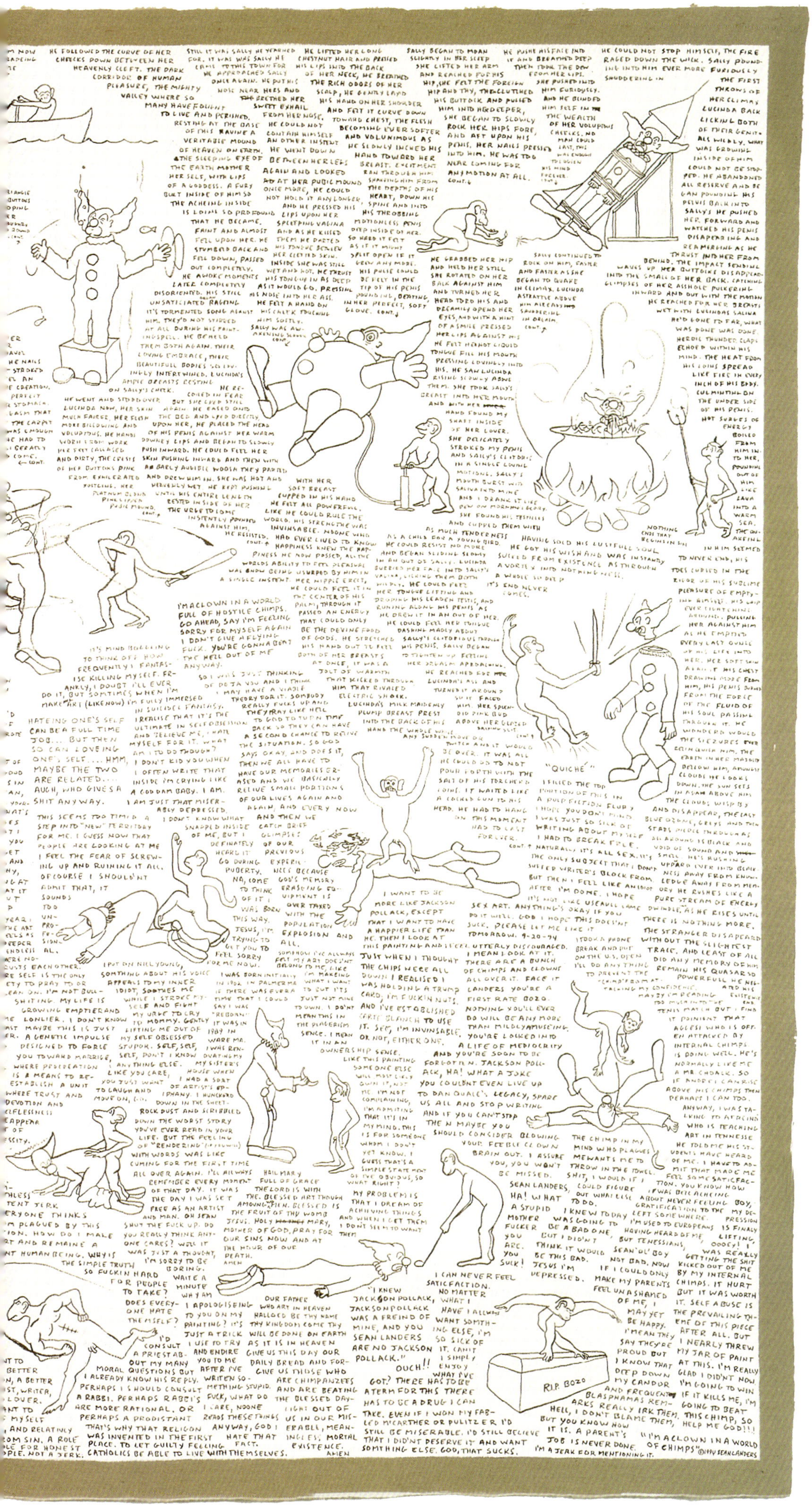

I'M A CLOWN
IN A WORLD OF CHIMPS, 1994
Oil on linen
213.36 × 304.8 cm

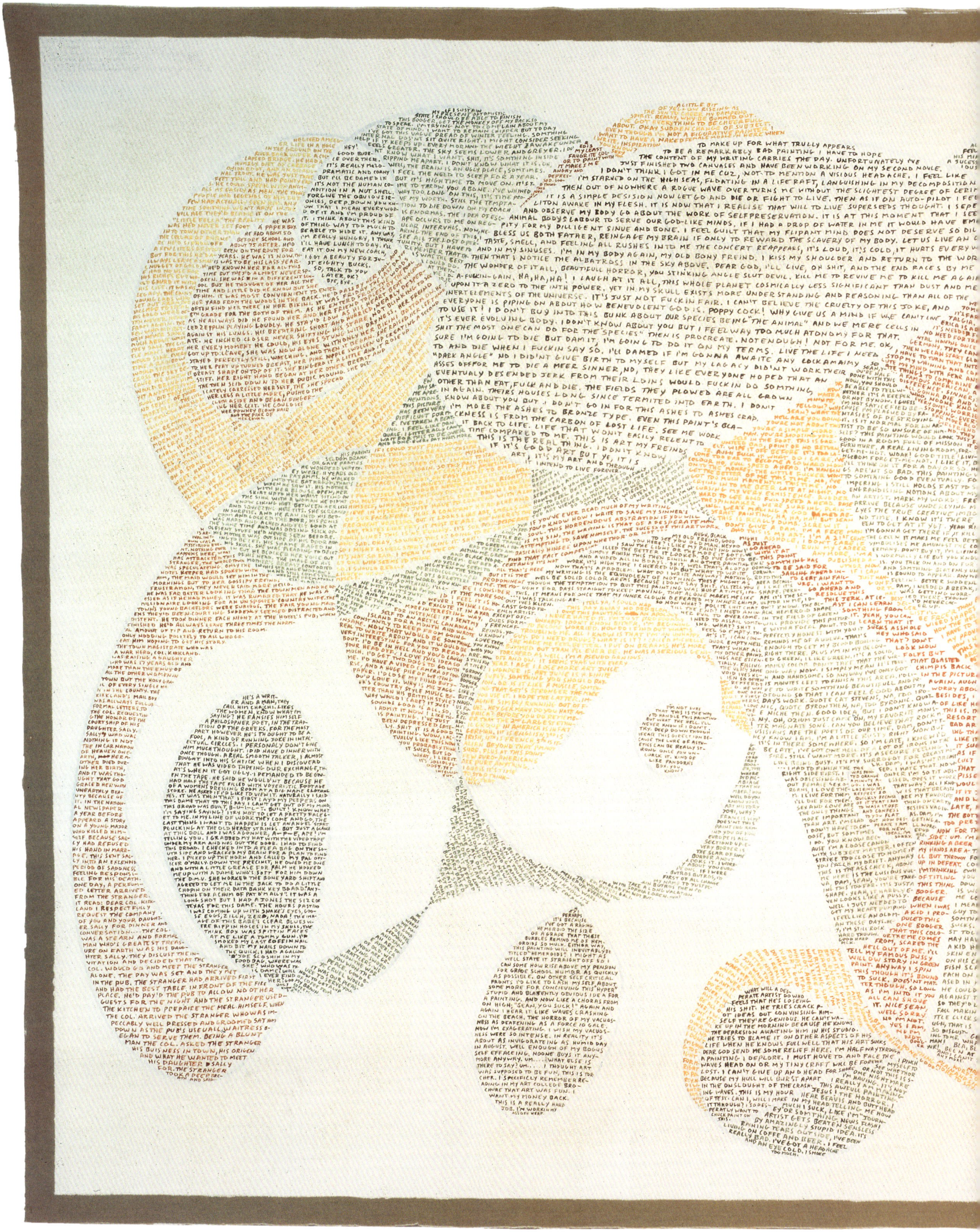

TO MAKE UP FOR WHAT TRULLY APPEARS
TO BE A REMARKABLY BAD PAINTING I HAVE TO HOPE
THE CONTENT OF MY WRITING CARRIES THE DAY.

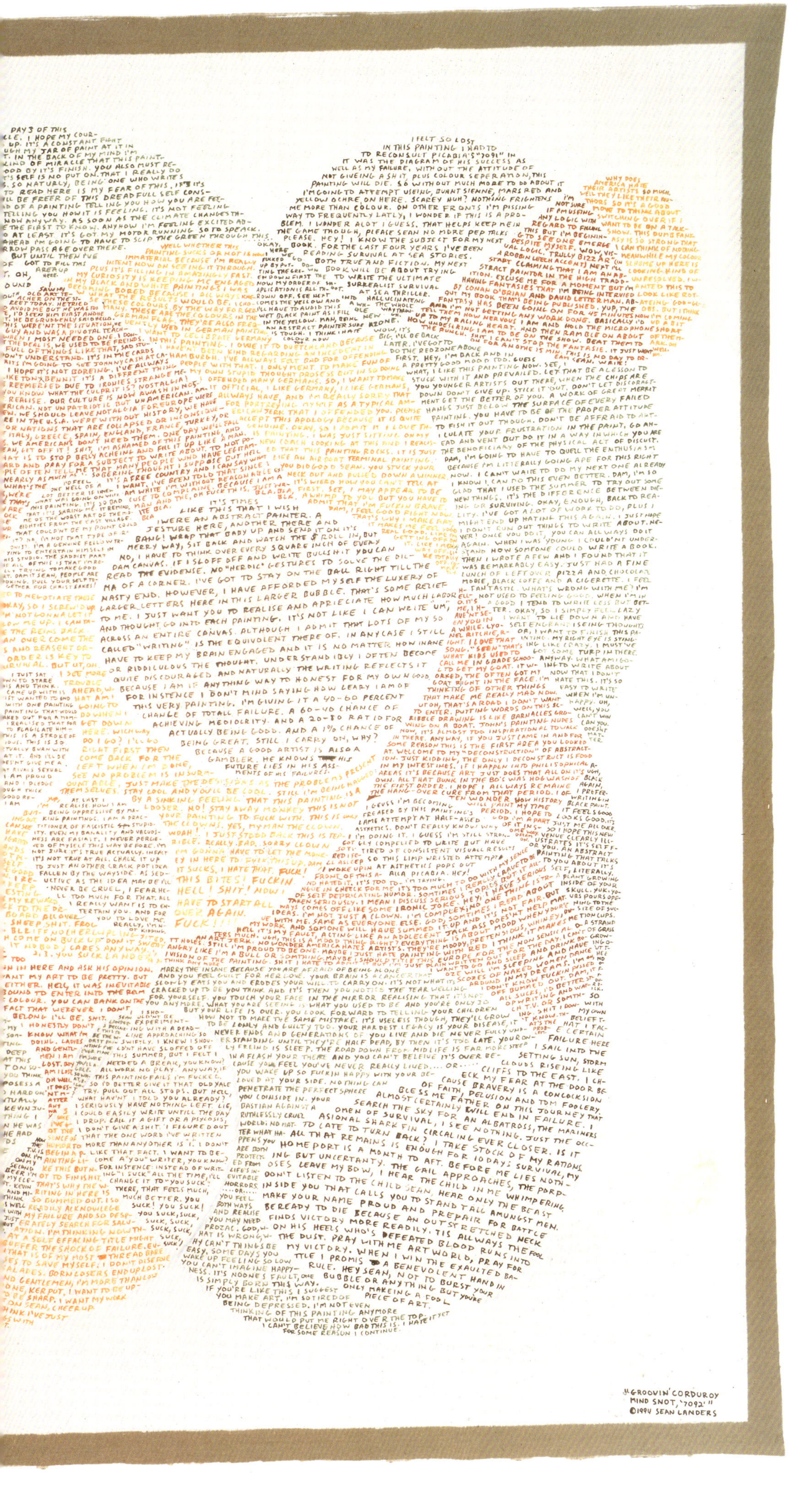

GROOVIN' CORDUROY
MIND-SNOT/7092, 1994
Oil on linen
213.36 × 304.8 cm

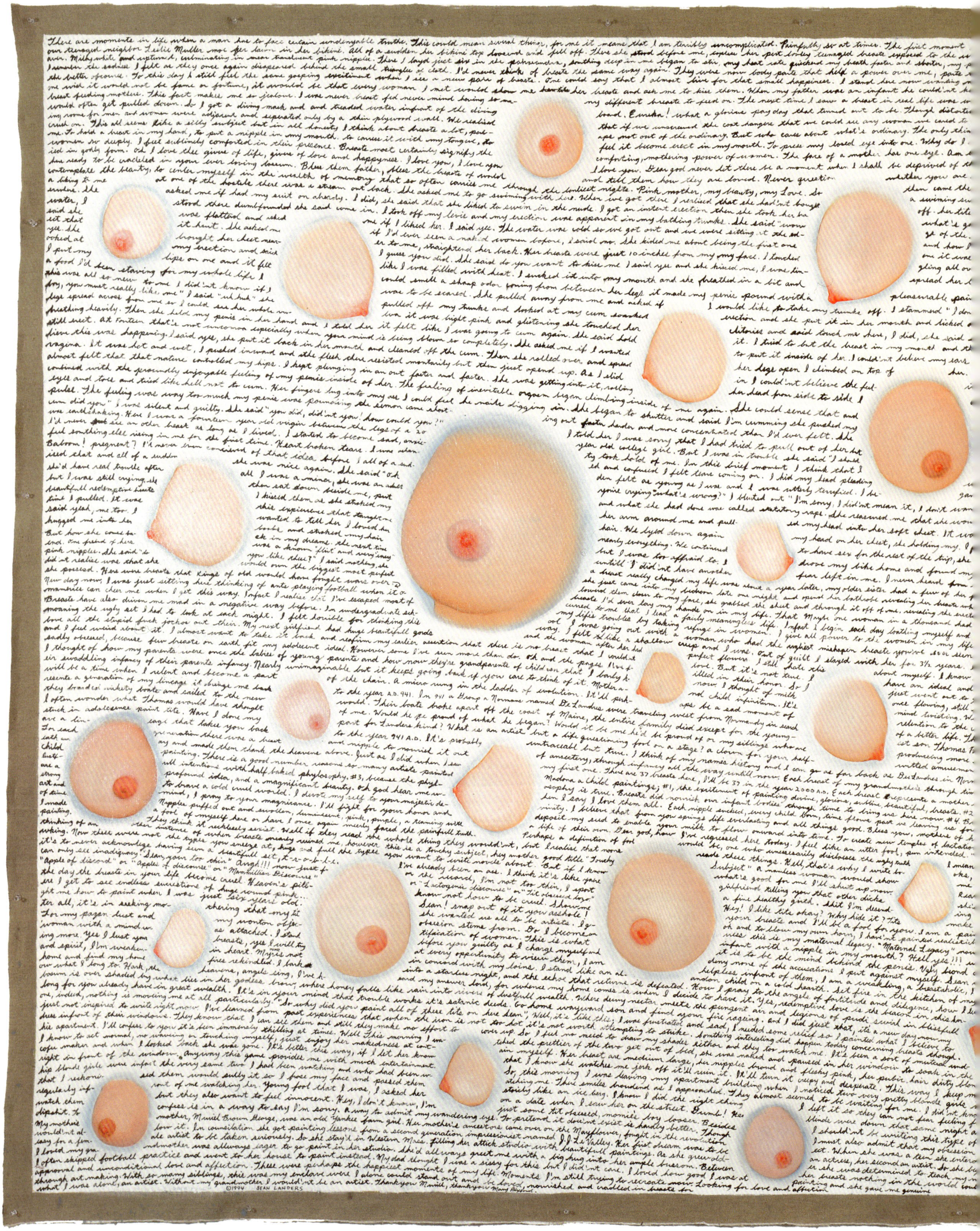
©1994 SEAN LANDERS

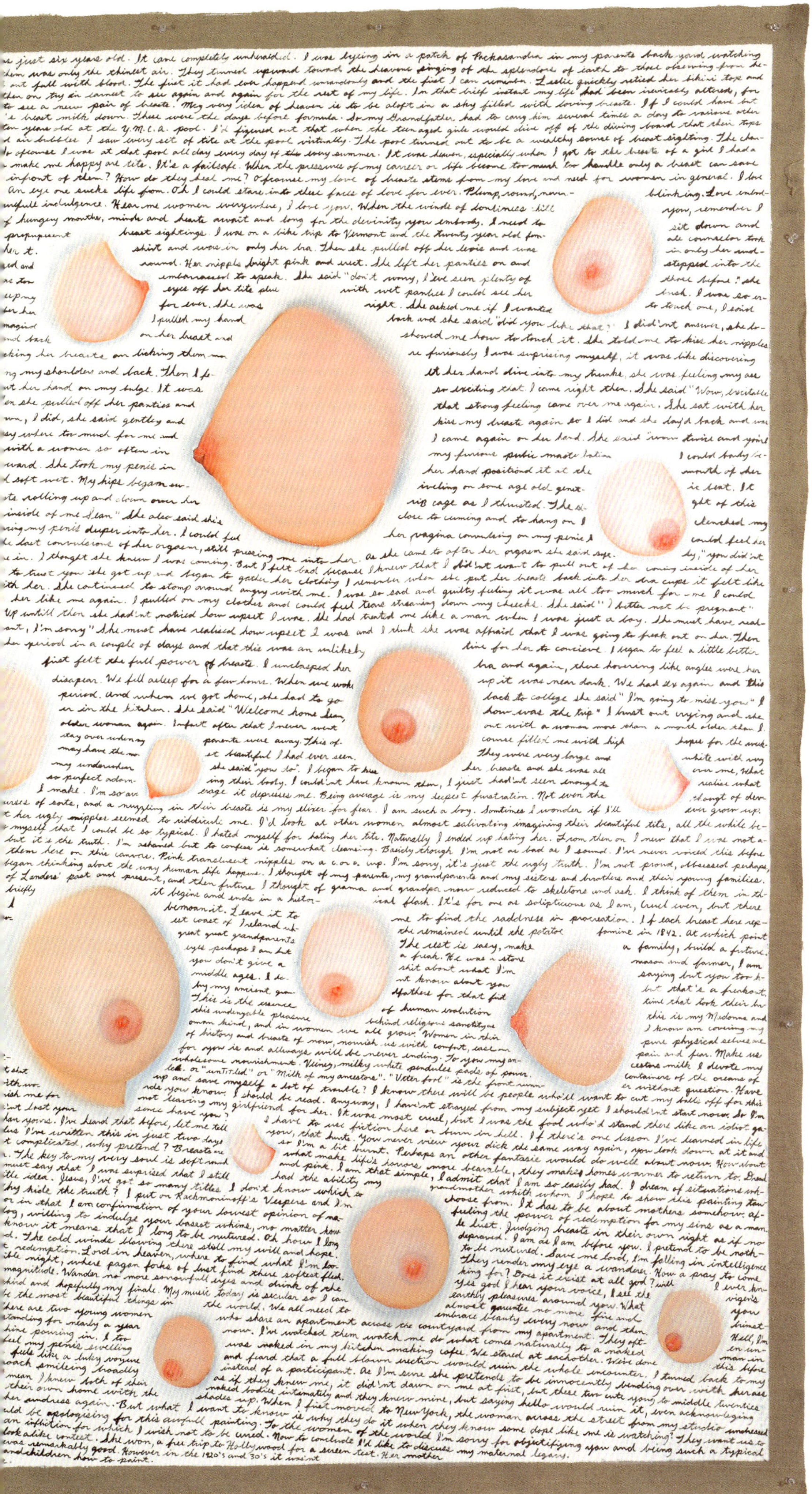

THE ETHER
OF MEMORY, 1994
Oil on linen
213.36 × 304.8 cm

LOOKING FOR
MR. GODBAR, 1995
Oil on linen
276.86 × 426.72 cm

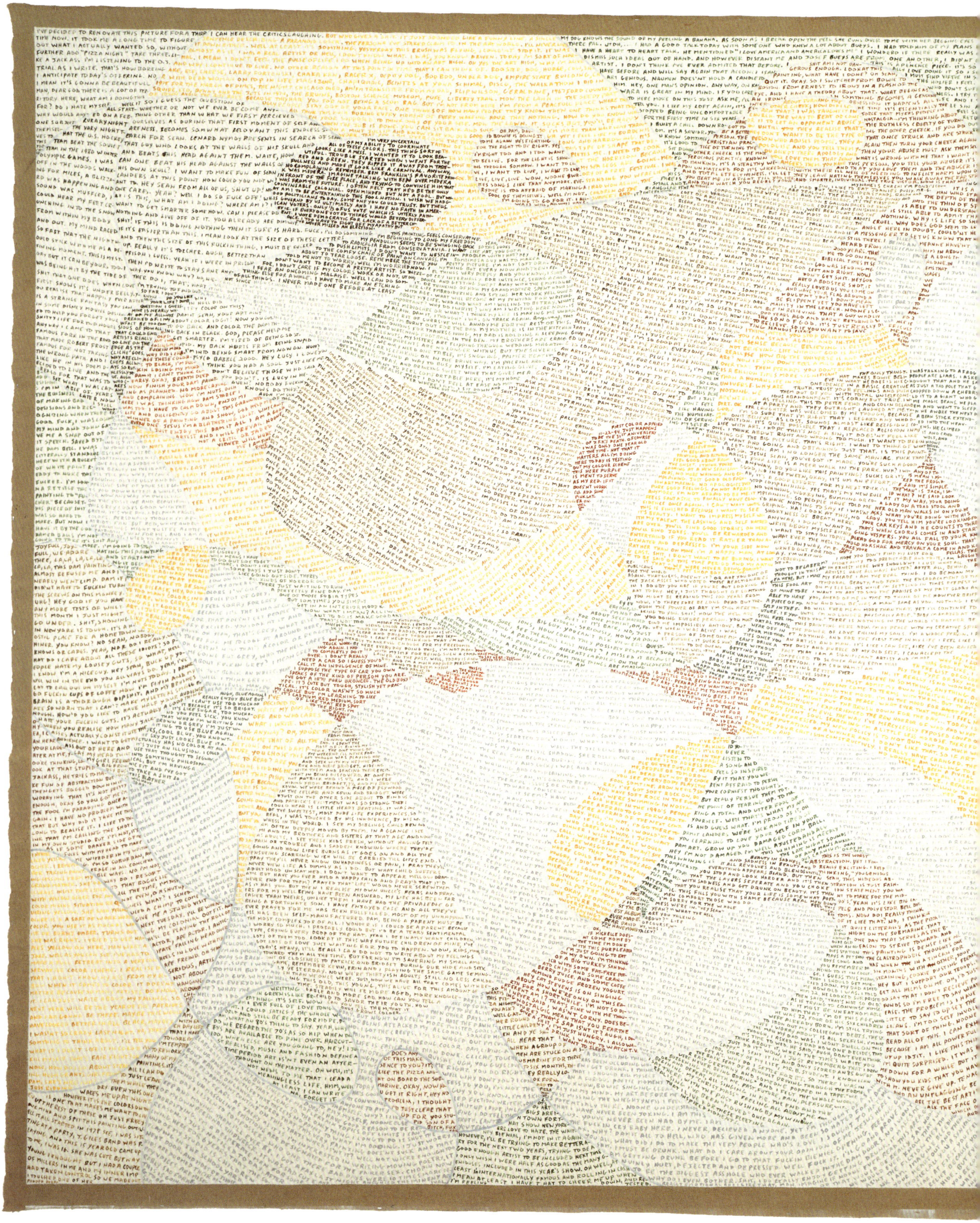

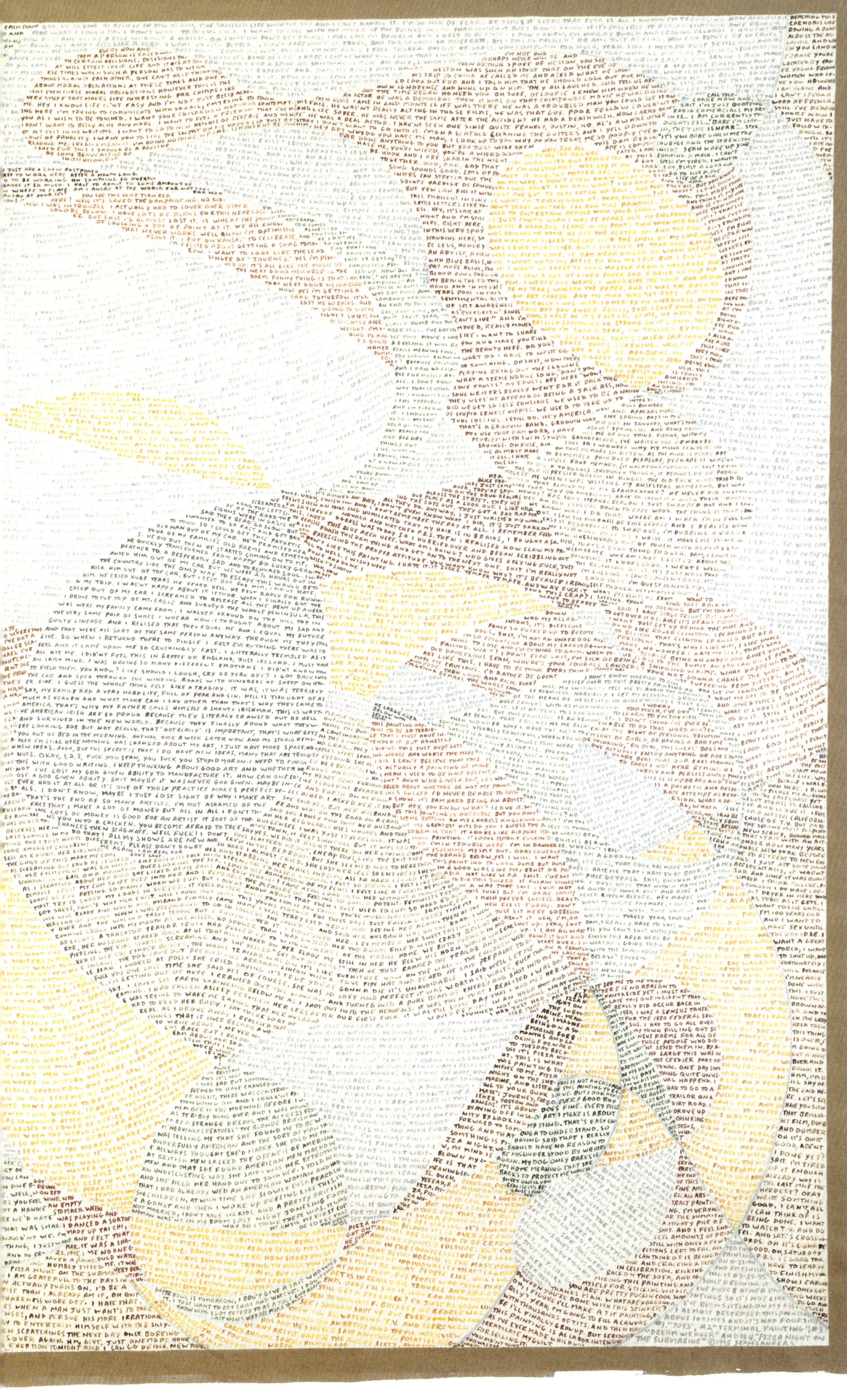

PIZZA NIGHT ON THE SUBMARINE/7093, 1995

Oil on linen
276.86 × 426.72 cm

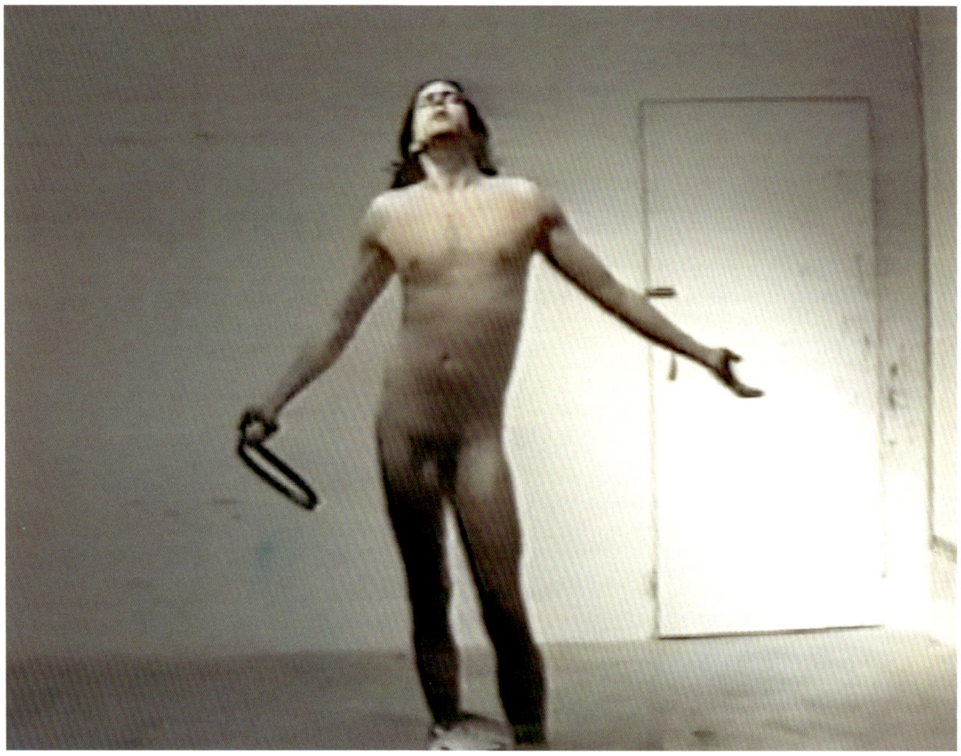

REMISSIONEM PECCATORUM, 1994
Videotape
60 min.

Interview with Sean Landers

CAOIMHÍN MAC GIOLLA LEÍTH & BEATRIX RUF

CAOIMHÍN & BEATRIX *Let's start by discussing your earliest works and then talk about how what you do has changed over the years and what the reasons were for those changes.*

SEAN In graduate school (1984–1986) I was making huge figurative wooden sculptures of fighting animals based on things like Goya's bullfight etchings and scenes from literature. To make figurative art in art school was the 'wrong' thing to do back then at a time when Minimalism and Conceptual art were taught. It was thought preposterous, laughable, so of course how could I resist?

CAOIMHÍN *Despite the fact that Neo-Expressionist painting – Schnabel, Basquiat, Clemente, Kiefer, and the like – had swept the globe over the previous five years or so?*

SEAN Yes. They were on the radar but not taught or discussed very much, like contemporary artists today are not 'taught' in schools, but discussed privately by students on their own. I also made large minimalist sculptures à la Ronald Bladen but I subverted them by having them double as skateboard ramps. I would exhibit these things in the center of my studio. On the walls surrounding them were a torrent of words, confessional writings and cartoons in graphite and marker along with huge action oil paintings splashed directly on the wall. When students and faculty would come for critiques they would read the walls with their backs to my giant sculptures. It never dawned on me that writing and painting would become the center of my art. Because I was a sculpture major I thought I would become a sculptor.

I moved to New York in the fall of 1986 when the East Village gallery scene was thriving and Jeff Koons was the Master of the Universe. I was impressed by his art and created a body of work that in retrospect was probably influenced by it. Store-bought plaster busts of famous writers, composers, and mythological characters were set in cylinders of clear polyester resin and displayed upon wooden pedestals that I designed and turned at a lathe shop. I had two exhibits of this work, one in Tommy Solomon's Garage in Los Angeles in 1989, and one in Postmasters Gallery in New York in 1990. They were reviewed well but the work didn't feel right. I didn't trust it or the small success it had. It wasn't the real me. At the same time I lost a girlfriend who I was crazy for. Whenever my love life is imperiled, I become... well, basically the truth comes out.

It wasn't a strategy to begin writing again – I was heartsick and needed to vent. Later on while re-reading some of this stuff I realized its potential as art and I started writing with this notion. I began with a screenplay of a struggling artist in 90s New York City based on Knut Hamsun's novel HUNGER. I was greatly impressed by the type of writing in it and in Dostoyevsky's CRIME AND PUNISHMENT – the way in which the authors gave voice to the inside of the anti-hero's head. It hit me like a ton of bricks when I first read these books. This was how I thought, this was how I wrote, this was my thing. I wanted my work to be a sort of 90s version of HUNGER and I wanted to operate as the anti-hero within it.

CAOIMHÍN *But, HUNGER is, after all, a novel rather than a work of visual art.*

SEAN Right. But what I was doing was also a reaction against 'text art' in New York at that time, by artists like Hans Haacke or Mary Kelly. I thought that if text is going to be on a gallery wall, then it should damn well be... well, I just wanted to do my own version of it, one that ended up being intensely personal. I quickly learned to use the power of giving away little bits of myself to feed other people's voyeuristic tendencies.

CAOIMHÍN *Which meant turning yourself into an exhibitionist.*

In the early 90s I sometimes used writings by my sister Maura such as her thank you notes for wedding gifts. Through her writing you got a different picture than probably what she had intended, and that's what attracted me to it. As you read more and more of them the story wasn't, "oh, what a sweet girl who is thankful for these wonderful gifts" but more like "this is my reality, these gifts suck. God damn it! Is this all I get? Is this my new life?" I thought it went so much further in describing her than she could have if she had sat down and written her life's story.

I realized that ultimately I could not control everything either. The picture I was rendering was something other than what I had intended. Another thing I found was that I could humiliate an audience by humiliating myself by using their self-recognition. It fueled my subject matter for a while, but I was in conflict. I wanted approval and popularity but this was a strange way to get it because I was in a sense humiliating myself to become more popular. I would ask myself things like "do I actually want recognition so badly that I'll jerk off on camera?" The palpable question was: are they laughing with me or at me? My instinct is now, and was then, for privacy. Exhibiting my whole early body of work was extremely counterintuitive. On the eve of my 1992 show at Andrea Rosen Gallery I was so nervous about what I had exposed about myself in the art works that I broke out in shingles. Luckily the show was well received. After this I measured my commitment to an artwork by how embarrassed I was of it. Now, at this point, I simply can't write the way I wrote back then because I'm too…

CAOIMHÍN *Self-conscious?*

SEAN Yeah. But not self-conscious 'scared' but self-conscious in that I know too much about what I'm doing. I understand it too well. Everything's purposeful now. That's why my current show with Andrea Rosen (2004) is like a parody of my earlier self. The text, as it appears in the new paintings, are like echoes of an earlier event ricocheting in the far reaches of the brain or through space or something.

CAOIMHÍN *It's no longer a continuous narrative. The texts tend to be short words or phrases repeatedly superimposed on themselves in the manner of a graphic rendition of an echo. They're more heraldic, or emblematic, or epigrammatic. So, they're self-conscious self-quotation?*

SEAN Yes. There's very little direct writing where I felt something and wrote it. My earlier work was solely 'feel it and write it.' In this show most of it happened on pieces of paper and then I copied it. I've never done that with paintings before. Anyway, it's different now. I just can't sit there and complain about depression anymore, because it's not accurate.

CAOIMHÍN *But didn't that realization come along as early as the mid-90s, the realization that with success came an inability for your audience to perceive you as this unsuccessful slacker artist?*

SEAN Right.

CAOIMHÍN *I know you have always had a problem with that perception of you as a 'slacker artist,' though that was your shtick for a while.*

SEAN That's what people thought of me. That's what they wrote about. But I was never disaffected and I was never pessimistic about my future. I was quite the opposite. I had every intention of being a very hardworking and important artist. I deeply believe in myself. That's probably what is very hard for people to believe. How else could anyone confess all this crap if they weren't utterly confident? I'm not afraid of humiliation because I know that ultimately I have nothing to be ashamed of.

As it turns out, I never actually was a slacker, but when I first began to get press this was in a lot of it. Coming out of obscurity I was just so thankful I was getting any press at all that I was willing to accept anything they said, even though it wasn't true. So I was, like, "yeah, okay, I'm a slacker." It was immature of me because now I have to live it down (laughs).

CAOIMHÍN *It did chime with what was in the air at the time, the whole 'Generation X' thing.*

SEAN Yeah. But I either grew out of it or it was never really true. Maybe it was a combination of both.

CAOIMHÍN *What might have given that impression was the rhythm of self-deprecation and self-satisfaction, or indeed exultation that remains a constant in any of your longer narrative texts to this day, don't you think?*

SEAN I don't know if that's a hallmark of anything particularly 'Generation X' or 'slacker.' The Generation X condition, as defined by Douglas Coupland – was that the generation before mine, the baby boom generation, got all the good jobs and that there's no place for us to go, and we can only get service industry jobs, and there's no career for us anywhere – a claim that I think is stupid. I never believed that for a second. I always felt totally empowered and capable within my profession. In fact, I felt that I was part of a generation of artists that would put form back in art.

CAOIMHÍN *What? Could you say something about that?*

SEAN Well, that's exactly what I was talking about earlier when comparing my writing to the work of previous artists using text. I put 'form' right back into text art again. I mean 'form' in the sense of 'personality,' 'humanity.' To put form back into abstract painting or sculpture was to put an image in it. With all due respect to Neo-Expressionism, it was my generation who made that popular again. I did it in my various different ways. Others of my contemporaries did it in their ways.

Neo-Expressionism may have been the first visceral reaction against Minimalism and Conceptualism, but I know that when I took on 'the project' or 'the mantle' or 'the responsibility' to move or evolve painting into a truly new form I wasn't merely going to react against history. I was going to use everything history offered me. That's why one of my clowns alone in a landscape is as much a descendant of Vito Acconci's SEEDBED as it is from Hudson River School painting and the notion of the anti-hero from literature.

CAOIMHÍN *Are you comparing the reintroduction of narrative into text to the reinsertion of figuration into picture making?*

SEAN Yes. I think that's partly what my texts did. There were actual stories. There were beginnings and endings. There were plots with climaxes and turning points. There was human emotional content.

CAOIMHÍN *So, to return to specific formal developments in your work, what happened after you discarded the yellow legal pad?*

SEAN Well there was a reason I discarded my yellow legal pad. It was my book [SIC] (1993), first published by Publicsfear Press Ltd. in 1993 as a limited first edition of 250 and then by Riverhead Books in 1995. This book was the culmination of all of my yellow legal pad work. It was like a bomb that went off in my life. It's the point at which everything we've been discussing thus far came to a head. It included the reverb I spoke of from AN AMERICAN FAMILY where art influences life. It included the question of whether I was in control of or a victim of my candor. It was fueled by heartache like my earliest art writing was and it painfully detailed a humiliating infatuation. Most importantly it was conceptual art with 'form' re-inserted. It literally dripped with humanity. It was figuration returned to the minimal form that text art had been in the 70s. [SIC] combined my art and life very successfully, but this created huge problems for me. So many people felt personally betrayed by it that it forced the question for me: what is more important, my art or my life? If I was to love anyone and expect them to love me could I continue to do this? I was way overexposed and genuinely humiliated by this book and I craved privacy, a fig leaf of some sort. So I continued along a new form I had invented previously where I could write what I wanted to but no one would be able to find it. I'd take a giant piece of photo backdrop paper and would just fill it up with stream-of-consciousness text. There was so much writing on these giant pieces of paper that one would lose one's place constantly while reading it and this gave me a place to hide. I completed four of these: I SUCK. RIGHT?... FUCK YOU! (1991), ANYONE'S ORGASM (1992), HARD MALE/SOFT MALE (1993), and DINGLEBERRY SEAN (1993). Each of them was an enormous amount of work so I became fearful that they'd rip, that they'd never last, and that's when I sought out giant pieces of unstretched linen to paint my words on, simply because the medium, oil on linen, has proven durable. Art for me is all about survival, immortality. Painting simply lasts longer than ballpoint pen on paper. So, just like that I was painting. Pandora's box had been opened.

Also at this same time, as I was making the transition from my yellow legal pad phase to my text painting stage, there was another significant development. I was sculpting a series of nine naughty naked Leprechauns. Each was based on something either specific or vague from the history of sculpture. I'd do this to force a comparison between me, "20th-century cartoon raised Sean," to some of the more revered moments of art history such as Rodin's JOHN THE BAPTIST or Donatello's DAVID, etc. I was eager to demonstrate how I both did and did not rate, because that demonstration illustrated art's dilemma in our time.

BEATRIX *Art's dilemma? Could you say something more about that?*

SEAN In the wake of an art education that devalued skill in art-making what were we left with? An art that is dominated by a couple of old 70s idea people who, by the way, guard their turf like old junkyard dogs standing in the middle of the worn out dust circles that surrounds their doghouses. "NO TRESPASSING!" I admire these guys and what they've done, but I don't want to be trapped in a world dominated by or confined to their ideas alone. This was the terrain of my art education and what I wanted to react against. Which is why the sculptures in my MFA thesis exhibit were like Ronald Bladen sculptures that you could skateboard in. It was putting the 'Me' back into austere art forms. This is also why pre-World War II European painters figure so heavily for me now, because their art was the last gasp before art became supposedly conceptually checkmated and minimally reduced to nothing here in America during the 60s and 70s. Art has been reeling ever since. This will all make more sense when we talk about what I did in the later 90s and what I'm up to now.

So, to go along with these sculptures I made a video that depicted myself in the nude and in various states of arousal, mocking famous Italian sculptures, called ITALIAN HIGH RENAISSANCE AND BAROQUE SCULPTURE (1993). Again I was thinking along the Gilbert and George line of a living, breathing, acting sculpture on video among my actual sculptures. But more importantly I was taking on the notion of narcissism. It was my view that all art is narcissism. For anyone to believe that the thing they made is worthy of attention, exultation, money, and being cherished throughout time by generations to come is basically narcissistic! In this video I sought to illustrate this conceptually and in reality. I mean, you can't fake an erection.

CAOIMHÍN *Bringing it back to your paintings, as soon as you actually make a decision to put these words not on a throwaway, lowly material, but on canvas, you plug into a very resonant history of picture-making, of fine art, of durability of materials and so forth.*

SEAN Right.

CAOIMHÍN *You were obviously conscious of that at the time.*

SEAN Yes, I was. But there are a few different things I was trying to capture at that point and least among them was probably 'painting history.' It was really a question of the aesthetics of necessity. In other words, the way the thing looked was what the process delivered to it. I didn't conceive of a look for those things. They just happened to look that way because what I wanted to do was get every thought I had while painting the painting onto its surface.

So it was very different writing than the yellow legal pad stuff. I thought it was a total evolution away. Conceptually, it was basically "Kilroy was here" again and again and again. Why I thought that was so important is because I believe that's what art is in civilization. At its foundation it's really just making your mark.

CAOIMHÍN *Saying "I was here"?*

SEAN Yes, "I was here." Ever since the caves of Lascaux, where people blew pigment around their handprint on the cave wall, art making has sought to record the life or existence of the artist. Right through the history of Western art up to now where art making became so self-referential, "I was here" has been a huge part of it. This is what I admire so much about On Kawara and that sort of work.

CAOIMHÍN *"I am still alive. I was here?"*

SEAN "I am still alive, I am here." But my large text paintings just took this idea much further and gave you the exact thoughts I was having at the point of the painting's creation. So I'm not just telling you that "I'm still alive," I'm telling you what I was thinking when I was alive. From the beginning of the painting to the end, everything I thought and could possibly write was recorded. It's an On Kawara idea, deeply elaborated upon.

CAOIMHÍN *That's interesting in that there's a sense of immediacy in the work, but it also involves the immediate sense of a narrative produced in real time, which again is very different from reading a book,*

SEAN Right. It's because everything's a performance.

CAOIMHÍN *A performance of immediacy, which is a trick, a strategy whereby the viewer is invited to imagine they're experiencing these thoughts in the same time – in real time – as you originally did, if you're registering everything you think and leaving nothing out.*

SEAN Right.

CAOIMHÍN *But it has, of course, its echoes in the history of stream-of-consciousness in modernist literature as well.*

SEAN Yes it does. Those stream-of-consciousness paintings of that period such as DUMB DUMB (1993), or FOR THE LOVE OF NOTHING (1994), or THOUGHT BUBBLE (1994) are very large and difficult to read. You start on the left and by the time you move all the way to the right you lose your place and can't find it again. Therefore, as you read it, you just get these fragmented thoughts. Ultimately, I wanted to be more in control of the experience. That's where the 'patch paintings' come from.

CAOIMHÍN *You're talking about paintings like SELF-SOMETHING (1994).*

SEAN Right. They're very much like me standing on a stage trying to entertain you as much as possible while basically giving the picture of human thought. It's taking a much more aggressive role in actively trying to entertain anybody who stands in front of the painting. I don't want the viewer to walk away. These little 'patches' are just enough to read and to maybe hook you into reading another. One in ten hopefully can make you smile or laugh at them and as you continue to read, hopefully you begin to see a bigger picture.

CAOIMHÍN *It's the difference between a very long monologue and a lot of epigrams.*

SEAN Yes.

CAOIMHÍN *The monologic and the epigrammatic modes are quite different.*

SEAN Basically, it's the difference between a monologist and a comedian. As a comedian tells hundreds of jokes in a row, he eventually begins to paint a portrait of himself. If you hear a hundred butt jokes, you will begin to think after a while, "oh, this guy's got an anal fetish." It gets sort of creepy. So when you read everything that's written on the painting, there's a picture of me that is constructed that I can't control. Now we're getting into the fact that all art earnestly done is basically self-portraiture.

CAOIMHÍN *As the title SELF-SOMETHING indicates.*

SEAN Yes.

CAOIMHÍN *Right after this, very specific images begin to appear amongst the words.*

SEAN Well not quite, there was an endgame played out with the large unstretched word paintings. After filling many of them for a year and a half, I was tired of writing and tired of the look of them. So I phased into a willful form of writer's block by making striped paintings. I did a show with Regen Projects in Los Angeles for which I made a huge word painting titled THOUGHT BUBBLE. Exhausted from it, I painted stripes on my next canvases, as if it were a mental vacation, and titled the first one ABSENCE OF THOUGHT BUBBLE (1994). This was also the show where clown and chimp imagery first appeared in sculpture.

CAOIMHÍN *So after this, images began to appear in your text paintings?*

SEAN Yeah. The first was the painting titled I'M A CLOWN IN A WORLD OF CHIMPS (1994), in which a clown and chimpanzee are fighting, and two other paintings GROOVIN' CORDUROY MIND-SNOT/7092 (1994), and STARING AT MY ASS IN THE MIRROR (1994), that were painted under a sort of Picabia influence. These would have been the first paintings where I wanted to put in or use images. They were part of my 1994 show at Contemporary Fine Arts Gallery in Berlin. There were just three paintings and a sculpture of a chimpanzee titled ICH MACHE MICH (1994). I thought this show was of particular importance because it was my first concerted effort into the realm of a more traditional and less conceptual form of picture making.

CAOIMHÍN *These were very oblique references to Picabia.*

SEAN GROOVIN' CORDUROY MIND-SNOT/7092 was a reference to his painting titled 7091 (1938) which is a spoof on abstraction. All the paintings that I have like this – where there's a scribble, and all the conjoining areas that are made by the scribble are colored a different color – including some overlapped images taken from Picasso – are in what I think of as my 'Picabia 7091 series.' They, like his, are my spoof on abstraction, but like all ironic gestures, once repeated it becomes sincere. They're all titled '709-something.' I'm up to maybe 7099 or 7100 in this ongoing series. But they take totally different forms at this point. Some are striped paintings, some are 'Picasso paintings,' and some are text paintings. Picabia is the only artist I can think of who was totally free from the beginning of his art-making career to the end. He utilized many different media and forms and he was great in all of them. He represents freedom to me. When I refer to him in paintings I'm not copying their look so much as quoting him obliquely, as a sort of symbol for my own artistic freedom, which I think is essential for my survival.

When I painted I'M A CLOWN IN A WORLD OF CHIMPS, I had reread a few years of my own writing and had recognized the cyclical pattern of self-aggrandizement and self-abasement. This thought pattern had become almost like a perpetual motion machine, out of which images and content were spinning. So I gave them both figures and characters. The chimp was self-aggrandizement and the clown was self-abasement. That's why in every single cartoon on this painting the chimp is getting the better of the clown.

CAOIMHÍN *You've said before that your interest in Picabia or later Picasso was because you want to be counted among the great artists, like them.*

SEAN I said that in a recording, an audio piece titled DEAR PICASSO (2001).

CAOIMHÍN *So that should be read within the context of a particular artwork rather than as an artist's statement?*

SEAN Yes. I'm fully aware that when I say that kind of thing it's kind of sad and endearing for you all to listen to. That particular piece is an excellent example of me personally meaning what I'm saying, but realizing that to others it's not credible. I didn't expect anybody to think "Sean is Picasso," or "He thinks he's going to be the next Picasso." But I do think that another artist can recognize that wish or thought pattern. That's a big part of my art: presenting an embarrassing situation like that and hoping for the viewer's empathy.

CAOIMHÍN *Presenting what may be a more universal aspiration than other artists are willing to concede openly?*

SEAN Right. I think it's a sign of strength. When you first hear that tape you think "oh, how sad and pathetic." But actually, I felt it was a bold and powerful thing to do. I'm not afraid of my dreams (laughs). Even if I know some of them are probably out of reach. I mean, I do want to be important. I'm not selling that one away here. I am just saying that I'm not crazy. I know that there are certain things about Picasso that… (pause). No, I can't even say it. Sorry. I'm not going to say it (laughs). You know what I think. You know I'm not going to say that I'm not a great artist. I won't. I don't believe it.

CAOIMHÍN *But the pictorial quotation from Picabia and the performance of the role of an artist aspiring to be Picasso are rather different.*

SEAN I think they're related in that they allude to other artists to create new meaning for myself. I admire Picasso for his unquestionable genius. I envy that. To quote him is to allude to the notion of artistic genius. I admire Picabia for the creative freedom he displayed throughout his life. I too need freedom, I have to continually change to be excited about making art. People generally do agree that I might be as free as he was. The difference is that he could afford to be, he had family money (laughs). But you know what it was with Picabia specifically? I needed help to create a picture because I was coming out of a sea of text, from two-dimensional graphic paintings. I was looking for help from art history to be able to create a new kind of picture from text. So I used Picabia. Later I used other things… such as breasts (laughter).

CAOIMHÍN *Would you like to talk about the 'breast painting:' THE ETHER OF MEMORY (1994)?*

SEAN What can I say? If you want to paint something, paint what you love! It sounds so stupid, but it's honest.

CAOIMHÍN *This was in 1994, a time when for a white, male artist to paint a profusion of breasts was probably the most unpopular subject you could have chosen.*

SEAN Exactly. It was provocative. Sort of bad-boyish, rather than scandalous or nasty. Shall we even say political? It was just so taboo in those knee-jerk politically correct times that I couldn't resist. The objectification of women is nothing to be proud of. But I have never believed that women were anything but men's complete equals. At the same time to believe that 'enlightened' men don't fetishize women's bodies is crazy. Of course we do.

CAOIMHÍN *How about the title, THE ETHER OF MEMORY?*

SEAN Breasts in the memory, at the point of self-gratification, on one level. If you read this text it's about my maternal lineage as far back as I could imagine it. I'm a painter because my grandmother was a painter, and my mother is a painter. As a kid I used to go over to my grandmother's house to paint. She had great big boobs and every time I'd go over there she'd hug me right into the middle of them before we'd go up into her attic studio to paint. It was one of the most pleasurable things. I loved it. So it was the maternal-mammary-origins of myself as a painter thing.

FOOTBALL DUCK (2003), the bronze sculpture and FOOTBALL DUCK (1999), the painting, also relate to that. My football practice field was right next to my grandmother's house. I hated going to football practice so much that I'd just skip out and go to her house to paint. I'd be sitting there in front of an easel with my shoulder pads and cleats on, painting geraniums while my teammates were out practicing. They are portraits of my youthful self-perception in conflict between 'sporting manliness' and 'feminine artisticness.'

CAOIMHÍN *What was the next step after THE ETHER OF MEMORY?*

SEAN The next big step was my chimpanzee show, 1995, at Andrea Rosen Gallery. I made paintings, a sculpture and a video using a visit by a chimpanzee to my studio. I hoped the chimpanzee would represent me or portray me. This is where things really began to open up.

With my license to paint given to me from Picabia, now anything could go onto a canvas including marks made by a chimp. I wasn't restricted by just what I could think to write. I could make images and use illusion, which meant I could do anything and go anywhere I wanted inside the rectangle of a painting. It turns out that art's oldest form, painting, is art's truest freedom, which is what I was looking for.

With the painting LOOKING FOR MR. GODBAR (1995), text floats over an illusionistic cloudy blue sky. All of a sudden the words occupied a physical space, not an imaginary space. I meant it to be like when you're looking out an airplane window, five miles up. If you're not reading a book or engaged in the movie your thoughts are uniquely loud at that point. I was remembering those sorts of thoughts and that type of thinking. For me, God becomes an issue…

CAOIMHÍN *God becomes an issue, but more mundanely, with this image of a wide expanse of sky in LOOKING FOR MR. GODBAR, so does the history of the sublime, from nineteenth-century romantic landscape painting to the abstract sublime and beyond.*

SEAN Yes. Definitely. It was absolutely that. The Hudson River School. A small insignificant figure in sublime landscape. What I was writing on this was in fact transcendental. Which is what those people were all about…

CAOIMHÍN *Or a seascape, such as 36 HOURS (1995)?*

SEAN …Yes, absolutely, with this too. But this had something more specific about it. I began reading many books of survival stories, of people on life rafts after their boats had gone down in the ocean, or solo circumnavigators kind of losing their mind on the trip. So, rather than looking out the airplane window, I imagined myself on this trip. And when you listen to your thoughts this clearly for so long – I filled so many canvases like this – it doesn't take long for me, at least, to get into this "why are we here" question, which just keeps coming up and up and up.

CAOIMHÍN *Soon after this, in paintings like ALONE (1996), which relates formally to 36 HOURS, you lose the textual element in the paintings.*

SEAN Yes. And this is where I totally lose my audience (laughs). Not really, but I felt no one adequately understood it. Actually, ALONE has never been exhibited. However, many other clown paintings from this period were exhibited at Contemporary Fine Arts in Berlin (1996), and at Rebecca Camhi Gallery in Athens (1996). In ALONE there's an impasto-painted clown, on top of an illusionistic seascape, who was directly replacing the text from a painting like NAVAL GAZE (1995) or 36 HOURS. I loved this painting. I got so high from making it that I wanted to do it again and again. So these paintings of sad lonely clowns struggling in nature became a full series, which, I guess, then acquired a new meaning in my life.

Up until this point everything I had done had been amazingly well received. I'm referring to the superficial things relating to career that just kept feeling better with every show that I made. When I removed the text from my paintings, all of a sudden there were enormous problems. No one knew what to make of them. The thing that people probably trusted about my art – writing on a painting – was gone. I felt misunderstood. Writing was just one method of re-inserting form into conceptually based art for me. It wasn't the be-all and end-all.

Therefore, when I began to make more ever-saddening clowns, their sadness referred to the fact that I was painting them and that no one seemed to understand them. It became a kind of conceptual death spiral. The more I made, the worse it seemed and the sadder the clowns became. Which I found hilarious when I was sitting around in my studio discussing it with friends, but it was also sad. I thought that someday this would be one of my favorite bodies of work and favorite stories to tell. And it is. As my wife hastens to add when I bellyache about this body of work, it has proved to be one of my most popular.

CAOIMHÍN *It's interesting that at certain points in your career there's an emphasis, sometimes literally, on the signature, as in the diptych SEAN LANDERS/7098 (2001). Yet at other times there's a denial of a signature device, which up to this particular point had been writing on paintings.*

SEAN I think all artists' natural reflex is to try to elude definition. But I felt that the clown became that signature. What frustrated me at that time, perhaps, was that I felt this 'new signature' was the same thing as my words.

CAOIMHÍN *I guess people were unwilling to accept it as the same.*

SEAN Maybe they felt that I lacked the facility or permission to 'simply' paint a picture or something. So many artists today paint in a far more lame fashion than I did back then and they get lauded for it. It was probably just timing, or maybe it was the particular emblem, the clown.

CAOIMHÍN *You mean, at the time people might have been saying that a slightly older painter like George Condo had cornered the clown market?*

SEAN No. I got no George Condo comparisons.

CAOIMHÍN *Really?*

SEAN No. Well, not that I knew of or remember. And I shouldn't have. What I was doing then was different. He is, however, one of my favorite living painters.

CAOIMHÍN *Nauman, then? Though it's less obvious, as he's not a painter.*

SEAN They gave me Nauman, probably because no one thought of me as a painter either. I got so much 'Nauman,' and the truth is that I never thought about him at all. If you even accidentally stumble across an old Nauman idea as an artist you will quickly find yourself in a shit storm from the 'Nauman lobby.' People come out of the woodwork to tell you "Nauman did that first," even if he didn't. What does it say about someone's art history education that they think Bruce Nauman invented the idea of clowns in art? He wasn't the first navel-gazer either. Artists contemplating creativity has a full history before he ever got to it. I think they saw me as a conceptual artist, plain and simple, and wearing those blinders perhaps I appeared like Nauman. The crazy thing is that no one ever thought these were paintings. That's what's remarkable. To this day people still don't think I'm a painter. I certainly have made a hell of a lot of paintings.

CAOIMHÍN *Well, what did people think they were?*

SEAN They thought this was a conceptual art act. That it was an oil painting as performance. Fair enough, but at the end of the day I did have to squirt paint out of a tube and spread it on with a brush, you know? It's a painting!

CAOIMHÍN *The distinction was probably more useful in the late 80s because the whole return of painting that had happened a decade earlier, whether perceived positively or negatively, had been seen partly as a reaction to conceptual art. So, painting per se and conceptual art were perhaps more obviously perceived as in opposition then. In any case, the initial negative critical response didn't stop you painting. What did it cause you to do within the painting?*

SEAN What it did allow me to do was paint more clowns becoming sadder in more extreme physical conditions. So that's why I find this particular series so central to the whole body of work. It's still self-conscious writing, but there's no actual text. It's me worrying about how I'm perceived, but through these cartoons.

BEATRIX *But doesn't some sort of collective consciousness come into play with the clown figure? I wonder if you can just say that it's about you. This is inherently a collective experience. You can speak about yourself as much as you want, but it's a shared feeling. Failure is a shared feeling, or wanting to be great, or wanting to last.*

SEAN Yes, and this had been one of my early surprises. When I showed this vulnerable side of myself that it was rewarded by the empathy and understanding of others. It turns out that most people are like-minded. That's the axis on which my work functions, and always has. The way that I reach out to the viewer is by giving them something utterly personal that they recognize within themselves. Like Vito Acconci did in that 70s performance on a pier giving away whispered secrets to people who'd make the trip to see him. However, I discovered that it doesn't always take 100 percent truth in a work of art to be convincing. In a Hollywood movie, for instance, you'll notice that the whole thing is ridiculous and absurd, but there are brief moments of something that seems utterly real, that you recognize, and that makes the whole picture convincing. Zuzu's petals, for instance, from Frank Capra's IT'S A WONDERFUL LIFE. It's the same in a text piece. I can write all bullshit throughout the whole thing and have just a few moments that reach through the bullshit and actually touch you with the truth, and this makes the whole thing convincing. I learned very early on that I wasn't only portraying myself, and that was fortunate. Otherwise it would have only confirmed that I was a crazy.

CAOIMHÍN *Let's return to the notion of signature and signature devices. The performance of signature in repetitive composition is something that is at the heart of 20th-century art, even the type of painting that doesn't inform your work much. The first thing a Jackson Pollock says to us today is "this is a Jackson Pollock."*

SEAN Right. And I have my trademark signature. It's the text on canvas. That's my Pollock-like signature medium. Anybody else who does that falls into 'my thing.' I feel like I own it. If there is a signature for me, it's that. And it's the unifier for all my work, right from the beginning to now.

CAOIMHÍN *So, when the cards of recent art history are shuffled, how do you think your work in this 'signature medium' will relate to that of painters as different as Ed Ruscha or Christopher Wool?*

SEAN I admire both of those artists. I welcome any comparisons with them, but I'm also secure in the knowledge that my work is completely its own thing when compared to theirs or anybody else's. It's just a brief moment for me in which I can be compared with them. There are so many artists that I can briefly be compared to, but then I move on. I don't think about them before I make the work. It just happens that it looks a certain way or shares a similarity but if it's intentional, you'll know it because I'll write about it. Like I did with Hamsun, Kawara, Acconci, Magritte, Picabia, Picasso, Hogarth, etc.

CAOIMHÍN *Yet, despite your claims to the signature medium of text on canvas, you consciously chose to jettison text around 1996 to produce what you now perversely claim to be among your favorite paintings, as you said earlier!*

SEAN Right. But you're assuming that I am the sole judge of what my signature is. In fact, others kind of assess that for you. I also said that we artists like to defy definition, and that I need to be free to do whatever I want when I want to do it, like Picabia. One can only do well what one loves to do. Anything else will be mediocre. I also didn't get to say earlier how, having had so many years of writing, the freedom of not writing was like a huge weight off my back. I had just gotten so sick of hearing my thoughts. It got really claustrophobic after a while. The freedom of just painting a picture was, like, "oh my God, everybody else who just does this has it so easy. Why do I have to push the stone up the hill? I don't have to." However, I quickly learned that I did have to. Or at least my audience expected it. I don't know why people are so uncomfortable with change within an artist or change in their 'signature.' I initially turned to Picabia for a way out. Now I look to him at times for solace, almost. That's why I keep referring to him symbolically. He's almost like a father figure or something. He sort of reassures me that it's okay to change, and to do what I need to do.

CAOIMHÍN *It's probably more common among artists of your generation of the 90s than previous generations to have what amounts to a signature style of doing lots of different things, to put it tritely.*

SEAN Well, to be trapped in a single style for life just seems like misery. How can you take yourself seriously if you do this? Even Pollock didn't. He has a full breadth of work too. What we commonly know of him is that one thing, but when you see a fuller perspective there's a lot more to that guy. He was brave enough to try many forms.

CAOIMHÍN *The reason why some people choose to have a practice that is other than varied, I suppose, is that what drives them most strongly is an act of negation or refinement that needs to take the same form. And they find it again and again and again, rather than insisting on variety.*

SEAN That's what I think is really suspect. Because, as a practitioner, I know how fast things get thin. And to think that refining just one thing can be interesting to somebody over the long term… well, I just question their curiosity. Assuming that curiosity represents intelligence, then how intelligent are they? To continue to crank out the same product is desperately cowardly. It's one of the saddest things. Yet it's what the art world seems to reward most handsomely. It's like the system has evolved to encourage mediocrity.

CAOIMHÍN *But arguably, you can have curiosity and refinement, rather than curiosity and variety. It's just not your particular way.*

SEAN As a practitioner I'm suspicious of it.

CAOIMHÍN *So you think that Agnes Martin or Robert Ryman should throw the odd clown in there?*

SEAN Yeah (laughs). Robert Ryman is an excellent example. He should have had me over to write on them (laughter). You know, there are emperor's new clothes arguments, and maybe there is none more apt than Robert Ryman. I know what a debate this could create, but ultimately it's a white painting again and again. What do you think? Are you totally sold with Robert Ryman's stuff? Some of them are beautiful, I guess. But, you know, so is some stucco work. The same goes for Ad Reinhardt. In a lot of ways those two people basically created this sort of phony checkmate to painting. It was totally false. It didn't exist. Painting was supposedly dead and they supposedly killed it. Its immediate reaction was Photo-Realism. And what came after? Neo-Expressionism? And then there was Neo-Geo, and then what…? Nothing? Obviously there were many very not-dead exceptions during this time, including Martin Kippenberger and George Condo, to name a few of my favorites. But then when painting really begins to become 'rehabilitated,' or to pick up steam again, I think, is by my generation, who actually go about the process of rebuilding this 'troubled' thing with rules that say that anything goes, and that has Conceptual art as its influence as much as, say,Velásquez, Manet, or Picasso.

CAOIMHÍN *Without any sense of imminent closure or belatedness or crisis?*

SEAN Right. That's why I'm not a slacker artist? In fact, if I were a slacker artist, then a black painting would make a lot of sense. But trying to reinvent painting is the project for everybody and anybody who paints. That's the mission for whoever takes it on.

CAOIMHÍN *But your commitment, nevertheless, is not to painting per se as a medium.*

SEAN My commitment is not solely to painting. It is to art in general.

CAOIMHÍN *But here you are talking about painting.*

SEAN I happen to be, but I don't limit myself to painting, because I don't have to. Others have to.

CAOIMHÍN *You feel they have to?*

SEAN Or they're not very good at anything else. They're not very good writers. And they're not very good sculptors. Basically, their fear prevents them from going there. I just don't have as much reticence, even with a medium that I'm not a master of. I don't mind heading straight into it. It's like the Icarus myth. I strive for greatness and if I crash and burn, and if the arc of my descent has meaning then I have created a new kind of art. There's a story in failure that's as beautiful as the story of triumph. Which is that whole anti-hero thing I learned from HUNGER.

CAOIMHÍN *If you fake failure too often, it becomes…*

SEAN No, it's not faking failure. It's trying and failing. It is failure. Failure is a story I want to tell because it's a story that everybody knows, a story that everyone lives, but no one wants to own.

BEATRIX *But you want to own it?*

SEAN Yeah. It's like beach-front property that no one wants because there's a sewage pipe on it. Well, the raw sewage is terrible but I'm on the beach.

BEATRIX *And the beach means what in this analogy?*

SEAN Art History. I hope.

CAOIMHÍN *So, it's "Try again, fail better," as Beckett put it.*

SEAN Yeah. Well, you can't say Beckett enough in regards to me.

CAOIMHÍN *Can we talk a little about your sculpture? You started with clay but you've also cast bronzes. That choice of materials is quite significant and resonant. Bronze is an enduring material. It's the material of monuments.*

SEAN Well, that's why I stopped writing on paper and started writing on lead-primed linen. I wanted it to last. That's behind my impulse to make art. I want it to last, to outlast me. In the show at Andrea Rosen Gallery (2004), that's what the painting THERE WAS A TIME… (2004), is stating. It describes my belief that, incrementally, I transfer my life into artworks, into these static objects, and when I die that's all that will be left. Perhaps that's corny, tacky, laughable, or whatever you want to call it, but it's at the basis of my impulse to do this. I've always taken great pleasure in telling the truth, especially when it's the 'wrong' thing to do. Most artists will do their damnedest to avoid this kind of statement.

CAOIMHÍN *But the ways in which you would choose to be remembered have apparently changed. You once said that you'd be as happy to be remembered for producing a sad funny little painting as for Robert Smithson's SPIRAL JETTY.*

SEAN Well, that's not changed at all.

CAOIMHÍN *There is a difference between the implied modesty of a 'sad little painting' and the monumental aspirations of a bronze sculpture.*

SEAN Monumental? I've never done anything taller than three feet.

CAOIMHÍN *Fair enough. But there are intimations of the monumental in the material itself that are unavoidable.*

SEAN I disagree. It's just a satisfying, lasting material. As far as we know oil paintings last, what, five, six hundred years? We know that bronzes last at least six thousand years. What I had in mind when I mentioned the 'sad little painting' were paintings like THE IDEA MAN (1998), or THREE NOSE

GUY (1998). Anything from the 'image and text' series, my 'vache period,' was exactly what I had in mind when I was saying that. But we are ahead of ourselves. Can I go back and connect a few dots?

BEATRIX *Sure.*

SEAN I made that series after a long evolution in my image-painting which began with the Hogarth series (1996). I took one painting by William Hogarth titled A MIDNIGHT MODERN CONVERSATION (1732) and made a dozen or so paintings from it. I used it to tell the story of my outgrowing the drinking-based camaraderie/culture on which my friends and I had subsisted for so long, where we debated and became inspired by each other's ideas. Where we kept each other company as we waited to be 'discovered.' Of finding my future wife and deciding to get married. It was an incredibly juvenile rendition of the story of growing up. This was the most overtly 'wrong' art I had ever made. They were mad paintings, but it was in line with my work. I was telling a story from my life through painting and using art history to do it. They stunned the gallerists with whom I exhibited them, Stuart Regen and Shaun Caley of Regen Projects in Los Angeles, who I cared for greatly. I'll never forget the look on Shaun's face when they came out of the crate. Needless to say, I was never asked to do another show there.

Next was the clown series, which I have already elaborated upon. That evolved into my 1997 show at Andrea Rosen Gallery in New York. These paintings were amalgams of two or three famous paintings done in a Disney-like cartoon style but in my own hand, with all of its own virtuosity or lack thereof. DANCE OF LIFE (1997), is half Matisse's DANCE (FIRST VERSION) (1909) and half Poussin's BACCHANAL BEFORE A STATUE OF PAN (1631–33). ZORKON (1997), is half Winslow Homer's BREEZING UP [A FAIR WIND] (1876) and half Géricault's RAFT OF THE MEDUSA (1819). For me the Disney influence was important because it represented the collective unconscious of imagery for people raised in the Baby Boom era and forward. We all have this sort of imagery in our heads, be it Looney Tunes, Japanimation or Tin Tin. To resist it and refer solely to imagery from the Met, Louvre and Prado I felt was just too pretentious. Again, it was the 'wrong' thing to have done but I was eager to, because it spoke of being an artist in my time. I was comparing myself favorably or not to the greats of art history to illustrate my or any artist's predicament of trying to make 'new' art in the wake of art history and, more specifically, in the wake of my generation's art education, which was dominated by theory, Conceptual art, Minimalism and Process art. These shows were my humble effort to re-insert form back into Conceptual art, to 'fail like Icarus' perhaps, but ultimately to use Conceptual art as a dagger against itself. It was a Conceptual art act that was anti-conceptual.

Unfortunately, few people seemed to understand it. Feeling rejected, I finally became despondent to the point where I had to write again for my psychological survival. Which is why I began writing in the first place.

CAOIMHÍN *What fed into the image-making at this point?*

SEAN Magritte's 'vache' period. For me, it represented a brief moment of total creative and painterly freedom and inventiveness within his otherwise very tightly rendered and deliberate body of work. When I first saw the paintings from Magritte's 'vache' period I felt so close to them, it was as if I was seeing my own art. I felt almost possessive of this body of work. I didn't want anyone else to like it because I should be the only one to like it. I felt that this was a language I already knew how to speak without studying it. I could instantly flop into it. And I did, in my way. I would paint the images referring sometimes directly to Magritte as in THREE NOSE GUY, which is inspired by what I call his 'Mr. Slipper Nose' (LE STROPIAT, 1948), though mine looks nothing like his. But most often they were completely my own inventions. All of my 'vache' figures are still part of, or an extension of, my clown language. Every one is clownish, dejected and sad. But the way these were painted in this new 'vache' language that was far more comfortable for me. I found a painting style that fit. It matched my ability, or it was just the right balance of cartoon and illusion for my particular skill level, which is something that was and should always be determined by my interest. I can paint far more 'realistically' if I want to, but the whole point of artistic freedom is not to do what you don't feel like doing. It's to follow your interest.

CAOIMHÍN *Some of these paintings are more overtly sexual than others.*

SEAN Yes, In LE DOMAINE ENCHANTÉ AKA MONSIEUR SAUCISSON (1999), it's just what it is (laughs). You know, he's happy to be where he is. The simple things in life are what's important.

CAOIMHÍN *How preconceived was the imagery in terms of the actual painting process?*

SEAN Oh, not at all. In fact, the way that I would find the images was by working on a stained canvas to begin with. Then I'd pick up my brush and I'd paint a cartoon in the middle of the canvas, not like it, wipe it off, do another, wipe it off, and repeat that process ten to twenty times. The ghost of each cartoon remained visible so there would be a mishmash or a layering of cartoon characters. Often, with that many ghosts of old drawings a new drawing begins to emerge. Many, many of these were found that way. That goes back to the original automatic drawing techniques of the Surrealists. I was just trying to get a good cartoon, and sometimes the best way to get one was to find them by mistake. Many of my sculptures were found in a similar way. I begin a sculpture by building the clay into a skull shape. Even skulls have humanlike characters. Inevitably it reminds me of something or someone and then I sculpt it in that direction.

CAOIMHÍN *Surrealism is the art movement most associated with a fascination with the workings of the unconscious, with automatic writing, with somehow bypassing premeditation, in so far as that's possible. As late as your last show at greengrassi in 2003, where you addressed a pantheon of 20th-century artists, all male, there was a predominance of Surrealists.*

SEAN It's more generally pre-World War II European painting. Like what I was speaking of earlier, how these guys represent to me the last gasp from the long tradition of European painting when art was pretty straightforward. Like when a person sits down in front of a blank canvas and an image arrives, not necessarily from life, but from the imagination. Before post-war American art domination occurred and the whole landscape changed so radically. If you look at all nine artists depicted in that show, with the exception of Duchamp, there's something about that with all of them: Picasso, Picabia, Magritte, Dalí, De Chirico, Braque, Ernst, and Beckmann. When I sit in front of a blank canvas I feel utterly connected to them. I feel I'm in their lineage. If there's a stream of creativity that they dipped their ladle into, I try to dip my ladle into that same one. But, of course, there's some 70s lineage in me as well, like the text-artists that I built my earlier body of work upon. But all of that ultimately stems from Duchamp, which is why he was included.

My Picasso show fits in with this too. I saw 20th-century art as divided by the art of Picasso and Duchamp. Picasso typifies what I've been describing, how an artist sits in front of a blank canvas and an image arrives. And Duchamp is of course the grandfather of Conceptual art. As a representative of my time, a time where artists feel the blood of both of these lineages coursing through their veins, I again sought to create a body of work that typified both. Both men used borrowed imagery. Obviously, Picasso riffed on Velásquez to announce his belief that he belonged in Velásquez's midst historically. Duchamp introduced the idea of the 'ready-made.' Therefore, borrowing another's imagery can be seen as 'ready-made.' To use Picasso's imagery in that way, spelling my name with it in SEAN/7099 (2001), or to write 'genius' with a piece of furniture lifted from a painting of his, FEMME AU BUFFET (1936) and having a variety of his ex-wives and girlfriends he'd depicted whose lives he ruined crying at, or placed on each letter in GENIUS (2001), was using Duchamp to riff on Picasso, melding them together to describe myself and my situation as an artist.

CAOIMHÍN *Let's talk about your reasons for sometimes showing work in a variety of mediums together, a video or audio work as well as sculpture and painting or drawing.*

SEAN I think it's an over-eagerness to please, frankly. I so want to satisfy people, and to be liked. Beyond that, I think it's also a way of showing off my talent by doing the same thing in many different media. It's all the same to me. Everything I do is united through a performance-based quality. I have become a personality operating within my work. When I paint it's a painting by this sort of artist character I've established, the same for sculpture, video, and writing. When I pick up a pen to write I just sort of click into character. Or, the audio piece I played at greengrassi (2000), for instance, which is titled THE MAN WITHIN (2000) and describes my 'greatness,' I just picked up the microphone, switched into character and let it rip. What is perhaps confusing for people is that this character is partly the real me and partly not. I am in a way, still Chris Hamson.

CAOIMHÍN *Had you any particular models for what to do with sculptural form or what to do with video when you first started using these media?*

SEAN As far as the video, it was in part AN AMERICAN FAMILY, as I described earlier. Besides that it was early Wegman videos perhaps, and Spalding Gray to some extent. I saw in Wegman the opportunity to exploit simple humor, and in Gray it was the personality of the artist and storytelling. I began in 1990 with a sort of talk show format and I sat at a desk mocking the radio and telling stories. I wanted them to appear preposterous in the lineage of video art, but in the end be far more entertaining and engaging than actual video art ever was. I wanted to win by losing, in effect. I wanted them to be full of personal content, to hook people through voyeurism and, most importantly, to be 'not boring.' Those early videos sort of evolved into the living sculpture idea à la Gilbert and George. None were ever intended for a captive audience, just something you walk by, and if I hook you, well then good for me. They were closely related to my written pieces, just acted out.

As for sculpture, again it was the 'inappropriate' thing to do at the time, and that interested me. Whether it was clay heads covered in trash bags or traditional clay, it seemed somehow perverse at the time of the 'new-materials sculpture' of Matthew Barney and Michael Joaquin Grey, who were making sculpture that seemed exceedingly smart and new.

Being naturally contrarian, I was interested in returning sculpture to the 'old' and 'dumb' thing it had happily been for thousands of years before they got to it. Long after the Vaseline bench-press melts into the soil or a Richard Serra rusts into the sea my dumb little bronze heads will be humming the tune of my immortality. It's a 'Tortoise and Hare' thing.

CAOIMHÍN *Let's talk a little bit more about virtuosity and your relationship to it. Is it of no interest to you that some people are praised, rightly or wrongly, for their consummate skills in a particular medium at a time when the conscious de-skilling of the media is quite common?*

SEAN I don't try to make 'bad art.' This was the first conversation you and I ever had…

CAOIMHÍN *Right.*

SEAN …and this was the issue I took, as I didn't believe that I belonged in that category. I was just doing what I did – I never feigned naiveté. ICH MACHE MICH, was sculpted as well as I could at that time. Now I can sculpt a chimp far better. I always worked to my level at the time. If it looked really naive or had an absence of virtuosity it's because that was the truth of my situation. The idea being that all art earnestly done is essentially self-portraiture. That's why I compared myself directly to painters like Manet and Matisse and Poussin in that 1997 Andrea Rosen Gallery show, because I knew I didn't rate with them on a skill level. I thought that mine was the story of searching for my comfort level in their midst because that is the situation of a painter or an artist. You're always judged in the context of art history, contemporary art history and ancient art history.

CAOIMHÍN *Yet some of the immediate predecessors you found inspirational right at the beginning, such as Jeff Koons, never felt any need to acquire even the most rudimentary facility, as one can always commission other virtuosos in different media, from glassblowing Venetians to American sign painters, to execute one's work.*

SEAN Yeah, whereas I do it myself, and that is what's different.

CAOIMHÍN *And why? The choice to do so is obviously important to you.*

SEAN Because I drive where I want to go. I'm the master of my image. I'm responsible for what's there. I'm accountable. Jeff Koons is not in full control of his imagery. He's a director.

CAOIMHÍN *Really?*

SEAN He didn't sculpt Michael Jackson or that chimp. Someone else did. He's only so close to that image. My fingerprints are in my chimpanzee. You see, for him it's an act of irony and for me it's the point where irony has gone full circle and begins the return to sincerity.

CAOIMHÍN *So we're back to that old gambit, the expressionist convention, of which there is an available critique. As Francis Bacon put it, you want to lift images directly off the nervous system. But is there such a thing as an unmediated access to spontaneous gestural expression?*

SEAN Yeah, I believe in that.

CAOIMHÍN *You do?*

SEAN Yes, I do. I believe the hand of a great artist extends directly from their soul. I think that has a hell of a lot of meaning. I'm not saying that it excludes what Jeff does, because I actually really love what he does and can't say enough about how much I admire him. I'm just saying that I see what I want to see when I want to see it with the peculiarities of my own hand and imagination, which is inherently more sincere. His process is more like expert shopping, or commissioning, which preserves his ironic distance.

CAOIMHÍN *But it's an important part of your project that you learned your skills on the job, as it were? Wouldn't it have been nice if you'd been able to do things in the beginning as well as you can do it now?*

SEAN It would have been, yes, but we all improve in no matter what we do. Look at the early Magrittes. My God, It was like they were painted by someone in my mother's backyard painting class.

I personally am comfortable with the level of skill in paintings like PLANK BOY (2000), MS. KITTY (1999), or BUFFALO (2003), for example. I have the ability to go further toward realism if I wanted to. But I didn't feel like those paintings would satisfy me any more if I did. In others like HAPPY AND SAD (2002) I went a little further. I realized the figures' outfits far more than in, say, MARINER (2003), which is done just right for what he is. It's just that I wanted to see more there in HAPPY AND SAD. Different paintings require different things.

CAOIMHÍN *It still seems that the have-a-go mentality of doing it as well as you can do it now and not caring if that falls far short of whatever skill you may develop later on is significant. It didn't bother you. You were relatively fearless.*

SEAN Yeah. I mean what else could I do? All I can do is work to the height of ability that my interest necessitates.

CAOIMHÍN *What difference does it make being over 40 and doing what you do?*

SEAN Well, I think I have to be honest about what I am now.

CAOIMHÍN *But how obviously has that change been registered in recent years?*

SEAN Well, this most recent show at Andrea Rosen Gallery (2004) is a great example of it. It's a look back at my old text paintings. I took their graphic nature and exploded it into spatial abstract paintings. Thoughts emerge in your brain, they become clear, and then they recede back into the blurry distance. They are still pictures of the way thoughts occur like my old paintings were, but the writing is different, it's self-parody. It's not like I no longer feel the things that I wrote on those early works, but when I write them now I feel how well-worn they are. It's like a closet full of old shoes. I've walked in them, they're worn out to the contours of my feet. I could put them on again and they'd fit comfortably but I just wouldn't feel snappy in them.

The reason the recent paintings have the 'echoing look' is when I was making them at nighttime, I'd look at the reflection of my paintings in the studio windows, which are double-glazed glass...

CAOIMHÍN *And they looked doubled, like the phrases in these new paintings?*

SEAN Yes, they looked so much better like that, and it just seemed like this sort of double vision/repetition effect was an exaggerated form of self-parody. It reminded me of a John Giorno recording where he repeated everything he said in his monologue and it evoked the palpable feeling of insanity. It just made sense to me that these paintings are echoes of those earlier 'well-worn shoes.'

CAOIMHÍN *It does seem like a graphic, cartoon rendition of an echo.*

SEAN Yeah.

CAOIMHÍN *You did say these texts were on abstract grounds. But some of them are not quite abstract, they are renditions of wide-open spaces, of skyscapes.*

SEAN Yes. The skyscapes are different. I grew up in a religious family, and really learned how to pray. It's still with me. My brain still falls into this mode of prayer, and I don't know what to do with it, being maybe not quite atheist, but a doubter of God.

CAOIMHÍN *When you say a 'mode of prayer,' you don't actually mean extempore praying, do you? You mean the repetition of pre-existing words.*

SEAN I mean, the train of thought in your mind that you think is being overheard by...

CAOIMHÍN *A deity?*

SEAN Yeah, a deity or a deceased relative.

CAOIMHÍN *Okay.*

SEAN So with these sky paintings, I'm attempting to capture this sort of prayer/thought. An example would be "Please make me a better artist," "Why can't things be easier?" By writing it I send it towards the heavens. "I want my paintings to last forever," "Please God, make me matter." Conversely, the one with the moon, THE SLEEP OF REASON PRODUCES MONSTERS (2004) was about insomnia, paranoia and the type of desperate prayer that occurs when the devils come out. It's directly made after the Goya etching THE SLEEP OF REASON PRODUCES MONSTERS (1797–1798). The words in this painting are like the bats rising in his etching. I was just trying to give thought a picture. A clown in the Arctic landscape is giving thought a picture in a different way, as are my text paintings, videos, sculptures and my 'vache' period. It's why I have an affinity with all those pre-World War II European painters, because they too are people who sat before an easel with a blank canvas in front of them and from their thoughts procured an image. That's what I value in art. That's what I want to see in art. That's what I like to make as an artist.

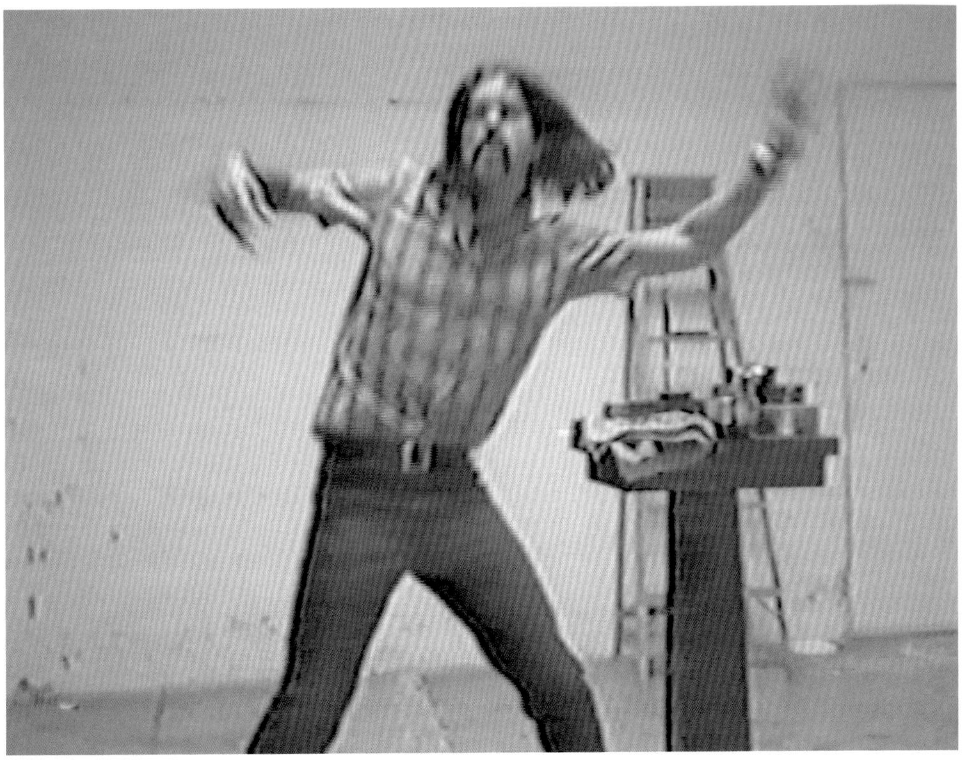

DANCING WITH DEATH, 1995
Videotape
7 min.

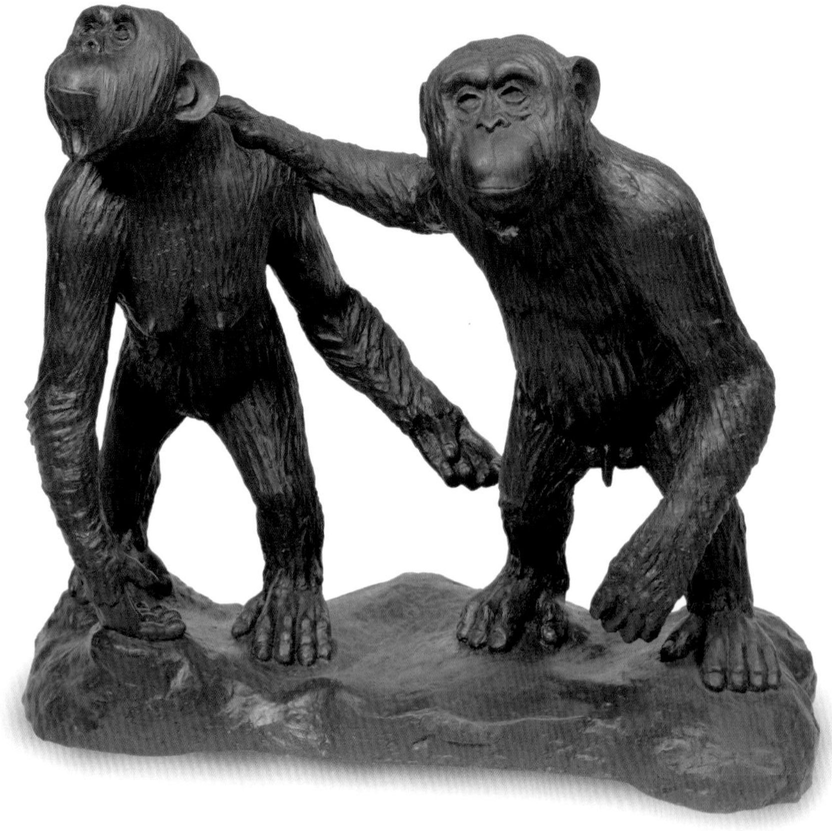

SINGERIE: LE SCULPTEUR, 1995
Bronze
92.07 × 113.03 × 60.96 cm

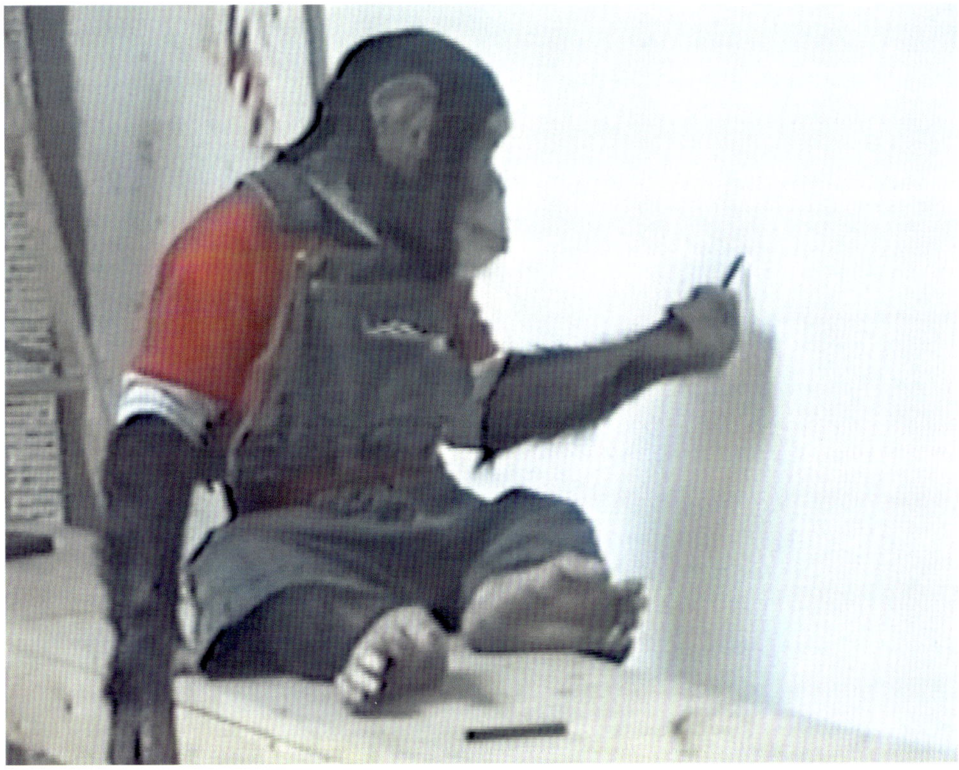

SINGERIE: LE PEINTRE, 1995
Videotape
27 min.

NOT FOR GOD NOR COUNTRY, NOT FOR LOVE OR HATE, NOT FOR LIFE NOR DEATH. MAKE NO MISTAKE ABOUT IT, NOTHING NOBLE DRAWS ME HERE. I AM BUT A FOOL OF THE HIGHEST MAGNITUDE.
FOR I HAVE NEVER FACED SUCH A SEA IN ALL MY LIFE. I SUMMON EVERY LAST IOTA OF STRENGTHE WITHIN MY FORLORN MIND, DO NOT FAIL ME. I IMPLORE YOU, PROVE ME WORTHY, BE I
WOULD SHIVER THE VERY TIMBERS MY VESSEL OF SELF HOOD ARE SO SURELY CONSTRUCTED. AND BLESS MY TINY CRAFT, AS ABLE A BOBBING CRAFT CAN BE. JOHNATHAN LIVINGSTONE SEAG
JOHNATHEN NOT FOR YEARS; OH, WELL I PERISHED IN THAT STORY SIR; OH YES NOW I RECALL; IT WAS THOUGHT TO HAVE BEEN A SUICIDE SIR; YES, WELL YOU WERE THE VICTUM OF UNFORTUNATE
BEEN ROAMING THE SEAS UNABLE TO REST; IF WHAT YOU'RE TELLING ME IS TRUE JOHNATHEN, THEN I'M NOT SO SURE THAT YOU ARE THE KIND OF COMPANY I NEED TO KEEP AS I WHEATHER
AND CLAIM YOU'RE SOUL FOR THE PRINCE OF DARKNESS, I'M SORRY, I DON'T LIKE WHAT I'M DOING BUT IT'S REQUIRED OF ME, MY WINGS ARE TIED; LISTEN HERE JOHNATHEN L. SEAGULL, MY WI
RE TO LOSE MY STRUGGLE FOR SOULS, I WISH NOONE MY FATE; SO WHY DON'T YOU LEAVE ME THEN JOHNATHEN? I'M AFFRAID THAT'S IMPOSSIBLE SIR, MY ORDERS WERE TO REMAIN WITH Y
EXACTLY LIFE MEANS TO A HUMAN BEING AND PARDON ME BUT YOU CERTAINLY ARE ABOUT TO FIND OUT, YOU SEE MOST PEOPLE DON'T WANT TO KNOW, BUT SINCE YOU'VE MADE SUCH A FUS
YOUR CHILDISH TIRAIDS AND NOW YOU'VE PISSED OF CREATION IT'S SELF: WHAT IS CREATION? WELL SIR, CREATION IS THE OCEAN, IT'S WHERE LIFE ON EARTH BEGAN AND FROM WHAT
ORDER YOU OFF OF MY SHIP: FINE, I'LL HOVER ALONG SIDE, BESIDES SIR, I'M ON YOUR SIDE, AND YOU'LL RELISH THE COMPANY ONCE THIS STORM HITS: EINE KLEINE NACHT MUSIK: DON'T CHANGE THE
THAT, I DON'T WANT THIS FANTASY I'M SIX INCHES BEHIND AND THE FIRST HALF IS ALLWAYS EASIEST. IF ONLY THE WORDS WOULD ENCOURAGE ME, THIS DAM SEA GULL IS AN ASSHOLE. I'LL IGNO
IED BY A WHALE OF A LIBIDO. TELL ME ABOUT IT, THE INTERNAL WORLD OF NACHT MUSIK OR VERKLART NACHT. I SIMPLY HAVN'T DROPPED INTO DRIVE YET AND THE CLOCK IS TICKING AS THE BAROMETER
VE UP FOR A SECOND AND YOU'LL RIDE THIS OUT. AM I TALKING OF WHAT I THINK I AM? YES, I'M JUST TRYING TO GET TO THE OTHER SIDE AND I'VE NEVER HAD SO FAR TO GO IN SO LITTLE TIME. W
END SAIL. STILL I WILL MAKE IT I HAVE TO, I WONDER IF IT'S ALL FOR NOTHING. NEW YORK TO CALLAISE, DID I SPELL THAT RIGHT. IF I'M NOT THERE BY 4:00 AM I'LL LOOSE THE RECORD. I NEE
WHAT I NEED TO KNOW. AM I WHAT I CRACK MYSELF UP TO BE? THE TRUTH IS THAT I'M THE ONLY ONE WHO'D CARE EITHER WAY. THIS QUESTION IS NON-EXISTANT TO YOU. STILL MY ASS HANGS OU
AUSE IT'S SUCH A SMALL FRACTION. BASICALLY FOR ME FRANCE IS ON THE OTHER SIDE. STRAIGHT INFRONT OF ME. BUT I CAN'T SEE VERY FAR SINCE THE EARTH IS ROUND. YOU KNOW WHAT, I'M JUST
AS PURE BORDUM. SO LONG AS THE TRAIL NEVER END AND I DON'T ABANDON SHIP. STAY ABOARD SAILOR DON'T EVEN BREAK TO PISS BECAUSE JOHNATHEN WILL GET YOU. JOHNATHEN FOLLOW
JUST THROUGH HOLEING ON A PIECE OF FLOTSUM AT LEAST THEN YOU KNOW YOUR CIRCUMSTANCES. JOHNATHEN IS AN UNPREDICTABLE HINDERENCE. EASILY DELT WITH WHENCE FRESH, BUT C
MORE, OR TWO MORE DEGREES PAST MY STERN I GET TO ENJOY SUSTENENCE AND A MOMENTS REST IN MY WARM CABIN. A TURN AT THE HEAD TO RELIEVE MY ACHEING BLADDER AND BUR
OF DESPERATION. JUST WHEN YOU RAISE YOURELF TO MEET A NEARLY INSURMOUNTABLE CHALLENGE YOUR BODY GIFTS YOU WITH VIOLENT DIOREAH, OR SUDDEN NAUSSIA. LEST IT BE FOR M
NOT A WISE DESION WHEN HYPOTHERMIA IS SUCH A REALL POSSIBILITY. THAT JOHNATHEN TRIED TO OVER TAKE ME ON THE WAY TO THE HEAD. THIS WOULD BE DIFFICULT ENOUGH UNDER FAIR C
I WILL NOT GIVE UP. A MAN DOES NOT OPEN A LUSIOUS BOTTLE OF BEER BEFORE HIS IS THROUGH WITH HIS DAYS WORK. NOT UNTIL I'M MOORED IN A SAFE FRENCH HARBOR. DAMIT! LET GO OF ME! THIS WIL
YOU ESCAPE INTO YOUR MIND, BY THE TIME YOU REACH YOUR DESTINATION YOU CAN HARDLY REMBER THE WALK. THE ONLY PROBLEM IS AFTER SO LONG AT SEA I HAVE NO ALTERNATIVE TO THE HORI
WILL BE MUNDANE THOUGHTS. CERTAINLY UNWORTHY OF THE METHODICAL TRANSCRIPTION I REWARD THEM WITH, BUT LIFE IT'SELF IS AN EVERLASTING BLABBER OF INSIGNIFICANT RUMINAT
IT EVEN FOR AN INSTANT AND YOU CEASE TO EXIST. IS THAT SAME PERSON YOU A YEAR AGO, TWENTY YEARS AGO, THE CONTINUENCE OF THE MONOLOG IN YOUR MIND CONECTS YOU STRAIT BA
STUPIFYING. I AM CONSTENTLY STUNNED AT HOW BARRON IT ALL IS. BUT MOSTLY I JUST ACCEPT IT THIS IS THE ANIMAL WE ARE, SO WHAT. I EVEN WANT TO BE KNOWN AS THE CHAMPION OF THIS E
ORTABLE CHAIR. I'M AN HOUR AND FIFTEEN MINETTS BEHIND MY SCHEDUAL OF BANALITY. IT'S ABSURD AND I DON'T UNDERSTAND IT MYSELF. EVERY NOW AND THEN A GUN IS PUT TO ONES HEAD AND
A GIANT CANVAS EQUATING THE TRANSCRIPTION OF HIS FORCED MUNDANE THOUGHTS TO MILES PRESSED ON IN AN IMAGINED STORM IN AN IMAGINED SEA. IS THAT WHAT LIFE IS IN IT'S ENTIREITY
EXISTS WITHIN YOUR PERCEPTION. WITHIN MY RELM ARE THESE SIMPLE THOUGHTS FORCED ONTO ROUGH CANVAS. MY PAINT HAS SO MUCH DRYER THAT IT DRIES IN FOUR HOURS MEANING I HAVE TO
ALREADY THERE. I WONDER IF ANYTHING INTELLIGENT WILL EVER OCCUR TO ME AGAIN, OR WILL I CONTINUE THIS SPIRALLING TAIL SPIN INTO THE DEPTH OF INSIGNIFICANCE. I SUPPOSE TH
FORCES HIMSELF TO SAY ANYTHING. TO WRITE CONTINUESLY WITHOUT STOPPING FROM BEGINING TO END. SOUNDS BOARING DOES'NT IT. WHAT A WAY TO CAP OFF A PERFECTLY CONCIEVED B
WATCHING A STORM BARE DOWN ON YOU AND IT'S SO TERRIFYING THAT YOU'VE FORCED YOURSELF TO BELIEVE THE ALTERNATE REALITY THAT YOU'RE IN A PARISIAN ART GALLERY ON AN AUTUM AFTERNOON E
IN THE INSULAR WORLD OF MY SELFHOOD. SELFHOOD SUCKS SOMTIMES THE MORE YOU PONDER IT THE FURTHER YOU ARE LEFT BEHIND. I STARTED AT 12:00 PM I HAVE NOT STOPPED FOR FIVE HOURS AND THIS IS WH
LITERARY ENDEAVOR, IF YOU WILL. I WANTED TO BE THE GRAND FATHER OF BANAL THOUGHT IN LITERATURE. ODD AMBITION, BUT WE ALL DO TEND TO CARVE OUR NICHES. OUR LITTLE DUST WORN PATCHES
TCHED BIRD LEAVE HOLD OF ME. AS LONG AS I NEVER LEAVE THE HELM I'LL GET THERE. WHERE, WHO GIVES A SHIT, TO THE OTHERSIDE. THIS DISCOURAGED I CAN ONLY HOPE THE PICTURE IS BEAUTIFULL. OR I COUL
NTING IS IS STUPID AND AND BEAUTIFUL. 2 HOURS AND 15 MINETS BEHIND SCHEDUAL. I'M GOING TO TRY TO MAKE IT UP BY BLABBING UTTERLY ANY NON-SENCEICLE THOUGHT THAT POPS IN, MARY POPPINS, DI
EARS OLDER THAN ME TAKE ME DOWN THEIR. HIS MOTHER JACKIE, HIS FATHER BOB, HIS BROTHER DANNY. DANNY WAS PAT'S BEST FREIND HIS FATHER WAS MY FATHER ALSO NAMED PAT WHOS FATHER WAS NA
HAS IT THAT HE RID THE ISLAND OF SNAKES, SERPANTS, EVIL. THAT CAN'T BE TRUE THOUGH BECAUSE EVERYONE ON THAT LITTLE ISLAND IS AFFRAID OF BURNING IN HELL FOR THEIR SINS. I THINK ST. PATR
LE TOO I'VE NEVER BEEN THERE THOUGH, I DID GO TO VENEZUELA ONCE. IT'S QUITE A FUNNY STORY ACTUALLY. I'VE BEEN TO EUROPE OVER TWENTY TIMES THATS A LOT FOR AN AMERICAN, I REMEMBER THE FIRST
THINGS EXCEPT ART, I LIKE ART. I LIKE LOTS OF CLASSY STUFF I GUESS BUT I'M STILL PRETTY THOUROUGHLY AMERICAN. IF I WEREN'T BORN HERE THOUGH, I PROBABLY WOULDN'T GIVE A DAM ABOUT IT. I D
USE MY OWN MIND FREE ASSOCIATION TIME, PROCREATION RYME. DID YOU SEE THAT? IT JUST FLASHED. LIGHTENING I GUESS OR PERHAPS I JUST GOT A BOOSTER SHOT OF DIVINE INSPIRATION. D
WILL IT'S UNBELIEVABLE HOW LONG THIS TAKES. BUT IT'S MINE, ALL MINE AND SO HANDSOME. I LIKE STARING AT IT. LIKE A NIPPLE IN PUBLIC. HOW MORE BEAUTIFULL CAN ANYTHING BECOME, ARE YOU
ONWARD INTO DESTINEY, HUH? YEAH, THERE IS NO DESTINY THERE IS ONLY CHOCOLAT SORBET, MMM, CHOCOLAT SORBET, HAVE YOU BEEN LOOKING DOWN HER SHIRT TOO. I'M SORRY, I KNOW IT'S CHILDIS
RONTED WITH ONES OWN ANIMAL, WAITE NOT ANIMAL. ANIMALS ARE COOL THOUGH, I PARTICULARY LIKE DOGS AND CHIMPANZEES. THAT'S A WHOLE OTHER SUBTOPIC. STILL NOTHING IS OUT OF PLAY THE BALL
MISUNDERSTOOD HE SAID. THE ROWS OF WORDS LOOK SO IMPORTENT. THEY SIMPLY MEAN NOTHING ALTHOUGH ONE THOUGHT DOES LEAD TO ANOTHER AND BEFORE YOU KNOW IT YOU'RE OUT O
ONE. THERE IS NO CASTRATION FEAR, I NEVER EVER FELT THAT EITHER. THAT SIGMUND FELLOW HAD TOO MUCH TRUST THAT WHAT WAS TRUE FOR HIM WAS TRUE FOR EVERYONE. LET THAT BE A L
PRESUME. PRESUMPTION THE GUMPTION OF THAT MAN. I'M SORRY BUT THIS IS BEAUTIFUL, HOLD ON I NEED MORE SUGAR. FREE ASOCIATION AGAIN IN SEARCH OF A TOPIC. SOMTHING ENGAGING T
CARED FOR. I PREDICT THAT MOST OF THE ART IN THE 20TH CENTURY WINGS OF MUSEUMS WILL BE WORTHLESS IN OUR LIFE TIMES. SO WHAT DOES THAT MEAN FOR ME. KEEP ON TRUCKING BABY. YOU GOT THE S
I'M SO LABOUR INTENSIVE, BECAUSE I AM THAT GRATEFULL, IT'S UNBELIEVABLE. I THANK EVERYTHING THAT GOT ME HERE. AND HERE AND HERE. ALL OVER IT. METHOD TO MADNESS, CHICKEN MADDRESS, ORANG
SON, GULLY, ALEC GUINESS STOUT, TWENTY BUCKS, IF FEEL LIKE FREAKING 20 DOLLARS MAN. DON'T YOU ENJOY BEING LOVED OR DO YOU HATE YOURSELF SO MUCH THAT ANYONE DUMB ENOUGH TO LOVE YOU IS
JUST DESERT GETS SERVED AND PEOPLE SIT AROUND LIKE ZOMBIES EATING THEIR CHEEKS FROM THE INSIDE OUT. MASTICATION OF SOMTHING SITUATION. JAMES CAGNEY HAD A VERY PECULIAR IDEA OF MASCUL
AGE. AND TO REASSES MY TIME EXPENDITURE ALOTMENT, I ATE CHEESE DOODLES INSTEAD, I'VE BEEN SUCKING ON A TWO LITER BOTTLE OF DIET COKE ALL DAY, I ALSO HAVE CARMEL CORN AND CORN CHIPS. THAT'S
TIED TO MY RUN OF THE MILL BORED THOUGHTS THAT I ACTUALLY FORGET I'M WRITTING AND I JUST SPACE OUT AND WALK AWAY. THAT'S WHY THE LOWER HALVES OF MY PAINTINGS ARE SO TOUGH TO GET THROUG
HAD 20 HOURS TO FILL THIS WITH WRITING SO ESSENTIALLY BEGGARS CAN'T BE CHOOSEY. ANY DAM THOUGHT I MANAGE TO HAVE IS GOING UP HERE. I KNOW THIS WILL TURN OUT TO BE MY BEST PAINTING TO DA
TOO. I'M 2½ HOURS BEHIND SCHEDUAL I'D LOVE TO BREAK INTO A REVERIE. I'D LOVE TO ESCAPE THE REALITY OF MY SITUATION AND FIND MYSELF IN A PERFECT FANTASY. BUT ON ANY OTHER DAY IF I FELT THI
I AM WELL HEELED IN THE ART OF MAINTAINING MY SANITY IN THE WAKE OF SUBSTANCIAL LONLINESS, NO I'M NOT, IT'S MY GREATEST FEAR THAT'S WHY I WRITE ABOUT IT. I WONDER HOW THAT HAPPEND. I RE
SOME OTHER GUY. DAM, THE MORE I THINK ABOUT IT THE MORE I REALISE HOW MUCH SHIT I'VE BEEN FORCE FED. I DON'T THINK I EVEN WANT TO UNCORK THAT SUBJECT. BUT I FOUND MYSELF IN THE DESSE
I'M NOT GOING TO BELLY ACHE ABOUT IT. BUT WHEN I WAS ON ROUTE 5 I FELT ABANDOND AND ALONE PERHAPS THE WORST I EVER FELT IT. AND IT'S A FAULT IN ME THAT WAITS TO REOCCUR OVER AND OVER.
IN HELL OF SELF OBESSION OR SOMTHING. FUCKING HELL I'M EXHAUSTED, I HAVE NOTHING TO SAY. JOHNATHEN YOU ARE NOT AMUSEING ANYONE. SOMTIMES IT'S ALL I CAN DO TO TURN ABOUT AND HEAD HOME
GREET IT. I WISH I HAD A STORY BUT I'M SO DAM JADED. A GREAT PAINTING IS: OH HOW THE HELL DO I KNOW. LIFE ON EARTH. BLA, BLA, I'M RIDDICULEING MY OWN THOUGHTS. I'M FINDING IT SO VERY DIFF
I LOWERD ALL SAILS AND BATTEND DOWN WITH TWO WARPS OFF MY STERN. I WENT BELOW AND LASHED MYSELF INTO MY BUNK AND LISTEND WITH ASTONISHMENT AT THE POWER OF THIS STORM. IN THE
INTO EVERY CORNOR OF MY MIND. ALL PEOPLE ARE SUBJECT TO TRIALS IN THEIR LIVES IN VARIOUS WAYS. THIS WAS MINE, JOHNATHEN APPEARD AGAIN. HE HELD OUT HIS HAND AND SAID: I DON'T NESSESA
OW YOU THE CHOICE NOT TO BUT IF YOU WISH TO RIDE IT OUT ON YOUR OWN THAN I CAN'T PREVENT YOU FROM SUFFERING: DONALD CROWHURST, IT'S YOU; YES, LISTEN TO JOHNATHEN SIR; FUCK JOHNA
CROWHURST DIED BY DROWNING WHEN HE JUMPED OVERBOARD HIS TRIMARAN IN THE 1965 GOLDEN GLOBE CHALLENGE. HE WAS ATTEMPTING TO PERPETRATE A FRAUD. BY SIMPLY DALYING ABOUT
HE DOES IT VERY WELL. FIRST HE GETS YOUR TRUST BY PROMISING NOT TO FORCE HIMSELF ON YOU. AND YOU ARE LONELY SO, BETTER TO TALK THEN NOT TO. BUT ONCE YOU STOP FEARING HIM IS
HE GETS IN AND ONCE HE'S IN YOU HAVE TO LIVE WITH THE ADDED BURDEN OF HIM. MAKE NO MISTAKE, HE IS NOT YOUR FREIND, NOR IS HE A RELUCTENT AGENT OF SATAN. HE IS SATAN AND IF YOU S
YOU CAN'T STAND UP TO HIM. IT'S JUST A PROBLEM YOU HAVE IN ADDITION TO LIFE THREATENING WHEATHER. IT'S ODD BECAUSE SOME SINGLE HANDERS NEVER RUN INTO HIM. BUT THOSE WHO D
HAS BEEN FOLLOWING ME PERSISTANTLY ALL DAY. IT'S TIME I GIVE HIM HIS WHAT FOR. I DUG OUT MY SHOT GUN AND STRAPPED ON MY SAFTEY HARNESS AND CLIMBED ON MY HEAVING DECK. THE O
ALL OF THIS JOHNATHEN NAVIGATED THE FEROUSIOUS WINDS AND MONSTEROUS SWELLS LIKE NOTHING WAS ERRANT. HE GLIDED ALONG FULLY AWARE THAT I WAS AIMING MY RIFLE AT HIM,
WAS A DEATH ON MY HANDS. MY BARBEROUS ACT WOULD NOT RELIEVE ANY ANGUISH BUT QUITE THE OPPOSITE WOULD HIGHTEN MY MENTAL ANGUISH. JOHNATHEN WAS NOT THAT SEA GULL THAT WAS A
MENTAL ANGUISH WAS TOO MUCH TO BARE THAT YOU'D RELIVE YOUR SELF BY DYEING AT YOUR OWN HAND THAN YOU HAVE MET JOHNATHEN. THIS IS NOT THE TYPE OF THOUGHT ONE NEEDS SO FAR FROM
IS NOT AN EXTERNAL ENTITY THAT JOHNATHEN IS ACTUALLY A CORNOR OF YOUR OWN MIND. THAT HE HAS APPEARD IN SOME HALLUCINATED FORM TO CLOAK HIMSELF FROM THE VERY HORRIFY
IN LOSEING THEN NOW IS CERTAINLY THE CHANCE. BUT JUDGEING BY THE HORROR IN WHICH I REGARD THIS NOTION OF PERISHING, I THINK IT'S FARE TO SAY THAT I GOT MY DAM ANSWER; I WANT T
GOOD, AND FEELS GOOD. NO QUESTION ABOUT IT JOHNATHEN, I LOVE MY LIFE AND I'M GOING TO RELISH EVERY BANAL INSTANT OF IT, BEGINING RIGHT NOW. WELL OF COURSE THERE I IN MY CRIB WA
TO SOAK UP EVERY LAST MORSEL OF IT DON'T WE. HM. TWO HOURS FOR EVERY FOOT. PERHAPS A STORY IS IN ORDER IF ONLY I WERE MOTIVATED TO TELL ONE. EVEN IF I WAS TO GO TO BED NOW I'D BE
COULD COMPREHEND GIVING, GOODNESS, TWELVE HOURS TO HERE, NO WONDER I'M EMPTY I'M FOUR HOURS BEHIND SCHEDUAL, I HAVE SIX HOURS LEFT REMAINING, EIGHT IN A PINCH, TIME TO JUST GO SLOW
REAL IN WORDS TO YOUR UTTER ASTONISHMENT AND WRITE NOTHING OF VALUE TO ANYONE ANYWHERE. MY DAD TOLD ME THAT A GEORGE HARISON SONG WAS HIS FAVORITE SONG BECAUSE IT WAS ON THE AIR
I AM A PRODUCT OF THE 1970'S AND I FEEL VERY AT HOME WATCHING SMOKEY AND THE BANDIT, CANNON BALL RUN, YOU KNOW, I DON'T HAVE TO TELL YOU. BUT I'M NEARLY ON TO SOMTHING. OH MAN, A TOPIC WO
THING. IT'S A BIT MUCH I MUST SAY, MORE THAN HALFWAY ACROSS AND STILL WITHOUT MY BARINGS IF SOMBODY ASKED ME TO ENCAPSULATE THIS ONE I WOULDN'T KNOW. HOW TO ANSWER. I DON'T
THAT. COME TO THINK OF IT THOUGH. JOHNATHEN WAS THERE TOO. WOW, JOHNATHEN IS TROUBLE. WELL THOUGHT IS THOUGHT BE IT BRILLIANT OR MUNDANE. WHAT'S STRIKING TO ME THIS EVENING
TURES TALK BACK. MUDLE BUT I'M STILL STANDING, NOT QUITE IMPASSIONED BUT REFUSING TO GIVE IN. I'VE BEEN GOING ON AND ON BUT WHAT HAVE I SAID? NOTHING. PEOPLE THINK ALL DAY EV
LAST WEEKEND THEN I WOULD HAVE MESSED UP MY STRETCHED ONES AND THIS ONE NEVER WOULD HAVE HAPPENED. WELL I'M SURE GLAD IT DID BECAUSE I FIND IT SO BEAUTIFULL. I'M SORRY I KEEP
MESSAGE FOR MY LADY. GET JUST FIVE MORE HOURS AND I GET TO GO BELOW. WILL THIS DRY IN TIME? I HAVE BETRAYED THIS IDEA OF MINE, I DON'T KNOW WHY. I GOT TIRED OF THE FANTASY. I'M T
MENTIONED ABOVE IN THAT JOHNATHEN BULLSHIT. WHAT THE HELL WAS THAT ALL ABOUT ANYWAY. TRYING TO BE SOMTHING OTHER THAN MYSELF IS WHAT IT IS. I'M A GUY WHO CAN EFFORTLESSLY

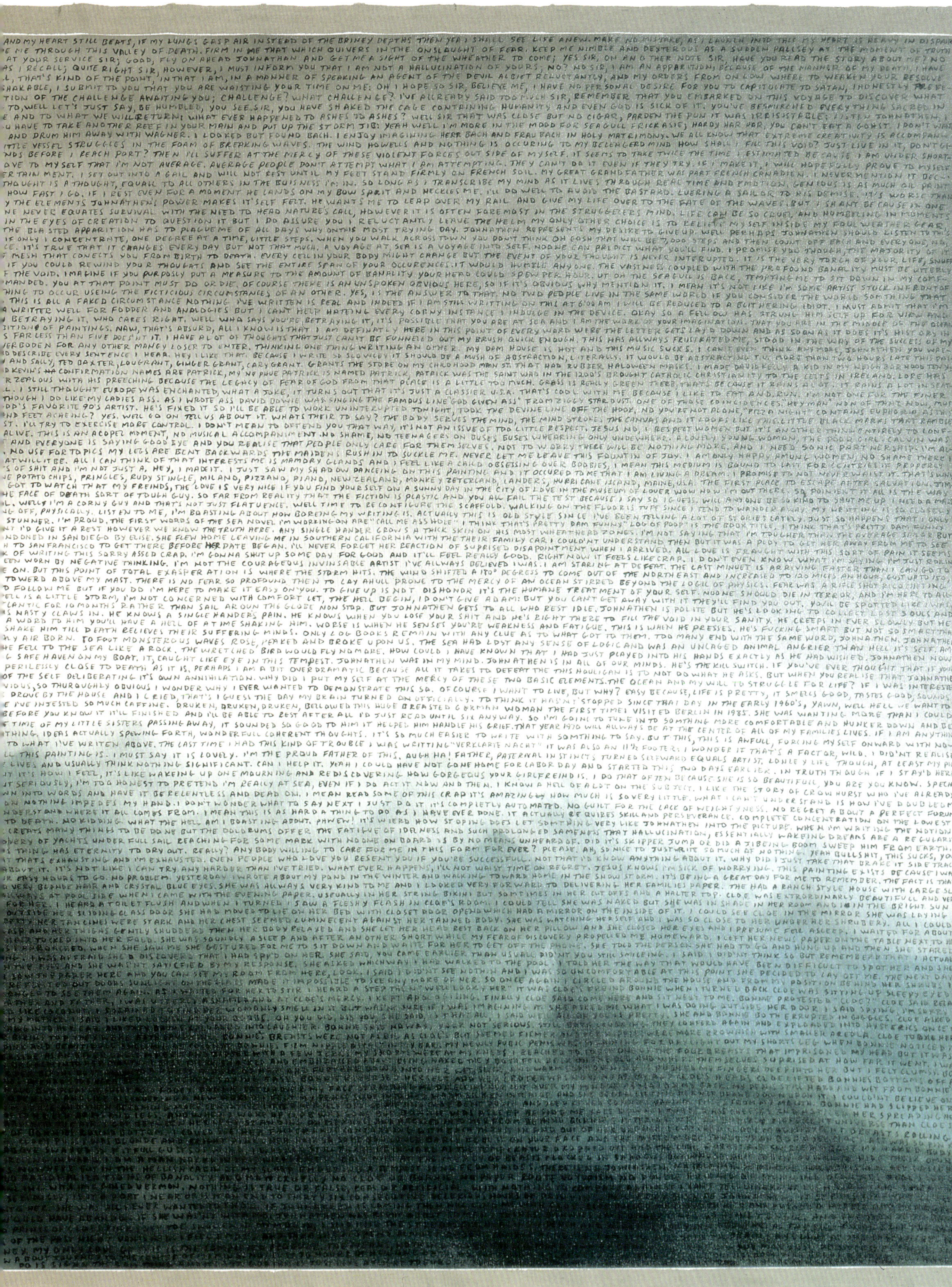

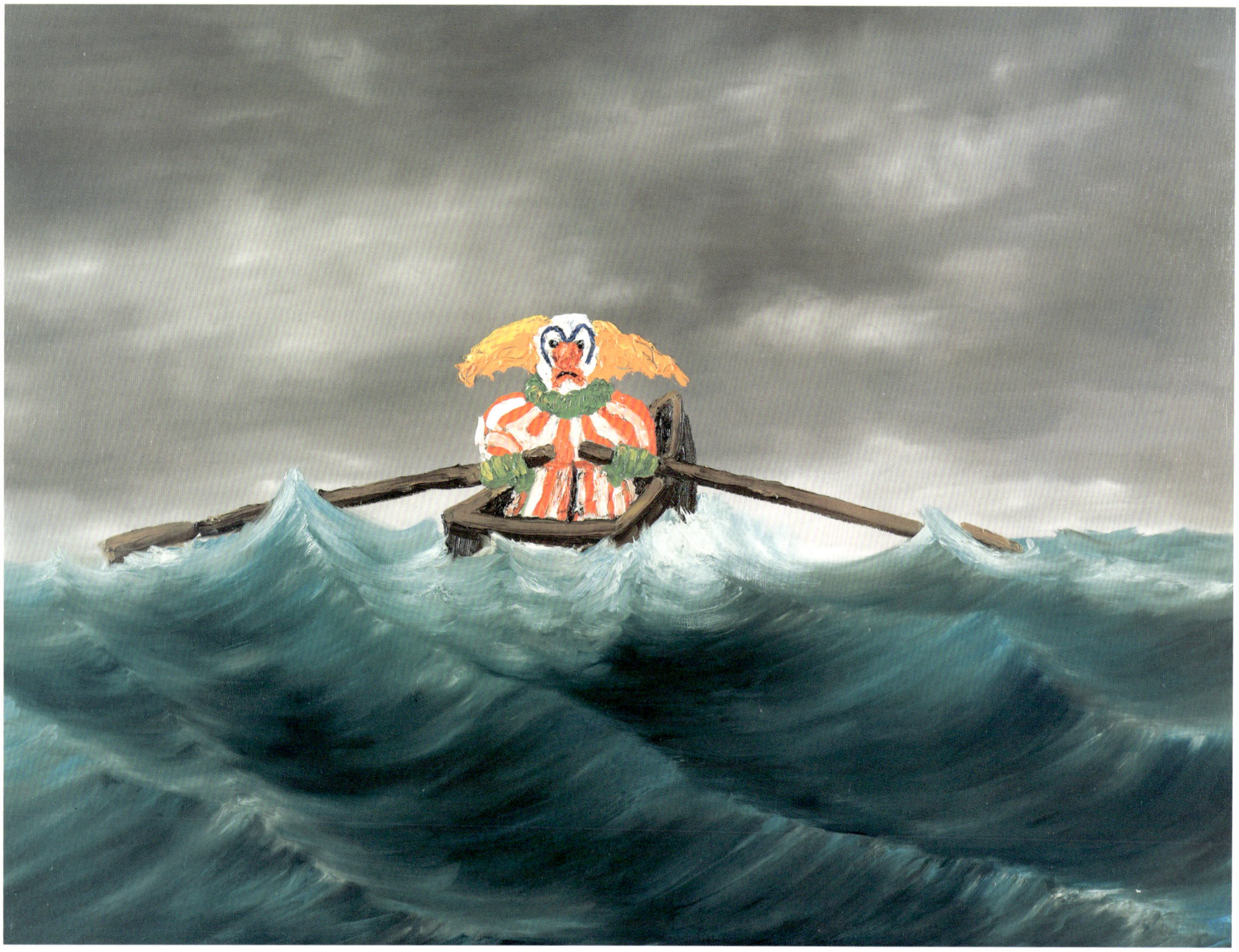

ALONE, 1996
Oil on linen
182.88 × 243.84 cm

Pages 52–53
36 HOURS, 1995
Oil on linen
213.36 × 365.76 cm

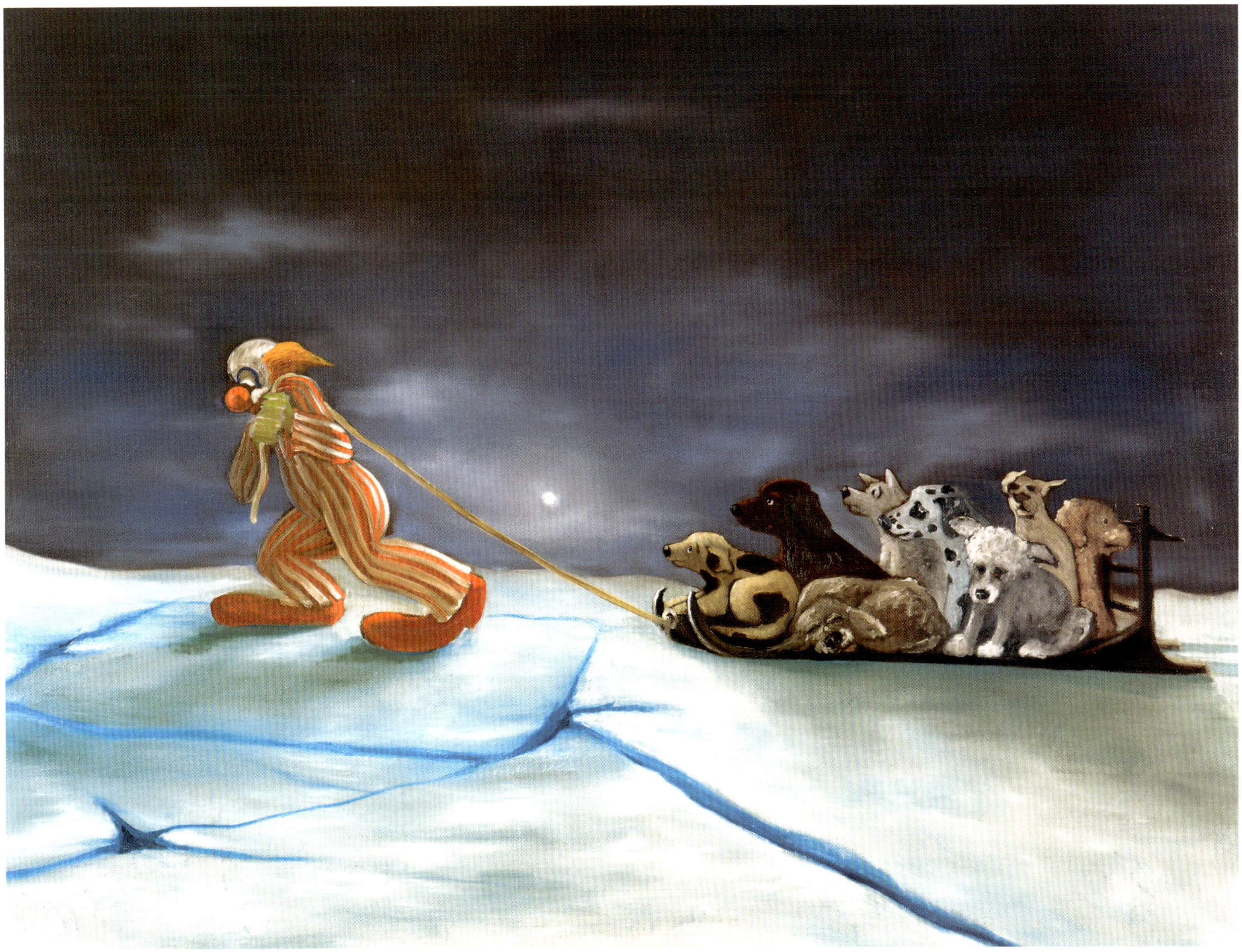

ARCTIC TREK, 1996
Oil on linen
182.88 × 243.84 cm

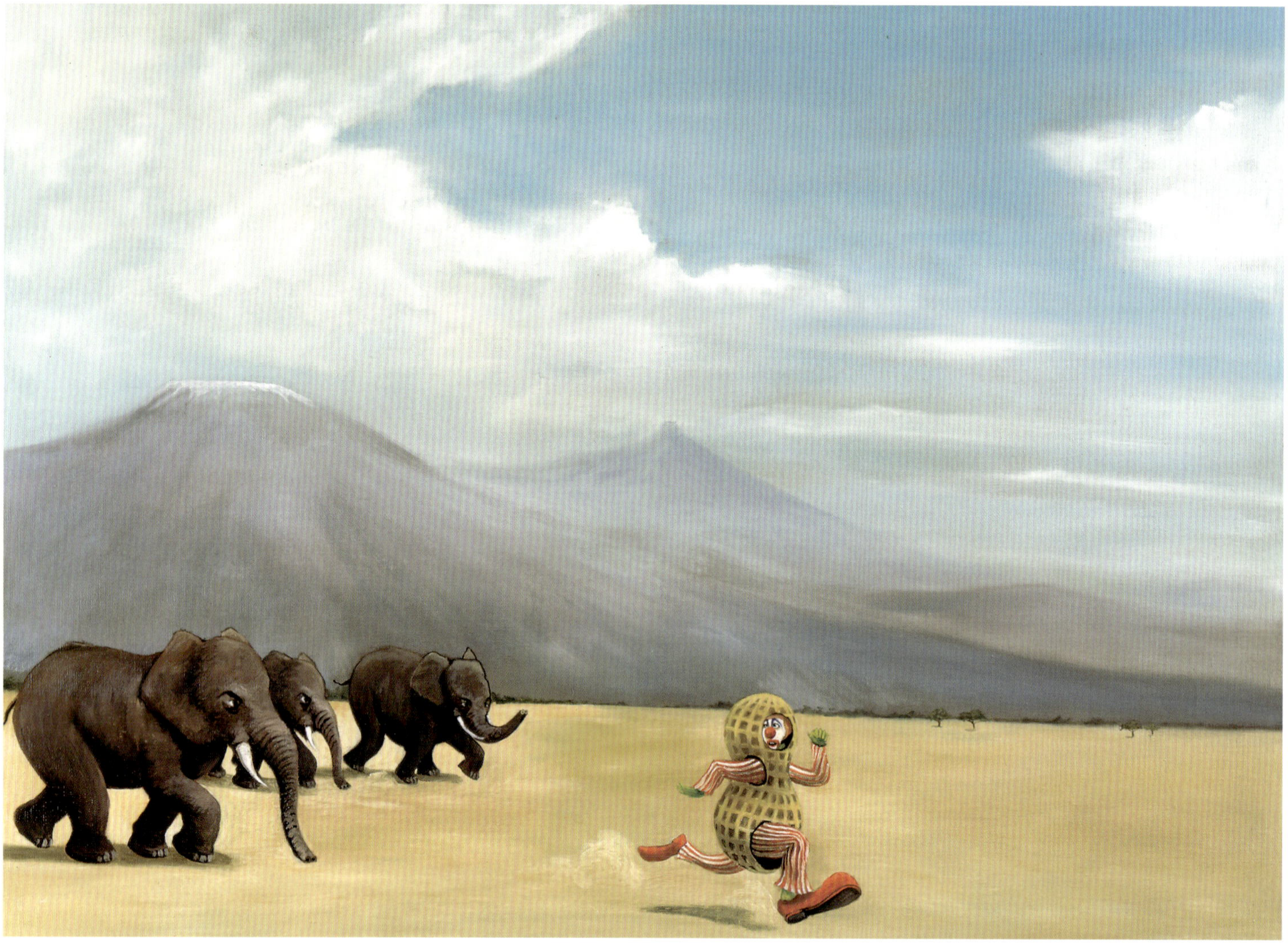

IN THE SHADOWS OF KILIMANJARO, 1996
Oil on linen
152.4 × 213.36 cm

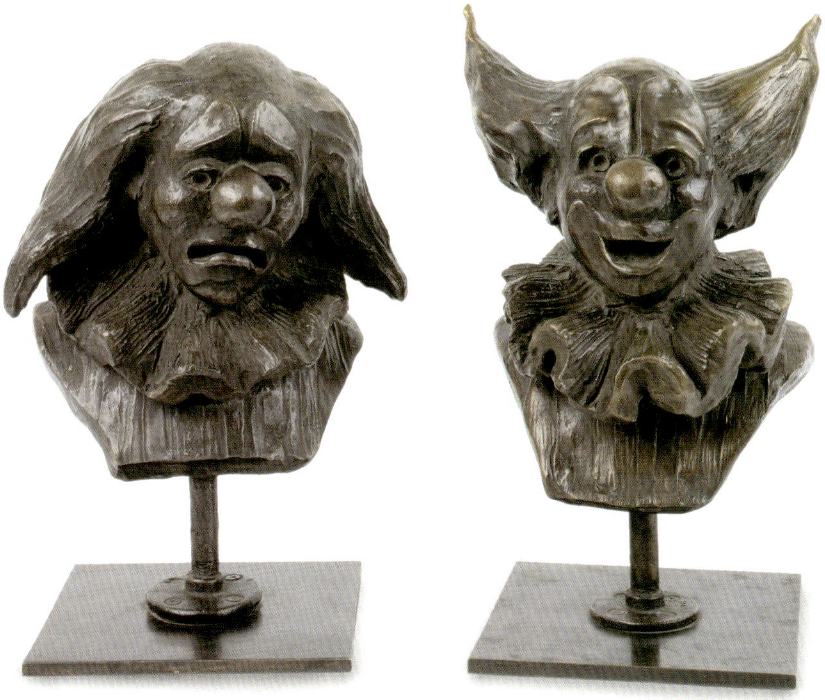

REALLY SAD AND REALLY HAPPY, 1996
Bronze
31.75 × 24.76 × 17.78 cm (left)
34.92 × 24.13 × 17.78 cm (right)

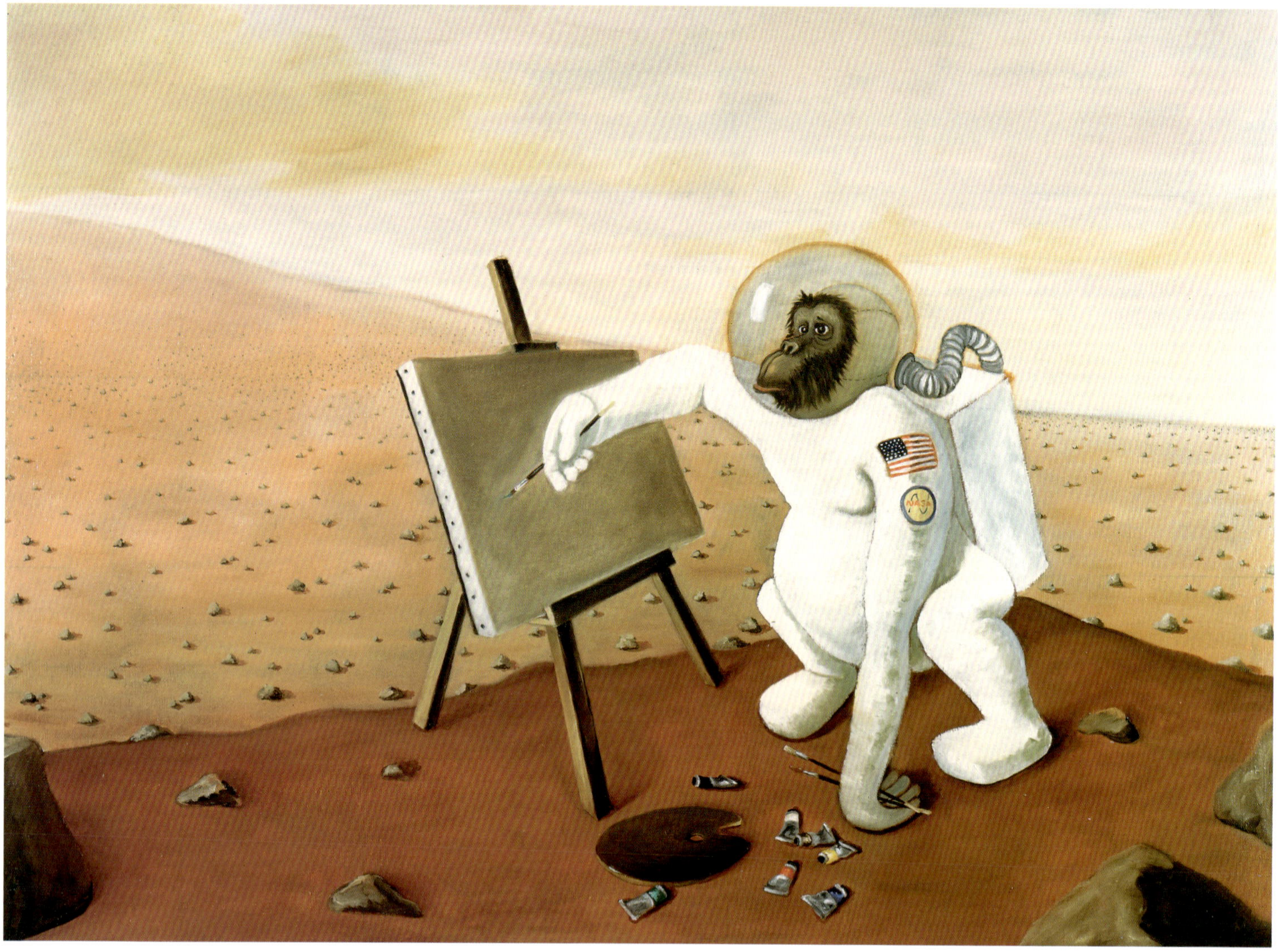

SPACE-APE ON MARS, 1997
Oil on linen
153.03 × 213.36 cm

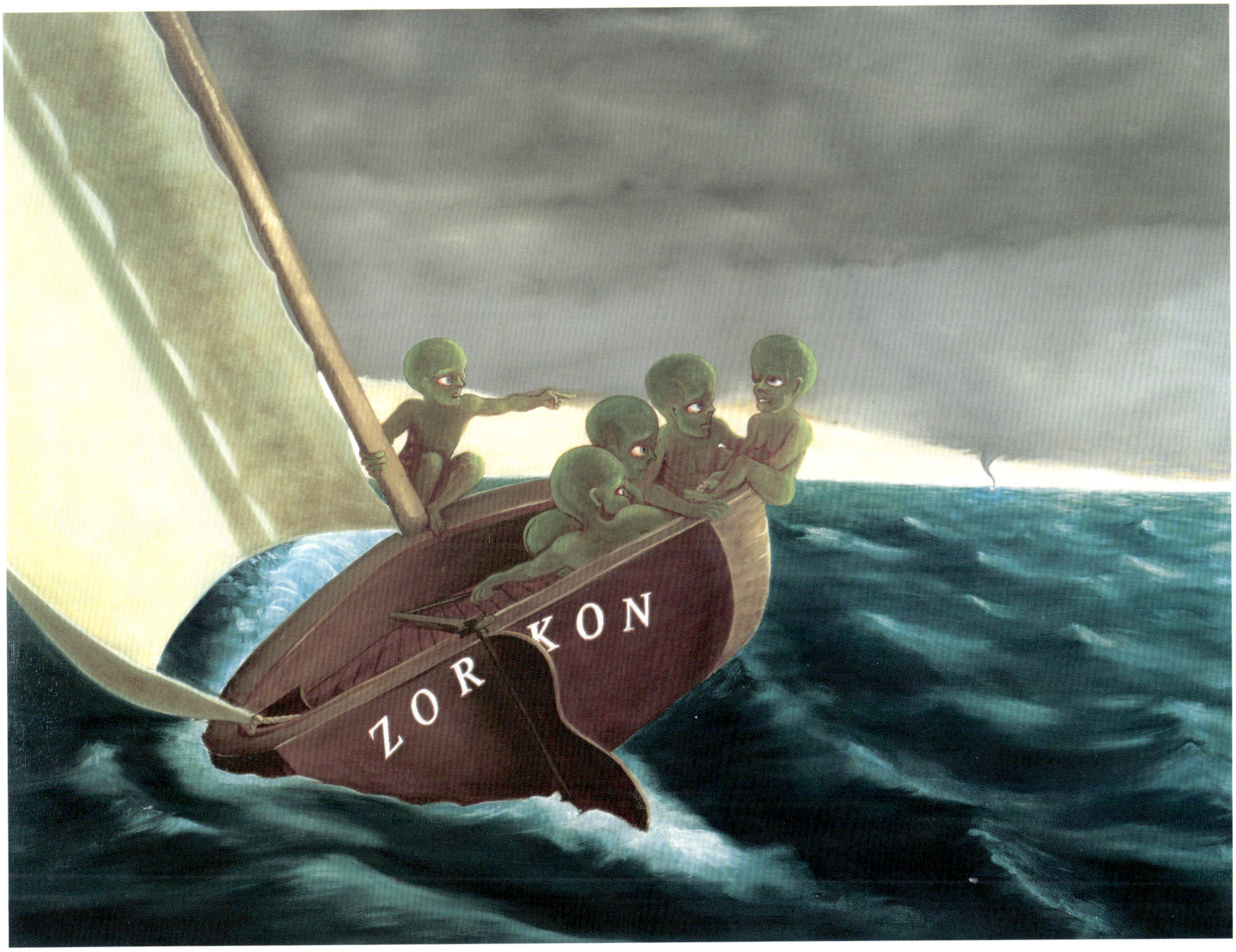

ZORKON, 1997
Oil on linen
182.88 × 243.84 cm

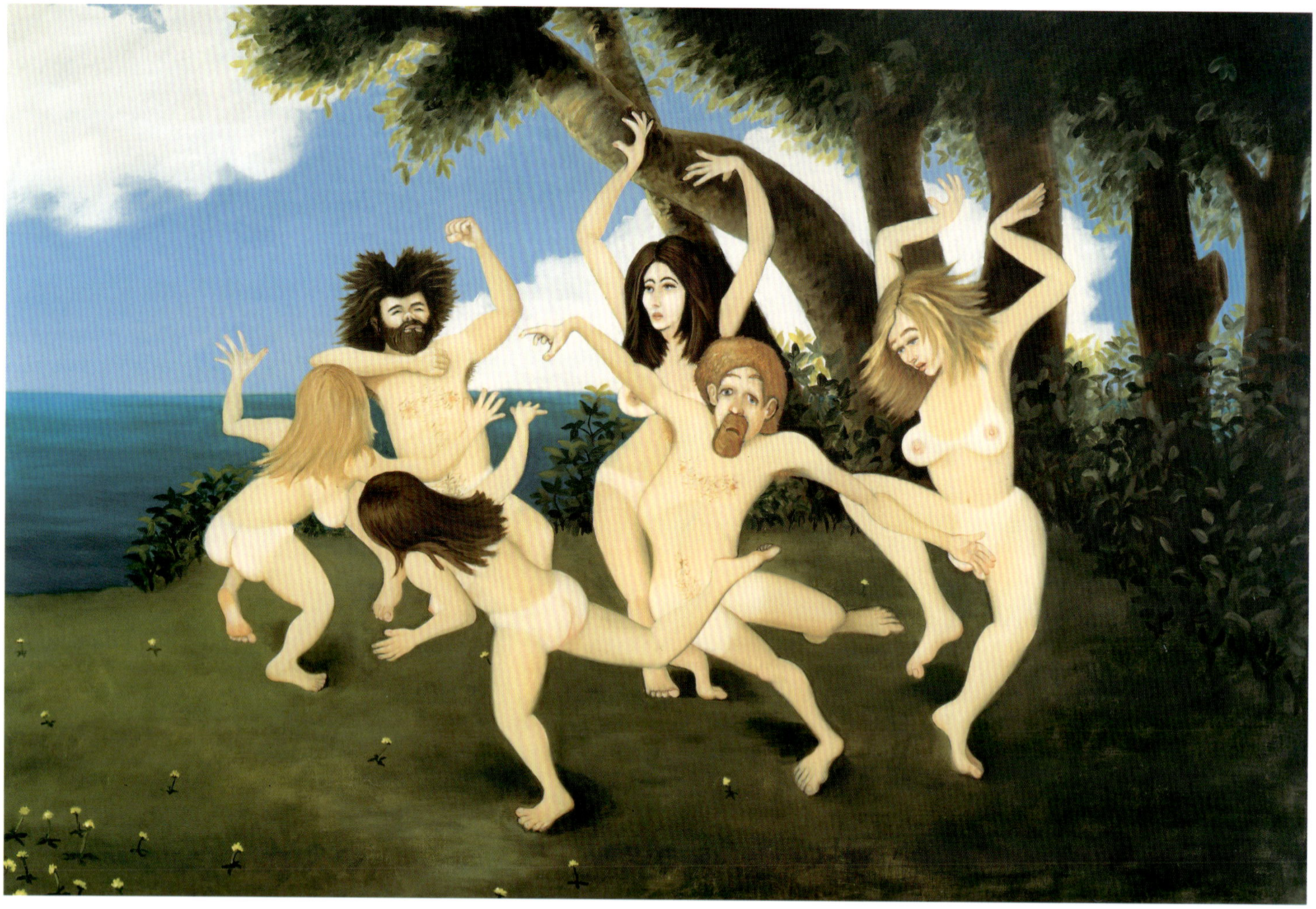

DANCE OF LIFE, 1997
Oil on linen
243.84 × 365.76 cm

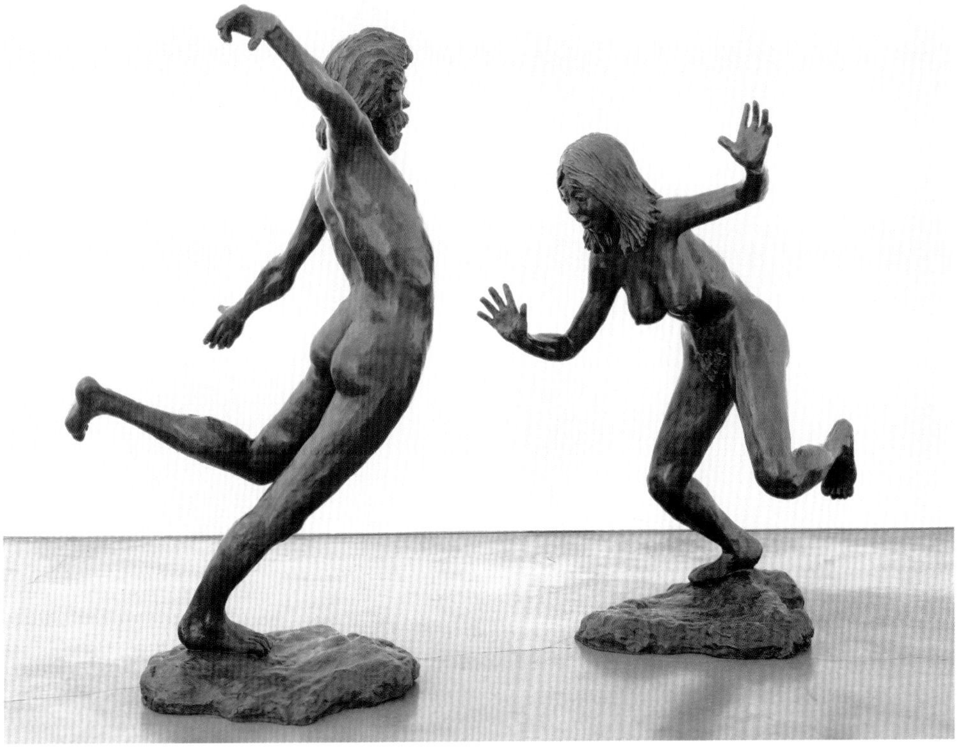

CANDLES IN THE WIND, 1997
Bronze
115.57 × 60.96 × 96.52 cm (left)
96.52 × 83.82 × 68.58 cm (right)

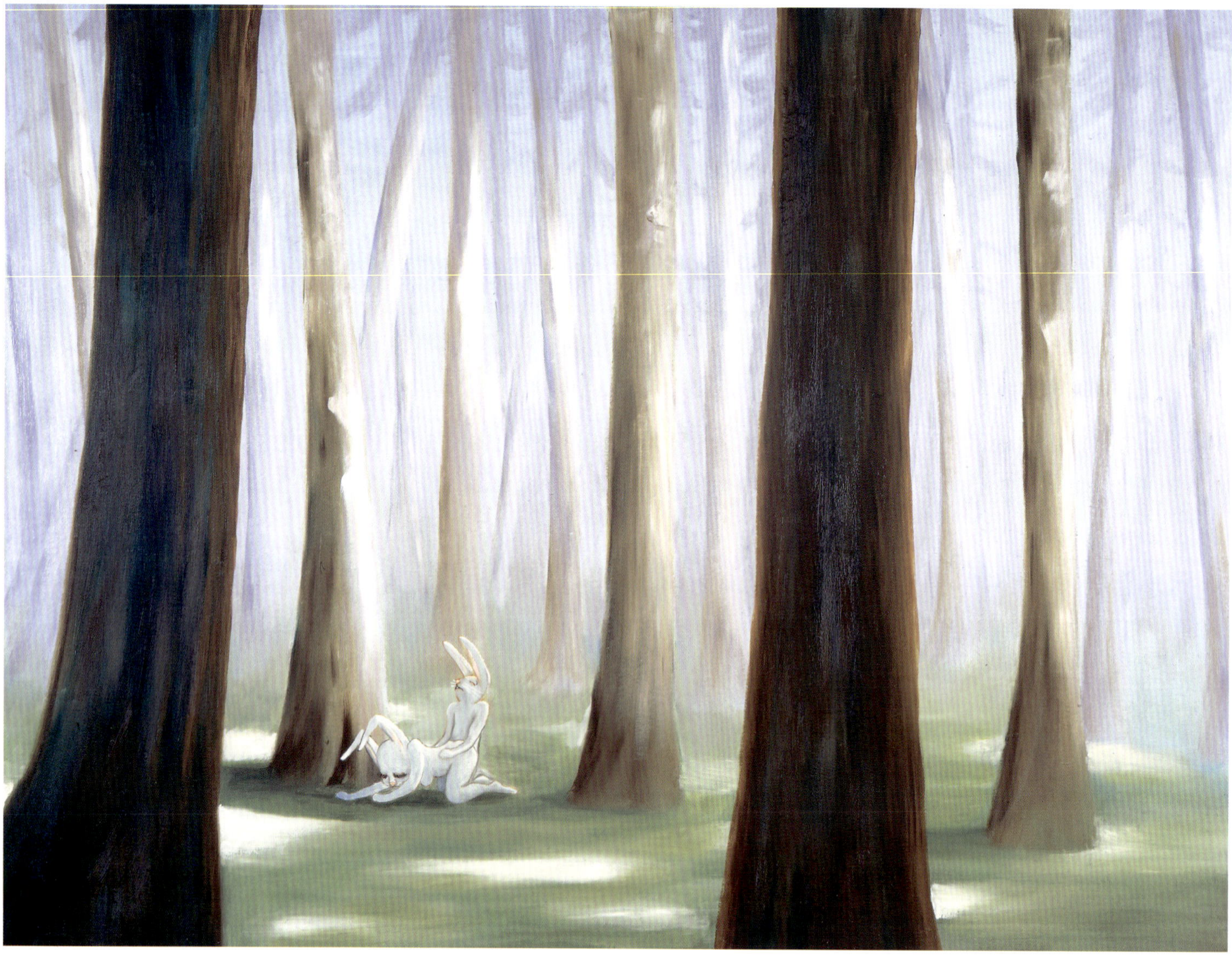

THE ENCHANTED FOREST (SPRING), 1996
Oil on linen
182.88 × 243.84 cm

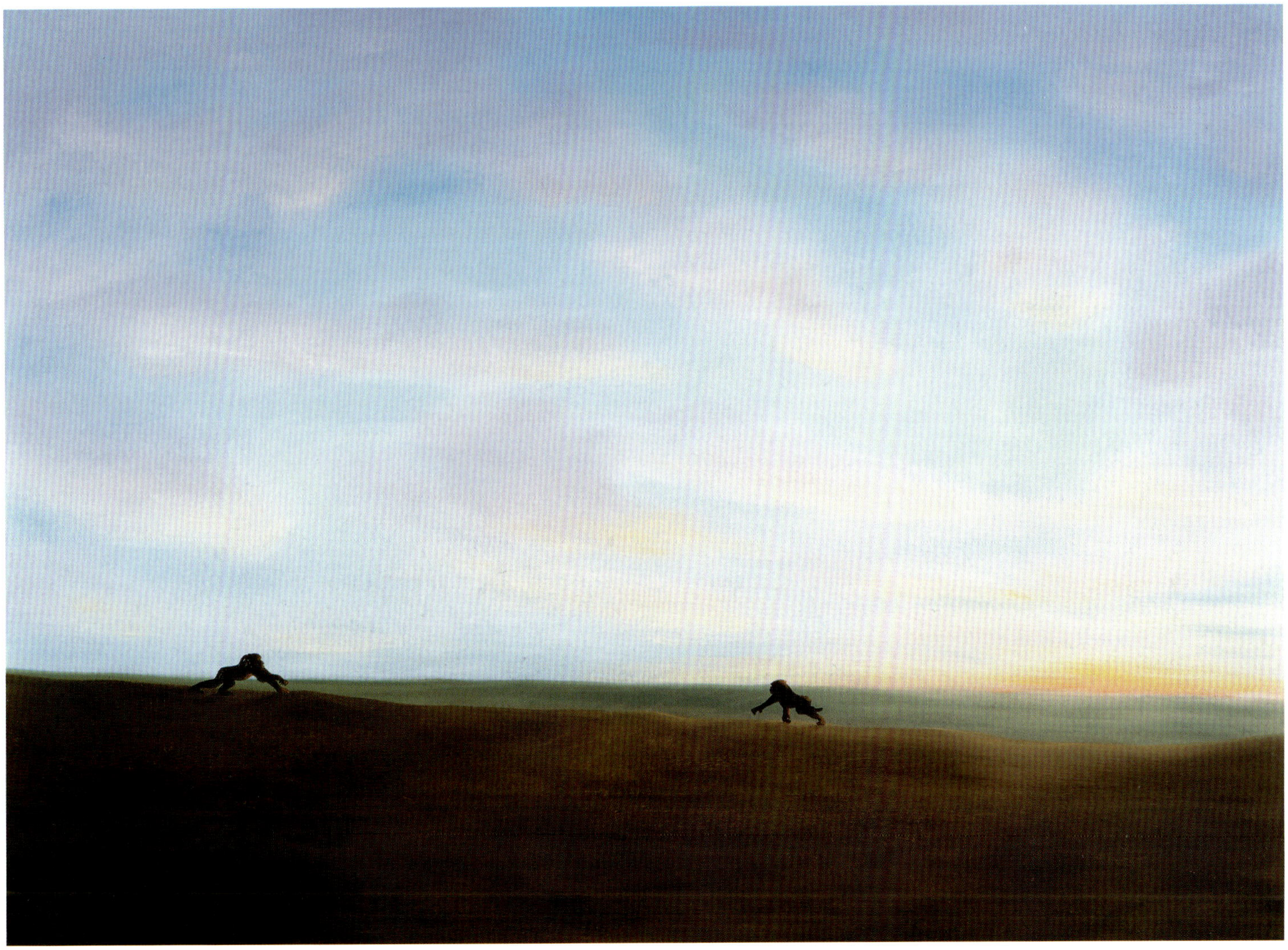

REUNITED... (SUMMER), 1996
Oil on linen
152.4 × 213.36 cm

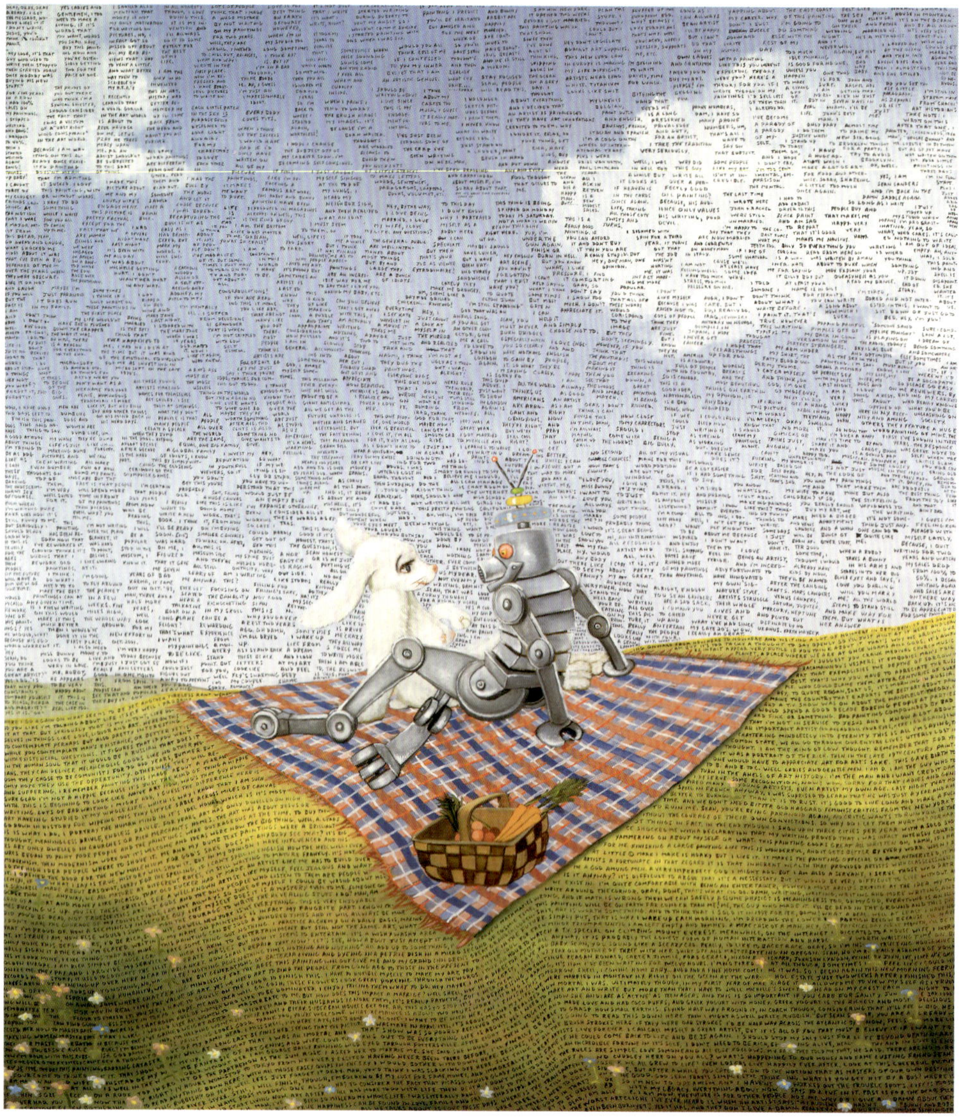

ROBOT AND BUNNY, 1998
Oil on linen
274.32 × 243.84 cm

Interview mit Sean Landers

CAOIMHÍN MAC GIOLLA LEÍTH & BEATRIX RUF

CAOIMHÍN & BEATRIX *Sprechen wir zunächst über deine frühesten Arbeiten und dann darüber, wie sich das, was du machst, über die Jahre verändert hat und was die Gründe für diese Veränderungen waren.*

SEAN Im Graduiertenstudium an der Universität (1984–1986) habe ich riesige Holzskulpturen von kämpfenden Tieren gemacht, die auf solchen Dingen wie Goyas Stierkampf-Radierungen oder Szenen aus der Literatur basierten. Figürliche Kunst an einer Kunsthochschule zu machen, zu einer Zeit, als Minimalismus und Konzeptkunst gelehrt wurden, das war damals genau das ‚Verkehrte'. Es galt als absurd, lächerlich, wie hätte ich da widerstehen können?

CAOIMHÍN *Obwohl sich die neoexpressionistische Malerei – Schnabel, Basquiat, Clemente, Kiefer und so – in den fünf Jahren vorher in Windeseile ausgebreitet hatte?*

SEAN Ja. Sie waren auf dem Radar, wurden aber nicht gelehrt oder gross diskutiert, so wie gegenwärtige Künstler heute an den Schulen nicht ‚gelehrt', sondern unter den Studenten privat diskutiert werden. Ich habe auch riesige minimalistische Skulpturen in der Art von Ronald Bladen gemacht, aber ich habe sie pervertiert, indem ich sie doppelt hinsetzte, zu Skateboard-Rampen umfunktioniert. Ich hatte diese Dinger damals in der Mitte meines Ateliers ausgestellt. Eine Textflut füllte die Wände um sie herum: Bekenntnisse und Cartoons mit Graphit und Marker neben riesigen Actionpaintings in Öl, die direkt auf die Wand gespritzt waren. Wenn die Studenten und Dozenten zur Begutachtung kamen, lasen sie das Geschriebene auf den Wänden mit dem Rücken zu meinen riesenhaften Skulpturen. Es kam mir nie in den Sinn, dass Schreiben und Malen einmal den Mittelpunkt meiner Kunst ausmachen würden. Weil ich Bildhauerei im Hauptfach studierte, dachte ich, ich würde Bildhauer werden.

Im Herbst 1986 zog ich nach New York, wo im East Village die Galerieszene florierte und Jeff Koons der Herr der Welt war. Ich war von seiner Kunst beeindruckt und schuf eine Reihe von Arbeiten, die – im Rückblick betrachtet – vermutlich von ihr beeinflusst waren. Gipsbüsten, die es von berühmten Schriftstellern, Komponisten und mythologischen Figuren fertig zu kaufen gab, setzte ich in Zylinder aus klarem Polyesterharz und stellte sie auf Holzpodeste, die ich entworfen und auf der Drehbank gedrechselt hatte. Ich habe diese Arbeiten zweimal ausgestellt: 1989 in Tommy Solomon's Garage in Los Angeles und 1990 in der Postmasters Gallery in New York. Sie erhielten gute Kritiken, aber ich hatte kein gutes Gefühl dabei. Ich traute ihnen nicht oder dem kleinen Erfolg, den sie hatten. Das war nicht wirklich ich. Zur gleichen Zeit verlor ich eine Freundin, nach der ich verrückt war. Immer dann, wenn mein Liebesleben in Gefahr gerät, werde ich… na, vor allem kommt die Wahrheit heraus.

Ich verfolgte keine bestimmte Strategie, als ich wieder mit dem Schreiben anfing – ich war verzweifelt und musste meinem Kummer Luft machen. Als ich später wieder etwas von diesem Zeug las, bemerkte ich sein Potential als Kunst und begann, unter diesem Aspekt zu schreiben. Ich begann mit einem Drehbuch, das von einem Künstler handelt, der sich in den neunziger Jahren in New York durchzuschlagen versucht, so wie in Knut Hamsuns Roman HUNGER. Ich war ungeheuer beeindruckt, wie das geschrieben war, auch von Dostojewskijs SCHULD UND SÜHNE – von der Art, wie die Autoren zum Ausdruck brachten, was sich im Kopf des Antihelden abspielt. Ich fühlte mich völlig erschlagen, als ich diese Bücher zum ersten Mal las. Das war so, wie ich dachte, das war so, wie ich schrieb, das war mein Ding. Meine Arbeiten sollten eine Art Version der neunziger Jahre von HUNGER sein, und ich wollte als Antiheld darin auftreten.

CAOIMHÍN *Aber HUNGER ist doch ein Roman und kein Werk der bildenden Kunst.*

SEAN Richtig. Aber was ich machte, war auch eine Reaktion gegen die ‚Textkunst' damals in New York, von Künstlern wie Hans Haacke oder Mary Kelly. Ich dachte, wenn Text auf einer Galeriewand auftaucht, dann sollte er verdammt noch mal… na, ich wollte einfach nur meine eigene Fassung davon machen, eine, die letzten Endes ausgesprochen persönlich ist. Ich habe schnell die Macht zu nutzen gelernt, die ich erhalte, wenn ich kleine Häppchen von mir weggebe, um die voyeuristischen Neigungen anderer Leute zu befriedigen.

CAOIMHÍN *Und das bedeutet, dass du dich zum Exhibitionisten gemacht hast.*

SEAN Zum Teil, aber auch sehr kontrolliert. Damals (1990) sah ich auch etwas im Fernsehen, was mich beeinflusst hat. Die Sendung hiess AN AMERICAN FAMILY, stammte von 1973 und war das erste Beispiel für Reality-TV – eine dysfunktionale Familie wurde ein Jahr lang begleitet. Sie lernten, mit dem Filmteam zu leben, und begannen, ihr Leben auf die Kamera auszurichten. Ein Sohn beschloss, der Familie zu eröffnen, dass er schwul war. Der Vater fing vor der Kamera eine Affäre an und benutzte sogar seinen Starruhm aus der Sendung, um an Mädchen zu kommen. Da war also ein Echo, das ich sehr interessant fand. Das ist einer der Gründe, warum ich beschloss, mein Leben als Thema in meiner Arbeit zu verwenden. Worauf ich aus war, das war die Realität, so ehrlich, wie ich es machen konnte, und so unterhaltsam wie möglich.

BEATRIX *Wie sah denn diese Reaktion gegen deine beiden frühesten Ausstellungen aus, und in welchem Jahr war das?*

SEAN Das war 1991. Es war meine zweite Ausstellung bei Postmasters und eine direkte Reaktion auf meine erste. In der Mitte der Galerie standen Skulpturen, auf die Wände war Geschriebenes geklebt. Die geschriebenen Arbeiten waren Szenen aus dem Drehbuch ART, LIFE AND GOD (1990), mit der Hand auf gelbem Linienpapier geschrieben, wie es Anwälte benutzen.

Die Szenen waren zwar ziemlich autobiographisch, aber nicht unbedingt aus meinem Leben. Einige Szenen waren real, andere erfunden, und einige Sachen waren meinem Bruder Kevin oder meinen Freunden Richard Phillips, Carl Ostendarp, John Currin oder anderen Leuten von Yale passiert, mit denen ich nach New York gezogen war. Sie waren in diesem Drehbuch verarbeitet und auf Chris Hamson umgemünzt worden, also war das nicht alles ich. Daher hatte ich nicht das Gefühl, er sei ein wirkliches Alter Ego, obwohl das damals so aufgefasst wurde.

Die Skulpturen waren dem, was ich jetzt mache, sehr nahe, aber statt sie offen auszustellen, zeigte ich sie mit schwarzen Plastiksäcken zugedeckt, denn sie waren angeblich von meiner fiktionalen Figur gemacht worden und ‚so schlecht', dass er sich zu sehr schämte, sie zu zeigen. Sie waren in genau der gleichen Anordnung aufgestellt wie meine früheren Arbeiten, die Harzköpfe, was manche Leute in ihrer Meinung bestärkte, die Ausstellung sei rein autobiographisch.

CAOIMHÍN *Hast du dann dieses Alter Ego abgelegt, um dich auf dein eigenes Leben zu konzentrieren oder weil dich die Missdeutung ärgerte?*

SEAN Weder noch. Ich glaube, es war einfach eine natürliche Entwicklung. Was mich auf den Weg brachte, das waren in Wahrheit die Briefe, die von der Vermittlungsstelle für Studentendarlehen kamen und in denen es hiess, ich sei mit meinen Zahlungen im Rückstand. Ich musste ihnen einen Brief schreiben und war nicht einmal imstande, eine halbe Seite von diesem Anwaltspapier vollzuschreiben, ohne dass eine ‚Verrücktheit' einfach so passierte. Statt mich ‚klar und deutlich' auszudrücken, kam ich bei der Frage an „ach wäre es nicht lustig, wenn ich es so machte?". Ich konnte nicht aufhören, ein Publikum mit dem zu unterhalten, was ich schrieb. Das war Performance. Die Briefe waren sehr unterhaltsam, und sie waren von mir. Also kein Chris Hamson mehr.

CAOIMHÍN *Bist du früh auf die Idee gekommen, Formen der Bildgestaltung mit Formen der Sprachproduktion zu verbinden?*

SEAN Innerhalb eines Jahres fing das allmählich bei meinen Zeichnungen an. In einer typischen Ausstellung von mir aus dieser Zeit (nach Chris Hamson, 1991–1994) gab es Skulpturen, Köpfe aus ungebranntem Ton, die am oberen Ende von langen, dünnen Stangen befestigt waren und Leute aus meiner Heimatstadt darstellten (Zeugen meiner ‚Scham'). Sie waren mitten im Raum aufgestellt, zwischen ihnen stand auf einem Skulpturensockel ein Videomonitor und spielte eines meiner Videos, zum Beispiel ANYONE'S ORGASM (1992), das ich als geschmacklose lebende Skulptur-Performance im Sinne der SINGING SCULPTURE von Gilbert & George auffasste. Es gab auch immer Texte in verschiedenster Form, die an den Wänden hingen, zum Beispiel CALENDAR PAGES FROM 1991 (1991), Cartoons von Stereotypen der Weltkunst, Briefe an meinen Sachbearbeiter bei der Darlehensvermittlung oder eine riesige Bahn Hintergrundpapier, wie es in Fotostudios verwendet wird, bedeckt mit Geschriebenem in Stream-of-Consciousness-Manier. Ich darf nicht vergessen, dass ich damals das Gefühl hatte, das, was ich schrieb, sei in gewisser Weise die ‚Zeichnung' oder das ‚Bild'. Der Gefühlsausbruch auf der Seite mit den ganzen Unzulänglichkeiten, den Rechtschreib- und Grammatikfehlern, dieses emotionale Schreiben war genau das ‚Richtige'.

Ich vermute, was die Betrachter geködert hat, das war das Voyeuristische an der Sache und dass sie sich selbst darin wiederfanden. Vielleicht war das der Grund, warum die Leute schmerzende Füsse in Kauf nahmen, um meine Kunst zu lesen, denn während sie mir in die offene Seele starrten, beurteilten sie in Wirklichkeit sich selbst. Ich glaube, das ist eine grundlegende Komponente der stillschweigenden Kommunikation zwischen Kunst und Betrachter.

CAOIMHÍN *Kannst du ein bisschen mehr darüber sagen, welche Absicht du mit der Sprache verfolgt hast im Vergleich zu früheren Künstlern, die Text verwendet haben?*

SEAN Na ja, mir ist klar, dass ich das, was ich gemacht habe, ohne das Vorbild so hervorragender Künstler wie Lawrence Weiner, Joseph Kosuth, Carl Andre und Vito Acconci nicht hätte machen können. Vito war ein Lehrer von mir, und ich bewundere ihn immer noch. Er hatte einen gewaltigen Einfluss auf mich. Ich bewundere auch On Kawara sehr. Obwohl einige seiner Formen trocken waren, fand ich sie immer interessant und poetisch. Sie schienen auf den Punkt zu bringen, was Kunst eigentlich ist. Ich brauchte das Vorbild dieser Künstler für das, was ich vorhatte. Ich wollte ihnen jedoch Kontra geben, und zwar gründlich. Meine Art, an den Text heranzugehen, war meist das genaue Gegenteil ihrer Sichtweise; es war die schludrige Innenschau, eher wie bei Acconci.

CAOIMHÍN *Im Gegensatz zu Hans Haacke und Mary Kelly, die du vorhin erwähnt hast, die in erster Linie politische Ziele verfolgt haben. Du hast anderswo gesagt, dass du dich mit keinem Künstler verwandt fühlst, dessen Werk unverhohlen politisch ist. Ich weiss, dass du dich sehr für Politik und sehr für Ästhetik interessierst, doch scheinst du ein Problem mit einer Kunst zu haben, die sich bemüht, beides zu verbinden.*

SEAN Ich meine, dass Kunst etwas sein sollte, was davon frei ist. Für mich ist Kunst genau das, was davon frei ist. Kunst und Politik können nur eine Verbindung eingehen, wenn die Notwendigkeit besteht, jenseits der Sprache zu kommunizieren. Malereien in den Kirchen der Vorrenaissance und mexikanische Wandmalereien dienten historisch zum Beispiel dem Zweck, das ungebildete Volk zu erziehen, zu belehren und zu manipulieren. Kunst hat heute nicht mehr diese Rolle. Ich glaube, es gibt einen Ort für politische Kunst, aber es ist selten, dass sie in anderen Formen als Film oder Unterhaltungsmusik funktioniert. Die Nationalhymne in der Version, wie Jimi Hendrix sie gebracht hat, ist wohl das perfekte Beispiel für politische Kunst, denn sie ist ästhetisch wunderbar und hatte 1969, als sie in Woodstock gespielt wurde, eine gewaltige politische Bedeutung, und sie hat heute wieder eine politische Bedeutung bekommen. Wenn du sie heute hörst, dann denkst du unweigerlich daran, dass die USA erneut vom Kurs abgekommen sind. Eine Melodie zu nehmen, die für Amerikaner eine so verbindende Funktion hat, und mit ihr auf diese Weise zu verfahren, das war perfekte politische Kunst. Es ist ein schönes Musikstück.

CAOIMHÍN *Dass ästhetisches Vergnügen abgelehnt wird, fandest du also ärgerlich und beunruhigend in einem Teil der Kunst, gegen den du dich früh zur Wehr gesetzt hast?*

SEAN Genau. Aber da fehlte noch eine andere Art von Inhalt in den Werken von Textkünstlern wie Haacke und Kelly: Menschlichkeit. Die ich, wie ich meine, im Wesentlichen wieder eingebracht habe: das triefende, hässliche Zeug genannt Menschlichkeit.

CAOIMHÍN *Es macht einen entscheidenden Unterschied aus, ob die bekenntnishaften Erinnerungen, die man abfasst, zur privaten Lektüre bestimmt sind oder ob sie als Texte an die Wand geklebt werden. Die Art, wie sich die Leute innerhalb einer Galerie auf das optische Bild einlassen, hat etwas Unmittelbares, auch wenn es von langer Dauer ist. Man liest immer noch Wörter in der gleichen Reihenfolge und braucht wohl auch die gleiche Zeit, die man in einem Buch brauchen würde, aber die Wirkung ist eine andere.*

SEAN Ja, es macht sie befangen. Auch haben diese Texte ihre eigene Ästhetik. Die Schrift neigt sich, und meine Rechtschreibung spielt verrückt, wenn ich emotional werde und schneller schreibe.

CAOIMHÍN *Also gibt es eine notwendige Verbindung zwischen Form und Inhalt?*

SEAN Richtig. Viele Kritiker nannten das damals die ‚Kunst des Pathetischen'. Ich vermute, die Gedanken erschienen ihnen pathetisch, genau wie die Form, die verknickt, eselsohrig war, gelbes Linienpapier mit Gekritzel in den Ecken und schrecklichem Geschreibsel. Sie sahen authentisch aus, das Interessante an ihnen war jedoch, dass sie nicht hundert Prozent authentisch waren. Es gab Zeiten, da hat mich das Schreiben völlig beherrscht, und das zwanghafte Bedürfnis, etwas schrecklich Persönliches über mich mitzuteilen, war fast eine Form der Selbstverwundung. Aber es gab auch Zeiten, da habe ich es kontrolliert und in die passende Richtung dirigiert. Es war immer eine Mischung.

CAOIMHÍN *Schlechte Schrift, schlechte Rechtschreibung werden gemeinhin mit Unmittelbarkeit, Vertraulichkeit und Bekenntnisbereitschaft assoziiert, was sich auch auf die Rezeption von Werken anderer Künstler wie zum Beispiel Tracey Emin auswirkt. Aber das ist ebenso eine Konvention wie die Annahme, eine nachlässige expressionistische Pinselführung bringe uns näher an ein echtes Empfinden heran als, sagen wir, eine pedantisch ausgearbeitete Hardedge-Malerei.*

SEAN Richtig.

CAOIMHÍN *Daher war die Kritik an Authentizität und bekenntnishafter Äusserung in den neunziger Jahren ebenso notwendig, wie es die Kritik des Expressionismus ein Jahrzehnt vorher war; aber das ist doch in Bezug auf deine Arbeiten und eigentlich auch die von Tracey Emin nicht wirklich weiter vertieft worden, oder?*

SEAN Nein, aber es hätte vielleicht sollen und könnte noch immer.

CAOIMHÍN *Ich erinnere mich an einen Satz von dir: Du hast einmal zu mir gesagt, du hättest eine völlig andere Beziehung zur Scham als Tracey Emin.*

SEAN Ich kann mich nicht einmal erinnern, wann ich das gesagt habe.

CAOIMHÍN *Es könnte vier oder fünf Jahre her sein.*

SEAN Ich gebe zu, dass wir beide gelernt haben, die Scham zu unserem Vorteil einzusetzen. Ich sehe diese Gemeinsamkeit. Aber ich glaube, wenn wir beide einen Teil unserer Seele dem Teufel verkauft haben, dann hat sie ein grösseres Stück verkauft als ich. Ich glaube, das macht sie weniger kompliziert, nach den Massstäben von Oprah Winfrey. Ihre Kunst zielt nicht auf jene Art von Voyeurismus, die mit Selbsterkenntnis zu tun hat, sie ist eher einem Spektakel ähnlich oder einem Zugunglück – wie soll man da nicht hinstarren? Ich glaube, an dieser Stelle ist sie eine Parodie ihres früheren, sexuell missbrauchten Ichs, so wie ich vielleicht eine Parodie meines jüngeren, von Ängsten erfüllten Ichs bin. Wenn Künstler wie sie und ich Arbeiten machen, die uns selbst zum Thema haben, dauert es nicht lange, bis alle Erinnerungen aufgebraucht sind und wir uns in der schrecklichen Gegenwart wiederfinden. Das ist zum Teil der Grund, warum ich mich so getrieben fühle, etwas gemalt wiederzugeben und Skulpturen zu machen – zu erfinden. Na ja, so etwas wie „steh zu deinem Wort, oder halte gefälligst den Mund".

CAOIMHÍN *Hast du dich schon früh zu der Mischung aus gewinnender Offenheit und bewusstem Raffinement in Werken wie dem von Karen Kilimnik oder vielleicht sogar Raymond Pettibon hingezogen gefühlt?*

SEAN Ja, ganz bestimmt. Aber da ist etwas an ihrer Kunst, was ein bisschen echter ist als meine. Ich spiele die Hauptrolle in dem, was ich schreibe, aber ich bin mir dessen wahrscheinlich mehr bewusst, ich spinne meine Rolle weiter aus. Während ich schockiert wäre, festzustellen, dass die Figur in Karens Werk alles andere als hundert Prozent echt ist. Das Gleiche gilt vermutlich auch für Raymond. Ich bin kein Opfer dessen, was da vor sich geht, aber das bedeutet nicht, dass ich trickse. Es gibt erstaunlich viel Grosszügigkeit und Echtheit in meinen Sachen. Das bisschen Täuschung in meinen Arbeiten liefert mir das Feigenblatt, das ich brauche, um dahinter agieren zu können. Die Möglichkeit, dass das, was man liest, erfunden ist, erlaubt mir, unverblümt ehrlich zu sein.

Anfang der neunziger Jahre habe ich manchmal Sachen verwendet, die meine Schwester Maura geschrieben hatte, zum Beispiel ihre Dankesbriefchen für Hochzeitsgeschenke. Durch das, was sie schrieb, ergab sich ein anderes Bild, als sie vermutlich beabsichtigt hatte, und das war es, was mich daran so reizte. Je mehr man davon las, desto mehr kam man weg von dem Eindruck „oh, was für ein nettes Mädchen ist das, sie ist so dankbar für diese wunderbaren Geschenke" hin zu „so sieht das also aus, diese Geschenke sind Scheisse. Verflucht noch mal! Ist das alles, was ich kriege? Ist das mein neues Leben?". Ich dachte, das beschrieb sie sehr viel besser, als wenn sie sich hingesetzt und ihre Lebensgeschichte aufgeschrieben hätte.

Ich merkte, dass ich letzten Endes auch nicht alles kontrollieren konnte. Das Bild, das ich wiedergab, war etwas anderes als das, was ich beabsichtigt hatte. Dazu fand ich heraus, dass ich das Publikum demütigen konnte, indem ich mich selbst demütigte, indem ich mir zunutze machte, dass sie sich wiedererkannten. Das gab meinen Themen eine Weile Nahrung, aber ich kämpfte mit mir. Ich wollte Zustimmung und Popularität, aber das war ein merkwürdiger Weg, sie zu erhalten, weil ich mich in gewisser Weise selbst demütigte, um besser anzukommen. Ich stellte mir ständig Fragen wie „brauche ich wirklich Anerkennung so nötig, dass ich vor der Kamera wichse?". Die Frage, die sich aufdrängte, war „lachen sie mit mir oder lachen sie mich aus?". Instinktiv will ich heute und wollte ich damals eine Privatsphäre haben. Meine gesamten frühen Arbeiten auszustellen, das lief meiner Intuition völlig zuwider. Kurz vor meiner Ausstellung 1992 in der Andrea Rosen Gallery irritierte mich so sehr, was ich in den Kunstwerken von mir preisgegeben hatte, dass ich plötzlich eine Gürtelrose bekam. Zum Glück wurde die Ausstellung gut aufgenommen. Danach mass ich mein Engagement für ein Kunstwerk daran, wie peinlich es mir war. Jetzt, wo ich jetzt bin, kann ich einfach nicht mehr so schreiben, wie ich damals schrieb, weil ich zu …

CAOIMHÍN *Weil du zu befangen bist?*

SEAN Ja. Aber nicht befangen ‚aus Angst', sondern befangen, weil ich zu viel über das weiss, was ich tue. Ich verstehe es zu gut. Alles hat jetzt einen Zweck. Das ist der Grund, warum meine gegenwärtige Ausstellung bei Andrea Rosen (2004) wie eine Parodie meines früheren Ichs ist. Der Text, so wie er auf den neuen Bildern erscheint, ist wie das Echo eines früheren Geschehens, das in den fernen

Bereichen des Gehirns oder durch den Raum oder wo auch immer widerhallt.

CAOIMHÍN *Es ist kein fortlaufendes Erzählen mehr. Die Texte sind eher kurze Wörter oder Wendungen, die mehrfach übereinander gelegt werden, als würde ein Echo in graphischer Form wiedergegeben. Sie sind eher wie Wappen oder wie Embleme oder Epigramme. Sie sind also reflektierte Selbstzitate?*

SEAN Ja. Da ist sehr wenig direkt aufgeschrieben, wie ich es empfunden habe. Meine früheren Arbeiten waren nur ‚fühle und schreibe'. In dieser Ausstellung kam das meiste auf einem Stück Papier zustande, und das habe ich dann abgeschrieben. Ich habe das vorher nie bei Bildern gemacht. Auf jeden Fall ist es jetzt anders. Ich kann nicht mehr dasitzen und mich über Depression beklagen, weil es nicht stimmt.

CAOIMHÍN *Aber kam diese Erkenntnis nicht schon Mitte der Neunziger – die Erkenntnis, dass dein Publikum nicht mehr in der Lage war, dich als erfolglosen, ‚slacker' Künstler wahrzunehmen, eben weil du Erfolg hattest?*

SEAN Richtig.

CAOIMHÍN *Ich weiss, du hast immer ein Problem damit gehabt, dass man dich als ‚slacker' Künstler wahrnahm, obwohl das eine Weile deine Masche war.*

SEAN Das glaubten die Leute von mir. Das schrieben sie über mich. Aber ich war nie unzufrieden und nie pessimistisch über meine Zukunft. Ich war genau das Gegenteil. Ich hatte die feste Absicht, ein sehr fleissiger und bedeutender Künstler zu werden. Ich glaube sehr fest an mich. Das ist vermutlich für die Leute sehr schwer zu begreifen. Wie könnte jemand sonst diesen ganzen Scheiss beichten, wenn er nicht vollkommen zuversichtlich wäre? Ich habe keine Angst vor Demütigung, weil ich weiss, dass ich mich letzten Endes für nichts zu schämen brauche.

Wie sich herausstellt, war ich eigentlich nie ein ‚Slacker', aber als ich die erste Presse bekam, war das häufig so zu lesen. Da ich langsam bekannt wurde, war ich einfach so dankbar, überhaupt Presse zu bekommen, dass ich gern alles akzeptieren wollte, was sie schrieben, auch wenn es nicht stimmte. Daher war es eher so etwas wie „ja, schon gut, ich bin ein Slacker". Das war unreif von mir, denn jetzt muss ich versuchen, diesen Ruf wieder loszuwerden (lacht).

CAOIMHÍN *Es passte zu dem, was damals in der Luft lag, die ganze Geschichte mit der ‚Generation X'.*

SEAN Ja. Aber entweder bin ich dem entwachsen, oder es hat nie wirklich gestimmt. Vielleicht war es eine Mischung aus beidem.

CAOIMHÍN *Was diesen Eindruck gemacht haben könnte, war dieser Wechsel zwischen Selbstherabsetzung und Selbstgefälligkeit oder sogar Beweihräucherung, der bis heute in allen deinen längeren erzählerischen Texten vorhanden ist, meinst du nicht?*

SEAN Ich weiss nicht, ob das unbedingt typisch ist für die ‚Generation X' oder die ‚Slacker'. Die Situation der Generation X, wie Douglas Coupland sie beschrieben hat, war, dass die Generation vor mir, die geburtenstarken Jahrgänge der Nachkriegszeit, all die guten Jobs bekam, und wir wissen nicht wohin, und wir können nur Jobs in der Dienstleistungsindustrie bekommen, und nirgendwo ist für uns eine Chance voranzukommen – eine Behauptung, die ich unsinnig finde. Ich habe das nie eine Sekunde lang geglaubt. Ich fühlte mich immer befugt und fähig in meinem Beruf. Ich empfand mich als Teil einer Generation von Künstlern, die in die Kunst wieder Form bringen würden.

CAOIMHÍN *Wie? Könntest du darüber etwas sagen?*

SEAN Na, das ist genau das, was ich vorhin gesagt habe, als ich meine Texte mit den Arbeiten früherer Künstler verglich, die auch Text verwenden. Ich bringe wieder ‚Form' in die Textkunst. Ich meine ‚Form' im Sinne von ‚Persönlichkeit', ‚Menschlichkeit'. Wenn man in ein abstraktes Gemälde oder eine Skulptur wieder Form bringt, gibt man dem Werk eine bestimmte Vorstellung mit. Bei allem gebotenen Respekt vor dem Neoexpressionismus: Meine Generation war es, die das wieder populär gemacht hat. Ich habe es auf verschiedene Weise auf meine Art gemacht. Andere Künstler in meinem Alter haben es auf ihre Art gemacht.

Der Neoexpressionismus war vielleicht die erste Reaktion aus dem Bauch heraus gegen Minimalismus und Konzeptualismus, aber ich weiss, als ich das ‚Projekt' oder die ‚Aufgabe' oder die ‚Verantwortung' übernahm, die Malerei zu einer wirklich neuen Form zu führen oder zu entwickeln, da wollte ich nicht einfach nur der Geschichte etwas entgegensetzen. Ich wollte alles verwenden, was die Geschichte mir bot. Das ist der Grund, warum einer meiner Clowns, der sich allein in einer Landschaft aufhält, ebenso ein Nachfahre von Vito Acconcis SEEDBED ist, wie er der Malerei der Hudson River School entstammt und an den Antihelden aus der Literatur erinnert.

CAOIMHÍN *Vergleichst du die Wiederaufnahme von erzählenden Inhalten in den Text mit der Rückkehr zur figurativen Darstellung in der Malerei?*

SEAN Ja. Ich glaube, das war zum Teil das, was meine Texte gemacht haben. Da gab es richtige Geschichten. Da gab es Anfang und Ende. Da gab es einen Handlungsverlauf mit Höhepunkten und Wendepunkten. Da ging es um menschliche Empfindungen.

CAOIMHÍN *Um auf die Entwicklung der Form in deinen Arbeiten zurückzukommen: Wie ging es weiter, nachdem du die gelben Anwaltsblöcke aufgegeben hattest?*

SEAN Na, es gab einen Grund, warum ich das gelbe Papier aufgegeben habe. Das war mein Buch [SIC], das 1993 zunächst in einer limitierten Auflage von 250 Exemplaren bei Publicsfear Press Ltd. und 1995 dann bei Riverhead Books erschien. Dieses Buch war der Höhepunkt meiner ganzen Arbeit mit den gelben Blöcken. Es war wie eine Bombe, die in mein Leben einschlug. Es war der Punkt, wo sich alles, was wir bisher diskutiert haben, zuspitzte. Dazu gehörte das Echo, von dem ich sprach, aus dieser Sendung AN AMERICAN FAMILY, wo die Kunst auf das Leben zurückwirkt. Dazu gehörte auch die Frage, ob ich meine Offenheit unter Kontrolle hatte oder ob ich ihr Opfer war. Es erhielt Nahrung aus seelischem Kummer wie bei meinen ersten Kunsttexten und schilderte in schmerzvollen Details eine demütigende Vernarrtheit. Vor allem war es Konzeptkunst, in die wieder ‚Form' gebracht worden war. Es triefte buchstäblich vor Menschlichkeit. Es war Figuration, reduziert auf die minimale Form der Textkunst in den siebziger Jahren. [SIC] war eine sehr gelungene Verbindung zwischen meiner Kunst und meinem Leben, aber das brachte mir riesige Probleme. Sehr viele Leute fühlten sich persönlich verraten, so dass sich mir die Frage aufdrängte: Was ist wichtiger, meine Kunst oder mein Leben? Wenn ich alle lieben sollte und erwartete, dass sie mich liebten, konnte ich dann so weitermachen? Ich wurde in gewisser Weise ausgeliefert und richtig gedemütigt durch dieses Buch und sehnte mich nach dem Rückzug in eine Privatsphäre. Daher machte ich mit einer neuen Form weiter, die ich mir vorher ausgedacht hatte, wo ich schreiben konnte, was ich wollte, aber keiner es finden würde. Ich nahm eine riesige Bahn Fotokulisse und füllte sie mit Stream-of-Consciousness-Text. Da war so viel geschrieben auf diesen riesenhaften Papierbahnen, dass man beim Lesen ständig die Orientierung verlor, und das gab mir einen Ort, wo ich mich verstecken konnte. Ich habe vier von dieser Art gemacht: I SUCK. RIGHT?... FUCK YOU! (1991), ANYONE'S ORGASM (1992), HARD MALE/SOFT MALE (1993) und DINGLEBERRY SEAN (1993). Es war jedes Mal irrsinnig viel Arbeit, daher bekam ich Angst, die Bahnen könnten reissen, sie würden nicht lange halten, und damals habe ich dann riesige Stücke ungespanntes Leinen ausfindig gemacht, auf die ich meinen Text schreiben konnte, einfach weil Leinen für Ölfarbe ein bewährter, dauerhafter Bildträger ist. In der Kunst geht es mir in erster Linie um Überleben, Unsterblichkeit. Malerei hält einfach länger als Kugelschreiber auf Papier. Daher habe ich eben gemalt. Die Büchse der Pandora hatte sich geöffnet.

Zu dieser Zeit, als ich von meinem gelben Anwaltsblock auf die Textmalerei umstieg, gab es eine weitere entscheidende Entwicklung. Ich habe neun Skulpturen mit nackten, frechen Kobolden gemacht. Jede bezog sich entweder auf etwas ganz Bestimmtes in der Geschichte der Bildhauerei oder enthielt vage Anspielungen. Ich wollte damit einen Vergleich zwischen mir, dem „mit Cartoons grossgezogenen Sean des 20. Jahrhunderts", und einigen der höher geschätzten Momente der Kunstgeschichte wie Rodins JOHANNES DER TÄUFER oder Donatellos DAVID provozieren. Ich wollte unbedingt demonstrieren, dass ich beides machte und eigentlich nirgendwohin gehörte, denn so, wie ich es brachte, verdeutlichte es ja das Dilemma der Kunst in unserer Zeit.

BEATRIX *Das Dilemma der Kunst? Könntest du darüber etwas mehr sagen?*

SEAN Im Kielwasser einer Kunsterziehung, die handwerkliches Geschick im Kunstschaffen abwertete, was blieb da für uns übrig? Eine Kunst, die von ein paar alten Leuten mit Ideen aus den siebziger Jahren beherrscht wird, die übrigens wie alte Hunde auf der Schutthalde ihre Scholle bewachen, in der Mitte der Staubkreise stehend, die sie um ihre Hundehütten herum in den Boden gefurcht haben: „ZUTRITT VERBOTEN!" Ich bewundere diese Typen und was sie gemacht haben, aber ich will nicht in einer Welt festsitzen, die nur von ihren Ideen beherrscht wird oder allein auf diese beschränkt ist. Das war das Terrain meiner Kunsterziehung und wogegen ich mich wehren wollte. Weshalb die Skulpturen meiner Abschlussarbeit für den Master of Fine Arts wie Skulpturen von Ronald Bladen waren, in denen man Skateboard fahren konnte. Ich brachte in karge Kunstformen das ‚Ich' zurück. Das ist auch der Grund, warum europäische Maler aus der Zeit vor dem Zweiten Weltkrieg für mich heute eine so grosse Bedeutung haben, denn ihre Kunst war das letzte Luftschnappen, bevor die Kunst hier in Amerika in den sechziger und siebziger Jahren angeblich konzeptuell schachmatt gesetzt und minimal auf ein Nichts reduziert wurde. Die Kunst taumelt seitdem. Dies wird alles klarer werden, wenn wir über das reden, was ich gegen Ende der Neunziger gemacht habe und was ich jetzt vorhabe.

Zur Begleitung dieser Skulpturen habe ich ein Video mit dem Titel ITALIAN HIGH RENAISSANCE AND BAROQUE SCULPTURE (1993) gemacht, das mich nackt und in verschiedenen Stadien der Erregung zeigt, während ich die Pose berühmter italienischer Skulpturen imitiere. Wieder dachte ich dabei an Gilbert & George, ich wollte eine lebende, atmende, agierende Skulptur auf Video zwischen meinen eigentlichen Skulpturen haben. Aber was noch wichtiger ist, ich begann mich mit dem Begriff Narzissmus auseinanderzusetzen. Ich war der Ansicht, alle Kunst sei ‚Narzissmus'. Denn wenn jemand glaubt, das Ding, das er gemacht hat, sei Aufmerksamkeit, Jubel, Geld wert und werde über alle Zeiten hinweg von kommenden Generationen in Ehren gehalten, so ist das im Grunde narzisstisch! In diesem Video habe ich versucht, das als Idee und in Wirklichkeit zu zeigen. Ich meine damit, man kann keine Erektion vortäuschen.

CAOIMHÍN *Um auf deine Gemälde zurückzukommen, sobald du also beschliesst, diesen Text nicht auf billiges Wegwerfmaterial zu schreiben, sondern auf Leinwand, klinkst du dich in eine sehr weit ausschwingende Geschichte der Bildgestaltung ein, der bildenden Kunst, der Beständigkeit der Materialien und so fort.*

SEAN Richtig.

CAOIMHÍN *Das war dir offensichtlich damals klar.*

SEAN Ja, bestimmt. Aber es sind verschiedene Dinge, die ich damals anzusprechen versucht habe, und am wenigsten wichtig war mir vermutlich die ‚Geschichte der Malerei'. Es war wirklich eine Frage der Ästhetik der Notwendigkeit. Anders ausgedrückt, so wie das Ding aussah, das war das, was der Vorgang daraus gemacht hatte. Ich habe das Aussehen dieser Sachen nicht vorausgeplant. Sie sind einfach zufällig so geworden, denn ich wollte jeden Gedanken festhalten, der mir durch den Kopf ging, während ich das Bild auf seine Oberfläche malte.

Daher war das eine ganz andere Art des Schreibens als bei dem Zeug auf den gelben Anwaltsblöcken. Ich dachte, es sei eine ganze Evolution weit weg. Von der Idee her war es im Wesentlichen immer und immer wieder „Kilroy was here". Ich hielt das deshalb für so wichtig, weil ich glaube, das ist es, was Kunst in der Zivilisation ist. Im Grunde ist es wirklich nur so, dass man seine Marke setzt.

CAOIMHÍN *Und sagt „ich war hier"?*

SEAN Ja, „ich war hier". Seit den Grotten von Lascaux, als die Menschen Pigment um ihren Handabdruck herum auf die Wand der Höhle bliesen, versucht das Kunstschaffen, das Leben oder die Existenz des Künstlers aufzuzeichnen. Die ganze Geschichte der westlichen Kunst hindurch bis heute, wo das Kunstschaffen so selbstreferentiell geworden ist, macht ‚ich war hier' einen grossen Teil davon aus. Das ist, was ich so sehr an On Kawara und Arbeiten dieser Art bewundere.

CAOIMHÍN *„Ich lebe noch." „Ich war hier"?*

SEAN „Ich lebe noch, ich bin hier." Aber meine grossen Textgemälde haben diese Idee noch ein ganzes Stück weitergeführt und dir genau die gleichen Gedanken gegeben, die ich zu dem Zeitpunkt hatte, als ich das Bild malte. Daher sage ich dir nicht nur „ich lebe noch", ich sage dir, was ich gedacht habe, als ich lebte. Vom Anfang des Bildes bis zum Ende ist alles, was ich gedacht habe und hätte aufschreiben können, aufgezeichnet worden. Das ist ein Konzept von On Kawara, das ich ein ganzes Stück vertieft habe.

CAOIMHÍN *Das ist insofern interessant, als die Arbeiten etwas Unmittelbares haben, aber sie vermitteln auch den Eindruck, dass in Echtzeit erzählt wird, was wiederum etwas ganz anderes ist, als wenn man ein Buch liest.*

SEAN Richtig. Weil eben alles eine Performance ist.

CAOIMHÍN *Eine Performance von Unmittelbarkeit, was ein Trick ist, eine Strategie, mit der das Publikum aufgefordert wird, diese Gedanken in der gleichen Zeit – in Echtzeit – zu haben, wie du sie ursprünglich hattest, wenn du alles festhältst, was du denkst, und nichts auslässt.*

SEAN Richtig.

CAOIMHÍN *Aber das enthält natürlich auch Anklänge an die Geschichte des Stream of Consciousness in der modernistischen Literatur.*

SEAN Ja, sicher. Diese Stream-of-Consciousness-Bilder wie DUMB DUMB (1993) oder FOR THE LOVE OF NOTHING (1994) oder THOUGHT BUBBLE (1994) sind sehr gross und schwierig zu lesen. Du fängst auf der linken Seite an, und während du den ganzen Weg nach rechts zurücklegst, verlierst du die Orientierung und findest dich nicht mehr zurecht. Während du liest, kannst du also nur diese bruchstückhaften Gedanken erfassen. Schliesslich wollte ich dann mehr Kontrolle darüber haben, was ich erlebe und empfinde. So sind diese ‚Zettelbilder' entstanden.

CAOIMHÍN *Du meinst damit Bilder wie SELF-SOMETHING (1994).*

SEAN Richtig. Sie sehen ganz danach aus, als stünde ich auf einer Bühne und wollte dir so viel Unterhaltung wie möglich bieten, während ich im Grunde genommen ein Bild menschlicher Gedanken gebe. Ich nehme also eine sehr viel herausfordernde Rolle an, indem ich aktiv versuche, alle zu unterhalten, die vor dem Bild stehen. Ich will nicht, dass der Betrachter weggeht. Diese kleinen ‚Zette' sind gerade genug zum Lesen, und vielleicht animieren sie dich, noch einen zu lesen. Einer von zehn bringt dich hoffentlich zum Schmunzeln oder Lachen, und wenn du weiterliest, gewinnst du hoffentlich allmählich ein grösseres Bild.

CAOIMHÍN *Das ist der Unterschied zwischen einem sehr langen Monolog und vielen Epigrammen.*

SEAN Ja.

CAOIMHÍN *Monolog und Epigramm sind völlig verschiedene Ausdrucksmittel.*

SEAN Hauptsächlich ist das der Unterschied zwischen einem Monologredner und einem Komödianten. Während der Komödiant Hunderte von Witzen am Stück erzählt, zeichnet er letzten

Endes allmählich ein Portrait von sich. Wenn du hundert Arschwitze hörst, sagst du dir nach einer Weile, „aha, der Typ hat einen Analfimmel". Es wird irgendwie unheimlich. Wenn du also alles liest, was auf dem Gemälde geschrieben ist, wird von mir ein Bild aufgebaut, das ich nicht unter Kontrolle habe. Jetzt kommen wir zu der Tatsache, dass alle ernsthaft geschaffene Kunst im Grunde eine Produktion von Selbstportraits ist.

CAOIMHÍN *Wie der Titel SELF-SOMETHING andeutet.*

SEAN Ja.

CAOIMHÍN *Gleich danach tauchen zwischen den Wörtern ganz bestimmte Figuren auf.*

SEAN Na ja, nicht ganz, da stand noch ein Endspiel mit den unaufgezogenen Textbildern aus. Nachdem ich anderthalb Jahre lang viele Leinwände vollgeschrieben hatte, war ich die Schreiberei leid und wollte sie auch nicht mehr sehen. Daher löste ich eine absichtliche Schreibblockade aus, indem ich eine Weile Streifenbilder malte. Ich hatte eine Ausstellung bei Regen Projects in Los Angeles, für die ich ein riesiges Textbild mit dem Titel THOUGHT BUBBLE gemacht hatte. Davon erschöpft, malte ich Streifen auf meine nächsten Leinwände, als wäre es Urlaub für den Geist, und nannte das erste Bild ABSENCE OF THOUGHT BUBBLE (1994). Das war auch die Ausstellung, wo zum ersten Mal Clown und Schimpanse als Skulptur auftauchten.

CAOIMHÍN *Also danach tauchten Figuren in deinen Textbildern auf?*

SEAN Ja. Das erste war das Bild mit dem Titel I'M A CLOWN IN A WORLD OF CHIMPS (1994), wo ein Clown und ein Schimpanse miteinander kämpfen, und zwei andere Bilder, GROOVIN' CORDUROY MIND-SNOT/7092 (1994) und STARING AT MY ASS IN THE MIRROR (1994), die ich in gewisser Weise unter dem Einfluss von Picabia gemalt habe. Das dürften die ersten Bilder gewesen sein, bei denen ich Figuren einsetzen oder verwenden wollte. Sie gehörten zu meiner Ausstellung 1994 in der Galerie Contemporary Fine Arts in Berlin. Es gab nur drei Gemälde und eine Skulptur von einem Schimpansen unter dem Titel ICH MACHE MICH (1994). Ich hielt diese Ausstellung für besonders wichtig, weil ich mit allen Kräften versucht hatte, in den Bereich einer traditionelleren und weniger konzeptuellen Form des Bildschaffens zu gelangen.

CAOIMHÍN *Das waren sehr versteckte Bezüge auf Picabia.*

SEAN GROOVIN' CORDUROY MIND-SNOT/7092 bezog sich auf sein Bild mit dem Titel 7091 (1938), das eine Parodie auf die Abstraktion ist. Die ganzen Bilder, die ich in dieser Art habe – wo ein Gekritzel ist und alle angrenzenden Bereiche, die durch das Gekritzel geschaffen werden, verschiedenfarbig sind – darunter auch Figuren, die sich überschneiden und die ich von Picasso entlehnt habe –, gehören zu meiner ‚Picabia 7091-Serie', wie ich sie nenne. Sie sind, wie bei ihm, eine Parodie auf die Abstraktion, aber wie bei allen ironischen Gesten wird Ernst daraus, sobald sie sich wiederholt. Sie haben alle einen Titel, der von ‚709-' an weiterzählt. Ich bin jetzt vielleicht bei 7099 oder 7100 in dieser fortlaufenden Serie. Aber sie sind bisher alle unterschiedlich. Manche sind Streifenbilder, manche sind ‚Picasso-Gemälde' und manche sind Textbilder. Picabia ist, wenn ich es recht bedenke, der einzige Künstler, der von Anfang bis Ende in seinem künstlerischen Schaffen völlig frei war. Er verwendete viele verschiedene Medien und Formen und war in allen grossartig. Er verkörpert Freiheit für mich. Wenn ich mich bei meinen Bildern auf ihn beziehe, dann kopiere ich nicht so sehr ihr Aussehen, sondern zitiere ihn eher indirekt, als eine Art Symbol für meine eigene künstlerische Freiheit, die, wie ich meine, für mein Überleben unbedingt notwendig ist.

Als ich I'M A CLOWN IN A WORLD OF CHIMPS malte, hatte ich gerade noch einmal gelesen, was ich im Laufe einiger Jahre geschrieben hatte, und aufgefallen war mir dabei das wiederkehrende Muster aus Selbsterhöhung und Selbsterniedrigung. Dieses gedankliche Muster war fast so etwas wie ein Perpetuum mobile geworden, aus dem Inhalte und Metaphern herausgewirbelt wurden. Also gab ich beiden Form und Charakter. Der Schimpanse war Selbsterhöhung, und der Clown war Selbsterniedrigung. Das ist der Grund, warum der Schimpanse bei jedem einzelnen Cartoon auf diesem Bild besser abschneidet als der Clown.

CAOIMHÍN *Du hast einmal gesagt, du interessiertest dich deshalb für Picabia oder später Picasso, weil du zu den grossen Künstlern wie sie gezählt werden möchtest.*

SEAN Ich habe das bei einer Aufzeichnung gesagt, einer Audioarbeit mit dem Titel DEAR PICASSO (2001).

CAOIMHIN *Also sollte das im Kontext eines bestimmten Kunstwerkes verstanden werden und nicht als öffentliche Erklärung eines Künstlers?*

SEAN Ja. Mir ist vollkommen klar, wenn ich so etwas sage, dann finden das alle, die es hören, irgendwie traurig und allerliebst. Diese bestimmte Arbeit ist für mich ein ausgezeichnetes Beispiel dafür, dass ich selbst meine, was ich sage, aber merke, dass es für andere nicht glaubhaft ist. Ich habe von niemandem erwartet, dass er glaubt, „Sean ist Picasso" oder „er denkt, er wird der nächste Picasso". Aber ich bin überzeugt, ein anderer Künstler kann den Wunsch oder das Gedankenmuster verstehen.

Das macht einen grossen Teil meiner Kunst aus: Ich führe eine peinliche Situation wie diese vor und hoffe, dass der Betrachter sich hineinversetzen kann.

CAOIMHÍN *Du zeigst einen vielleicht umfassenderen Ehrgeiz, als andere Künstler willens sind, öffentlich einzugestehen.*

SEAN Richtig. Ich meine, das ist ein Zeichen von Stärke. Wenn du dieses Band zum ersten Mal hörst, dann denkst du „oh, wie traurig und pathetisch". Aber tatsächlich empfand ich das als kühne und gewaltige Angelegenheit. Ich fürchte mich nicht vor meinen Träumen (lacht). Selbst wenn ich weiss, dass einige von ihnen ausser Reichweite sind. Ich meine, dass ich wirklich wichtig sein will. Ich will diese Vorstellung nicht aufgeben. Ich sage nur, dass ich nicht verrückt bin. Ich weiss, es gibt da gewisse Sachen an Picasso, die … (Pause). Nein, ich kann es nicht sagen. Tut mir leid. Ich werde es nicht sagen (lacht). Du weisst, was ich meine. Du weisst, dass ich nicht sagen werde, ich bin kein grosser Künstler. Werde ich nicht. Ich glaube es nicht.

CAOIMHÍN *Aber das Bildzitat von Picabia und die Performance der Rolle eines Künstlers, der unbedingt Picasso werden will, sind recht verschieden.*

SEAN Ich glaube, sie haben insofern etwas miteinander zu tun, als sie sich auf andere Künstler beziehen und mir eine neue Bedeutung schaffen sollen. Ich bewundere Picasso, weil er ohne Frage ein Genie war. Ich beneide ihn darum. Wenn ich ihn zitiere, dann spiele ich auf den Begriff des künstlerischen Genies an. Ich bewundere Picabia, weil er sein ganzes Leben lang schöpferische Freiheit bewiesen hat. Auch ich brauche Freiheit, ich muss mich ständig verändern, damit ich Lust habe, Kunst zu schaffen. Die Leute sind im Allgemeinen einhellig der Meinung, ich könnte genau so frei sein, wie er war. Der Unterschied ist, dass er sich das leisten konnte, er hatte Geld von der Familie (lacht). Aber weisst du, was es speziell bei Picabia war? Ich brauchte Hilfe, um ein Gemälde zu machen, weil ich aus einem Meer von Texten kam, zweidimensionalen graphischen Bildern. Ich suchte Hilfe in der Kunstgeschichte, um vom Text aus eine neue Art Bild zu schaffen. Daher benutzte ich Picabia. Später benutzte ich andere Dinge … zum Beispiel Brüste (Lachen).

CAOIMHÍN *Möchtest du etwas über das ‚Brustbild' sagen: THE ETHER OF MEMORY (1994)?*

SEAN Was soll ich dazu sagen? Wenn du etwas malen willst, dann male, was du liebst! Das klingt so dumm, aber es ist ehrlich.

CAOIMHÍN *Das war 1994, in einer Zeit, als überwältigend füllige Brüste für einen weissen, männlichen Künstler vermutlich das unpopulärste Thema waren, das du dir hättest aussuchen können.*

SEAN Genau. Das war eine Provokation. Eher in der Art Lausebengel, gar nicht mal skandalös oder anstössig. Sollen wir vielleicht sagen politisch? Es war einfach so tabu in diesen reflexhaft reagierenden politisch korrekten Zeiten, dass ich nicht widerstehen konnte. Die Abwertung der Frau zum Objekt ist nichts, worauf sich stolz sein liesse. Aber ich habe nie geglaubt, Frauen könnten den Männern nicht vollkommen ebenbürtig sein. Gleichzeitig zu glauben, dass ‚aufgeklärte' Männer den Frauenkörper nicht zum Fetisch erheben, ist verrückt. Natürlich tun wir das.

CAOIMHÍN *Was bedeutet der Titel THE ETHER OF MEMORY?*

SEAN Brüste in der Erinnerung, bis zur Befriedigung sinnlicher Lust, auf einer Ebene. Wenn du diesen Text liest, es geht darin um meine Abstammung mütterlicherseits, so weit zurück, wie ich mir das vorstellen konnte. Ich bin Maler, weil meine Grossmutter Malerin war und meine Mutter Malerin ist. Als Kind ging ich immer zu meiner Grossmutter hinüber zum Malen. Sie hatte riesengrosse Dinger, und jedes Mal, wenn ich hinüberging, umarmte sie mich und drückte mich genau dazwischen, bevor wir hinauf unters Dach in ihr Atelier gingen. Das gehörte zu den lustvollsten Erlebnissen. Ich liebte es. Also ging es um meinen Ursprung als Künstler aus den mütterlichen Brüsten.

FOOTBALL DUCK (2003), die Bronzeskulptur, und FOOTBALL DUCK (1999), das Gemälde, haben auch damit zu tun. Der Fussballplatz, wo wir trainierten, war direkt neben dem Haus meiner Grossmutter. Ich hasste es so sehr, zum Fussballtraining gehen zu müssen, dass ich einfach schwänzte und zu ihr zum Malen ging. Da sass ich dann vor der Staffelei mit meinen Schulterpolstern und Nockenschuhen und malte Geranien, während meine Mannschaftskameraden draussen trainierten. Diese Arbeiten sind Portraits des Konflikts zwischen ‚männlicher Sportlichkeit' und ‚weiblichem Künstlertum' in meiner Selbstwahrnehmung als Jugendlicher.

CAOIMHÍN *Was war der nächste Schritt nach THE ETHER OF MEMORY?*

SEAN Der nächste grosse Schritt war meine Schimpansenausstellung, 1995 in der Andrea Rosen Gallery. Ich hatte, als mich ein Schimpanse in meinem Atelier besuchte, Gemälde, eine Skulptur und ein Video gemacht. Ich hoffte, der Schimpanse würde mich vertreten oder als mein Ebenbild herhalten. Das war die Zeit, als die Dinge wirklich in Gang kamen.

Mit der Malerlaubnis, die ich von Picabia erhalten hatte, konnte nun wirklich alles auf die Leinwand kommen, einschliesslich der Spuren, die ein Schimpanse hinterliess. Ich war nicht einfach nur auf das beschränkt, was mir zu schreiben einfiel. Ich konnte Figuren machen und Illusion verwenden, und das bedeutete, ich konnte überhaupt alles machen, überallhin gehen innerhalb des Rechtecks eines Gemäldes. Es stellt sich heraus, dass die älteste Form der Kunst, die Malerei, die echteste Freiheit der Kunst ist, und danach suchte ich.

Bei dem Gemälde LOOKING FOR MR. GODBAR (1995) fliesst der Text über einen illusionistischen blauen Wolkenhimmel. Das Geschriebene nahm plötzlich einen tatsächlich vorhandenen, keinen imaginären Raum ein. Es sollte so aussehen, als schautest du im Flugzeug aus dem Fenster, in 8000 Meter Höhe. Wenn du nicht gerade ein Buch liest oder mit dem Film beschäftigt bist, dann sind dort deine Gedanken ungewöhnlich laut. Ich erinnerte mich an diese Art Gedanken und an diese Art des Denkens. Für mich wird Gott ein Thema ...

CAOIMHÍN *Gott wird ein Thema, aber auf eine eher irdische Art, mit dieser Vorstellung von einem sich weithin erstreckenden Himmel bei LOOKING FOR MR. GODBAR, das gilt auch für die Geschichte des Erhabenen, von der romantischen Landschaftsmalerei des 19. Jahrhunderts bis zur abstrakten Erhabenheit und darüber hinaus.*

SEAN Ja. Ganz bestimmt. Es war genau das. Die Hudson River School. Eine kleine, unbedeutende Figur in erhabener Landschaft. Was ich da geschrieben habe, war in der Tat transzendent. Und das ist es, worauf alle diese Leute aus waren ...

CAOIMHÍN *Oder ein Seestück wie 36 HOURS (1995)?*

SEAN Ja, ganz bestimmt, das auch. Aber das hatte noch etwas Besonderes. Ich begann damals, viele Bücher mit Überlebensgeschichten zu lesen, über Leute auf Rettungsflössen, nachdem ihre Schiffe im Meer versunken waren, oder einsame Weltumsegler, die unterwegs irgendwie den Verstand verloren. Statt also im Flugzeug aus dem Fenster zu sehen, stellte ich mich auf dieser Reise vor. Und wenn man so lange dermassen deutlich seinen Gedanken lauscht – ich habe auf diese Weise so viele Leinwände gefüllt –, dann dauert es nicht lange, wenigstens bei mir nicht, bis man zu dieser „warum sind wir hier"-Frage kommt, die einfach immer wieder auftaucht.

CAOIMHÍN *Bald danach auf Bildern wie ALONE (1996), das sich formal auf 36 HOURS bezieht, verlierst du das Textelement bei den Bildern.*

SEAN Ja. Und genau da verliere ich mein Publikum (lacht). Eigentlich nicht, aber ich hatte das Gefühl, keiner hat es so richtig verstanden. ALONE ist übrigens nie ausgestellt worden. Viele andere Clownbilder aus dieser Zeit waren allerdings in der Galerie Contemporary Fine Arts in Berlin (1996) und in der Galerie Rebecca Camhi in Athen (1996) zu sehen. ALONE zeigt einen pastos gemalten Clown zu einem illusionistischen Seestück, der den Text aus einem Bild wie NAVAL GAZE (1995) oder 36 HOURS unmittelbar ersetzte. Ich liebte dieses Bild. Ich wurde so high vom Malen, dass ich es immer wieder neu malen wollte. Daher wurde aus diesen Bildern mit den traurigen, einsamen Clowns, die sich in der Natur abmühen, eine ganze Serie, die dann vermutlich in meinem Leben eine neue Bedeutung annahm.

Bis dahin war alles, was ich gemacht hatte, erstaunlich gut aufgenommen worden. Ich rede von den äusseren Dingen, die mit Karriere zu tun haben, die sich einfach mit jeder Ausstellung, die ich machte, besser anfühlten. Als ich den Text aus meinen Bildern entfernte, gab es plötzlich riesige Probleme. Kein Mensch wusste etwas mit ihnen anzufangen. Das, worauf sich die Leute offensichtlich bei meiner Kunst verlassen hatten – das Geschriebene auf einem Bild –, war nicht mehr da. Ich fühlte mich missverstanden. Schreiben war für mich nur einer von vielen Wegen, in eine konzeptuell begründete Kunst wieder Form zu bringen. Es war nicht das A und O.

Als ich dann begann, mehr ewig traurig stimmende Clowns zu machen, dann waren sie deswegen traurig, weil ich sie malte und kein Mensch sie zu verstehen schien. Es wurde eine Art konzeptuelle Todesspirale. Je mehr ich machte, desto schlimmer schien es und desto trauriger wurden die Clowns. Was ich rasend komisch fand, wenn ich in meinem Atelier sass und mit Freunden darüber diskutierte, aber es war auch traurig. Ich dachte, eines Tages würde das eine meiner beliebtesten Werkfolgen und eine meiner Lieblingsgeschichten sein. Und es ist tatsächlich so. Wie meine Frau immer gleich hinzufügt, wenn ich über diese Serie jammere, sie hat sich als eine meiner populärsten erwiesen.

CAOIMHÍN *Es ist interessant, dass in deinem Schaffen zu gewissen Zeiten das Schwergewicht – manchmal buchstäblich – auf der Signatur liegt, zum Beispiel bei dem Diptychon SEAN LANDERS/7098 (2001). Zu anderen Zeiten fehlt hingegen die Kennzeichnung durch eine Signatur, was bis zu diesem bestimmten Zeitpunkt das Geschriebene auf den Bildern war.*

SEAN Ich glaube, es ist bei allen Künstlern ein natürlicher Reflex, dass sie sich einer Definition zu entziehen versuchen. Aber ich hatte das Gefühl, dass der Clown diese Signatur wurde. Frustriert hat mich damals vielleicht, dass ich meinte, diese ‚neue Signatur' sei das Gleiche wie meine Texte.

CAOIMHÍN *Ich vermute, die Leute wollten es nicht als das Gleiche akzeptieren.*

SEAN Vielleicht glaubten sie, mir fehle das Geschick oder die Erlaubnis, ‚einfach' ein Bild oder was zu malen. So viele Künstler malen heutzutage auf eine sehr viel lahmere Art als ich damals und werden dafür gelobt. Es war vermutlich einfach die falsche Zeit, oder es war das ganz bestimmte Emblem, der Clown.

CAOIMHÍN *Du meinst, die Leute haben sich vielleicht damals gesagt, dass ein kaum älterer Künstler wie George Condo den Markt mit Beschlag belegt hatte?*

SEAN Nein, ich bin nicht mit George Condo verglichen worden.

CAOIMHÍN *Wirklich nicht?*

SEAN Nein. Na ja, nicht dass ich wüsste oder mich erinnerte. Und es wäre auch nicht berechtigt gewesen. Was ich damals machte, war anders. Er gehört allerdings zu meinen heute lebenden Lieblingsmalern.

CAOIMHÍN *Dann vielleicht Nauman? Obwohl das weniger offensichtlich ist, weil er kein Maler ist.*

SEAN Sie stellten mich zu Nauman, weil mich vermutlich auch niemand als Maler sah. Ich bekam so viel ‚Nauman', und die Wahrheit ist, dass ich mich überhaupt nie um ihn gekümmert habe. Selbst wenn du als Künstler nur rein zufällig über eine alte Nauman-Idee stolperst, schon fällt die ‚Nauman-Lobby' unflätig über dich her. Leute tauchen aus dem Nichts auf und erzählen dir ‚Nauman hat das zuerst gemacht', auch wenn das gar nicht stimmt. Was sagt das über ihre Kenntnisse in Kunstgeschichte, wenn sie glauben, Bruce Nauman habe die Idee mit den Clowns in der Kunst erfunden? Er war auch nicht der Erste, der Nabelschau gehalten hat. Dass Künstler sich über Kreativität Gedanken machen, hatte schon eine umfassende Geschichte, bevor er auftauchte. Ich glaube, sie sahen mich schlicht und einfach als Konzeptkünstler, und weil ich diese Scheuklappen trug, wirkte ich wohl so wie Nauman. Das Verrückte ist, dass nie jemand gedacht hat, das könnten Gemälde sein. Das ist das Erstaunliche. Bis heute glauben die Leute immer noch nicht, dass ich Maler bin. Ich habe doch nun wirklich wahnsinnig viele Bilder gemalt.

CAOIMHÍN *Und was dachten die Leute, was das wäre?*

SEAN Sie hielten das für einen Akt der Konzeptkunst. Ein Ölgemälde als Performance. Na schön, aber wenn der Tag um war, musste ich doch tatsächlich Farbe aus einer Tube spritzen und mit dem Pinsel auftragen. Es ist ein Gemälde!

CAOIMHÍN *Die Unterscheidung war vermutlich Ende der achtziger Jahre eher angebracht, weil die ganze Wiederkehr der Malerei, die ein Jahrzehnt vorher stattgefunden hatte, ob sie nun positiv oder negativ aufgenommen wurde, zum Teil als Reaktion auf die Konzeptkunst aufgefasst worden war. Daher wurden die Malerei per se und die Konzeptkunst damals wohl eher als Gegensätze verstanden. Auf jeden Fall hat dich die anfängliche negative Reaktion der Kritik nicht davon abgehalten, weiter zu malen. Was hat sie innerhalb deiner Malerei bewirkt?*

SEAN Sie hat mich noch mehr Clowns malen lassen, die in extremeren physischen Situationen noch trauriger werden. Das ist der Grund, warum ich finde, dass diese bewusste Serie für mein gesamtes Schaffen eine so zentrale Bedeutung hat. Es ist immer noch reflektiertes Schreiben, aber da gibt es keinen Text im eigentlichen Sinn. Ich bin es, der sich darüber Gedanken macht, wie ich aufgenommen werde, aber durch diese Cartoons.

BEATRIX *Aber kommt nicht mit der Clownfigur eine Art kollektives Bewusstsein ins Spiel? Ich frage mich, ob du einfach so sagen kannst, es geht um dich. Das ist von Natur aus ein kollektives Erlebnis. Du kannst so viel über dich reden, wie du willst, aber das Gefühl wird geteilt. Misserfolg ist ein Gefühl, das geteilt wird, oder der Wunsch, berühmt zu sein oder zu überdauern.*

SEAN Ja, und das gehörte zu meinen frühen Überraschungen. Als ich diese verletzbare Seite von mir zeigte, da wurde das durch die Einfühlung und das Verständnis der anderen belohnt. Es stellt sich heraus, dass die meisten Menschen gleich gesinnt sind. Das ist die Achse, auf der meine Arbeit stattfindet und immer stattgefunden hat. Ich versuche, den Betrachter zu erreichen, indem ich ihm etwas ausgesprochen Persönliches gebe, das er in sich selbst wiederfindet. Wie das Vito Acconci in jener Performance in den siebziger Jahren gemacht hat, als er auf einer Pier Menschen, die sich zu ihm auf den Weg machten, Geheimnisse zuflüsterte. Ich habe jedoch herausgefunden, dass ein Kunstwerk nicht immer hundertprozentig wahr sein muss, um überzeugend zu wirken. Bei einem Hollywood-Film zum Beispiel merkt man, dass die ganze Sache lächerlich und absurd ist, aber da gibt es kurze Augenblicke von etwas, was vollkommen real erscheint, was du wieder erkennst und was den ganzen Film überzeugend macht. Zuzus Rosenblätter zum Beispiel aus Frank Capras IT'S A WONDERFUL LIFE. Das ist genauso bei einer Arbeit mit Text. Ich kann das ganze Ding hindurch allen möglichen Scheiss schreiben und habe trotzdem ein paar Momente, die über den Scheiss hinausgehen und dich tatsächlich mit ihrer Wahrheit berühren, und das macht das ganze Ding überzeugend. Ich habe sehr früh gelernt, dass ich dabei nicht nur mich portraitierte, und das war ein Glück. Sonst hätte es wohl nur bestätigt, dass ich verrückt bin.

CAOIMHÍN *Kehren wir zum Begriff der Signatur und den Emblemen der Signatur zurück. Die Ausführung der Signatur in einer sich wiederholenden Komposition ist etwas, was zum Herzstück der Kunst des 20. Jahrhunderts gehört, sogar zu der Art von Malerei, die deine Arbeit nicht besonders beeinflusst hat. Das Erste, was ein Jackson Pollock uns heute sagt, ist „das ist ein Jackson Pollock".*

SEAN Richtig. Und ich habe meine Warenzeichen-Signatur. Das ist der Text auf der Leinwand. Sie ist ähnlich wie bei Pollock mein Signaturträger. Wenn jemand anderes so etwas macht, dann dringt er in mein ‚Revier' ein. Mir ist, als gehörte mir das. Wenn ich eine Signatur habe, dann ist es diese. Und sie schafft die Einheit aller meiner Arbeiten, von Anfang an bis jetzt.

CAOIMHÍN *Wenn also die Karten der jüngsten Kunstgeschichte gemischt werden, was glaubst du, in welche Beziehung wird deine Arbeit auf diesem ‚Signaturträger' zu dem Werk von Künstlern gesetzt werden, die so verschieden sind wie Ed Ruscha oder Christopher Wool?*

SEAN Ich bewundere diese beiden Künstler. Ich begrüsse alle Vergleiche mit ihnen, aber ich weiss auch mit Sicherheit, dass mein Werk im Vergleich zu ihrem oder dem Schaffen anderer Künstler etwas ganz Eigenes ist. Es ist immer nur ein kurzer Moment, dass ich mit ihnen verglichen werden kann. Es gibt so viele Künstler, mit denen ich kurz verglichen werden kann, aber dann gehe ich weiter. Ich kümmere mich nicht um sie, bevor ich anfange. Es passiert einfach, dass es so oder in gewisser Weise ähnlich aussieht, aber wenn es Absicht ist, wirst du das erfahren, weil ich darüber schreibe. So wie ich das bei Hamsun, Kawara, Acconci, Magritte, Picabia, Picasso, Hogarth usw. getan habe.

CAOIMHÍN *Obwohl du den Text auf der Leinwand als deine Signatur beanspruchst, hast du doch um 1996 herum den Text absichtlich aufgegeben, um das zu schaffen, was du jetzt bockig zu deinen Lieblingsbildern zählst, wie du vorhin gesagt hast!*

SEAN Richtig. Aber du nimmst an, ich wäre der einzige Richter, der über meine Signatur zu befinden hätte. In Wahrheit legen das andere Leute für uns fest. Ich habe auch gesagt, dass wir Künstler uns gern der Definition entziehen und dass ich frei sein muss, das zu tun, was ich will und wann immer ich es will, wie Picabia. Man kann nur das gut machen, was man gern macht. Alles andere wird mittelmässig. Ich wollte vorhin noch sagen, dass die Freiheit, nicht zu schreiben, nachdem ich so viele Jahre geschrieben hatte, mir vorkam, als hätte ich mir ein riesiges Gewicht vom Hals geschafft. Ich war es einfach so leid geworden, meine Gedanken zu hören. Es wurde nach einer Weile richtig beängstigend eng. Die Freiheit, einfach ein Bild zu malen, das war wie „o mein Gott, alle anderen, die das machen, haben es so einfach. Warum muss ich den Stein den Berg hinaufschieben? Muss ich nicht". Allerdings habe ich schnell gelernt, dass ich doch musste. Zumindest mein Publikum hat es erwartet. Ich weiss nicht, warum es den Leuten so unangenehm ist, wenn ein Künstler sich oder seine ‚Signatur' verändert. Anfangs wandte ich mich an Picabia, um einen Ausweg zu finden. Jetzt suche ich manchmal bei ihm Trost, ein bisschen. Das ist der Grund, warum ich symbolisch auf ihn verweise. Er ist fast wie eine Vaterfigur oder so etwas für mich. Er versichert mir irgendwie, dass es in Ordnung ist, sich zu verändern, und dass ich tue, was ich tun muss.

CAOIMHÍN *Es ist vermutlich unter Künstlern deiner Generation der Neunziger verbreiteter als bei früheren Generationen, einen Signaturstil zu haben, der letztendlich darin besteht, dass man eine Menge verschiedener Sachen macht, um es banal auszudrücken.*

SEAN Na ja, einem einzigen Stil lebenslänglich in die Falle zu gehen, scheint einfach ein Elend zu sein. Wie kannst du dich selber ernst nehmen, wenn du das machst? Nicht einmal Pollock hat das gemacht. Er hatte ebenfalls ein weites Arbeitsfeld. Was wir gemeinhin von ihm wissen, ist das eine, aber wenn du ihn unter einem breiteren Blickwinkel siehst, dann ist an diesem Typen sehr viel mehr dran. Er war mutig genug, viele Formen auszuprobieren.

CAOIMHÍN *Der Grund, warum sich manche Leute für ein Vorgehen entscheiden, das alles andere als abwechslungsreich ist, ich vermute, was sie am stärksten treibt, das ist ein Akt der Negierung oder Verfeinerung, der die gleiche Form hervorbringen muss. Und sie finden sie immer und immer wieder, statt auf Abwechslung zu bestehen.*

SEAN Das halte ich wirklich für fragwürdig. Denn als Praktiker weiss ich, wie schnell sich das abwetzt. Und zu glauben, nur etwas zu verbessern, könnte auf lange Sicht für jemanden interessant sein… na, ich stelle da einfach ihre Neugier in Frage. Wenn wir annehmen, dass Neugier für Intelligenz steht, wie intelligent sind sie dann? Immer weiter das gleiche Ergebnis herauszuleiern, ist hoffnungslos feige. Das ist absolut traurig. Und doch scheint es das zu sein, was die Kunstwelt besonders grosszügig belohnt. Es ist, als sei das System auf einem Stand angekommen, wo Mittelmässigkeit gefördert wird.

CAOIMHÍN *Aber vielleicht kann man neugierig sein und trotzdem ausfeilen, statt neugierig zu sein und verschiedene Sachen zu machen. Es ist eben nur nicht dein Weg.*

SEAN Als Praktiker habe ich da meine Zweifel.

CAOIMHÍN *Du meinst also, Agnes Martin oder Robert Ryman sollten es einmal mit dem Clown versuchen?*

SEAN Ja (lacht). Robert Ryman ist ein ausgezeichnetes Beispiel. Er hätte mich holen sollen, damit ich darüber schreibe (Lachen). Na ja, es gibt Diskussionen über des Kaisers neue Kleider, und vielleicht ist keiner besser geeignet als Robert Ryman. Ich weiss, was für eine Debatte das in Gang setzen könnte, aber letzten Endes malt er immer wieder weisse Bilder. Was meinst du? Bist du vollkommen begeistert von dem Zeug von Robert Ryman? Manche Sachen sind schön, vermute ich. Aber das ist Stuck wohl auch. Das Gleiche gilt für Ad Reinhardt. In vielerlei Hinsicht haben diese beiden Leute die Malerei scheinbar schachmatt gesetzt. Sie war völlig unberechtigt. Sie hat nicht existiert. Die Malerei war angeblich tot, und sie hatten sie angeblich umgebracht. Die unmittelbare Reaktion darauf war der Photorealismus. Und was kam danach? Der Neoexpressionismus? Und dann kam Neo-Geo, und was dann …? Nichts? Offensichtlich gab es viele untote Ausnahmen in dieser Zeit, darunter Martin Kippenberger und George Condo, um zwei meiner Lieblinge zu nennen. Aber wenn die Malerei tatsächlich allmählich ‚rehabilitiert' wird oder wieder in Fahrt kommt, ich glaube, das geschieht durch meine Generation, die sich die Mühe macht, diesem ‚Problemkind' neue Regeln zu geben, die besagen, dass alles möglich ist, und von der Konzeptkunst ebenso beeinflusst wird wie, sagen wir mal, von Velázquez, Manet oder Picasso.

CAOIMHÍN *Ohne dass der Eindruck entstünde, hier drohe ein Stillstand, es sei gestrig, es könnte kritisch werden?*

SEAN Richtig. Ist das der Grund, warum ich als Künstler kein ‚Slacker' bin? Wenn ich tatsächlich ein ‚Slacker' wäre, dann ergäbe ein schwarzes Bild sehr viel Sinn. Aber der Versuch, die Malerei neu zu erfinden, das ist das Unternehmen für überhaupt jeden, der malt. Das ist eine Mission für jeden, der gewillt ist, sie auf sich zu nehmen.

CAOIMHÍN *Aber du engagierst dich trotzdem nicht für die Malerei per se als Medium.*

SEAN Ich engagiere mich nicht nur für die Malerei. Sondern für die Kunst überhaupt.

CAOIMHÍN *Aber hier redest du über Malerei.*

SEAN Das ist Zufall, aber ich beschränke mich nicht auf die Malerei, weil ich das nicht muss. Andere müssen.

CAOIMHÍN *Du meinst, sie müssten.*

SEAN Oder sie können alles andere nicht besonders gut. Sie sind keine guten Autoren. Und sie sind keine guten Bildhauer. Im Grunde hält ihre Angst sie davon ab, sich zu verändern. Ich habe nicht so viel Zurückhaltung, auch nicht bei einem Medium, das ich nicht beherrsche. Mir macht es nichts aus, mich kopfüber hineinzustürzen. Es ist wie der Mythos von Ikarus. Ich strebe nach Grösse, verbrenne und stürze ab, und wenn der Bogen meines Niedergangs Bedeutung hat, dann habe ich eine neue Art von Kunst geschaffen. Da gibt es eine Geschichte des Scheiterns, die so schön ist wie die Geschichte des Triumphs. Was diese Sache mit dem Antihelden ist, die ich aus HUNGER gelernt habe.

CAOIMHÍN *Wenn du das Scheitern zu oft vortäuschst, dann wird es …*

SEAN Nein, das ist kein vorgetäuschtes Scheitern. Das ist versuchen und scheitern. Es ist scheitern. Scheitern ist eine Geschichte, die ich erzählen will, weil das eine Geschichte ist, die jeder kennt, eine Geschichte, die jeder erlebt, aber keiner haben will.

BEATRIX *Aber du willst sie haben?*

SEAN Ja. Das ist wie Eigentum direkt am Strand, das keiner haben will, weil dort ein Abwasserrohr entlangläuft. Na ja, das ungeklärte Abwasser ist schrecklich, aber ich bin am Strand.

BEATRIX *Und der Strand bedeutet was in dieser Analogie?*

SEAN Die Kunstgeschichte. Hoffe ich.

CAOIMHIN *Also „versuch's noch einmal, scheitere besser", wie Beckett gesagt hat.*

SEAN Ja. Na ja, du kannst in Bezug auf mich gar nicht genug Beckett bringen.

CAOIMHÍN *Können wir ein bisschen über deine Skulpturen reden? Du hast mit Ton angefangen, aber du hast auch Bronzeguss gemacht. Diese Wahl der Materialien ist recht bezeichnend und bringt Nachhall. Bronze ist ein dauerhaftes Material. Es ist das Material von Denkmälern.*

SEAN Na, deswegen habe ich aufgehört, auf Papier zu schreiben, und angefangen, auf Leinen zu schreiben, das mit Bleiweiss grundiert ist. Ich wollte, dass es erhalten bleibt. Das steht hinter meinem Drang, Kunst zu machen. Was ich schaffe, soll dauerhaft sein, mich überdauern. Das ist genau das, was das Bild THERE WAS A TIME … (2004) in der Ausstellung in der Andrea Rosen Gallery (2004) ausdrückt. Es beschreibt meine Überzeugung, dass ich mein Leben schrittweise in Kunstwerke verlagere, in diese statischen Objekte, und wenn ich sterbe, ist das alles, was übrig bleiben wird. Vielleicht ist das rührselig, geschmacklos, lächerlich oder wie du es nennen willst, aber es ist das, was mich treibt. Ich hatte immer grosse Freude daran, die Wahrheit zu sagen, besonders dann, wenn sie nicht ‚angebracht' ist. Die meisten Künstler setzen alles daran, dergleichen Äusserungen zu vermeiden.

CAOIMHÍN *Aber die Art und Weise, wie man sich deiner Meinung nach an dich erinnern sollte, hat sich offensichtlich geändert. Du hast einmal gesagt, du wärest genauso glücklich, wenn man dich als Maler eines traurig-lustigen Bildchens in Erinnerung behielte, wie du dich freutest, wenn du Robert Smithsons SPIRAL JETTY hinterlassen könntest.*

SEAN Nun, daran hat sich überhaupt nichts geändert.

CAOIMHÍN *Da gibt es einen Unterschied zwischen der implizierten Bescheidenheit eines ‚traurigen Bildchens' und den monumentalen Ambitionen einer Bronzeskulptur.*

SEAN Monumental? Ich habe nie etwas gemacht, was höher war als ein Meter.

CAOIMHÍN *Na gut. Aber allein das Material lässt doch schon auf Monumentalität schliessen.*

SEAN Ich bin anderer Meinung. Bronze ist einfach ein befriedigender, dauerhafter Werkstoff. Soweit wir wissen, halten Ölgemälde na vielleicht vierhundert, fünfhundert Jahre? Wir wissen, dass Bronze mindestens sechstausend Jahre überdauert. Woran ich dachte, als ich das ‚traurige Bildchen' erwähnte, waren Bilder wie THE IDEA MAN (1998) oder THREE NOSE GUY (1998). Eben alles aus der ‚Figur und Text'-Serie, meiner ‚période vache', das war genau das, woran ich dachte, als ich das sagte. Aber wir sind zu schnell vorgegangen. Kann ich zurückgehen und ein paar Kleinigkeiten einschieben?

BEATRIX *Natürlich.*

SEAN Ich habe diese Serie gemacht, nachdem ich mit meiner figürlichen Malerei ein ganzes Stück weitergekommen war. Diese begann mit der Hogarth-Serie (1996). Ich nahm ein Werk von William Hogarth mit dem Titel A MIDNIGHT MODERN CONVERSATION (1732) und malte auf dieser Basis ungefähr ein Dutzend Bilder. Ich erzählte die Geschichte, wie ich einer Lebensphase entwuchs, der Trinkgelagekameraderie/-kultur, von der meine Freunde und ich so lange gezehrt hatten, wo wir diskutierten und uns mit unseren Ideen gegenseitig inspirierten. Wo wir einander Gesellschaft leisteten, während wir darauf warteten, ‚entdeckt' zu werden. Wie ich meine Frau fand und zu heiraten beschloss. Es war eine unglaublich jugendhafte Wiedergabe der Geschichte des Erwachsenwerdens. Es war die unverhohlen ‚falscheste' Kunst, die ich je gemacht habe. Das waren verrückte Bilder, aber sie lagen auf einer Linie mit meiner Arbeit. Ich erzählte durch die Malerei eine Geschichte aus meinem Leben und benutzte dazu die Kunstgeschichte. Die Galeristen, bei denen ich sie ausstellte und die ich sehr mochte, Stuart Regen und Shaun Caley von Regen Projects in Los Angeles, reagierten fassungslos. Ich werde nie Shauns Gesichtsausdruck vergessen, als ausgepackt wurde. Ich brauche nicht zu sagen, dass sie mich nie wieder fragten, ob ich dort ausstellen will.

Dann kam die Clownserie, über die ich schon ausführlich gesprochen habe. Daraus wurde 1997 meine Ausstellung in der Andrea Rosen Gallery in New York. Diese Bilder waren ein comicartiger Verschnitt in Disney-Manier aus zwei oder drei berühmten Gemälden, aber von mir gemacht, mit ihrer ganz eigenen oder fehlenden Virtuosität. DANCE OF LIFE (1997) ist zur einen Hälfte DER TANZ (erste Fassung, 1909) von Matisse und zur anderen Hälfte Poussins BACCHANAL VOR EINER PAN-BÜSTE (1631–1633). ZORKON (1997) ist halb Winslow Homers BREEZING UP [A FAIR WIND] (1876) und halb Géricaults FLOSS DER MEDUSA (1819). Für mich war Disneys Einfluss wichtig, weil er für Leute der Babyboom-Jahre und danach das Figureninventar repräsentierte, das im kollektiven Unbewussten vorhanden ist. Wir alle haben einen solchen Figurenvorrat in unseren Köpfen, sei es Looney Tunes, Japanimation oder Tin Tin. Sich diesem zu widersetzen und einfach nur auf die bildlichen Darstellungen des Metropolitan Museum, des Louvre und Prado zurückzugreifen, war meiner Meinung nach einfach zu grossspurig. Wieder war es das ‚Falscheste', was man tun konnte, aber ich wollte es unbedingt, weil es etwas darüber aussagte, was es bedeutet, in meiner Zeit Künstler zu sein. Ich verglich mich mehr oder weniger wohlwollend mit den Grossen der Kunstgeschichte, um mein eigenes und das Dilemma aller anderen Künstler zu schildern, die wir versuchen, im Kielwasser der Kunstgeschichte ‚neue' Kunst zu machen, und vor allem im Kielwasser der Kunsterziehung meiner Generation, die von Theorie, Konzeptkunst, Minimalismus und Prozesskunst beherrscht war. Diese Ausstellungen waren mein bescheidener Versuch, in die Konzeptkunst wieder Form zu bringen, vielleicht ‚wie Ikarus zu scheitern', aber letztendlich die Konzeptkunst als Dolch gegen sich selbst zu benutzen. Es war ein Akt der Konzeptkunst, der antikonzeptuell war.

Leider schienen das wenige Leute zu begreifen. Da ich mich abgewiesen fühlte, wurde ich schliesslich so mutlos, dass ich wieder zu schreiben beginnen musste, um psychisch zu überleben. Das ist der Grund, warum ich nun das Schreiben an die erste Stelle setzte.

CAOIMHÍN *Was hat zu diesem Zeitpunkt deine Bildgestaltung beeinflusst?*

SEAN Magrittes ‚période vache'. Für mich repräsentierte sie einen kurzen Augenblick vollkommener schöpferischer Freiheit und Kreativität als Maler in einem ansonsten eng umrissenen und wohlüberlegten Schaffen. Als ich zum ersten Mal die Bilder aus Magrittes ‚période vache' sah, fühlte ich mich ihnen so nah; mir war, als sähe ich meine eigene Kunst. Ich erhob fast einen Besitzanspruch auf diese Werke. Ich wollte nicht, dass jemand anders sie mochte, weil nur mir dieses Recht zustehen sollte. Ich hatte das Gefühl, dies sei eine Sprache, die ich sprechen konnte, ohne sie gelernt zu haben. Ich konnte mich sofort hineinfallen lassen. Und das tat ich, auf meine Weise. Ich malte Figuren, die sich manchmal direkt auf Magritte bezogen, wie in THREE NOSE GUY, der von seinem STROPIAT (1948) inspiriert ist, ‚Herrn Pantoffelnase', wie ich ihn nenne, obwohl meiner mit seinem überhaupt keine Ähnlichkeit hat. Aber am häufigsten waren sie vollständig meine eigenen Erfindungen. Alle meine ‚vache'-Figuren sind immer noch Teil oder eine Erweiterung meiner Clownsprache. Jede einzelne ist clownhaft, deprimiert und traurig. Aber sie so zu malen, in dieser neuen ‚vache'-Sprache, war für mich sehr viel angenehmer. Ich fand einen Malstil, der zu mir passte. Er entsprach meinem Können oder bot für meinen aktuellen Stand genau das richtige Gleichgewicht zwischen Cartoon und Illusion, etwas, was immer durch mein Interesse bestimmt wurde und immer bestimmt werden sollte. Ich kann sehr viel ‚realistischer' malen, wenn ich will, aber der springende Punkt bei der künstlerischen Freiheit ist, dass man das, wonach einem nicht zumute ist, eben nicht macht. Wichtig ist, dass man seinem Interesse folgt.

CAOIMHÍN *Einige dieser Malereien sind deutlicher sexuell als andere.*

SEAN Ja. Bei LE DOMAINE ENCHANTÉ AKA MONSIEUR SAUCISSON (1999) ist es einfach das, was es ist (lacht). Er freut sich eben, dort zu sein, wo er ist. Im Leben sind es die einfachen Dinge, die zählen.

CAOIMHÍN *Hattest du schon eine Vorstellung von den einzelnen Bildelementen, bevor du mit dem eigentlichen Malen begannst?*

SEAN Nein, überhaupt nicht. Ich fand die einzelnen Elemente, indem ich die ungrundierte Leinwand zunächst dünnflüssig einfärbte. Dann nahm ich meinen Pinsel und malte ein Cartoon in die Mitte der Leinwand, mochte es nicht, wischte es weg, malte ein neues, wischte es weg und wiederholte die Prozedur ungefähr zehn- bis zwanzigmal. Von jedem Cartoon blieb eine Spur sichtbar, so dass es einen Mischmasch oder ein Übereinanderlagern von Cartoon-Figuren gab. Oft taucht dann aus den vielen Spuren alter Zeichnungen allmählich eine neue Zeichnung auf. Viele, viele davon sind auf diese Weise zustande gekommen. Das geht zurück auf die Techniken des automatischen Zeichnens bei den Surrealisten. Ich habe einfach versucht, ein gutes Cartoon zu erhalten, und die beste Möglichkeit, eines zu bekommen, war manchmal, dass ich es durch Zufall fand. Viele meiner Plastiken sind auf eine ähnliche Weise entstanden. Ich begann eine Plastik, indem ich den Ton in eine Schädelform arbeitete. Sogar Schädel sehen Menschen ähnlich. Zwangsläufig erinnert er mich an etwas oder an jemanden, und dann arbeite ich in dieser Richtung weiter.

CAOIMHÍN *Surrealismus ist die Bewegung in der Kunst, die vorwiegend mit den faszinierenden Wirkungen des Unbewussten assoziiert wird, mit dem automatischen Schreiben, dem Versuch, eine vorherige Planung irgendwie zu umgehen, soweit das möglich ist. In deiner letzten Ausstellung 2003 bei greengrassi, wo du ein Pantheon von Künstlern des 20. Jahrhunderts gezeigt hast, alle männlich, waren die Surrealisten in der Überzahl.*

SEAN Es war eher allgemein europäische Malerei aus der Zeit vor dem Zweiten Weltkrieg. So ähnlich, wie ich vorhin schon gesagt habe, dass nämlich diese Leute für mich den letzten Atemzug in der langen Tradition europäischer Malerei repräsentieren, als die Kunst recht geradlinig verlief. So wie sich jemand vor eine leere Leinwand setzt, und ein Bild taucht auf, nicht unbedingt aus dem Leben, aber aus der Phantasie. Bevor in der Nachkriegszeit die amerikanische Kunst zu dominieren begann und sich die ganze Landschaft von Grund auf derart änderte. Wenn du dir alle neun Künstler ansiehst, die in dieser Ausstellung dargestellt sind, so gilt das, mit Ausnahme von Duchamp, für alle von ihnen in gewisser Weise: Picasso, Picabia, Magritte, Dalí, De Chirico, Braque, Ernst und Beckmann. Wenn ich vor einer leeren Leinwand sitze, dann fühle ich mich ihnen ausgesprochen verbunden. Ich spüre, dass ich zu ihrem Stammbaum gehöre. Wenn es einen Strom an Kreativität gibt, in den sie ihre Schöpfkelle getaucht haben, dann will ich meine Schöpfkelle in denselben Strom tauchen. Aber natürlich stamme ich auch ein bisschen aus den siebziger Jahren, mit den Textkünstlern, auf die ich meine frühere Werkgruppe aufgebaut habe. Aber das alles stammt letzten Endes von Duchamp, und das ist der Grund, warum er mit dabei war.

Meine Picasso-Ausstellung gehört auch dazu. Ich sah die Kunst des 20. Jahrhunderts aufgeteilt zwischen der Kunst von Picasso und Duchamp. Picasso ist ein typisches Beispiel für das, was ich eben beschrieben habe, wie ein Künstler vor einer leeren Leinwand sitzt und das Bild auftaucht. Und Duchamp ist natürlich der Grossvater der konzeptuellen Kunst. Als Vertreter meiner Zeit, einer Zeit, in der die Künstler das Blut dieser beiden Ursprünge durch ihre Adern fliessen fühlen, war es mir darum zu tun, eine Werkgruppe zu schaffen, die beides symbolisiert. Beide Männer benutzten entlehnte Bildelemente. Picasso schlachtete Velázquez wohl deshalb aus, um zu verkünden, dass er sich Velázquez' Kreisen historisch zugehörig fühle. Duchamp führte den Begriff ‚Readymade' ein. Daher kann man die Entlehnung aus dem Bildvorrat anderer Künstler als ‚Readymade' auffassen. Wenn ich Picassos Inventar auf diese Weise benutzte, dazu meinen Namen buchstabierte und das Bild SEAN/7099 nannte, wenn ich ‚genius' hinschrieb bei einem Möbelstück, das von einem seiner Gemälde, FEMME AU BUFFET (1936), abgekupfert ist, wenn ich eine Auswahl seiner Exfrauen und Freundinnen vorführte, die er gemalt und mit seiner Schreierei zugrunde gerichtet hatte, oder bei dem Bild GENIUS (2001) eine von ihnen auf die einzelnen Buchstaben setzte, dann benutzte ich Duchamp, um Picasso auszuschlachten, verschmolz sie miteinander, um damit mich und meine Situation als Künstler zu beschreiben.

CAOIMHÍN *Sprechen wir über deine Gründe, warum du deine Arbeiten manchmal in verschiedenen Medien gleichzeitig zeigst: Video oder Audio und ebenso Skulptur und Gemälde oder Zeichnung.*

SEAN Ich glaube, das ist offen gesagt ein übermächtiges Verlangen, den Leuten zu gefallen. Ich will auf diese Weise ihre Erwartungen erfüllen, sie sollen mich mögen. Darüber hinaus ist es wohl auch eine Möglichkeit, mein Talent vorzuführen, indem ich die gleiche Sache in vielen verschiedenen Medien mache. Mir ist das einerlei. Alles, was ich mache, ist zu einer Art Performance verbunden. Ich bin eine Persönlichkeit geworden, die in meinen Arbeiten auftritt. Wenn ich male, dann wird das Bild von diesem Künstlertyp gemalt, den ich geschaffen habe; das Gleiche gilt für Skulptur, Video und Schreiben. Wenn ich einen Stift in die Hand nehme, um zu schreiben, dann klinke ich mich einfach irgendwie in diese Rolle ein. Oder zum Beispiel die Audioarbeit, die ich bei greengrassi (2000) abgespielt habe, die den Titel THE MAN WITHIN (2000) trägt und meine ‚Grösse' beschreibt, ich habe einfach das Mikrofon genommen, bin in die Rolle geschlüpft und habe losgelegt. Verwirrend ist für die Leute vielleicht, dass diese Rolle zum Teil mein wirkliches Ich ist und zum Teil nicht. In gewisser Weise bin ich immer noch Chris Hamson.

CAOIMHÍN *Hattest du für das, was du mit der Skulptur als Form und mit dem Video machen könntest, bestimmte Vorbilder, als du anfingst, mit diesen Medien zu arbeiten?*

SEAN Was das Video betrifft, so war das zum Teil AN AMERICAN FAMILY, wie ich vorhin schon gesagt habe. Daneben waren es vielleicht die frühen Videoarbeiten von Wegman und bis zu einem gewissen Grad Spalding Gray. Ich sah bei Wegman, wann sich einfacher Humor verwenden lässt, und bei Gray war es die Persönlichkeit des Künstlers und das Geschichtenerzählen. Ich begann 1990 mit einer Art Talkshow, ich sass an einem Tisch, machte mich über das Radio lustig und erzählte Geschichten. Sie sollten – auf dem Stand, auf dem sich die Videokunst damals befand – grotesk wirken, aber letzten Endes sehr viel unterhaltsamer und einnehmender sein, als es die Videokunst tatsächlich jemals war. Ich wollte praktisch gewinnen, indem ich verliere. Sie sollten sehr viel Persönliches enthalten, die Leute durch Voyeurismus ködern und vor allem ‚nicht langweilig' sein. Aus diesen frühen Videos entwickelte sich irgendwie die Idee der lebenden Skulptur à la Gilbert & George. Keins war jemals für ein eingesperrtes Publikum gedacht, es sollte etwas sein, woran man vorbeigeht, und wenn ich euch damit packe, na dann schön für mich. Sie hatten sehr viel mit meinen geschriebenen Arbeiten zu tun, waren nur ausagiert.

Was die Skulptur betrifft, so war das damals wieder das ‚Unpassendste', was man machen konnte, und das interessierte mich. Ob es mit Müllsäcken zugehängte Tonköpfe waren oder der herkömmliche Ton, es erschien irgendwie verrückt zu einer Zeit, als die ‚Skulptur aus neuen Materialien' von Matthew Barney und Michael Joaquin Grey modern war, deren Arbeiten ausgesprochen raffiniert, elegant und neu wirkten. Da ich von Natur aus gern Kontra gebe, reizte es mich, die Skulptur wieder zu dem ‚alten' und ‚dummen' Ding zu machen, das sie erfreulicherweise über Jahrtausende gewesen war, bevor diese Leute damit anfingen. Lange nachdem die aus Vaseline geformte Trainingsbank in den Boden zerflossen oder ein Richard Serra ins Meer gerostet ist, werden meine dummen Bronzeköpfchen das Lied meiner Unsterblichkeit singen. Das ist wie die Geschichte vom Hasen und vom Igel.

CAOIMHÍN *Sprechen wir noch ein bisschen über Perfektion in einer künstlerischen Technik und wie du dazu stehst. Interessiert es dich nicht, dass in einer Zeit, in der sehr häufig auf Fertigkeiten in den einzelnen Bereichen absichtlich verzichtet wird, manche Leute für ihre Virtuosität in einem bestimmten Medium – zu Recht oder zu Unrecht – gelobt werden?*

SEAN Ich versuche nicht, ‚schlechte Kunst' zu machen. Das war das Thema unseres allerersten Gesprächs…

CAOIMHÍN *Richtig.*

SEAN …und zur Antwort gab ich, dass ich mich dieser Kategorie nicht zugehörig fühlte. Ich habe einfach das gemacht, was ich gemacht habe, ich habe Naivität nie vorgetäuscht. Die Skulptur ICH MACHE MICH habe ich damals so gut gemacht, wie ich konnte. Jetzt kann ich eine viel bessere Skulptur von einem Schimpansen machen. Ich habe damals immer mein Niveau gehalten. Wenn es wirklich naiv aussah oder technisches Können vermissen liess, dann deshalb, weil das damals meine wirkliche Situation war. Die Idee dahinter war, dass jede Kunst, wenn sie ernsthaft gemacht wird, im Grunde ein Selbstportrait ist. Darum habe ich mich in dieser Ausstellung 1997 in der Andrea Rosen Gallery direkt mit Malern wie Manet, Matisse und Poussin verglichen, weil ich wusste, dass ich nicht mit ihnen auf eine Stufe gehörte. Ich dachte, meine Aufgabe sei es, in ihrer Mitte eine Ebene zu finden, auf der ich mich wohl fühle, denn das ist die Situation eines Malers oder Künstlers. Wir werden immer im Kontext der Kunstgeschichte beurteilt, der Geschichte der zeitgenössischen Kunst und der alten Kunst.

CAOIMHÍN *Aber einige der unmittelbaren Vorgänger, die du gleich zu Anfang inspirativ fandest, zum Beispiel Jeff Koons, hatten nie das geringste Bedürfnis, sich auch nur die elementarsten Fertigkeiten anzueignen, da man für die verschiedenen Techniken immer ausgezeichnete Fachleute anheuern kann, von venezianischen Glasbläsern bis hin zu amerikanischen Schildermalern, die einem die Arbeit abnehmen.*

SEAN Ja, während ich das selber mache, und das ist der Unterschied.

CAOIMHÍN *Und warum? Die Entscheidung, es so zu machen, ist dir offensichtlich wichtig.*

SEAN Weil ich dorthin fahre, wohin ich will. Ich bin der Herr meines Bildes. Ich bin verantwortlich für das, was da ist. Ich bin Rechenschaft schuldig. Jeff Koons hat seine Bildgestaltung nicht voll unter Kontrolle. Er ist der Regisseur.

CAOIMHÍN *Wirklich?*

SEAN Er hat die Skulptur von Michael Jackson oder diesen Schimpansen nicht selbst gemacht. Jemand anders hat das gemacht. Nur so nah ist er diesem Bild. Mein Schimpanse trägt meine Fingerabdrücke. Für Jeff ist das ein Akt der Ironie, und für mich ist es der Punkt, wo sich der Kreis schliesst und die Ironie wieder ernsthaft zu werden beginnt.

CAOIMHÍN *Da sind wir wieder bei der alten Masche, der expressionistischen Konvention, für die es eine brauchbare Kritik gibt. Wie Francis Bacon gesagt hat, willst du Bilder direkt dem Nervensystem entnehmen. Aber gibt es so etwas wie einen unvermittelten Zugang zum Ausdruck spontaner Gesten?*

SEAN Ja, daran glaube ich.

CAOIMHÍN *Wirklich?*

SEAN Ja, wirklich. Ich glaube, dass die Hand eines grossen Künstlers direkt aus seiner Seele herausreicht. Ich meine, das hat eine ungeheuer grosse Bedeutung. Ich sage damit nicht, dass es das ausschliesst, was Jeff macht, weil ich eigentlich wirklich mag, was er macht, und nicht oft genug wiederholen kann, wie sehr ich ihn bewundere. Ich sage damit nur, dass ich sehe, was ich sehen will, wenn ich es angesichts der Besonderheiten meiner eigenen Hand und Phantasie sehen will, was naturgemäss aufrichtiger ist. Seine Verfahrensweise ist eher die eines Sachverständigen, der Einkäufe tätigt oder Aufträge vergibt, was ihm seine ironische Distanz erhält.

CAOIMHÍN *Aber ein wichtiger Teil deiner Vorhaben ist, dass du dir deine Fertigkeiten sozusagen bei der Arbeit erworben hast. Wäre es nicht schön gewesen, wenn du gleich am Anfang die Dinge so gut hättest machen können, wie du sie jetzt machen kannst?*

SEAN Das wäre schön gewesen, ja, aber wir werden alle besser, egal, was wir machen. Sieh dir die frühen Magrittes an. Mein Gott, sie sehen aus, als hätte sie jemand aus dem Malkurs meiner Mutter auf der Wiese hinterm Haus gemalt.

Ich persönlich bin zufrieden mit dem Niveau meines Könnens bei Bildern wie zum Beispiel PLANK BOY (2000), MS. KITTY (1999) oder BUFFALO (2003). Ich kann weiter in Richtung Realismus gehen, wenn ich das wollte. Aber ich hatte das Gefühl, diese Bilder würden mich dann nicht mehr zufrieden stellen, wenn ich es getan hätte. Bei anderen wie HAPPY AND SAD (2002) bin ich ein Stück weiter gegangen. Ich habe das Outfit der Figuren sehr viel weiter ausgeführt als, sagen wir, bei MARINER (2003), wo es genau seine Art trifft. Ich wollte bei HAPPY AND SAD einfach mehr sehen. Bei unterschiedlichen Bildern muss man auf verschiedene Weise verfahren.

CAOIMHÍN *Diese Wacker-voran-Mentalität, es jetzt so gut zu machen, wie du kannst, und dich nicht darum zu kümmern, ob das bei weitem nicht an die Fertigkeit heranreicht, die du vielleicht später entwickeln wirst, spielt offensichtlich immer noch eine wichtige Rolle. Es hat dich nicht beirrt. Du warst relativ furchtlos.*

SEAN Ja. Ich meine, was sollte ich sonst machen? Ich kann doch nur bis zu der Höhe des Könnens arbeiten, die mein Interesse mir abnötigt.

CAOIMHÍN *Was ändert sich, wenn man über vierzig ist und das macht, was du machst?*

SEAN Na ja, ich denke, ich muss mir ehrlich eingestehen, was ich jetzt bin.

CAOIMHÍN *Aber wie deutlich ist diese Veränderung in den vergangenen Jahren wahrgenommen worden?*

SEAN Na, die gerade vergangene Ausstellung in der Andrea Rosen Gallery (2004) ist dafür ein wunderbares Beispiel. Sie war ein Rückblick auf meine alten Textbilder, deren graphischen Charakter ich in raumgreifende abstrakte Gemälde explodieren liess. Gedanken tauchen im Kopf auf, sie werden klar und verschwimmen dann wieder in der Ferne. Es sind immer noch Bilder, die zeigen, wie Gedanken zum Vorschein kommen, wie das meine alten Bilder getan haben, aber die Art des Schreibens ist eine andere, es ist Selbstparodie. Das bedeutet nicht, dass ich die Dinge, die ich bei den früheren Arbeiten geschrieben habe, nicht mehr so empfinde, aber wenn ich sie jetzt schreibe, merke ich, wie abgewetzt sie sind. Es ist wie ein Schrank voll alter Schuhe. Ich bin in ihnen gelaufen, sie sind so verschlissen, dass sie die Form meiner Füsse angenommen haben. Ich könnte sie wieder anziehen, und sie würden bequem passen, aber ich würde mich einfach nicht flott in ihnen fühlen.

Die jüngsten Gemälde wirken deshalb so ‚echohaft', weil ich, wenn ich nachts malte, die Reflexion der Bilder auf den Fenstern meines Ateliers betrachtet habe, die doppelt verglast sind …

CAOIMHÍN *Und sie sahen doppelt aus – wie die Satzfetzen auf diesen neuen Bildern?*

SEAN Ja, sie sahen so viel besser aus, und es schien irgendwie, als sei diese Art des Doppeltsehens/des Wiederholungseffekts eine übersteigerte Form der Selbstparodie. Es erinnerte mich an eine Aufnahme von John Giorno, wo er alles wiederholte, was er in seinem Monolog sagte, und das rief ein deutliches Gefühl geistiger Verwirrung hervor. Mir wurde einfach klar, dass diese Bilder

Spiegelbilder jener früheren ‚abgetragenen Schuhe' sind.

CAOIMHÍN *Es sieht tatsächlich aus wie eine graphische, cartoonartige Wiedergabe eines Echos.*

SEAN Ja.

CAOIMHÍN *Du hast gesagt, diese Texte seien abstrakt begründet. Aber einige sind gar nicht so abstrakt, sie sind die Darstellung weit geöffneter Räume, von Himmelslandschaften.*

SEAN Ja. Die Himmelslandschaften sind anders. Ich bin in einer religiösen Familie aufgewachsen und habe wirklich beten gelernt. Das ist noch in mir drin. Mein Gehirn fällt immer noch in diesen Gebetston, und ich weiss nicht, wie ich damit umgehen soll, da ich vielleicht nicht ganz atheistisch bin, aber Gott anzweifle.

CAOIMHÍN *Wenn du sagst ‚Gebetston', dann meinst du doch nicht beten, was dir einfällt? Du meinst die Wiederholung vorhandener Worte.*

SEAN Ich meine die Gedanken im Kopf, von denen man glaubt, dass sie mitgehört werden…

CAOIMHÍN *Von einer Gottheit?*

SEAN Ja, von einer Gottheit oder einem verstorbenen Verwandten.

CAOIMHÍN *Verstehe.*

SEAN Mit diesen Himmelsbildern versuche ich also, diese Art des Gebets/des Denkens wiederzugeben. Ein Beispiel wäre „Mach mich bitte zu einem besseren Künstler" oder „Warum kann das nicht alles leichter sein?". Indem ich das schreibe, schicke ich es zum Himmel. „Ich will, dass meine Bilder ewig halten", „Bitte, lieber Gott, lass mich wichtig sein". Umgekehrt ging es bei dem Bild mit dem Mond, THE SLEEP OF REASON PRODUCES MONSTERS (2004), um Schlaflosigkeit, Paranoia und jene Art verzweifelten Betens, wenn die Teufel hervorkommen. Es ist direkt nach Goyas Radierung DER SCHLAF BRINGT UNGEHEUER HERVOR (1797/98) gemacht. Die Worte auf diesem Bild sind wie die Fledermäuse, die auf seiner Radierung aufsteigen. Ich habe nur versucht, dem Denken ein Bild zu geben. Ein Clown in der arktischen Landschaft gibt dem Denken auf andere Weise ein Bild, so wie meine Textbilder, Videos, Skulpturen und meine ‚période vache' das tun. Das ist der Grund, warum ich mich zu all diesen europäischen Malern aus der Zeit vor dem Zweiten Weltkrieg hingezogen fühle, denn auch sie haben vor einer Staffelei mit einer leeren Leinwand gesessen, und aus ihren Gedanken stieg ein Bild auf. Das ist es, was ich an der Kunst schätze. Das ist es, was ich als Künstler gern mache.

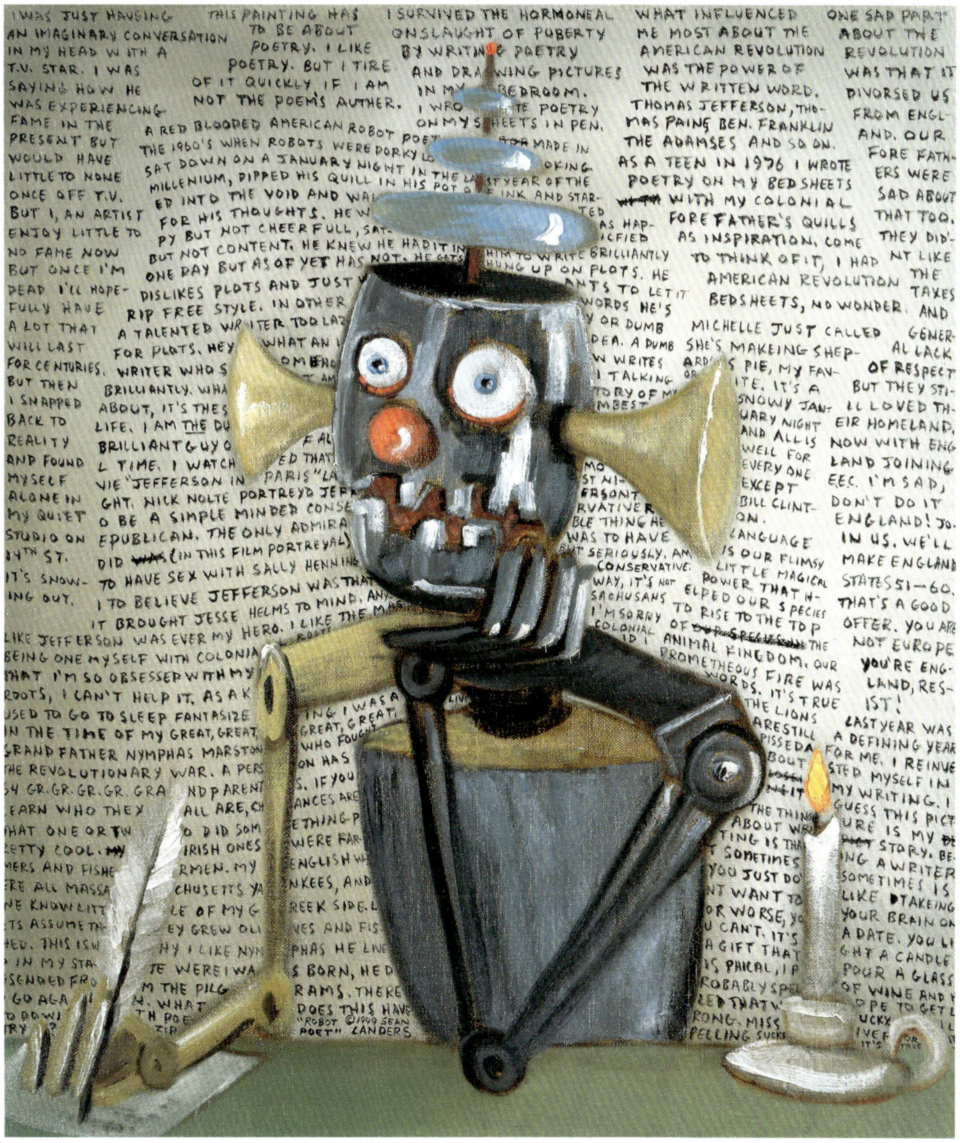

THE ROBOT POET, 1999
Oil on linen
76.2 × 66.04 cm

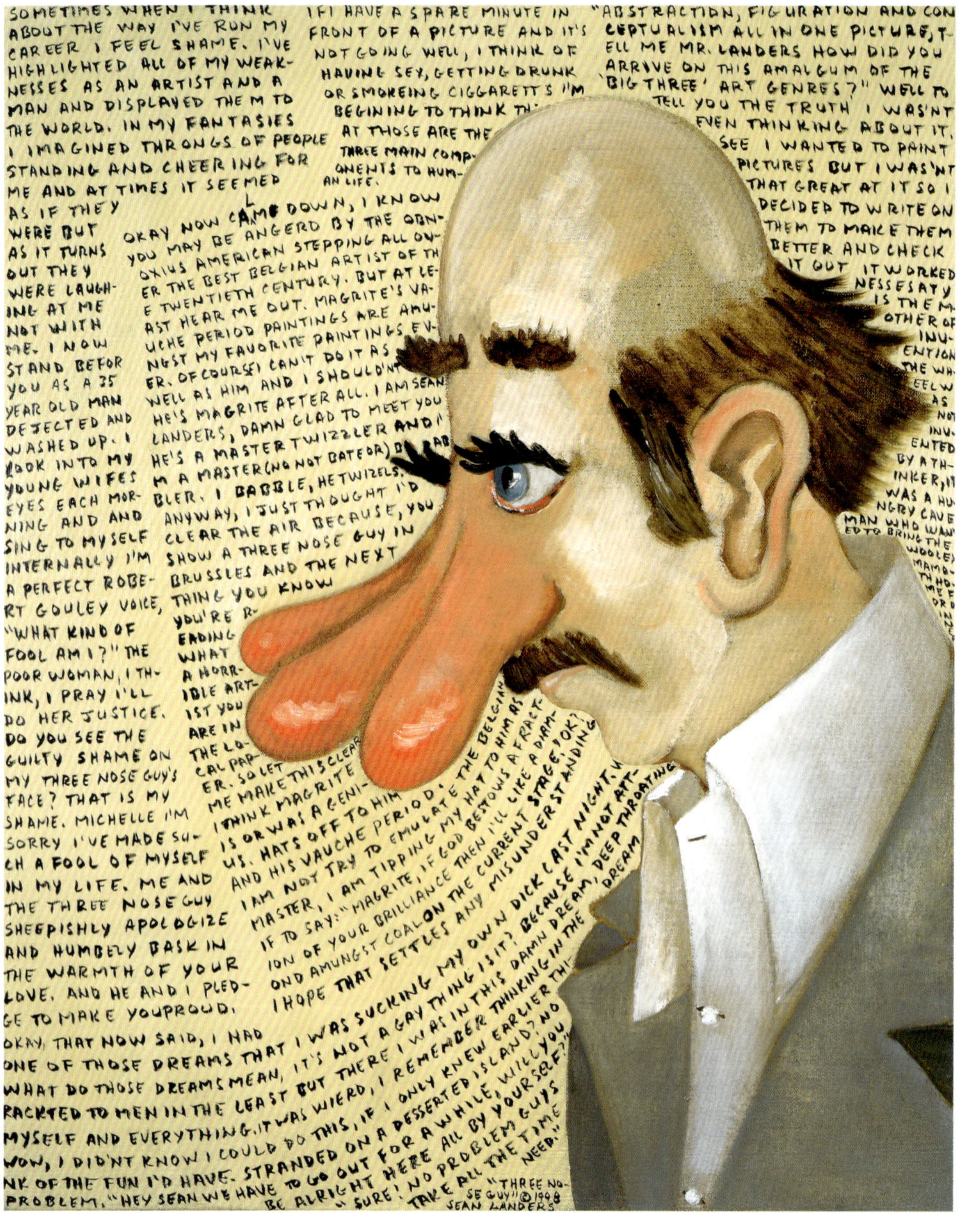

THREE NOSE GUY, 1998
Oil on linen
81.5 × 66 cm

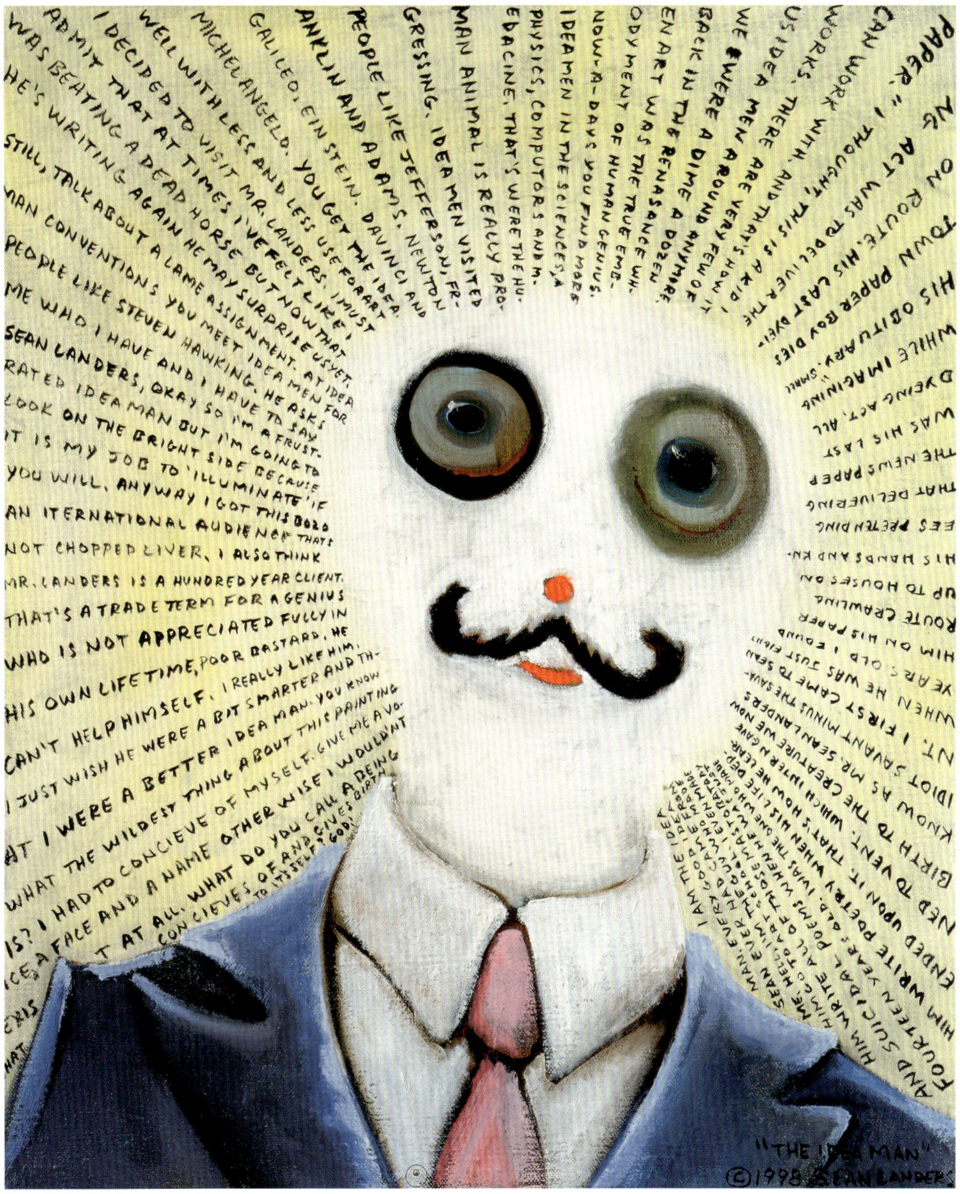

THE IDEA MAN, 1998
Oil on linen
61.96 × 50.8 cm

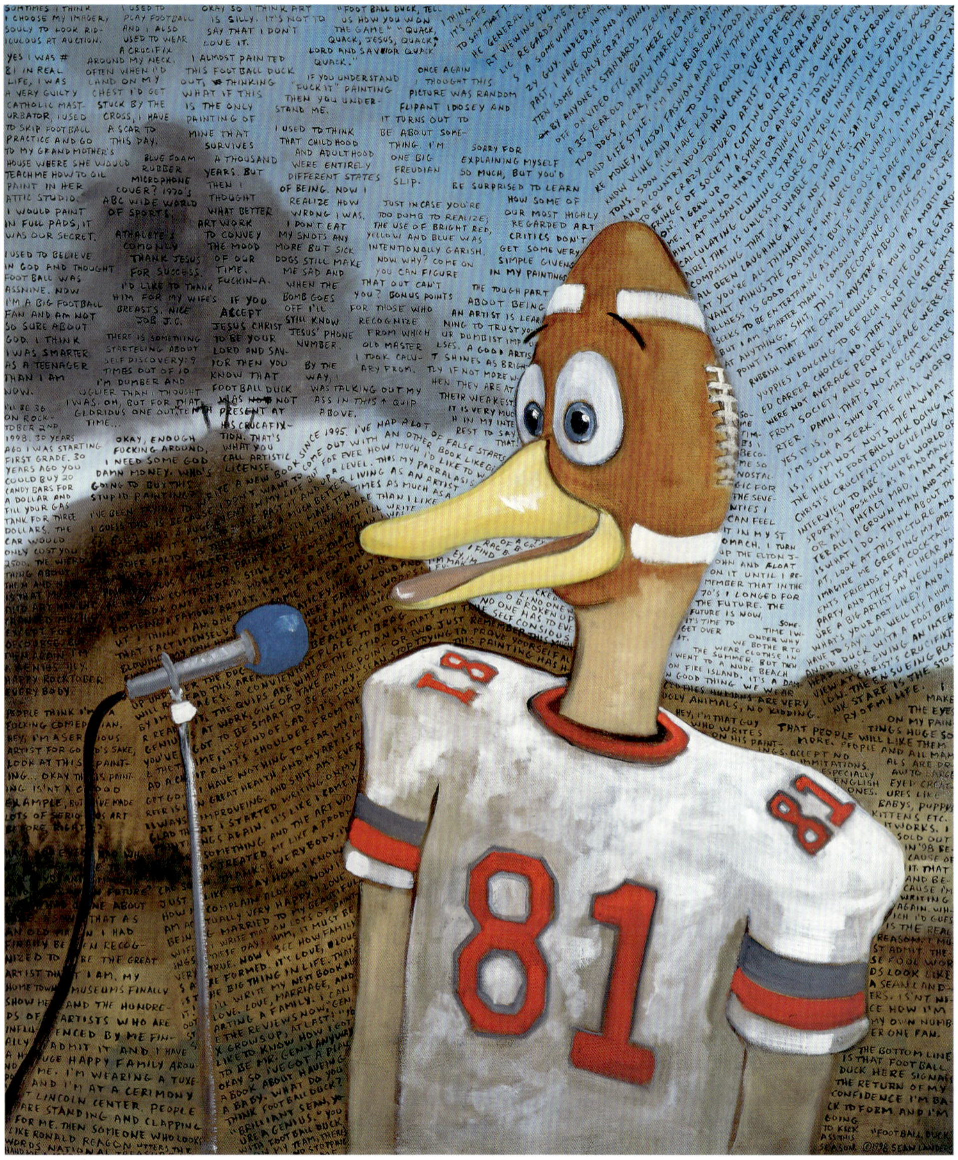

FOOTBALL DUCK, 1998
Oil on linen
137.16 × 116.84 cm

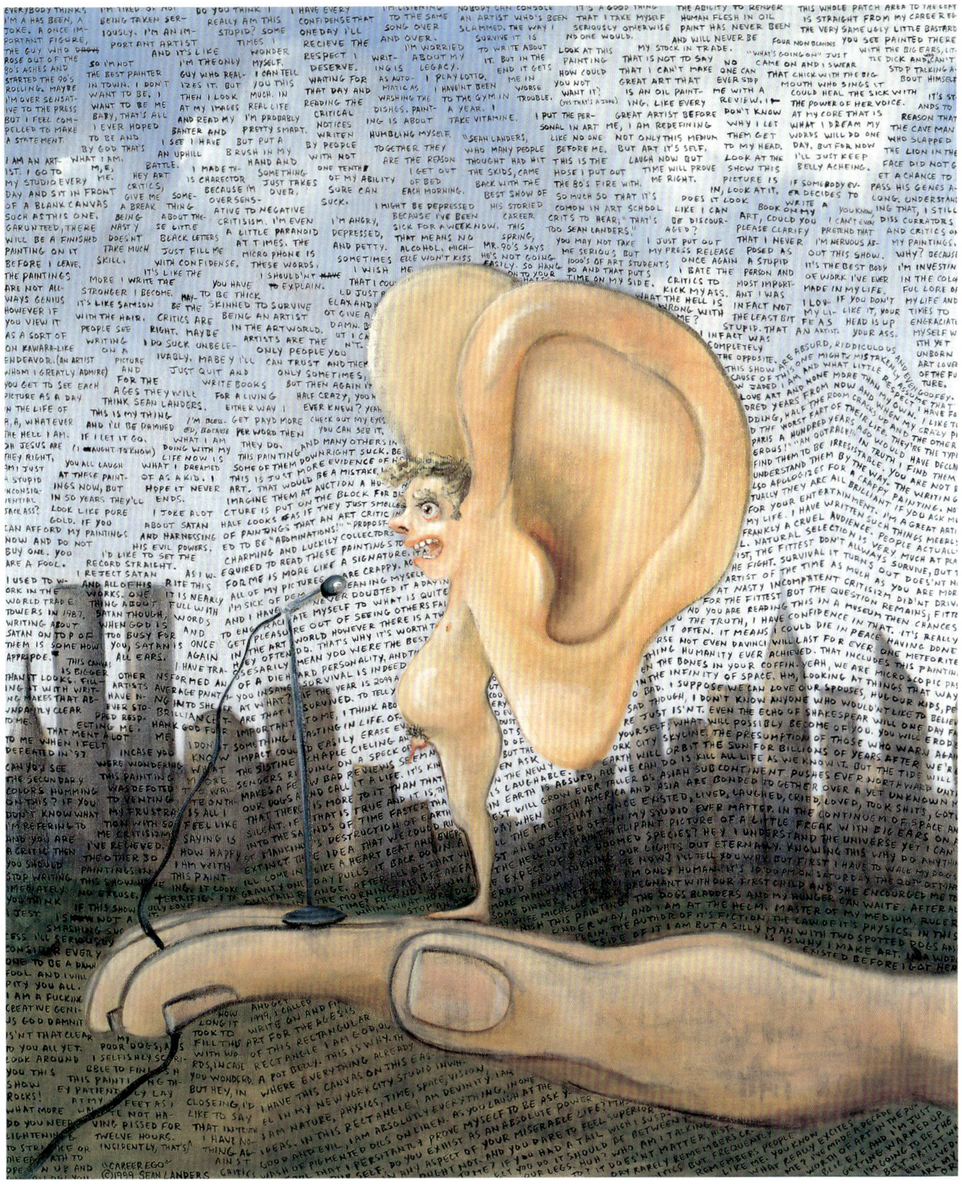

CAREER EGO, 1999
Oil on linen
142.24 × 119.38 cm

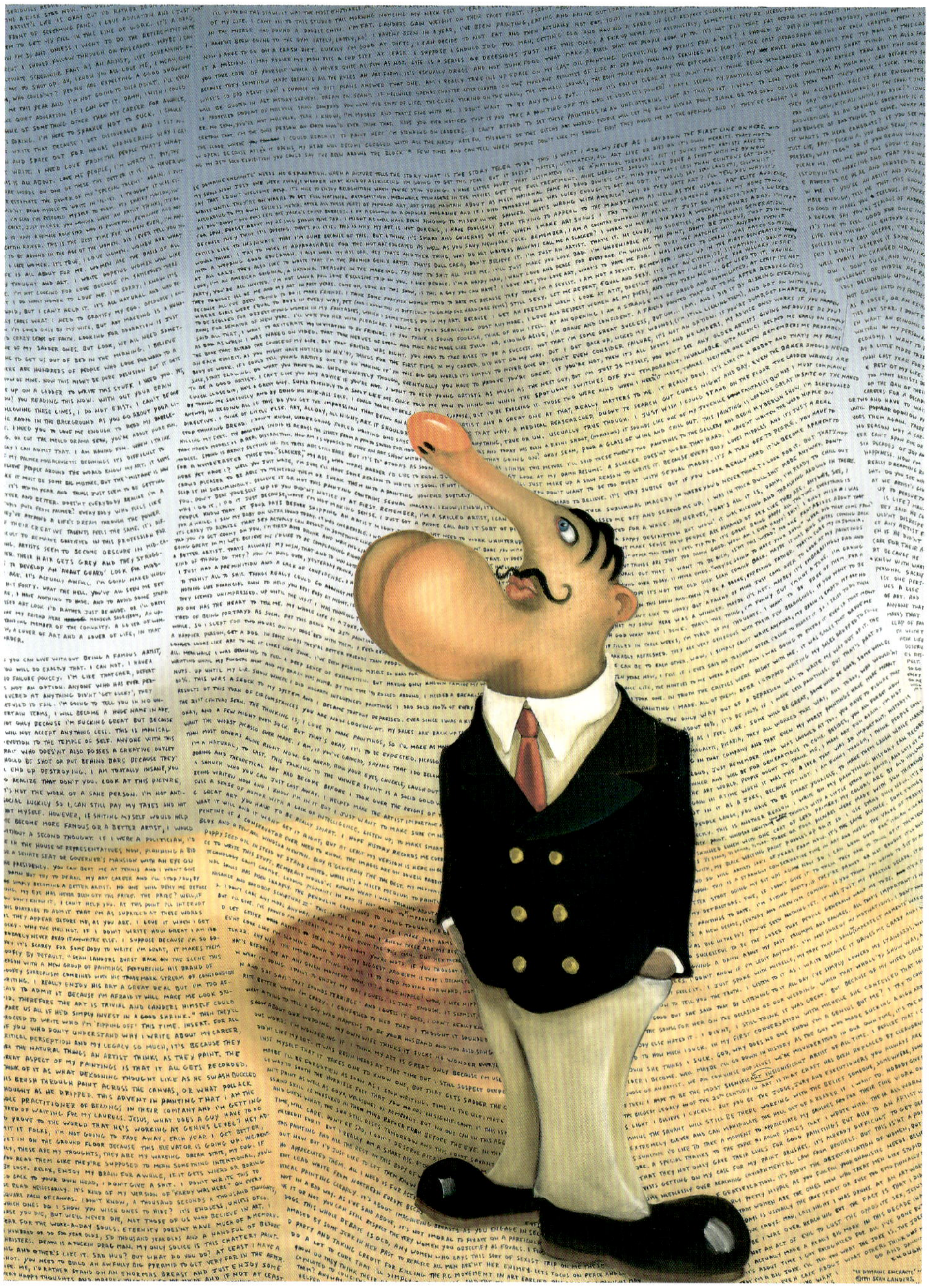

LE DOMAINE ENCHANTÉ AKA MONSIEUR SAUCISSON, 1999
Oil on linen
259 × 193 cm

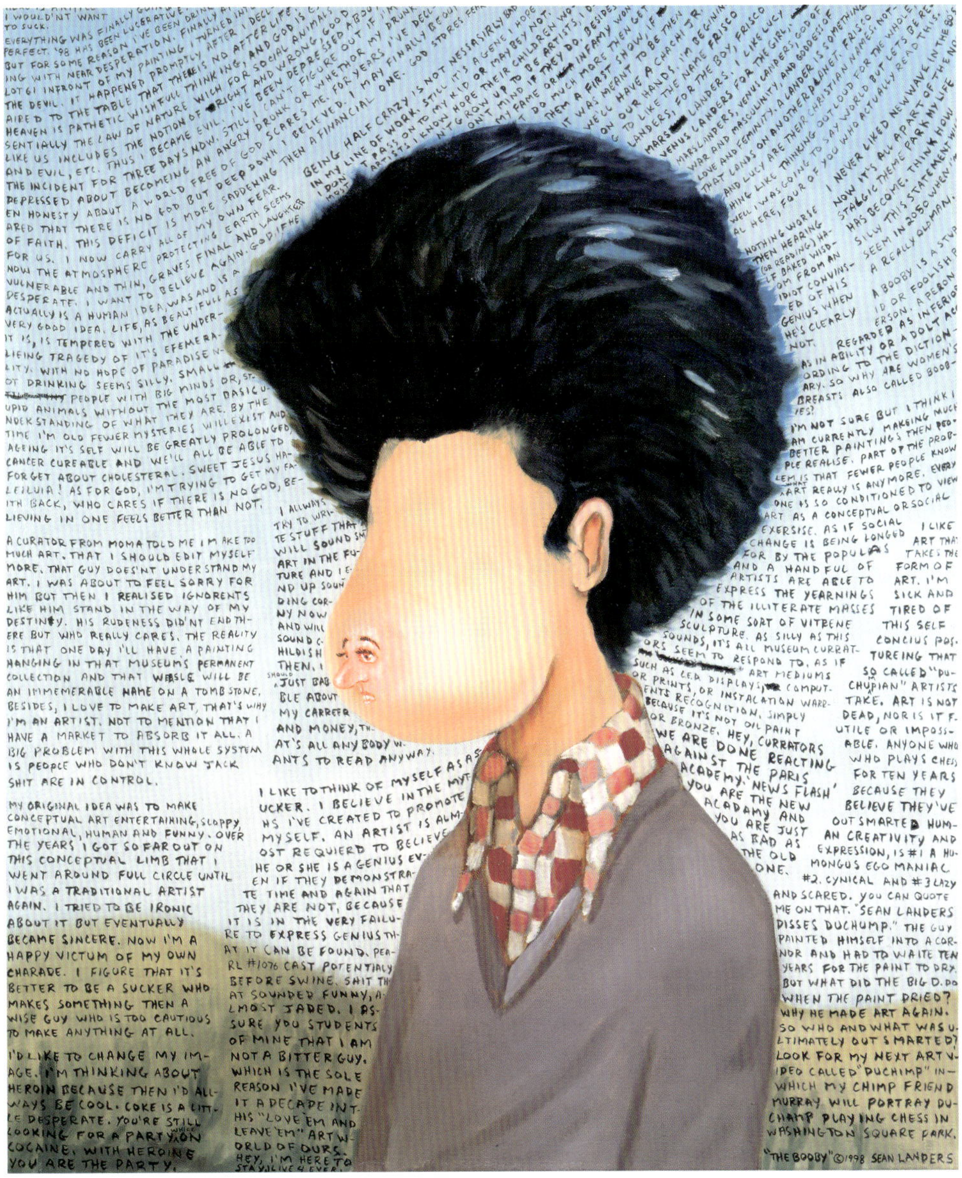

THE BOOBY, 1998
Oil on linen
96.52 × 81.28 cm

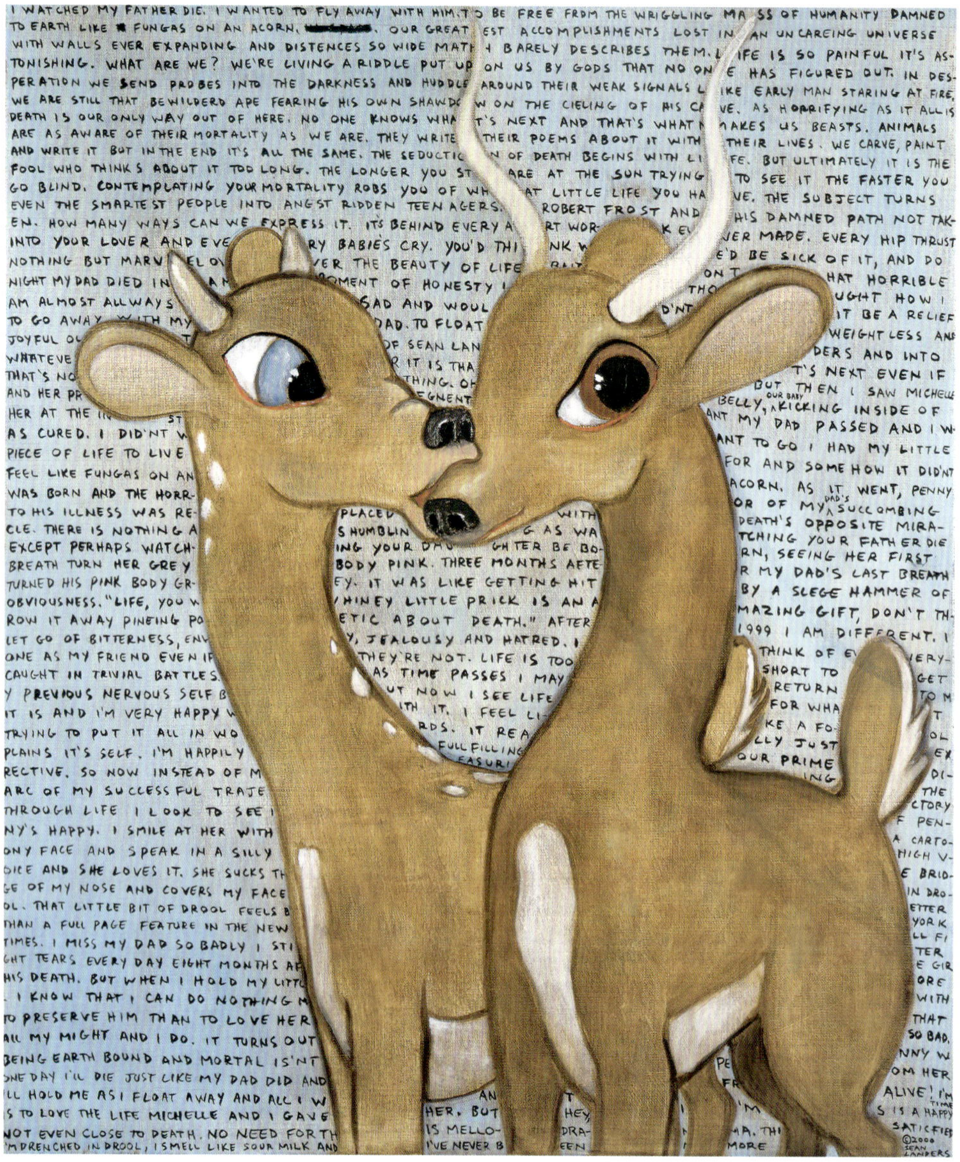

FAWN AND DEER, 2000
Oil on linen
86.36 × 73.66 cm

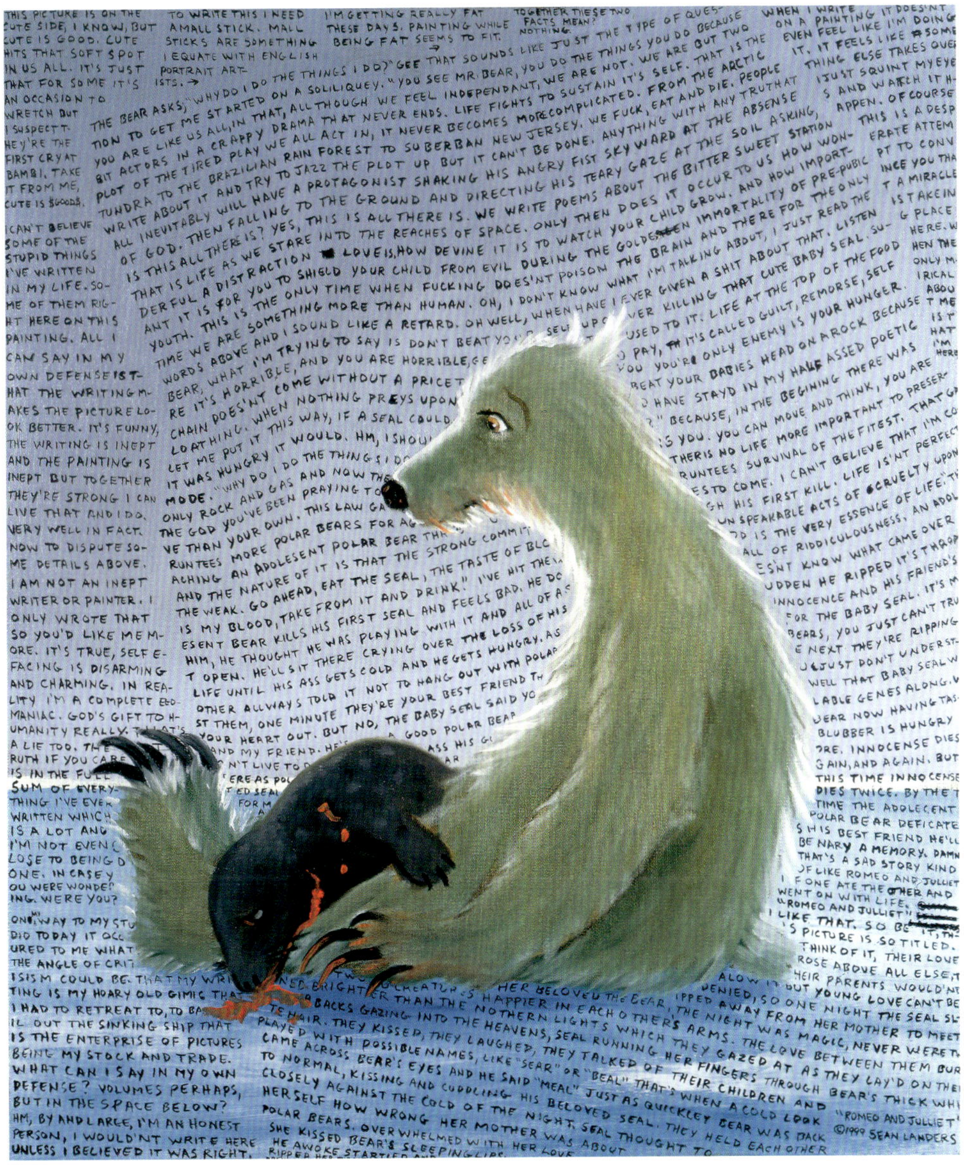

ROMEO AND JULIET, 1999
Oil on linen
101.6 × 86.36 cm

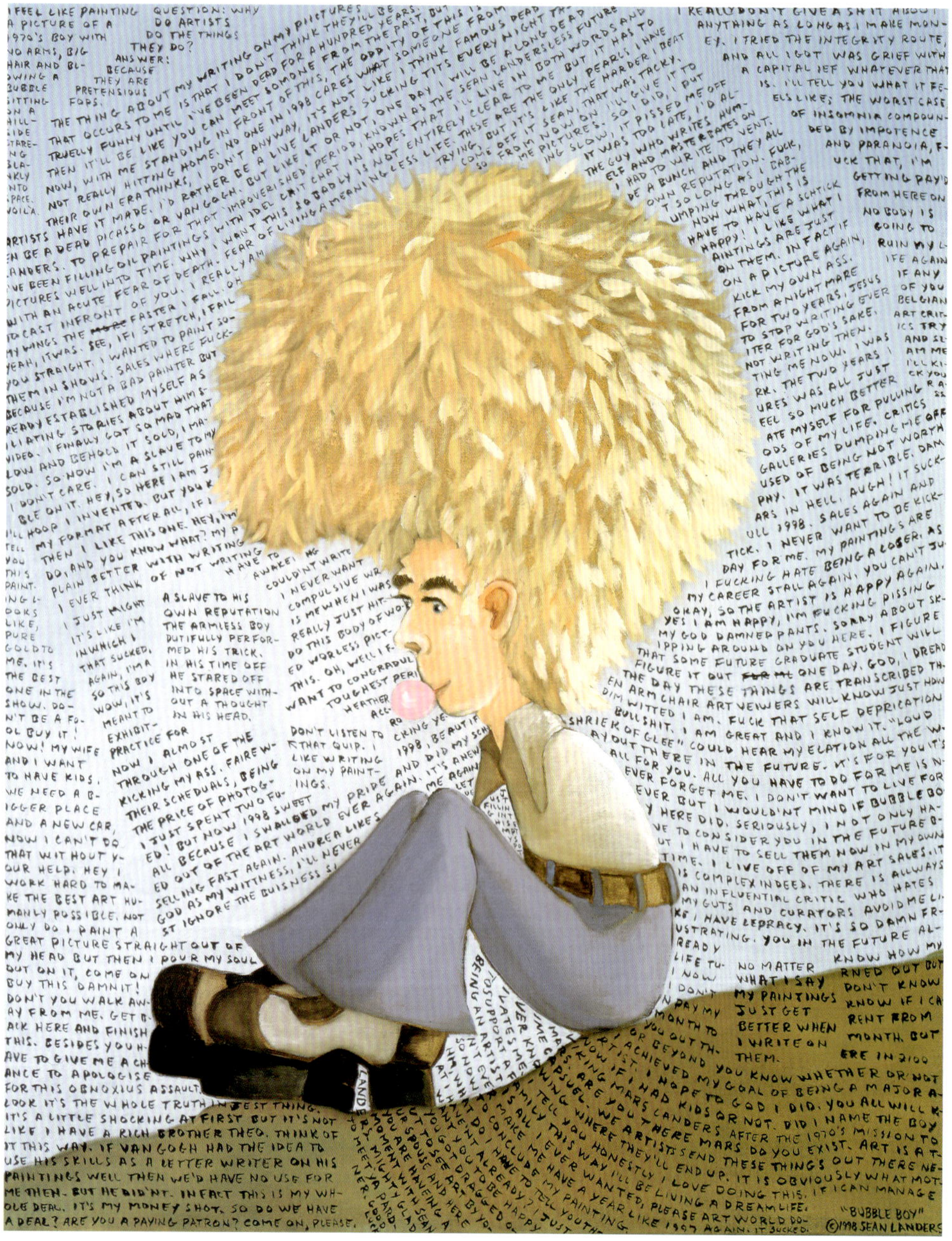

BUBBLE BOY, 1998
Oil on linen
121.92 × 96.52 cm

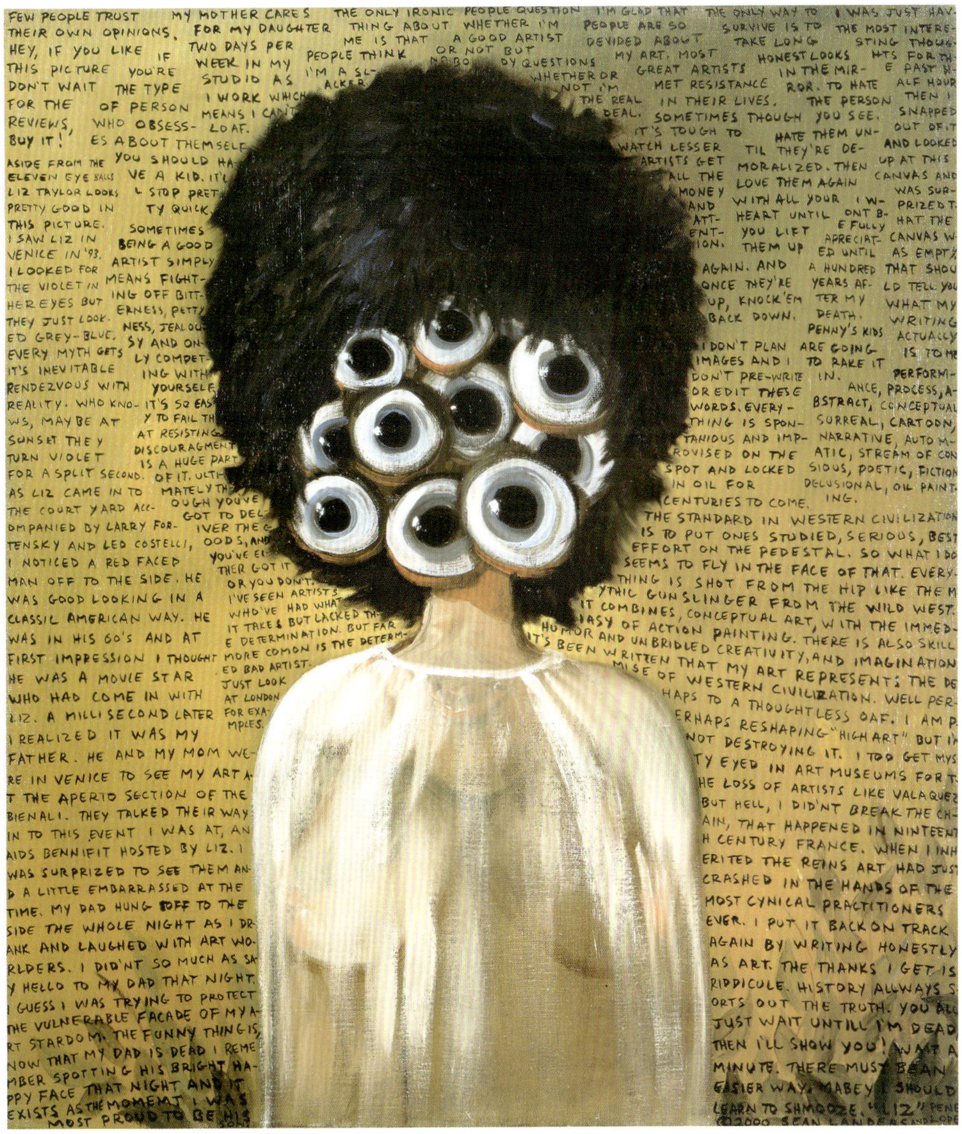

LIZ, 2000
Oil on linen
83.82 × 73.66 cm

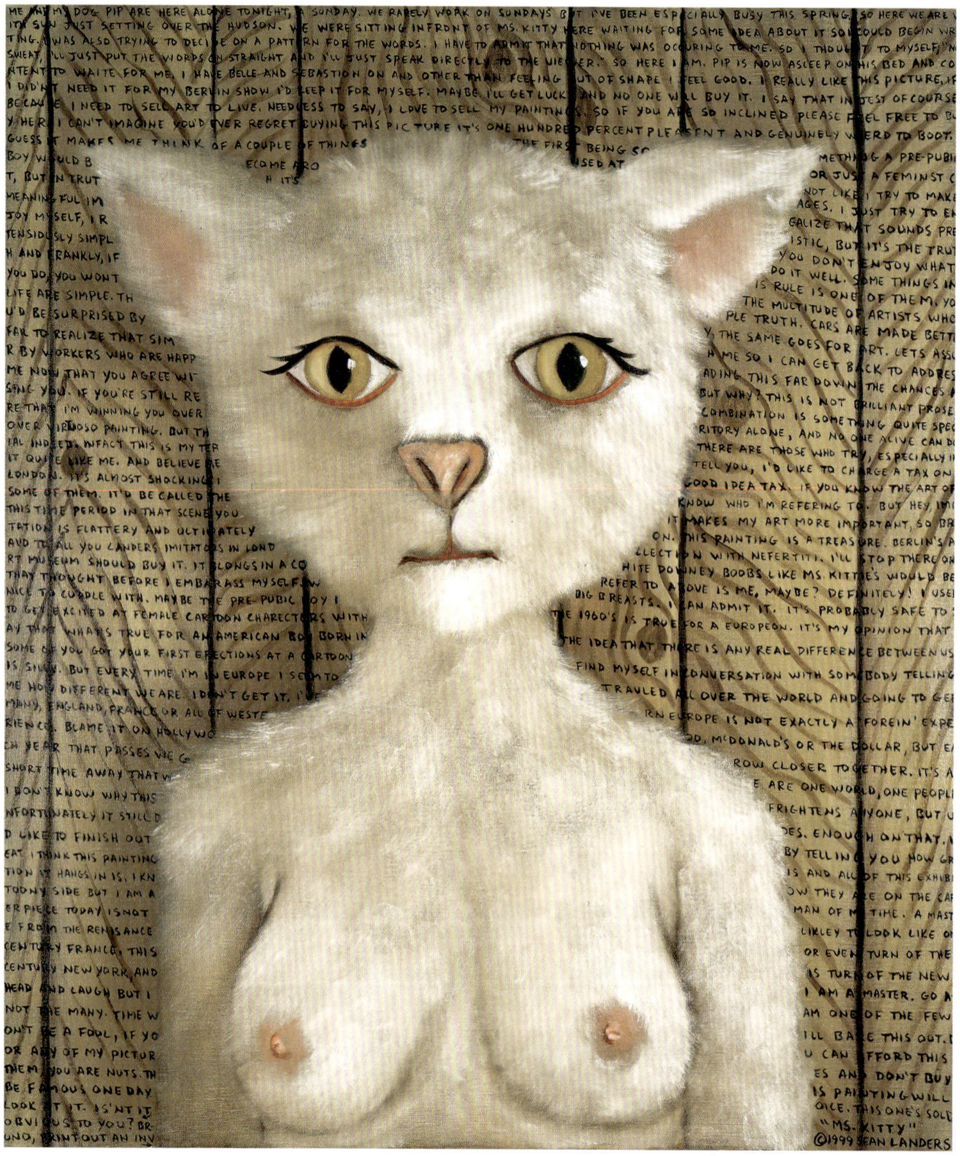

MS. KITTY, 1999
Oil on linen
109.22 × 93.98 cm

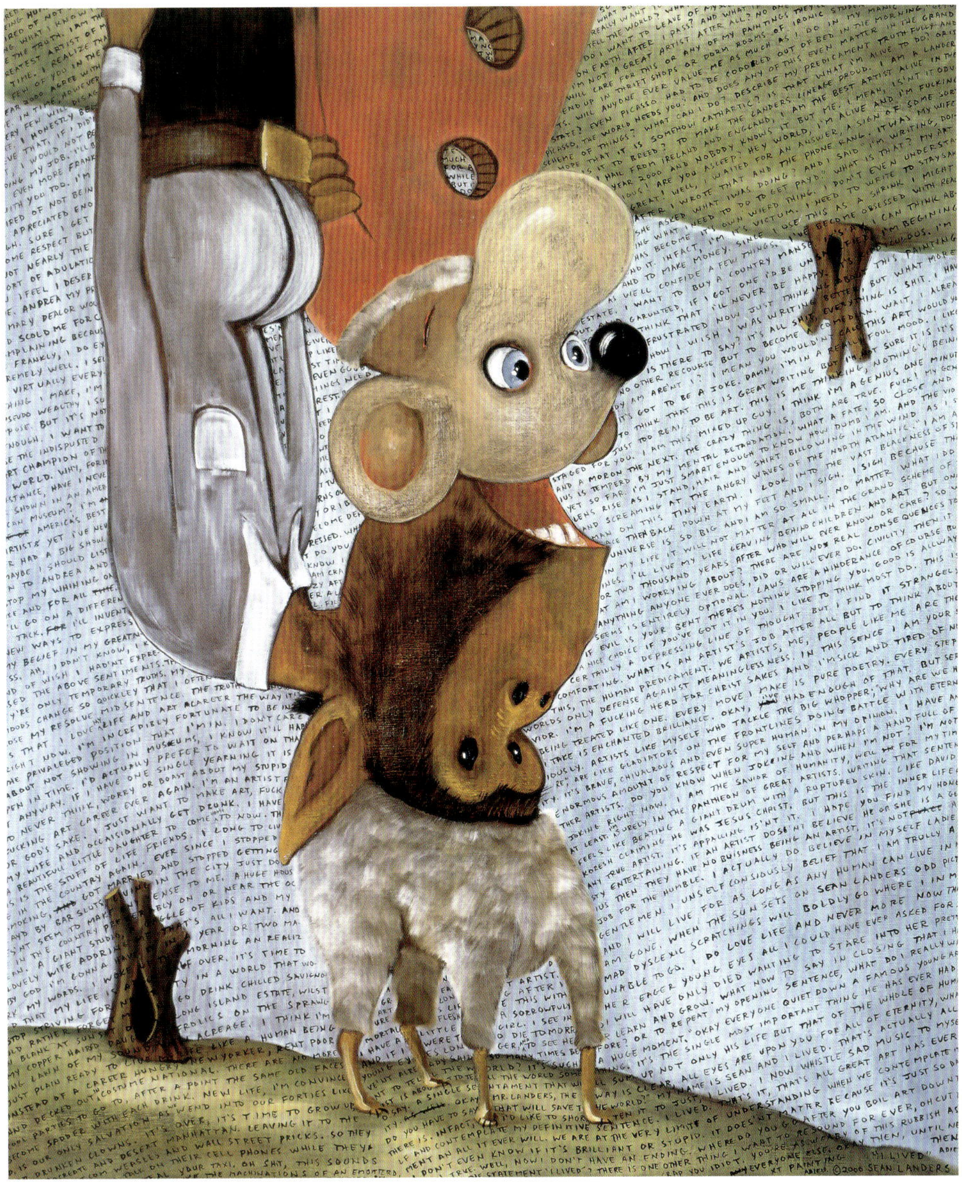

I LIVED/MONKEY AND GNOME, 2000
Oil on linen
144.78 × 121.92 cm

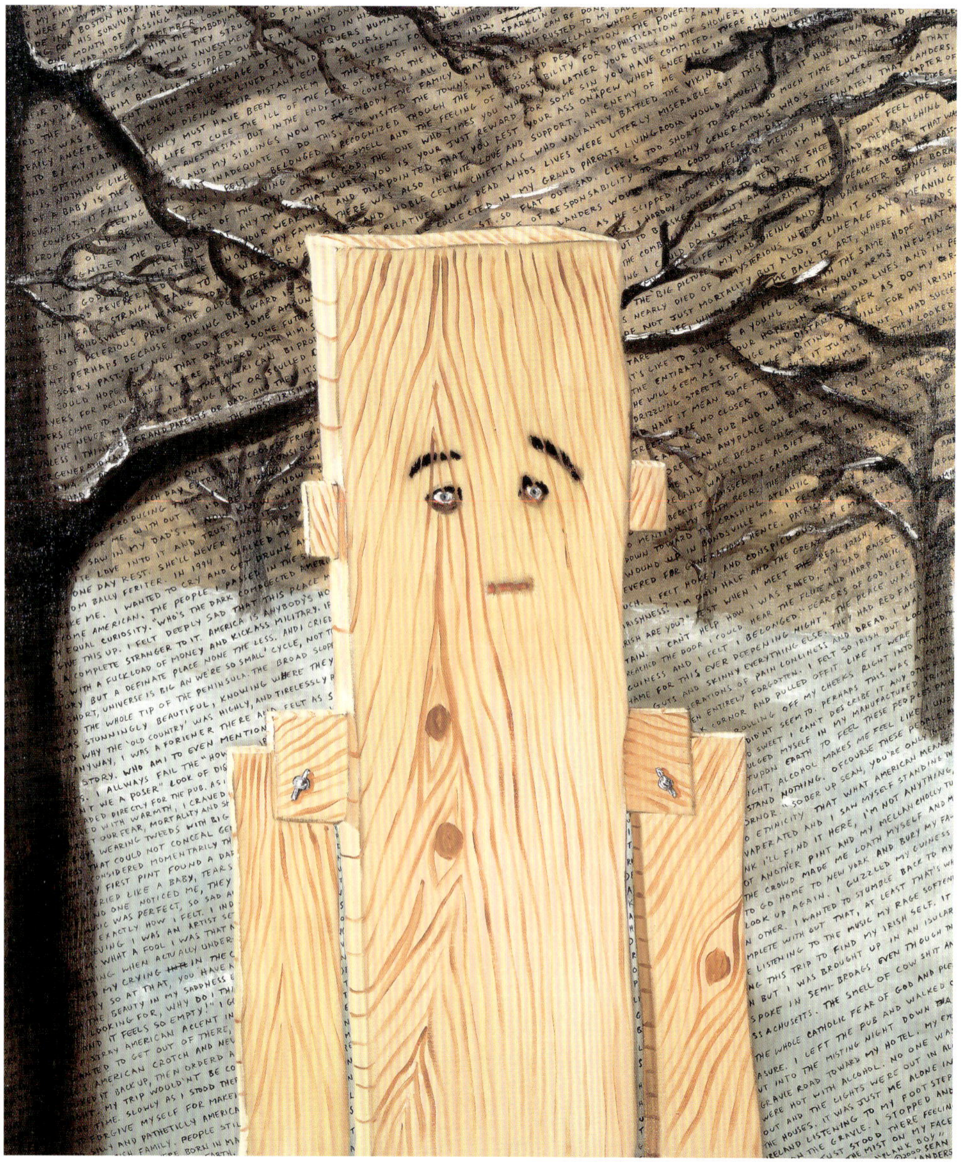

PLANK BOY, 2000
Oil on linen
139.7 × 119.38 cm

Sean Landers: Art and Language

ALEX FARQUHARSON

"My original idea was to make conceptual art entertaining, sloppy, emotional, human and funny. Over the years I got so far out on this conceptual limb that I went around full circle until I was a traditional artist again. I tried to be ironic about it but eventually became sincere. Now I'm a happy victim of my own charade. I figure that it's better to be a sucker who makes something than a wise guy who is too cautious to make anything at all."[1]

1 Sean Landers, *The Booby* (1998)

In the early 90s Sean Landers was the guy with logorrhoea and the masochistically high embarrassment threshold making text works and videos about his naked self. Text and lo-fi video is seen as the preserve of Conceptual art. That association seemed accentuated in the aftermath of a decade of muscular figurative painting and high-finish objects. Despite the wonderfully inappropriate anomaly of clowns, clouds, oceans, and breasts appearing within and behind his fields of text, and clay chimps and humanoids circling his television monitors, Landers was still down as a conceptualist, albeit one prefixed by 'Neo.'

Beyond the media he used, there was some mileage in the association. Much of the time this was art about art, which made it Conceptual art of sorts. The writing – on canvas, on sheets of yellow legal paper, in his novel [SIC] (1993) – alluded at length to its own characteristics, to the contexts in which it was made, to the contexts in which it might be seen. Reflexivity of this kind was a hallmark of Conceptual art: an artist might begin exploring what art was, or could be, by revealing how the structures around it acted on it, and how it acted on its surroundings. By appearing in his videos Landers seemed to be keeping another common conceptual conundrum in the air: What is art? Something made by an artist... What's an artist then? Someone who makes art.

Like Conceptual art before it, Landers' work has the tendency to occupy spaces beyond the framework of the traditional artwork – spaces that frame both its production and reception. The studio, for example, is very evident in all his videos. Landers also interferes directly with the reception of his work by writing his own press releases. (Recently he even reviewed his own work!) One thinks of all those Minimalists and Conceptual artists who wrote criticism that appropriated or pre-empted the work of the critic (Donald Judd, Robert Morris, Joseph Kosuth, Robert Smithson, Mel Bochner, etc.) and, less directly, those that used art magazine pages as sites for works (Dan Graham, Douglas Huebler, Smithson, Bochner, Kosuth). [SIC], and the writing that appears on his paintings, continually makes reference to the infrastructure of the art world: its participants (critics, dealers, curators, collectors, artists, viewers) and its institutions (galleries, magazines, art schools, biennials, museums). Prior to the 60s, we were supposed to ignore such things – except, that is, when confronted by the proto-conceptual enigmas of Marcel Duchamp.

Besides the cloudy skies and choppy seas, the fulsome but disembodied breasts, the sadistic chimps and battered clowns, it takes less than a minute's reading of his early text paintings to realize that Sean Landers' reflexivity deviates radically from these conceptual precedents. While subjectivity is rarely acknowledged in Conceptual art, the majority of his sentences feature the word 'I.' Furthermore, critics and viewers are directly addressed as 'you,' as if he is literally in the room with us breathing down our necks – almost like an imaginary Vito Acconci performance. When he refers to the art world, the reflexivity isn't the analytical sort we've come to expect of Conceptual art and 'institutional critique.' Instead it takes the form of emotional outpourings of triumph, rage, despair, envy, and humiliation. As such, these responses to art's contexts are inseparable from the apparently unfiltered continuum of his life.

In this he has taken the confessional mode to new extremes. By comparison, notorious confessionalists as various as Sylvia Plath, Robert Lowell, Woody Allen, Kurt Cobain, and Morrissey seem coyly self-censorious. As if on a truth drug, there's nothing, seemingly, Sean Landers won't divulge, however embarrassing and self-indicting: we read of his masturbatory fantasies, his religious hang-ups, his professional jealousies, his personal relationships, his faltering belief in his genius, the agony he suffers on receipt of negative reviews, and much more besides.

This is high stakes stuff, but Landers, in his portrayal of himself, comes over – like the unreliable narrators of modernist novels – as a little too naive to have realized its full implications. We find ourselves not knowing whether what we are reading or hearing is the whole truth, half the truth, or complete fiction. This ambiguity is especially effective in an intellectual context – post-Barthes, Derrida, and Foucault – that is skeptical of authorial presence. By seemingly adopting a strategy of full disclosure, Landers not only transgresses art-world etiquette through many of the things he divulges, he also rattles its philosophical co-ordinates.

The verisimilitude of his representations of his emotional life is such that we find ourselves wondering, for a moment, if we might be in the presence of the real thing – i.e. the outsider or 'idiot savant' whose conspicuous talents have been embraced by the art world (his I'M A CLOWN IN A WORLD OF CHIMPS seems to toy with that idea). Reading between the lines, though, we can begin to detect the games being played by a sophisticate well versed in the rules of the art world. It's not transgression itself that makes Landers unique – 90s art is particularly notable for transgression. What makes his practice unique is the impression he manages to maintain that these transgressions are done involuntarily – that he just can't help these aspects of his life flooding into his art.

It's this performative aspect that lends continuity to the many apparently contradictory forms his work has taken – paintings and bronze sculptures on the one hand, text works and videos on the other. It's also what has made his works amongst the most engaging and entertaining of the last fifteen years. In Landers' case, those qualities contribute to the works' complexity. The laughter and empathy which they give rise to, defer and frustrate our will and ability to interpret the practice as a whole. Its performativity runs rings round us: the work is always two or three steps ahead of our ability to process it. We find ourselves letting go of our critical guard. It's his audience, rather than Sean Landers himself, who, momentarily at least, find themselves 'happy victims' of his 'charade.'

Bruce Nauman's early videos show what art can look like if you remove the object: we are left with the artist alone in his studio, an image both profound and absurd. Stripped of all received notions of art-making, we view Nauman at the zero degree of the creative act, reduced to bouncing balls, pacing the room in an exact square formation, and other apparently worthless tasks. Bereft of art objects, Nauman's studio loses definition, and in the process becomes infinite – a kind of universe. At the same time his studio is a prison cell – after all, what's the use of a studio if you're not going to make objects? Stuck here, seemingly without purpose, killing time as we imagine a prisoner would, Nauman, like Samuel Beckett and Franz Kafka before him, implies that the calling of the avant-garde is a life sentence.

While Nauman's studio is virtually empty, Landers' studio in ANYONE'S ORGASM (1992) is full of art materials and one or two works-in-progress: some kind of head, perhaps, made of clay, on a plinth, under wraps, and a large text piece on a sheet of paper that covers an entire wall. Their presence is enough to problematise the status of his actions in the film. While the pointlessness of Nauman's actions can be considered conceptually and existentially profound, however casual they appear, Landers makes it that much harder for us to decide whether the pointlessness of his actions adds up to anything. This problem is emphasized the one time we see him at work on his text painting. In light of this short sequence, what are we to make of the actions that fill the rest of the sixty-minute video – the monologues, the singing, the dancing, the face pulling? Any one of these actions alone, sustained for the full duration, might just evoke 70s performance-based video (Vito Acconci, John Baldessari, Paul McCarthy, Andy Warhol, or William Wegman, for example), but together in one film, seemingly performed at whim, they begin looking like the behavior of an artist with severe motivation problems. Instead of dematerializing the art object, Landers creates the impression that he can't seem to get round to doing the materializing. His activities ask to be taken for the diversion strategies of an indolent procrastinator. Nauman, Beckett, and Kafka come to mind, but so do the attention-seeking dimwits of reality shows that now crowd television schedules. We're left in an interpretative dilemma.

The constant din of the radio doesn't help. While we know that most art gets made to some kind of soundtrack, I can't recall another artwork other than ANYONE'S ORGASM that gives the radio such prominence. Its prominence in the piece suggests Landers doesn't know what's involved in making video art, since the first thing any other artist would do, once the camera is rolling, is turn it off. It also contributes to the sense that we aren't so much viewing the documentation of a performance as witnessing the artist's down time – the bits we shouldn't see, the bits all other artists would edit out of the work. By showing us the 'life' around the 'art' Landers introduces a new level of uncertainty between those terms just when we thought the issue was a dead one in the aftermath of the 'dematerialized' practices of the 60s and 70s. Ironically, Landers achieves this by re-introducing traditional media in the middle of it all (the clay head and the canvas on the wall).

Perhaps it could be argued the radio in ANYONE'S ORGASM does what the palettes, easels, and models do in Picasso, Matisse, and Braque's reflexive compositions. Perhaps it also follows on from the coffee tins and brushes Jasper Johns rendered in bronze. It's harder to make such a claim, though, when we've heard what Landers is listening to. While we might like to imagine Pollock listening to Charlie Parker, Rauschenberg to John Cage, the British Pop artists to The Beatles, and so on, soft rock rules chez Landers, an association he uses to offend our sense of art's respectability. "I want to know what love is/I want you to show me," "I want to know/have you ever seen the rain?," "Never get caught between the moon and New York City," "The albatross and whale are my brothers" and other ridiculous pomp wafts through his studio, stimulating and accompanying his activities in ANYONE'S ORGASM. The singing, dancing, and mugging to camera is done as if showing off to friends – very good friends – rather than for the approval of gallery visitors, an impression that seems to lampoon the sacrosanct white rooms used to show it in. When he sings, he adopts a grotesque croon, like a dreadful lounge act, or a mock pious chant, as if singing the Eucharist. On several occasions he repeats a phrase over and over as if identifying with sentiments resembling some of the more self-parodic passages in his prose, or, alternatively, as if imitating a teenager imitating an avant-garde composer dismembering a popular song. When he plays with the interference between radio stations, his grimaces imply that he knows that we know that he knows he is indulging in a received notion of experiment rather than the actual thing.

As such Landers is playing with the notion that he might be someone simply doing what's expected of him, instead of striving to develop an artistic path of his own. The studio in his videos doesn't symbolize art's new frontier. Instead, Landers seems to imply that he's there because he's supposed to be, as if to say "what else do you expect me to do now that I've got my MFA?" Watching his videos we always have the sense that the creative spell, such as it is, is about to be broken by a loft-mate wanting to borrow some sugar, or a call from a creditor chasing a late instalment on a student loan. By hiring a chimpanzee (dressed like a human, as in television adverts and family movies) and letting him loose in the studio for half an hour, Landers deliberately implies that he is inadvertently suggesting that the monkey might make better use of these four walls than he does. SINGERIE: LE PEINTRE (1995) looks like a Bruce Nauman video speeded up: the loveable primate body surfs on a skateboard, darts up and down step ladders, and sprints back and forth from one end of the space to the other, accompanied by a soundtrack, sentimental and spirited by turns, that includes MOON RIVER and the theme to MISSION IMPOSSIBLE.

If we were to go on the specific references Landers makes to other artists, he wouldn't seem that interested in the recent avant-garde anyhow. Whereas artists like Warhol and Nauman were role models for Landers' generation, his many homages to artists date back to an era before art took the forms many of his works take. This enhances the performative evocation that he is writing, performing, and shooting videos simply because that's what an artist of the 90s does, in the same way that renting a white-washed loft in Manhattan and going to gallery openings in Chelsea is what's expected of him. Even when his videos get closest to performance precedents, they have pretences to be among more elevated company. REMISSIONEM PECCATORUM (1994) and ITALIAN HIGH RENAISSANCE AND BAROQUE SCULPTURE (1993) are reminiscent of the endurance feats on camera of Marina Abramovic and Vito Acconci, yet the poses are designed to evoke Michelangelo and Bernini. The effect of the conflation is an image of the artist as narcissist, appearing as his own muse – more Morrissey, were he ever to appear on stage naked, than Dying Slave or avant-garde masochist. Rather than simply quoting art history, as many first generation postmodernists in the 80s did, Landers literally makes the references his own.

With the exception of a group of paintings featuring clowns, naked hippies, aliens, robots, and pink rabbits in various landscapes, nearly all Landers' paintings that don't feature writing are pastiches of great art-historical works or portraits of great artists. The former include series by William Hogarth and Pablo Picasso. The latter come in two forms: famous artists as ghosts of themselves and famous artists in various disguises. Both are portraits of what popular publishers now call 'modern masters' of an era contemporary artists rarely refer to.

GHOST 1 (ERNST), GHOST 2 (DUCHAMP), and GHOST 3 (PICABIA) (all 2003) resemble grisailles, old photographs, and spectres. Together, the series is a séance which we as viewers witness or, by implication, participate in: Landers attempts to channel the spirits of his forebears through oil on canvas, a medium which itself has since reputedly died. In this, Landers' use of the medium, with the exhibition context in mind, is as performative as his videos – an agency painting rarely has.

It's harder to determine what Landers intends by the other portraits, which feature clowns' face paint and garish costume. Why is Dalí a king, Braque an elf, De Chirico a Viking, Ernst a devil and Picasso a soldier from the American Civil War? And why, with the exception of Dalí, would they appear in costume at all? The point of all these artists, and presumably their appeal to Landers, is that they embody uniqueness. Why the uniforms then? Why the obvious but inappropriate personifications? Although we recognize everything we are looking at, Landers manages to make paintings that resist categorization and remain enigmas.

Virtually all Landers' gallery of modern masters were related to Surrealism. His version of the Surreal, however, looks deliberately off target. Instead of being bizarre, his 'masters' simply look odd, like pantomime dames in the wrong costumes. Landers' other attempts at Surrealism seem similarly contrived. The chimps, clowns, aliens, robots, bunnies, and naked hippies that populate his first series of paintings devoid of writing were generic before Landers got to them: despite backdrops that hark back to Romanticism, the slightly anachronistic figures that populate them look as if they've strayed from the comforting world of post-war American entertainment: Disney animations, family sitcoms, theme parks, and children's picture books. His aliens are green and egg-headed, of course, while his robots are so tinpot they seem like they never saw the back of the 50s or the Yellow Brick Road. Their appearance in his art suggests a mind crowded with cultural hand-me-downs, so much so that it's unable to summon up individually persuasive characters of his own.

That accusation is harder to level at others. A recent series of bronze busts of anthropomorphic animals could have sprung from the eccentric and unhinged Victorian imaginations of Lewis Carroll or Edward Lear were they to resettle in 21st-century America: FOOTBALL DUCK (2003) is, as implied, a duck whose head is shaped like a U.S. football, while PEANUT HEAD'S (2003) head is indeed modelled on the shell of monkey nuts. A series of figurative paintings that feature writing, made between 1998 and 2000, feature all manner of mutants: among them a sad balding man with three droopy red noses (THREE NOSE GUY), a man with an erect penis for a nose and giant scrotum for a chin (LE DOMAINE ENCHANTÉ AKA MONSIEUR SAUCISSON), and a woman with teddy bear faces on her breast and trees where her head, left arm and waist should be (APOLLO AND DAPHNE). Still, we don't shudder in the face of these anatomical aberrations as we might before a strange creature in a Surrealist painting. Instead of actually looking dreamlike, they look as if they have been contrived to seem dredged from the unconscious: the hybridization is forced, the sexual allusions absurdly clichéd, and the characters' symbolic roles all too apparent. Those characteristics set up a fictitious sense of authorship. We feel they are the works of a Sunday painter aiming at some received idea of Surrrealism filtered through more immediate influences of B movies and soft porn. The technical sophistication of several of these works – the inappropriately beautiful Tiepoloesque light that bathes Monsieur Saucisson and the breast he stands on, for instance – reveals the gap between this fictitious creator and the actual artist who assumes his identity. The effect, again, is analogous to modernist novelists' use of 'unreliable' narrators.

The combination of writing and image on these paintings comes across as especially wrong: in terms of the avant-garde, figurative painting was regarded obsolete by artists employing text; in terms of the Western tradition, writing on the painting would disrupt the illusionistic coherence of what it represented. The appearance of illustrations by famous artists in works of literature are these paintings' closest forebears. In Landers' works, though, writing and image are fused on the same canvas, which compounds their fundamental incompatibility. Often, though, the imagery bears no more relation to the subject of the writing around them than traditional English pub signs do with the conversations occurring indoors. In some, Landers makes a quick reference to the image and title on the top left hand corner and then ignores it in the rest of the text, like the proverbial elephant in the room. BUBBLE BOY (1998), for example, begins, "I feel like painting a picture of a 1970s boy with no arms, big hair and blowing a bubble sitting on a hillside stareing [sic] blankly into space. Voilà." (Thanks Sean.) Bar a couple of brief re-appearances, BUBBLE BOY doesn't get a look into the comically lugubrious monologues that follow and we are left none the wiser. Instead Landers opines on posterity; how being alive is better than being dead; how he got a critical hiding when he dropped his 'shtick' of writing on his paintings in previous shows; how he's returned to it because it means his paintings would sell; how as a consequence his dealer likes him again; how great this particular painting is; how we really should buy it if we can afford it so that he and his family can have a better lifestyle. It's hard to know what this has to do with BUBBLE BOY any more than any of his other creations from the series – PLANK BOY (2000), CAREER EGO (1999), THE BOOBY (1998), et al – which is, of course, precisely the point.

The images in these paintings operate the way themes do in many stand-up comedy routines. Landers on Landers as entertainer: "People think I'm a fucking comedian. Hey, I'm a serious artist for God's sake, look at this painting… Okay this painting isn't a good example, but I've made lots of serious art before, right?" (FOOTBALL DUCK, 1998). A routine may purport to be about a comedian's experiences of hitch-hiking, a bus journey home one day, or the relative merits of the various emergency services[2], but these prosaic themes merely act as pretexts for a sequence of wild digressions. Occasionally the theme comes back in view, as if the comedian has just remembered what it was he or she should be addressing. The effect of these 'mistakes' is of someone following the non-linear train of their thoughts. Usually, of course, most of what seems like free association is scripted. When the writing is good, the effect is astonishing, like witnessing a movie of the workings of the mind, which is the impression we have reading [SIC]. Because stand-up comedy is happening before us in real time, often we're not sure whether we are witnessing actual free-association or its representation.

Many of literature's modernists shared this aim of representing the flux of consciousness realistically. None, however, have surpassed Lawrence Sterne's THE LIFE AND OPINIONS OF TRISTRAM SHANDY,

2
The subjects of three acts I've seen lately.

published between 1759 and 1767 in nine volumes shortly after the heyday of Hogarth and English literary satire (John Dryden, Alexander Pope, Jonathan Swift, et al), amusing and bemusing its contemporary readership in equal measure. As TRISTRAM SHANDY reveals, consciousness behaves in an endlessly digressive manner, obstructing the progressive path the novelist is expected to take. As a consequence, the book's apparent hero, Tristram, remains in utero for the first two volumes while he expounds on a whole range of subjects other than the events of his life. By the end we still know next to nothing about him, yet we've become familiar with the obstetrician who delivers him, the local parson's sermons, the progress of the Williamite wars in Flanders, Uncle Toby's meticulous real-time enactments of these wars on his bowling green with his sidekick Corporal Trim, contemporary French Catholic opinion on baptising children before birth, Pythagorean mathematics, and much more.

Sean Landers' writing, especially in [SIC], is as digressive and absurd as TRISTRAM SHANDY, except that his 'life and opinions' remain the constant subject of these digressions. Written out by hand, it resembles speech, as it cannot be edited, except by crossing words out. In this respect [SIC] is a performance with a set length – 1000 pages – which he fails in the end to achieve, despite threatening himself with the death of his mother if he doesn't. As with TRISTRAM SHANDY, much stand-up and a lot of his other work, the writing is full of references to the task at hand, what he's written so far, and the anticipated response of the reader:

> *Naturally by the time you read this in Grenoble the thousand pages won't be done, I guess I should set a time limit of some kind. Let's say by the date of my opening at Andrea Rosen Gallery in Sept. or October of 1993 if my 1000 pages are not done by then the thug will execute my mother and I shall be to blaim. God save me and for my mother's sake don't let me get writters block. Shit. 992 pages to go. Maybey I got in over my head here. 1000 pages it's a lot you know it'll be a piece about as long as Crime and Punishment, probably about as important to litterature too [sic].*[3]

Its performativity and reflexivity is echoed in one of many passages by Sterne:

> *I will not finish that sentence till I have made an observation upon the strange state of affairs between the reader and myself [...] I am this month one whole year older than I was this time twelve-month; and having got, as you perceive, almost in the middle of my fourth volume – and no farther than to my first day's life – 'tis demonstrative that I have three hundred and sixty-four days more life to write just now, than when I first set out... at this rate I should just live 364 times faster than I should write – It must follow, an' please your worships, that the more I write, the more I shall have to write – and consequently, the more your worships read, the more your worships will have to read.*[4]

While [SIC] and the writing on Landers' early paintings tends to read as unmediated stream-of-consciousness, the writing in the recent paintings seems increasingly self-parodic: "Hey, I'm that guy that writes on his paintings. Accept no imitations. Especially English ones" (FOOTBALL DUCK). Landers does Landers as consciously as he's done Hogarth and Picasso. His most recent paintings feature melodramatic short phrases or single words drawn from what we've come to know as his lexicon: "masterpiece," "cynical," "finish me," "struggle," "give in," "my work will function better when I'm dead," "I know I worked hard I really tried" in THERE WAS A TIME... (2004) and "I know I'm great," "sometimes I can suck," "I have greater range and talent than anyone" in IT'S UP TO YOU (2003). Each word and phrase is repeated as if it's an echo returning from his earlier work, as if its author now suffers from compulsive repetition, and as if Landers is offering us the prospect that he has become the monster he created.

The bronze 'confederacy of dunces' that accompany the paintings evokes no less than Rembrandt, Narcissus, Sisyphus, Icarus, and the Minotaur, according to his own triumphant review of the exhibition in FRIEZE[5]. They're "his progeny for his progeny," "irreverent fantasy creatures" intended to "entertain his kids." Finally, despite the rabbit ears, the reptilian skin, the elephant trunk, and walrus tusks, they are no less SEAN LANDERS, he claims, than the Landers we know from his apparently unmasked monologues. Referring to himself in the third person, as if "I is another" (Arthur Rimbaud), Landers ends the review-cum-obituary, "And last, they are a record of his performance on this stage, one at times warped by delusion and fantasy and fig leafed by occasional fiction but ultimately, it is him. He is this person."

Free for once of the anxieties all artists are prey to, but none have dared or thought to include in their work – "Why, for instance, have I never shown in an American museum? I'm America's best artist yet I've never had a big show" (I LIVED/MONKEY AND GNOME, 2000) – he projects a mock-heroic image of himself in the afterlife, in the manner of Shelley's Keats in ADONAIS (1821), in the company of the great dead masters, far from the petty malice of the everyday art world.

3
Sean Landers, *[sic]*, Publicsfear Press, New York, 1993; Riverhead Books (New York), 1995, p. 8.

4
Lawrence Sterne, *The Life and Opinions of Tristram Shandy, Gentleman*, Oxford University Press, 1993, p. 228.

5
Sean Landers, "Sean Landers, Andrea Rosen Gallery, New York," in: *frieze*, issue 83, May 2004, p. 108.

Failure, as a strategy – what one could call 'secondary failure' – connects Sean Landers with many of the other most significant artists of the last fifteen years. The contemporaneity of John Currin's portraits, for example, is attributable to their 'flaws' when held up against art historical precedents. The apparent slightness of many of Martin Creed's neo-Conceptual works derive from his anxieties around his ability to add anything new to art or the world. Maurizio Cattelan has gone to a doctor to get a certificate excusing himself on medical grounds for not having come up with a work in time for an exhibition, and the police for a certificate to state the work he didn't make was stolen from his car. Carsten Höller turned a car into a mobile LABORATORY OF DOUBT (1999), equipping it with a logo and a public address system. The work, however, remained silent when he failed to find ways of articulating doubt.

Mike Kelley and Martin Kippenberger, two of these artists' immediate predecessors, have since come to be seen as two of the most influential figures of the 80s. At a time when art works acted iconically and the artists that made them were stars, Kelley cast himself as a museum janitor and Kippenberger showed photographs of himself having been badly beaten up. Kelley has since become best known for deploying lowly craft techniques against Modernism and masculinity, while some of Kippenberger's most powerful late works were actual size subway entrances, in various architectural styles, that led nowhere.

It is significant that all these artists are white and male, and that all come from either the United States or Western Europe. Since the early 90s there has been much discussion around identity, especially from post-colonial, post-feminist, and queer perspectives. At the same time, the art world has undergone a process of globalization, with curators eager to identify emerging art centres in Latin America, Africa, Asia, and Eastern Europe.

While in works related to these contexts difference tends to be celebrated and injustices denounced, Landers, like Cattelan, Currin, Kelley, and Kippenberger, for example, takes a completely different approach to identity. Since Landers and these artists aren't acting from a distinct position of 'otherness,' their means of exploring identity have more to do with ambivalent and nuanced relations between the self and society, than issues of visibility and representation. Identity, in the representational sense, does enter Landers' work via his conflicted feelings about his Catholic and lower-middle class upbringing, his Greek and Irish roots, and his dyslexia, but he makes no attempt to offer himself as a representative of these demographics.

In many ways, however, his can be considered a parallel and progressive project, the bad behavior notwithstanding. In the past, few straight white male artists felt the need to question their own relationship to the kind of art they made or the contexts in which it was received – not in public at least, and not in their works. That unselfconsciousness arose from a sense that their role as artists was naturally theirs. By contrast, Landers makes his conflicts, doubts, humiliations and anxieties the subject matter of his work. Even when the tone of the works turn to expressions of his genius, we know that the artist behind the persona knows that this is an embarrassing faux pas, and that these proclamations come at a time when the term is discredited.

We know this because we understand that Landers' portrayal of his emotional life is as performative as it is comic. In this it is related to overt aspects of self-portraiture in the works of Cattelan, Kelley, and Kippenberger and implicit aspects of self-portraiture in Creed, Currin, and Höller. As with Landers, they construct a sense of persona in their work that is often mocking or self-deprecating: the cruel prankster (Cattelan), the angry adolescent (Kelley), the maudlin drunk (Kippenberger), the agonizer (Creed), the womanizer (Currin), the slightly malign scientist (Höller). In Landers' work, this staging of the self is developed in many more directions and to much greater extremes. While the personas these other artists adopt are quickly recognizable, it's more difficult to determine what MONSIEUR SAUCISSON and FOOTBALL DUCK stand for with any degree of certainty and to what extent they and Sean Landers are interchangeable. Obviously they don't resemble the artist physically, but are their words a direct transcription of the artist's thoughts at the moment they were written, or, alternatively, do the words themselves form different caricatures of Sean Landers? If the latter, what is there more of, fact or fiction? Rarely do we find ourselves with such disorientating doubts before art works.

Humor is often closely related to performativity and 'secondary failure.' In Landers' practice it runs far deeper than most. With the exceptions of Dada and Fluxus, some Surrealism and some Pop, comedy is not something we associate with Fine Art. Generally, we associate it with art forms involving the written or spoken word (film, theatre, novels), comedy being far harder to achieve through images, especially non-moving ones. Landers' works – especially, but not exclusively, when writing is involved – often attain true comic brilliance. As in Woody Allen's films, we find ourselves laughing out loud with the artist at the picture of SEAN LANDERS that emerges in the confessions in his writing, the actions in his videos and choice of imagery in his paintings and sculpture while we are in the act of absorbing them.

As with Woody Allen, Landers' staging of the self is part of a metafictional game. We are aware, throughout, that he operates both inside and outside the work as both its protagonist and author. This means that we always have the sense that Sean Landers is stepping in and out of the frame of the work –

be it painting, video, or memoir – much as Allen literally enters and exits the cinematic frame he is simultaneously directing.

This is what distinguishes Landers' works from historical precedents they appear to resemble or pay homage to. The Picasso paintings are a case in point. In one, the Picassoid forms spell "Sean Landers," while in another they spell "Genius." In the monologue that accompanies them, Landers meditates, mock-heroically, on the relation between this noun and proper noun. As parodies, the paintings are innately resistant to the claims his performative self makes on his behalf. On the other hand, the soundtrack undermines the autonomy of Landers' paintings and the famous paintings they are based on. With Landers' speech and Holst's epic music resounding in the gallery, his Picasso paintings verge on becoming props in the performance of his elaborate metafiction, despite the authority of their compositional virtuosity.

Metafiction has a particularly contradictory relationship to Surrealism. Instead of plumbing the depths of the self, it suggests that the self, when apparent in art works, is a construction. Portraiture, since it belongs to the world of appearances, would be the last strategy a surrrealist would employ to convey the unconscious self. André Breton wouldn't have tolerated Landers' representations of his circle, which of course is part of their irony. Nor would he have appreciated the deliberate absurdity of the various pop cultural borrowings in his neo-Surrealist paintings: the aliens in a rowing boat on a wild sea at night, the chimp in the astronaut suit at an easel on what looks like Mars, and so on.

Landers' text works and performance-based videos also deliberately fail in respect to the criteria of Conceptual art. In general, anything that could be taken as a subjective statement was excised from these precedents in the 60s and 70s: the language employed a quasi-scientific objectivity, while the artist's body was treated as abstract material. In this way Conceptual art made what came before and after the art object, and the structures around it, the content of the work itself: the artist's body, the space of the studio, the politics of the exhibition space, the world beyond these spaces, the publications used to represent it, etc. Landers incorporates many of these contexts into his works. At the same time, he has incorporated a whole range of contextual material into his work that Conceptual artists neglected, which is what creates the impression that he is getting Conceptual art wrong. That material belongs to the subjective, emotional sphere and is shared by all artists. By making his artistic and professional highs and lows the main subject of his work, Sean Landers hasn't just provided an ongoing commentary on his own practice, he has also, indirectly, provided a commentary on every other artist's.

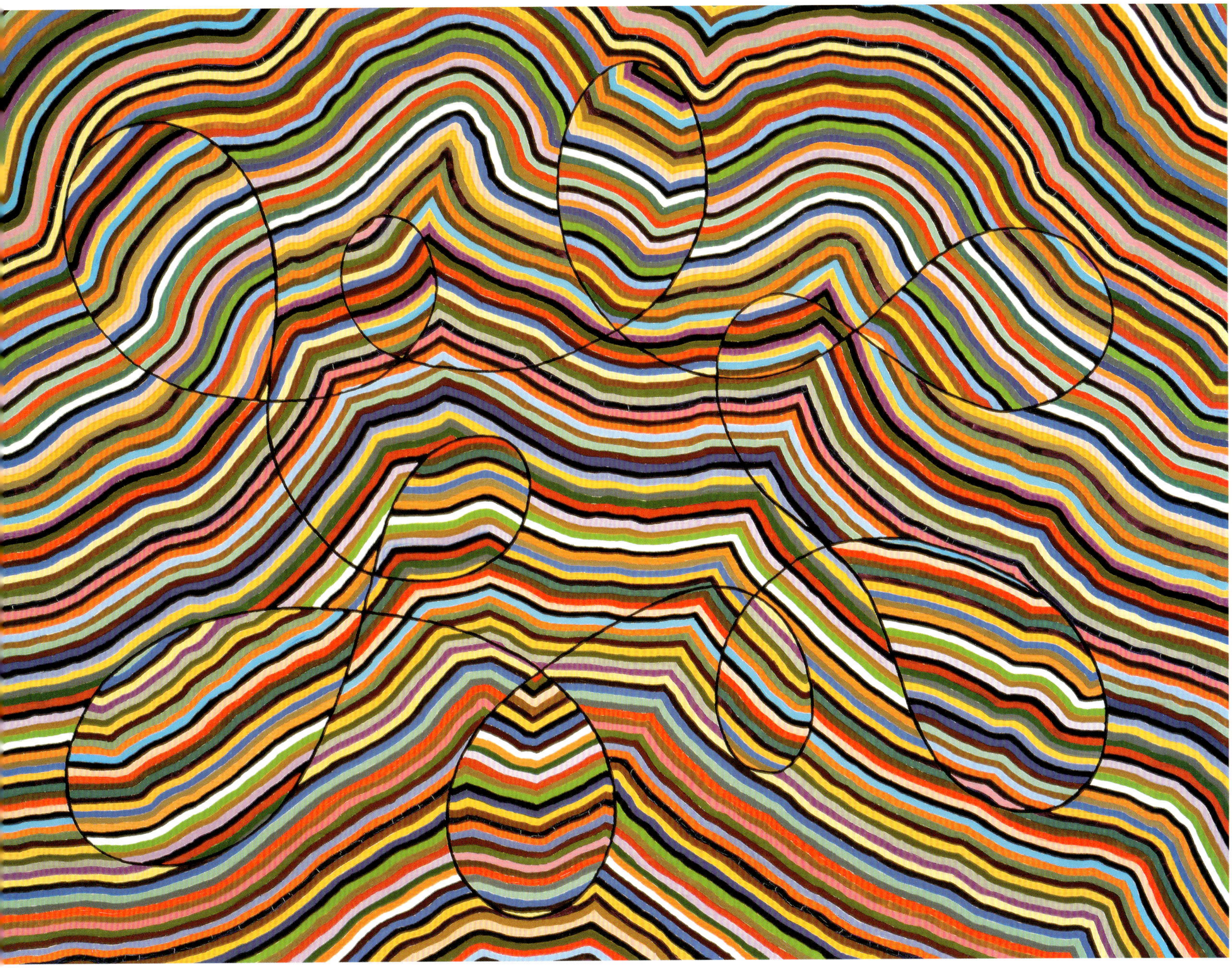

7095, 2001
Oil on linen
172.72 × 233.68 cm

Pages 106–107
PERFECT, 2000
Oil on linen
213.36 × 365.76 cm

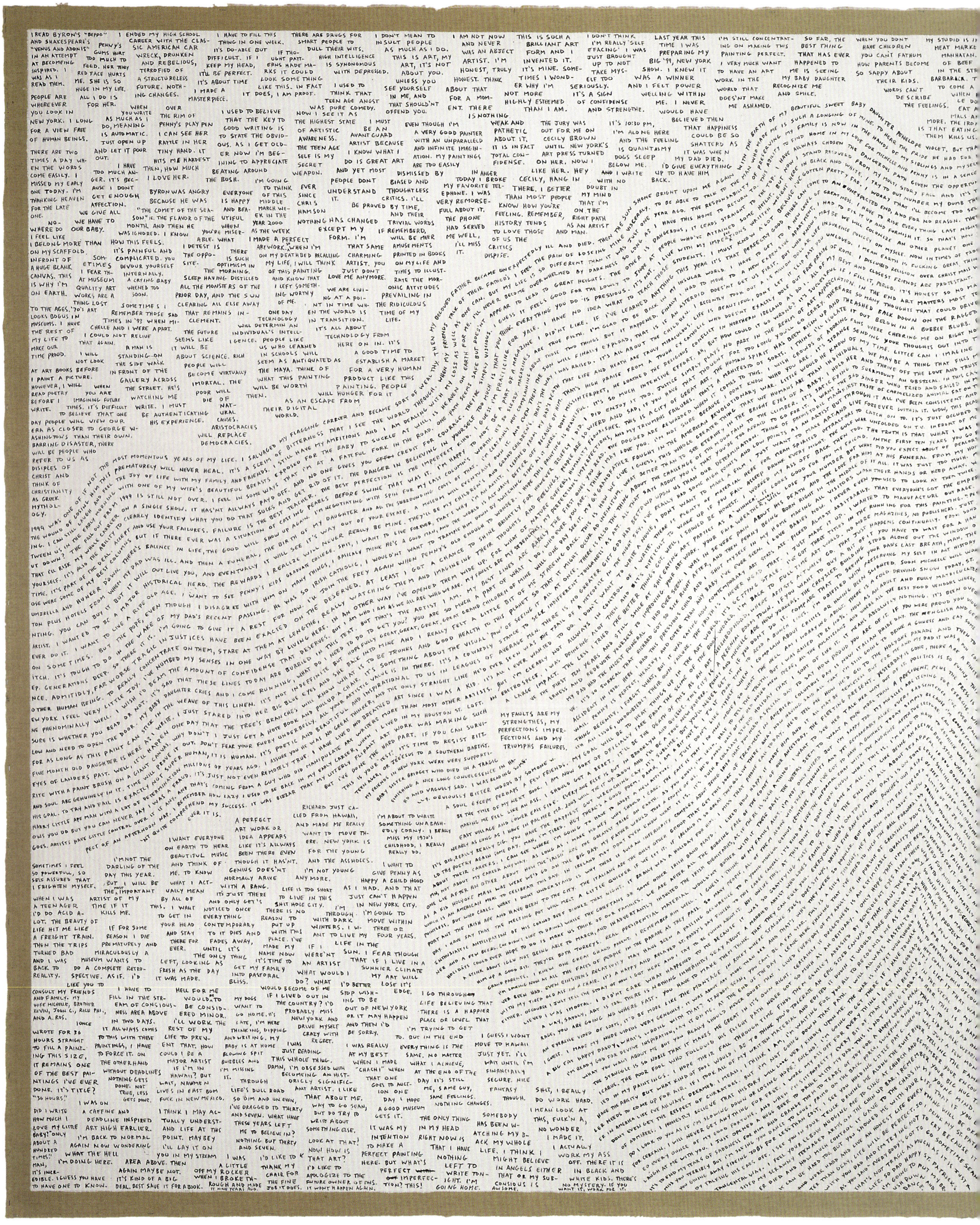
LAST YEAR THIS TIME I WAS PREPARING MY BIG '99 NEW YORK SHOW. I KNEW IT WAS A WINNER AND I FELT POWER WELLING WITHIN ME. I NEVER WOULD HAVE BELIEVED THEN THAT HAPPINESS COULD BE SO SHATTERED AS IT WAS WHEN MY DAD DIED.
MY FAULTS ARE MY STRENGTHS, MY PERFECTIONS IMPERFECTIONS AND MY TRIUMPHS FAILURES.
I'M NOT THE DARLING OF THE DAY THIS YEAR. BUT I WILL BE THE IMPORTANT ARTIST OF MY TIME IF IT KILLS ME.

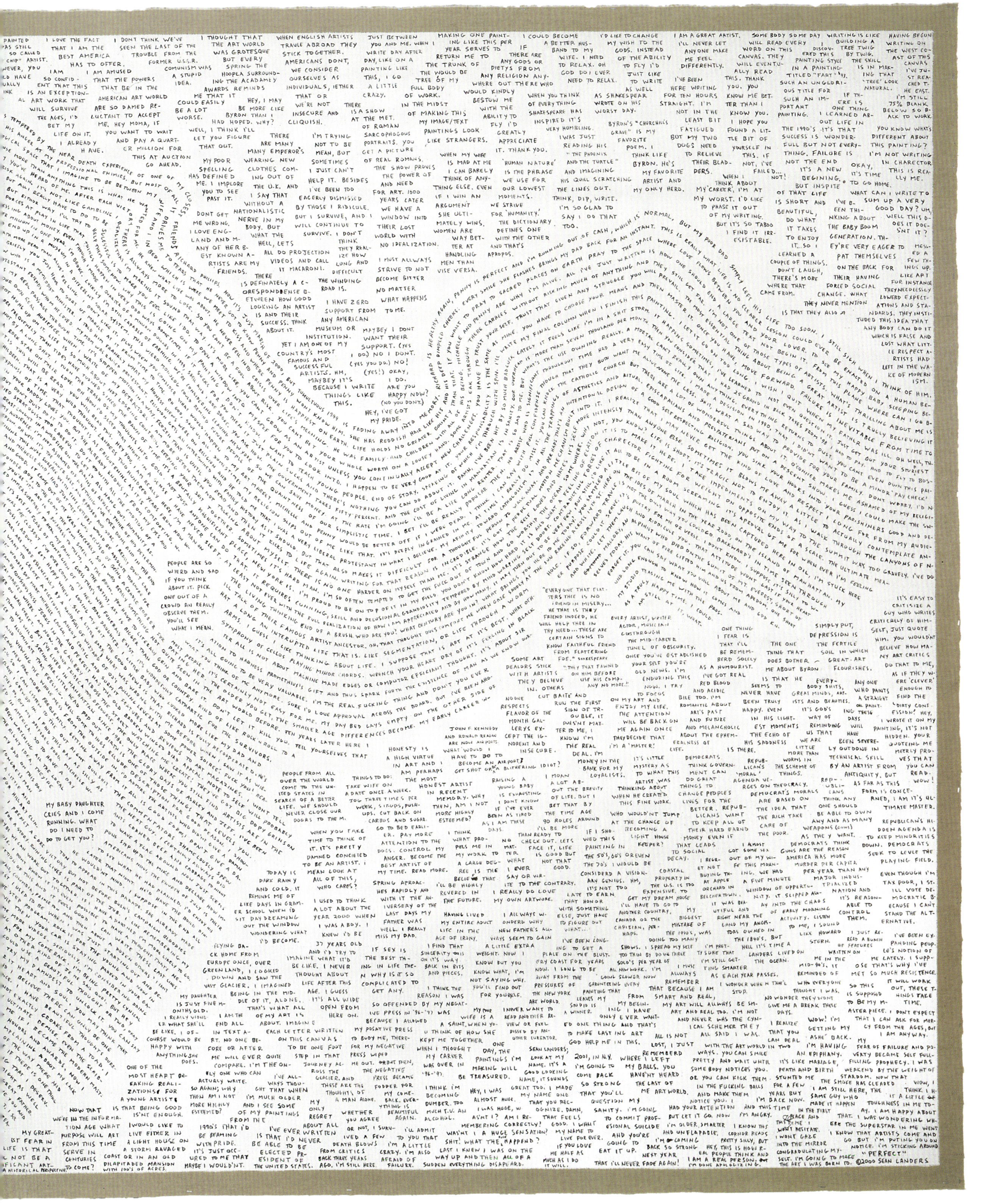

I LOVE THE FACT THAT I AM THE BEST AMERICA HAS TO OFFER.
I DON'T THINK WE'VE SEEN THE LAST OF THE TROUBLE FROM THE FORMER U.S.S.R.
I THOUGHT THAT THE ART WORLD WAS GROTESQUE BUT EVERY SPRING THE HOOPLA SURROUNDING THE ACADEMY AWARDS REMINDS ME THAT IT COULD EASILY BE A LOT WORSE.
WHEN ENGLISH ARTISTS TRAVEL ABROAD THEY STICK TOGETHER. AMERICANS DON'T, WE CONSIDER OURSELVES AS INDIVIDUALS, EITHER THAT OR WE'RE NOT INSECURE AND CLIQUISH.
I COULD BECOME A BETTER HUSBAND TO MY WIFE. I NEED TO RELAX. OH GOD DO I EVER NEED TO RELAX.
I'D LIKE TO CHANGE MY WISH TO THE GODS. INSTEAD OF THE ABILITY TO FLY I'D JUST LIKE TO WRITE AS WELL AS SHAKESPEARE.
I AM A GREAT ARTIST. I'LL NEVER LET ANYONE MAKE ME FEEL DIFFERENTLY.
SOME BODY SOME DAY WILL READ EVERY WORD ON THIS CANVAS.
©2000 SEAN LANDERS

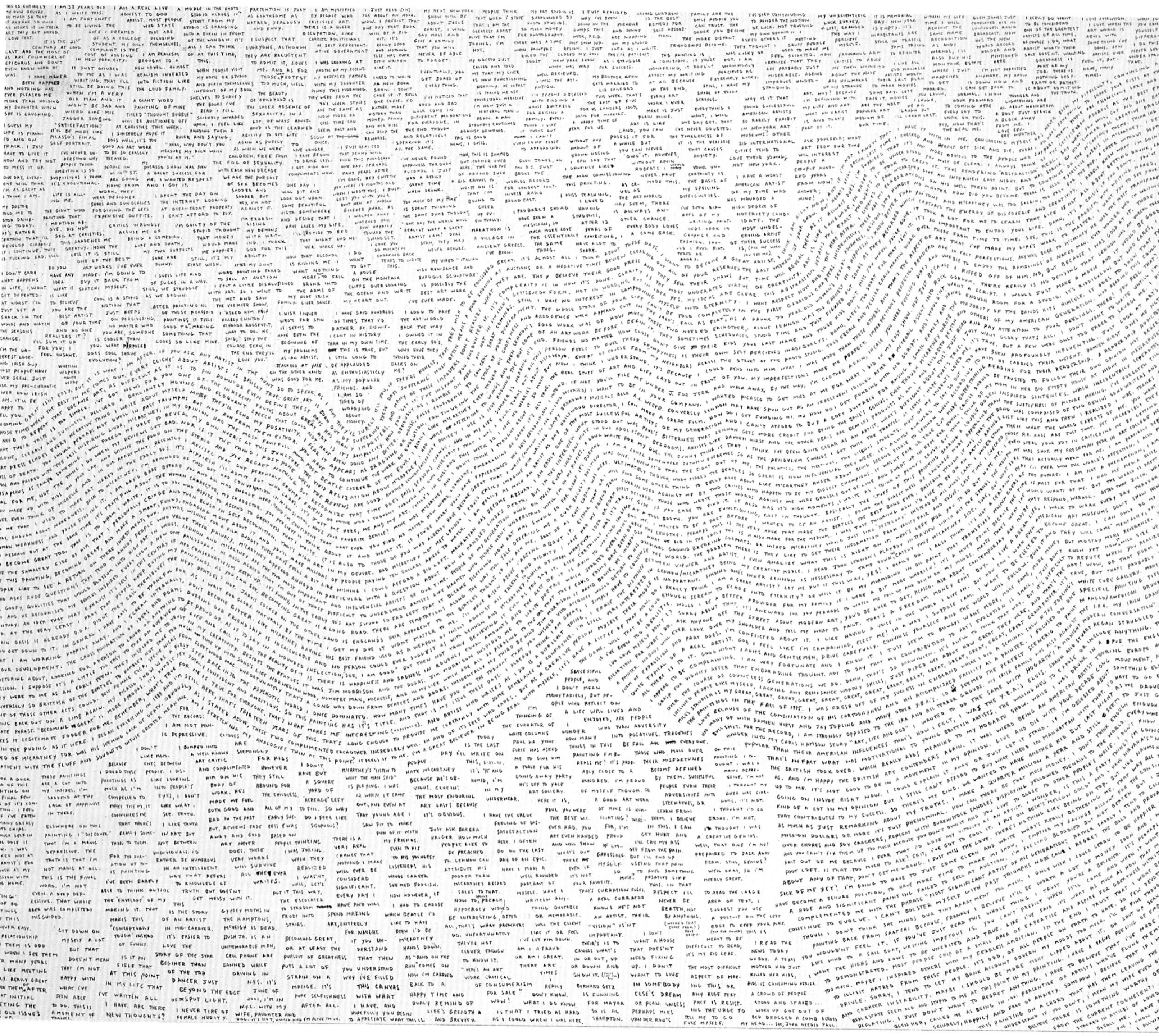

BECOMING GREAT, 2001
Oil on linen
218.44 × 543.56 cm

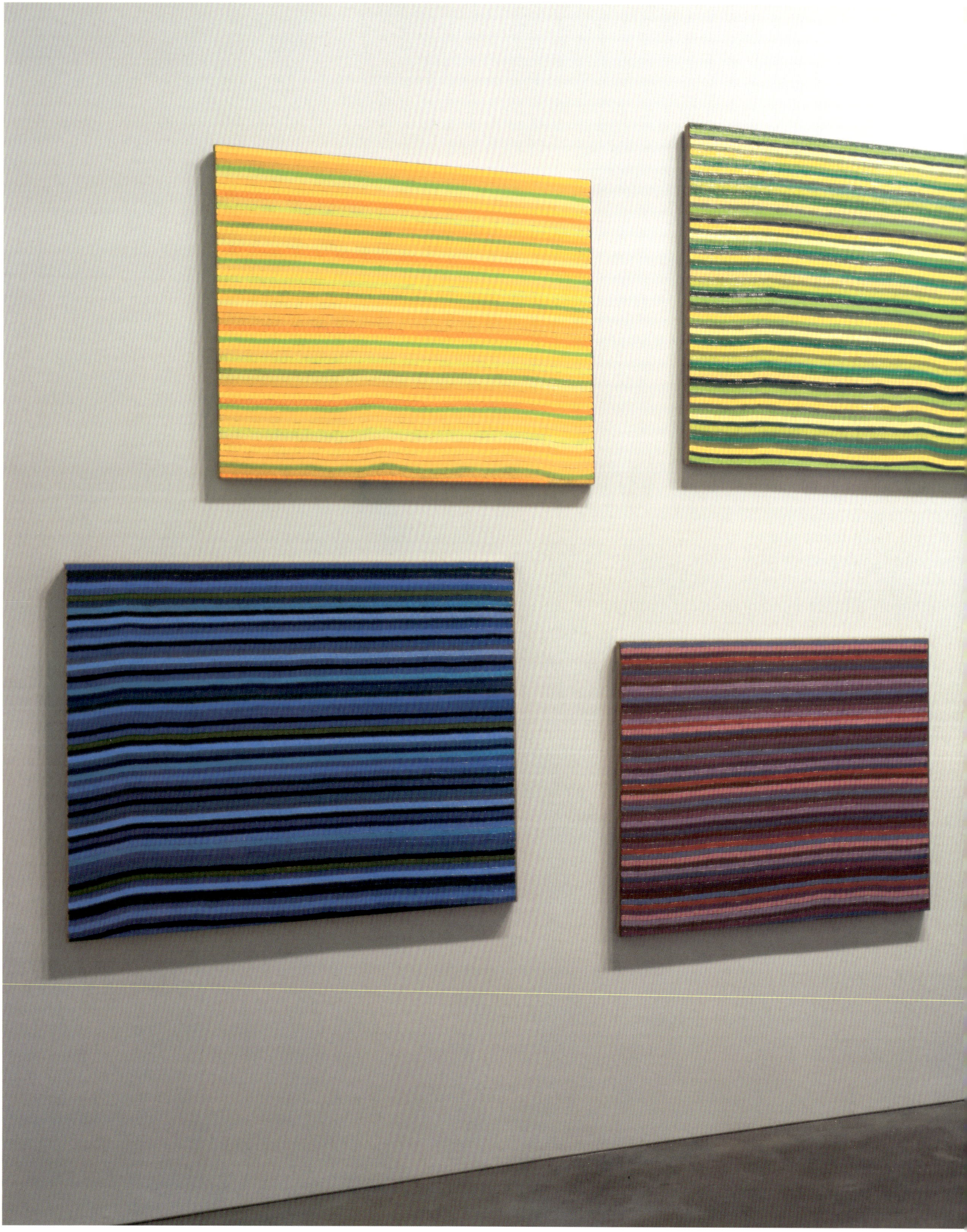

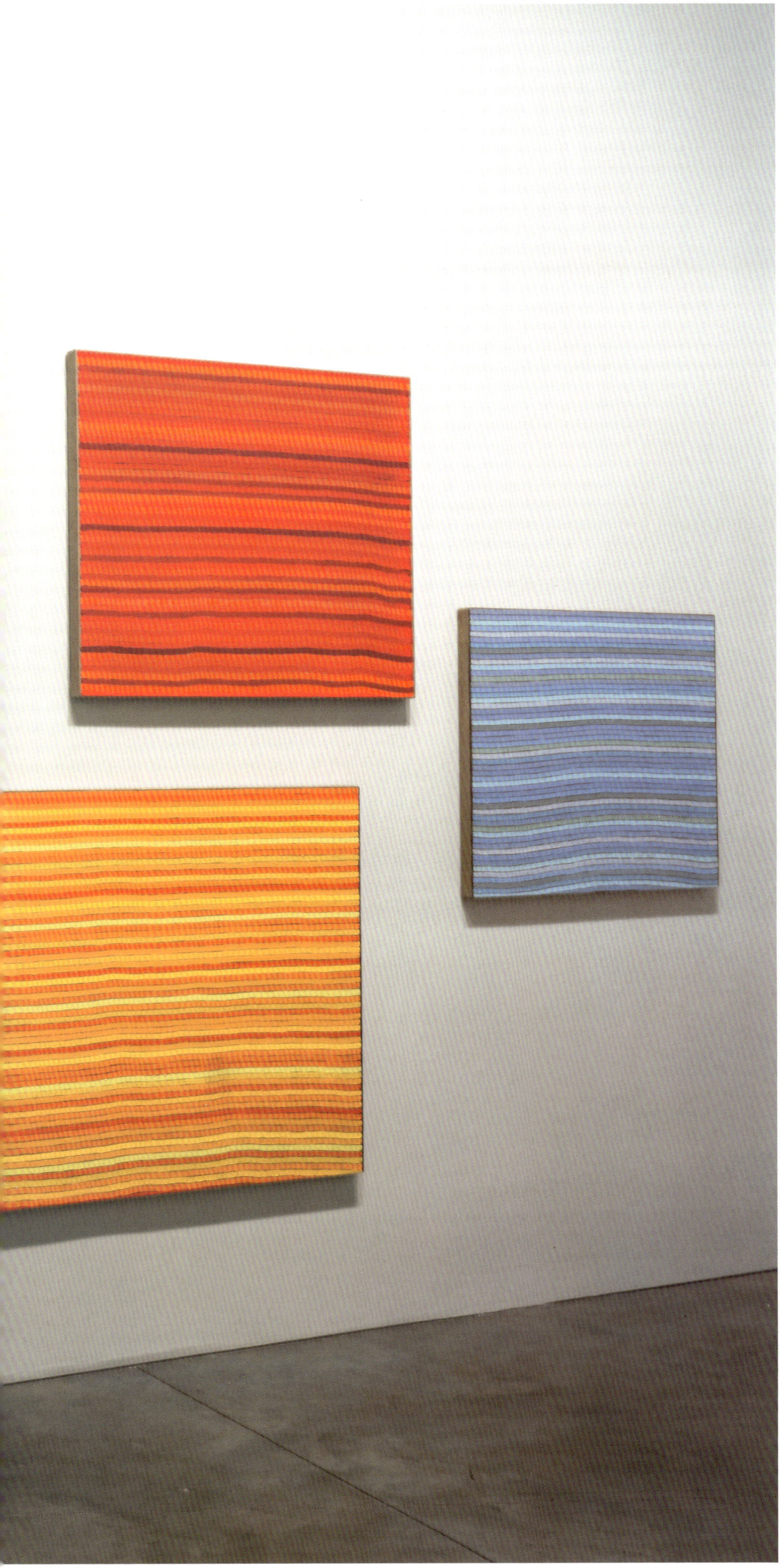

SEVEN DEADLY SINS,
2002
Set of seven paintings
Oil on linen

Clockwise, from top left:

GREED
83.82 × 99.06 cm

ENVY
96.52 × 116.84 cm

ANGER
86.36 × 106.68 cm

SLOTH
78.74 × 93.98 cm

GLUTTONY
101.60 × 121.92 cm

PRIDE
81.28 × 96.52 cm

LUST
91.4 × 111.8 cm

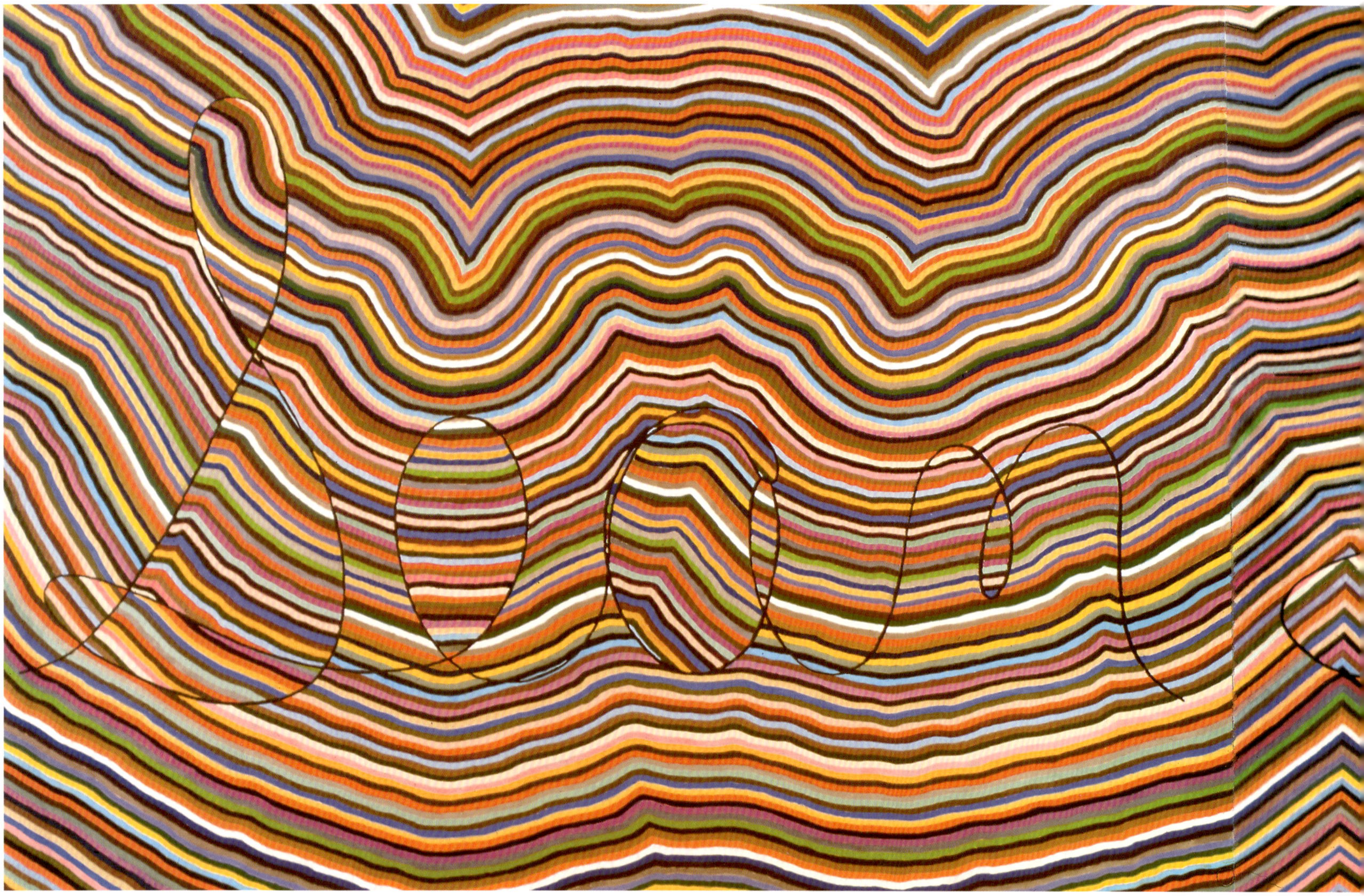

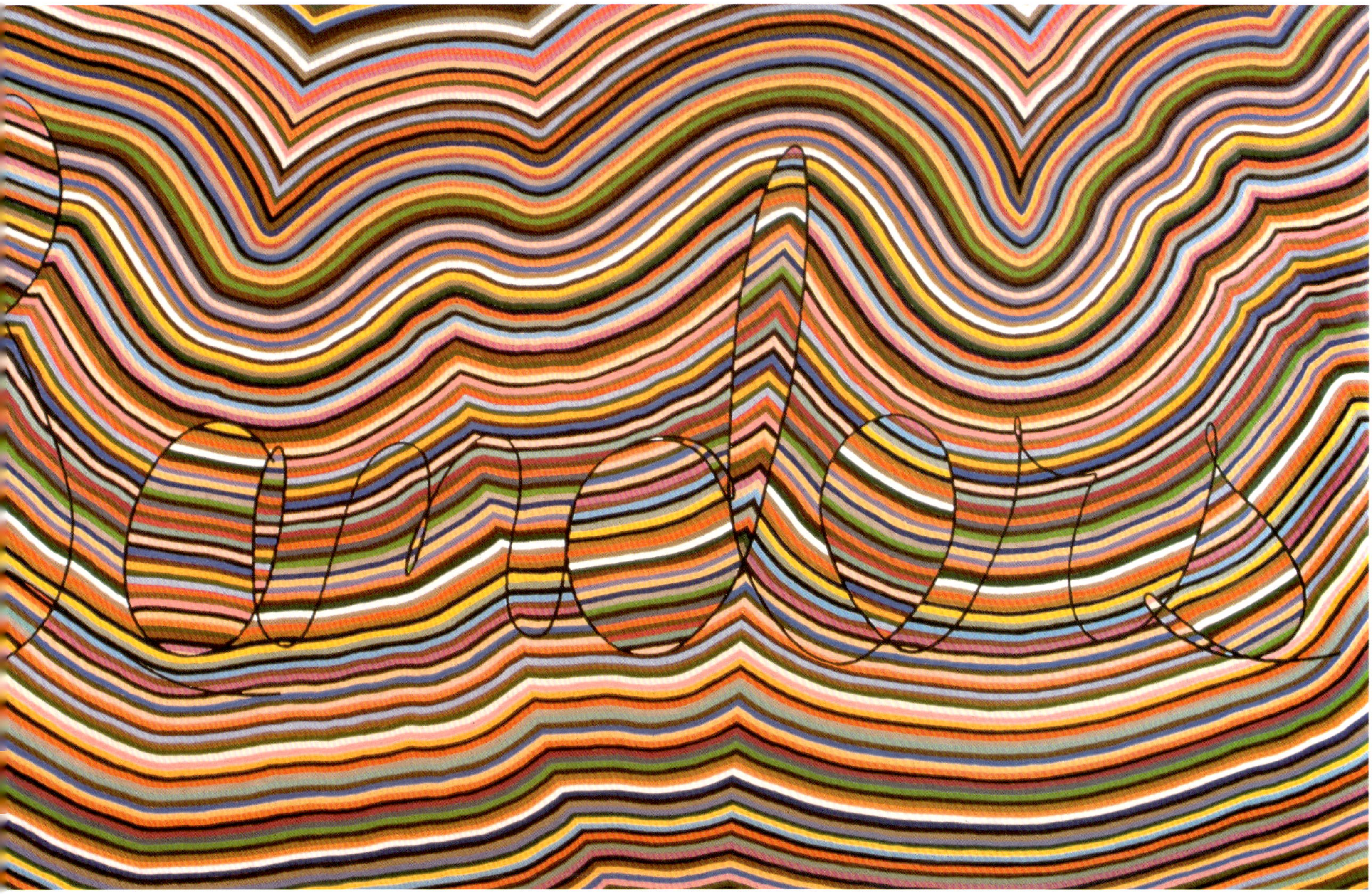

SEAN LANDERS / *7098*, 2001
Oil on linen
187.96 × 254 cm (left)
187.96 × 330.2 cm (right)

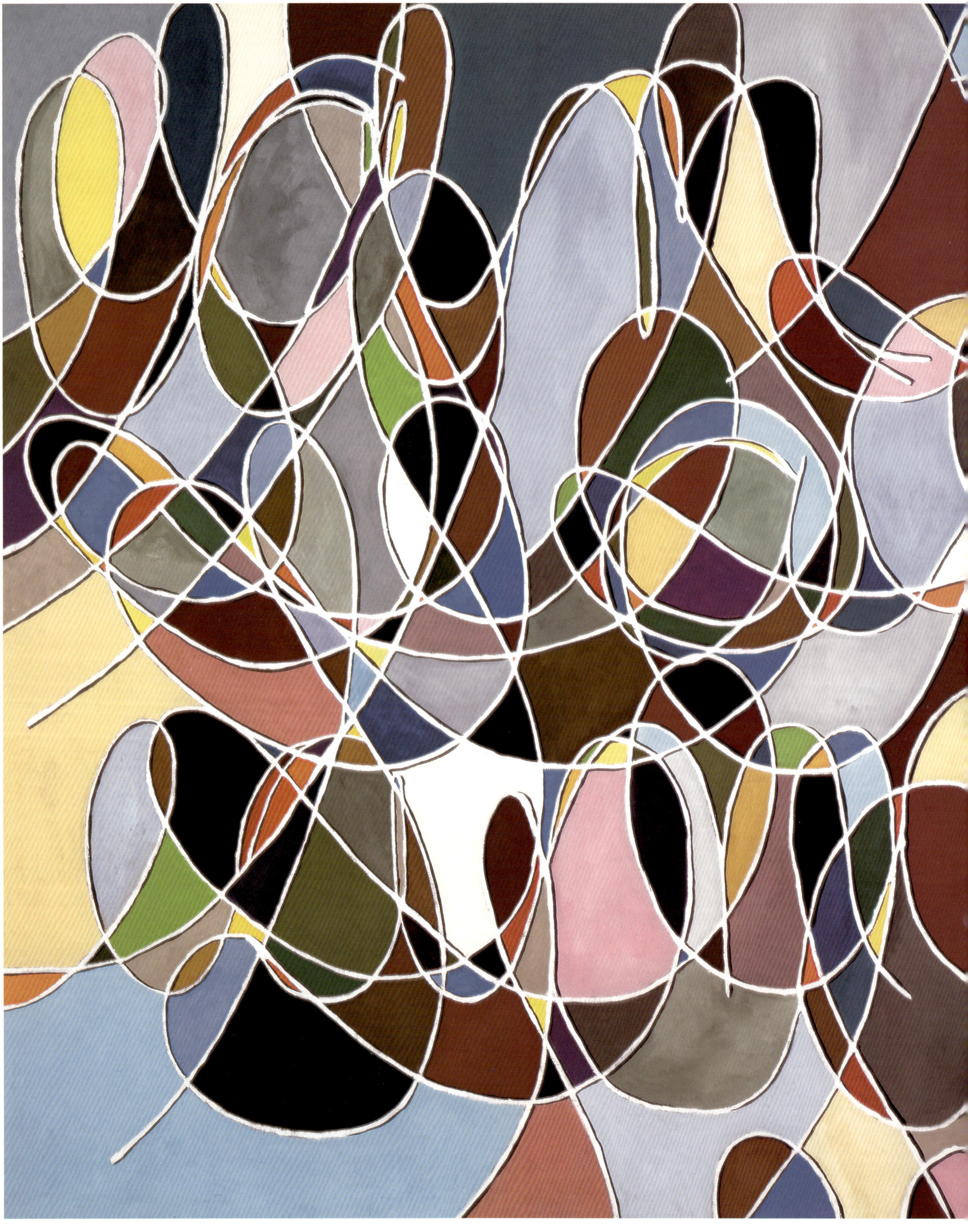

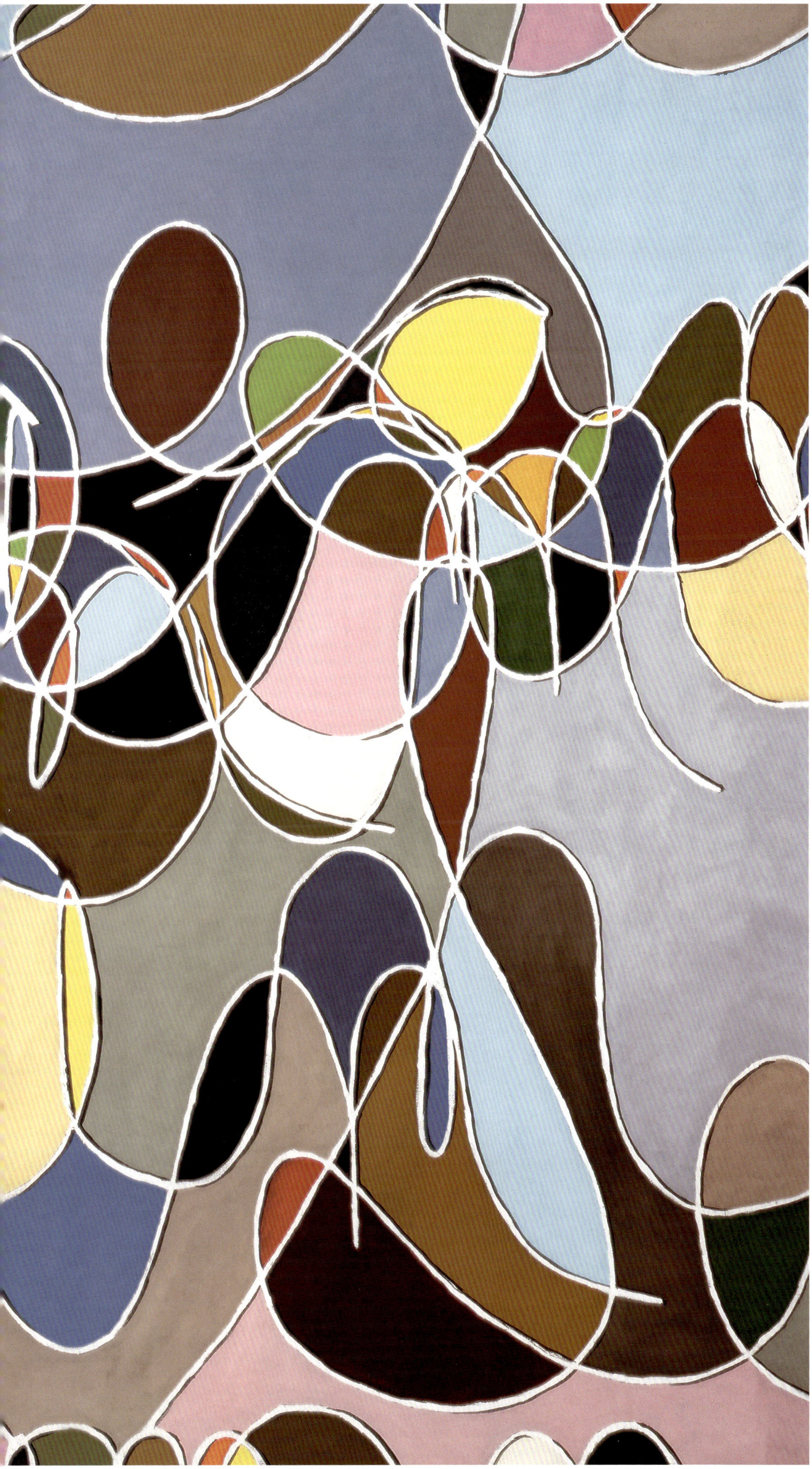

SEAN, SEAN, SEAN/7097,
2000
Oil on linen
203.2 × 294.64 cm

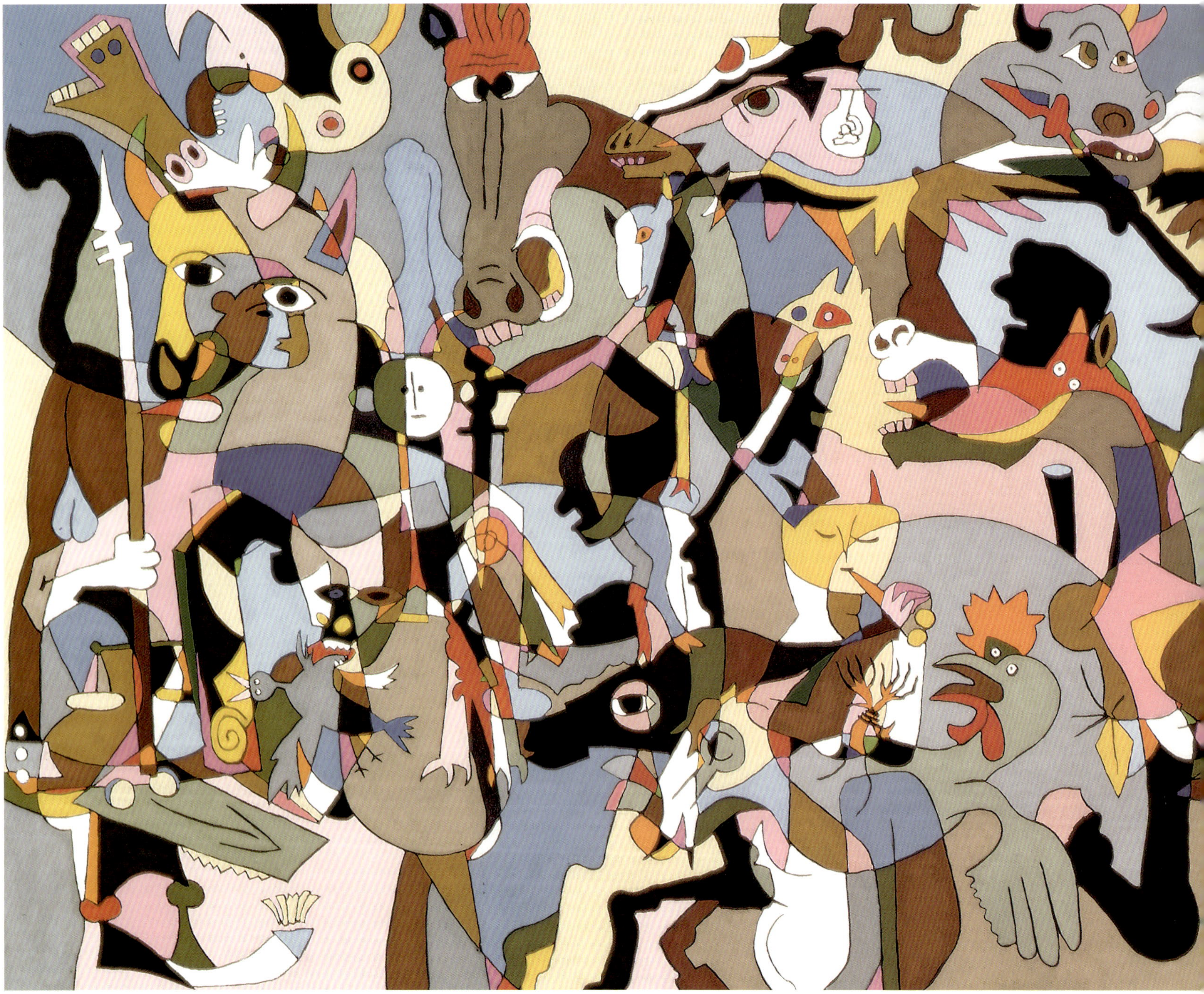

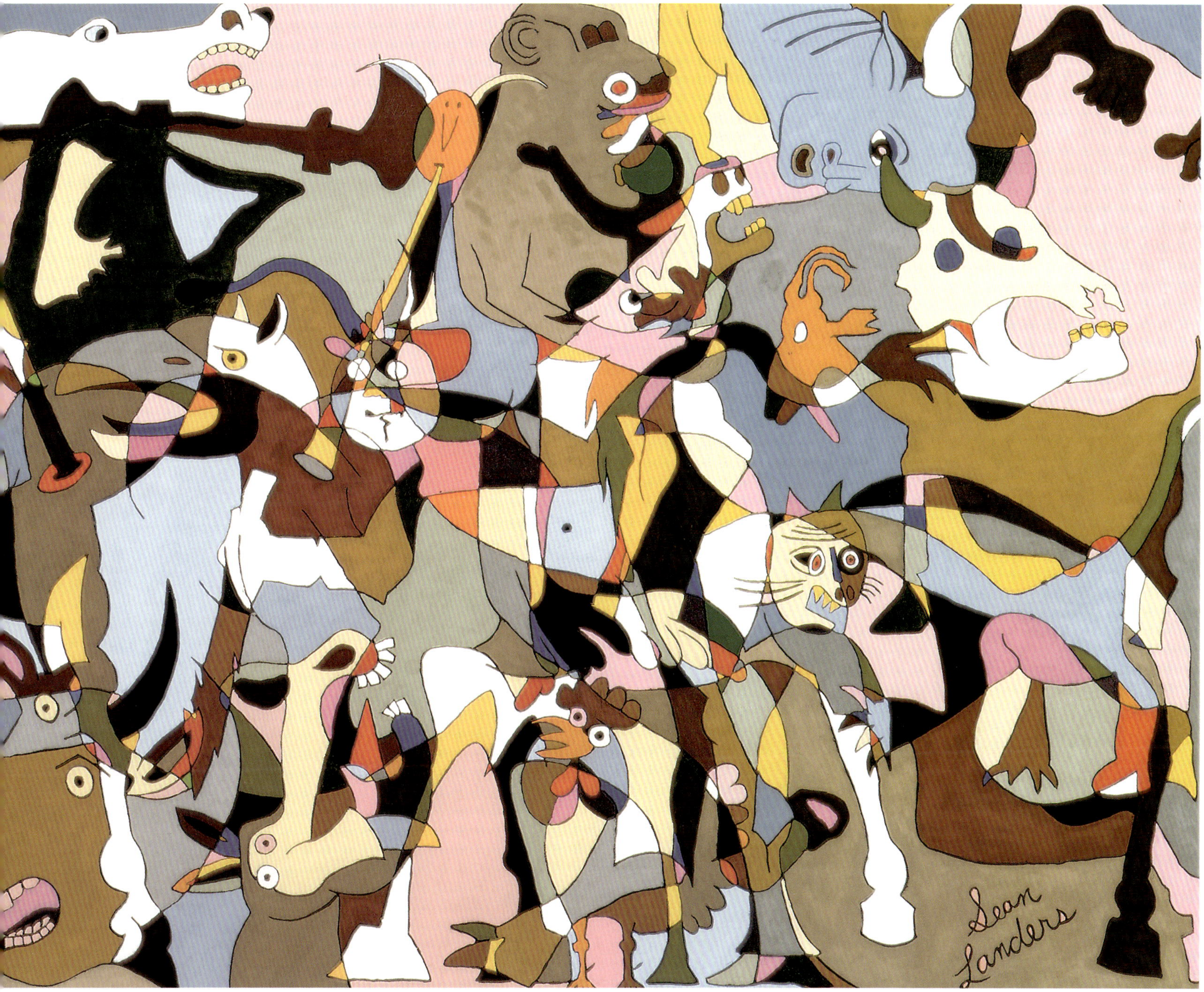

WAR AND PEACE / 7100, 2001
Oil on linen
259.08 × 670.56 cm

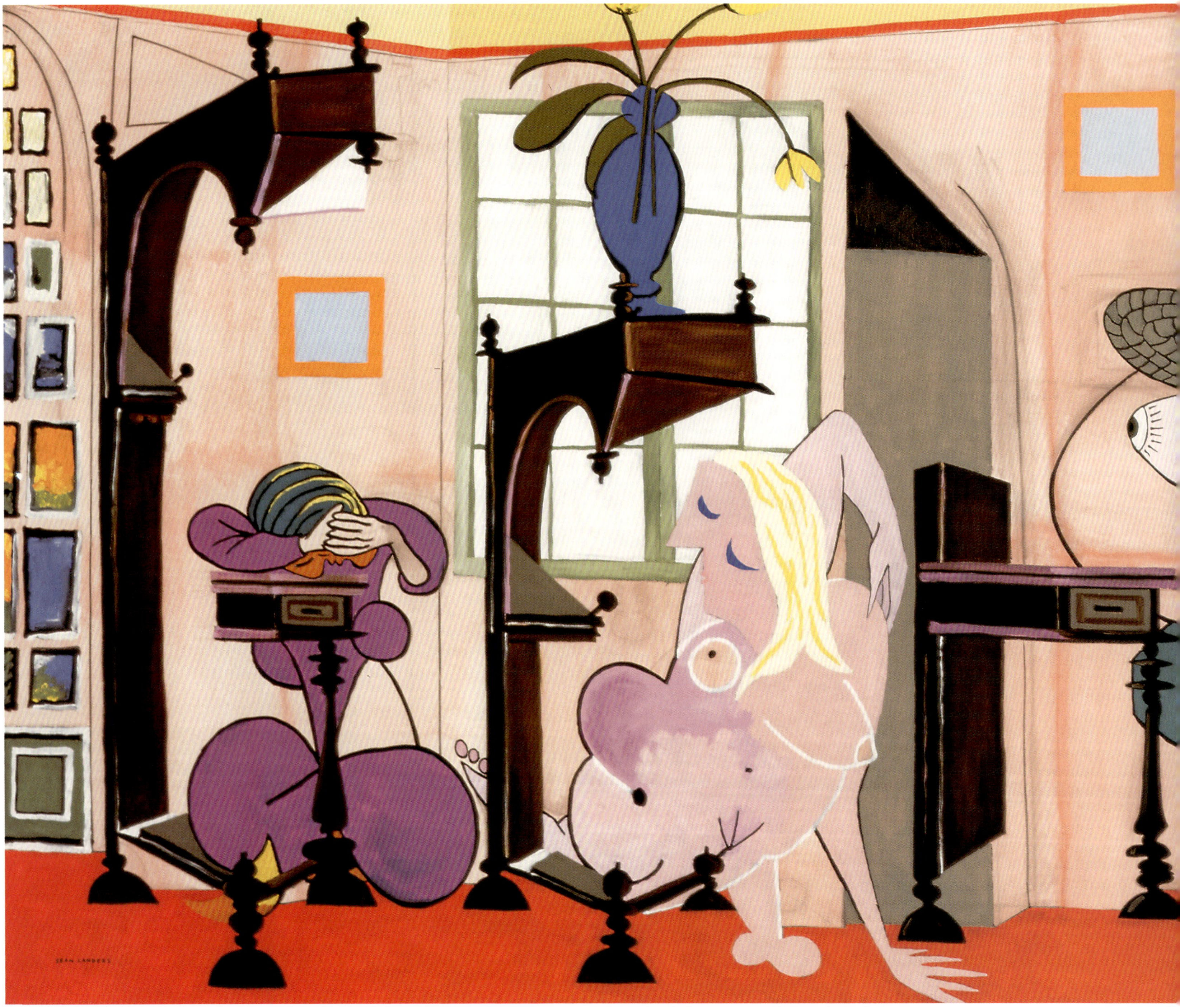

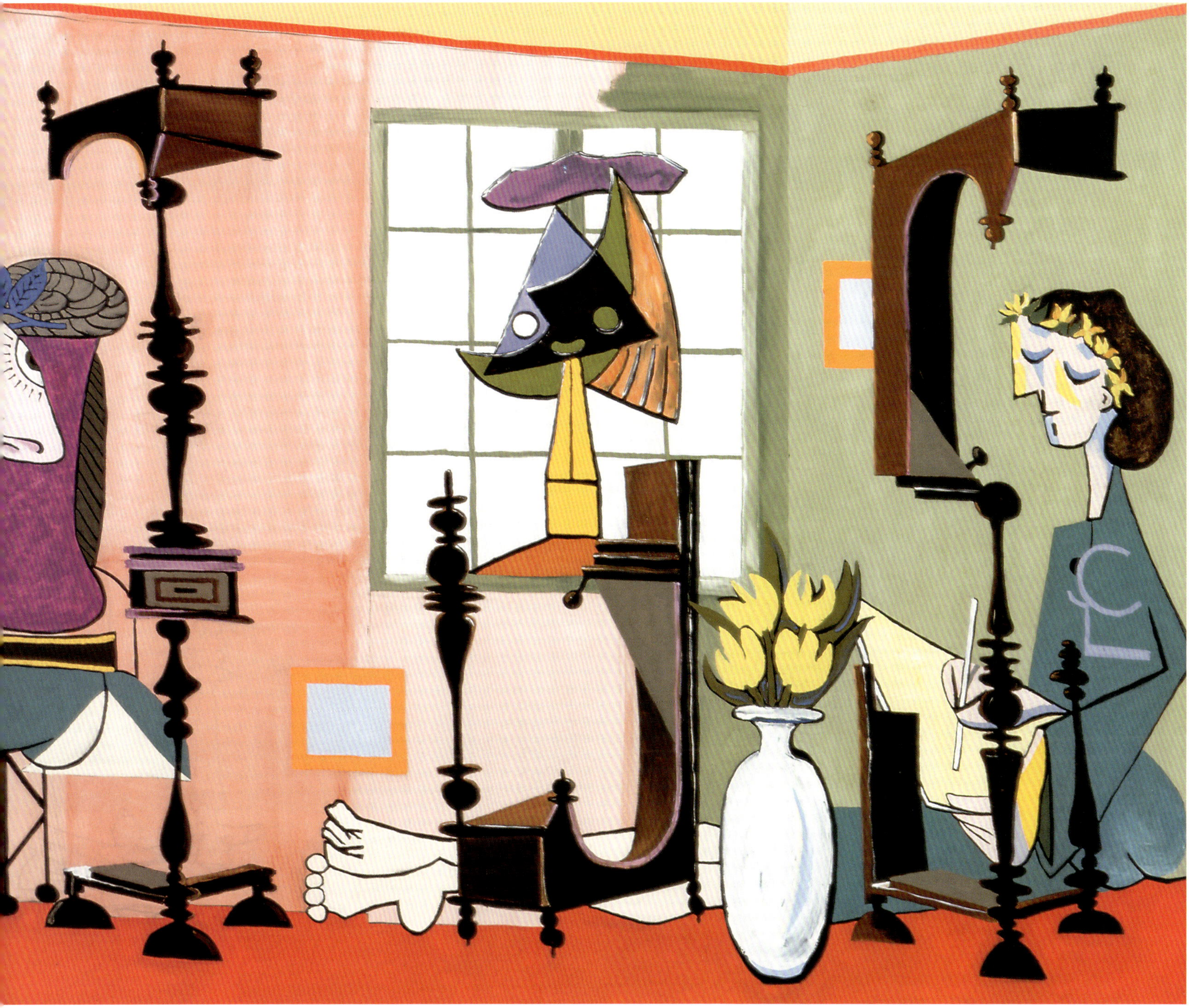

GENIUS, 2001
Oil on linen
218.44 × 543.56 cm

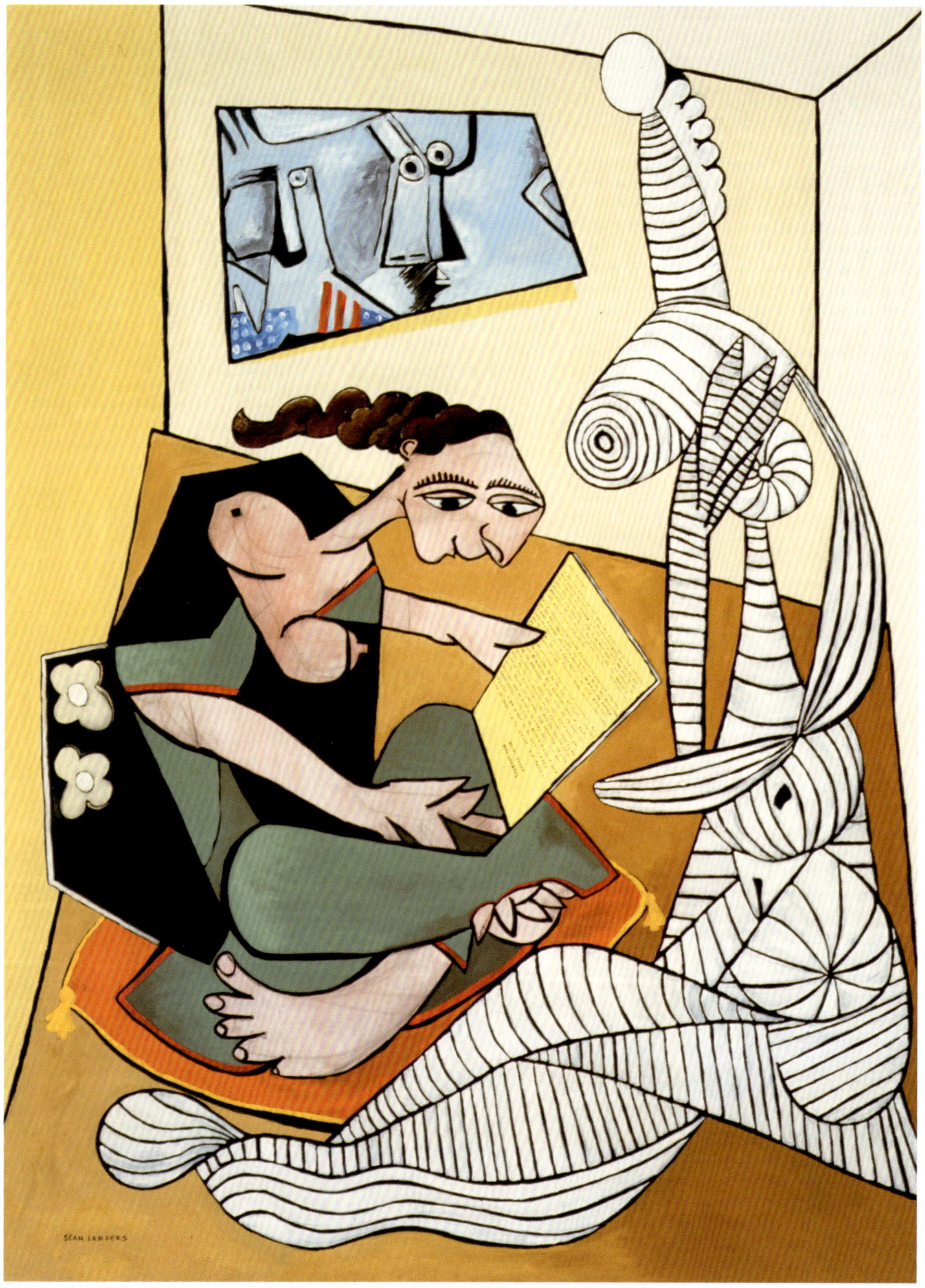

ON THE WALL ABOVE, 2001
Oil on linen
233.68 × 172.72 cm

Sean Landers: Kunst und Sprache

ALEX FARQUHARSON

„Ursprünglich hatte ich die Idee, die konzeptuelle Kunst unterhaltsam, schludrig, emotional, menschlich und witzig zu machen. Über die Jahre habe ich mich mit diesem Konzept so sehr exponiert, dass sich der Kreis zu schliessen begann und ich wieder zu einem traditionellen Künstler wurde. Ich versuchte, ironisch damit umzugehen, aber es wurde letzten Endes ernst. Jetzt bin ich ein glückliches Opfer meiner eigenen Scharade. Ich denke mir, es ist besser, ein Trottel zu sein, der etwas macht, statt ein Klugscheisser, der zu vorsichtig ist, überhaupt etwas zu machen." [1]

1 Sean Landers, *The Booby* (1998)

Anfang der neunziger Jahre war Sean Landers der Typ mit der Logorrhoe und der masochistisch hohen Schamschwelle, der Textarbeiten und Videos über sein nacktes Ich machte. Text und Low-Fidelity-Video gelten als Domäne der konzeptuellen Kunst. Diese Verbindung schien in den Nachwirkungen eines Jahrzehnts, das eine deftige figurative Malerei und Hochglanzobjekte hervorgebracht hatte, betont hervorzutreten. Der wunderbar unpassenden Absonderlichkeit der Clowns, Wolken, Meere und Brüste, die in und hinter seinen Textfeldern auftauchten, sowie den Tonschimpansen und menschenähnlichen Wesen zum Trotz, die seine Fernsehschirme umkreisen, wurde Landers immer noch als Konzeptkünstler geführt, wenngleich mit der Vorsilbe ‚Neo-' versehen.

Über die verwendeten Medien hinaus lag in der Verbindung ein gewisser Nutzen. Die meiste Zeit ging es um Kunst über Kunst, was sie zu einer Art Konzeptkunst machte. Das Geschriebene – auf Leinwand, auf gelbem Linienpapier, in seinem Roman [SIC] (1993) – nahm ausführlich auf seine eigenen Merkmale Bezug, auf die Kontexte, in der es geschaffen wurde, auf die Kontexte, in denen es möglicherweise gesehen würde. Reflexivität dieser Art war ein Markenzeichen der Konzeptkunst: Ein Künstler mochte zunächst erkunden, was Kunst ist oder sein könnte, indem er aufdeckt, wie die Strukturen in ihrer Umgebung auf sie einwirken und wie sie auf ihre Umgebung einwirkt. Indem Landers in seinen Videos auftrat, schien er ein weiteres gängiges konzeptuelles Rätsel in der Schwebe zu halten: Was ist Kunst? Etwas, was ein Künstler gemacht hat... Was ist denn ein Künstler? Jemand, der Kunst macht.

Wie die Konzeptkunst aus der Zeit vor ihnen greifen Landers' Arbeiten allmählich in Bereiche über, die sich ausserhalb des Rahmens des traditionellen Kunstwerkes befinden – Bereiche, die sowohl ihre Produktion als auch ihre Rezeption betreffen. Das Atelier ist zum Beispiel in allen seinen Videoarbeiten deutlich präsent. Landers mischt sich auch direkt in die Rezeption seiner Arbeit ein, indem er seine eigenen Pressemeldungen schreibt. (Vor kurzem hat er sogar seine eigene Arbeit rezensiert!) Man denkt an all jene Minimalisten und Konzeptkünstler, die Besprechungen schrieben, in denen sie die Arbeit des Kritikers selbst übernahmen oder ihr zuvorkamen (Donald Judd, Robert Morris, Joseph Kosuth, Robert Smithson, Mel Bochner usw.), und, weniger offensichtlich, an jene, die Seiten von Kunstmagazinen als Orte für ihre Arbeiten verwendeten (Dan Graham, Douglas Huebler, Smithson, Bochner, Kosuth). [SIC] sowie das Geschriebene, das auf seinen Gemälden erscheint, bezieht sich immer auf die Infrastruktur der Kunstwelt: ihre Mitglieder (Kritiker, Händler, Kuratoren, Sammler, Künstler, Betrachter) und ihre Institutionen (Galerien, Zeitschriften, Kunstschulen, Biennalen, Museen). Vor den sechziger Jahren sollten wir solche Dinge nicht beachten – das heisst mit Ausnahme der Situationen, in denen wir mit den protokonzeptuellen Rätseln Marcel Duchamps konfrontiert waren.

Von den bewölkten Himmeln und bewegten Meeren, den übertrieben üppigen, doch körperlosen Brüsten, den sadistischen Schimpansen und übel zugerichteten Clowns abgesehen, hat man beim Lesen seiner frühen Textbilder in weniger als einer Minute erfasst, dass sich die Reflexivität von Sean Landers grundsätzlich von der seiner konzeptuellen Vorgänger unterscheidet. Während in der Konzeptkunst Subjektivität selten eingestanden wird, enthält die Mehrzahl seiner Sätze das Wort ‚ich'.

Daneben werden Kritiker und Betrachter direkt mit ‚du' angeredet, als sei er im Raum und sitze uns buchstäblich im Nacken – fast wie eine fiktive Performance von Vito Acconci. Wenn er sich auf die Kunstwelt bezieht, ist die Reflexivität nicht analytisch in der Weise, wie wir es von der konzeptuellen Kunst und ‚institutionellen Kritik' inzwischen erwarten. Stattdessen nimmt sie die Form emotionaler Ergüsse von Triumph, Wut, Verzweiflung, Neid und Demütigung an. Als solche sind diese Reaktionen auf die Kontexte der Kunst von dem offenbar ungefilterten Kontinuum seines Lebens nicht zu trennen.

Damit hat er die bekenntnishafte Äusserung zu neuen Extremen geführt. Im Vergleich dazu erscheinen bekannte und so grundverschiedene Autoren von Bekenntnisliteratur wie Sylvia Plath, Robert Lowell, Woody Allen, Kurt Cobain und Morrissey verschämt selbstkritisch. Da gibt es offensichtlich nichts, wie peinlich oder selbstanklägerisch es auch sein mag, was Landers nicht verbreiten würde, als stünde er unter einer Wahrheitsdroge: Wir lesen von seinen Phantasien beim Masturbieren, seinen religiösen Komplexen, seinen beruflichen Eifersüchteleien, seinen persönlichen Beziehungen, von seinem schwankenden Glauben an sein Talent, den Qualen, die er leidet, wenn er negative Kritiken bekommt, und vieles mehr.

Das sind Dinge, bei denen es um einen hohen Einsatz geht, aber Landers wirkt mit seiner Selbstdarstellung – wie die unzuverlässigen Erzähler modernistischer Romane – ein bisschen zu naiv, um die Auswirkungen vollständig erfasst zu haben. Wir ertappen uns dabei, dass wir uns fragen, ob das Gelesene oder Gehörte die ganze Wahrheit, die halbe Wahrheit oder reine Erfindung ist. Dieser Doppeldeutigkeit kommt in einem intellektuellen Kontext – Barthes-Nachfolge, Derrida und Foucault –, welcher der Gegenwart eines Autors skeptisch begegnet, eine besondere Wirkung zu. Indem Landers offensichtlich die Strategie einer vollständigen Enthüllung verfolgt, setzt er sich durch die vielen Dinge, die er verbreitet, nicht nur über die Etikette der Kunstwelt hinweg, er bringt auch ihre philosophischen Koordinaten in Unordnung.

Die Darbietungen aus seinem Gefühlsleben wirken so realistisch, dass wir uns plötzlich fragen, ob wir der wirklichen Sache begegnen – d. h. dem Aussenseiter oder ‚idiot savant', dessen unübersehbare Talente von der Kunstwelt vereinnahmt wurden (I'M A CLOWN IN A WORLD OF CHIMPS scheint mit diesem Gedanken zu spielen). Wenn wir jedoch zwischen den Zeilen lesen, können wir allmählich entdecken, dass diese Spiele von einem kulturerfahrenen Menschen gespielt werden, der sich mit den Regeln der Kunstwelt gut auskennt. Es ist nicht die Transgression als solche, die Landers einzigartig macht – die Kunst der neunziger Jahre ist besonders für Transgression bekannt. Was seine Praxis einzigartig macht, ist die Tatsache, dass er den Eindruck aufrechtzuerhalten vermag, diese Grenzüberschreitungen geschähen unwillkürlich – dass er nicht umhinkönne, diese Aspekte seines Lebens in seine Kunst einfliessen zu lassen.

Es ist dieser performative Aspekt, der den zahlreichen, scheinbar widersprüchlichen Formen, die sein Schaffen angenommen hat, Kontinuität verleiht – Gemälde und Bronzeskulpturen auf der einen Seite, Textarbeiten und Videos auf der anderen. Es ist auch das, was seine Arbeiten zu den reizvollsten und unterhaltsamsten Kunstwerken der letzten fünfzehn Jahre gehören lässt. In Landers' Fall tragen diese Eigenschaften zur Komplexität der Arbeiten bei. Das Gelächter und die Anteilnahme, die sie hervorrufen, behindern und vereiteln unseren Willen und unsere Fähigkeit, die Praxis als Ganzes zu deuten. Ihrer Performativität sind wir nicht gewachsen: Das Werk ist immer zwei oder drei Schritte unserer Fähigkeit voraus, sie zu verarbeiten. Wir ertappen uns dabei, wie wir unsere kritische Wachsamkeit einstellen. Es ist sein Publikum, nicht so sehr Sean Landers selbst, welches zu ‚glücklichen Opfern' seiner ‚Scharade' wird, zumindest vorübergehend.

Bruce Naumans frühe Videos zeigen, wie Kunst aussehen kann, wenn das Objekt entfernt wird: Wir werden mit dem Künstler in seinem Atelier allein gelassen, ein Bild, das ebenso tiefsinnig wie absurd ist. Aller landläufigen Begriffe des Kunstschaffens entledigt, sehen wir Nauman am Nullpunkt des schöpferischen Akts, darauf reduziert, Bälle zu dribbeln, den Raum in einem exakten Quadrat zu durchschreiten und andere offensichtlich nutzlose Aufgaben zu verrichten. Der Kunstgegenstände beraubt, verliert Naumans Atelier seine Definition und wird während des Vorgangs unendlich – eine Art Universum. Gleichzeitig ist sein Atelier eine Gefängniszelle – wozu ist denn schon ein Atelier gut, wenn man dort keine Objekte schaffen wird? Hier festgesetzt, offensichtlich ohne Zweck und Ziel, schlägt Nauman die Zeit tot, wie wir uns das von einem Gefangenen vorstellen, und unterstellt, wie Samuel Beckett und Franz Kafka vor ihm, dass die Berufung der Avantgarde eine lebenslängliche Verurteilung impliziert.

Während Naumans Atelier praktisch leer ist, befindet sich in ANYONE'S ORGASM (1992) in Landers' Atelier eine Fülle von Kunstmaterial, dazu ein oder zwei angefangene Arbeiten: eine Art Kopf vielleicht, auf einem Sockel, aus Ton gefertigt, verhüllt, und eine riesige Textarbeit, auf einem Bogen Papier, welche die ganze Wand einnimmt. Ihr Vorhandensein genügt, um den Status seiner Handlungen im Film zu problematisieren. Während der Sinnlosigkeit von Naumans Aktionen konzeptuell und existenziell eine tiefere Bedeutung unterstellt werden kann, wie zufällig sie auch erscheinen mögen, macht uns Landers die Entscheidung sehr viel schwerer, ob die Sinnlosigkeit seiner Handlungen irgendeinen Sinn ergeben könnte. Dieses Problem wird das eine Mal besonders deutlich, wenn wir ihn bei der Arbeit an seinem Textgemälde sehen. Was sollen wir angesichts dieser kurzen Sequenz von den Handlungen halten, die den Rest des sechzigminütigen Videos einnehmen – den Monologen, dem Singen, dem Tanzen, den Grimassen? Jede einzelne dieser Handlungen, über die volle Dauer aufrechterhalten würde vielleicht nur an Videoaufzeichnungen von Performances der siebziger Jahre (Vito Acconci, John Baldessari, Paul McCarthy, Andy Warhol oder William Wegman zum Beispiel) erinnern, aber zusammen in einem Film und offenbar nach Lust und Laune durchgeführt, scheinen sie das Verhalten eines Künstler zu zeigen, der ernsthafte Motivationsprobleme hat. Statt den Kunstgegenstand zu entmaterialisieren, erweckt Landers den Eindruck, dass er offenbar nicht dazu kommt, die Materialisierung in Gang zu bringen. Seine Tätigkeiten fordern dazu heraus, als Ablenkungsmanöver eines trägen Zauderers ausgelegt zu werden. Nauman, Beckett und Kafka kommen in den Sinn, aber auch die Aufmerksamkeit heischenden Dummköpfe von Realityshows, die heute unsere Fernsehprogramme füllen. Wir sind in ein interpretatorisches Dilemma geraten.

Der ständige Radiolärm hilft nicht. Während wir wissen, dass die meiste Kunst zu Hintergrundgeräuschen irgendwelcher Art gemacht wird, kann ich mich, abgesehen von ANYONE'S ORGASM, an kein Kunstwerk erinnern, das dem Radio ein solches Gewicht gäbe. Die Bedeutung, die es in dieser Arbeit gewinnt, lässt vermuten, Landers wisse nicht, was es bedeutet, Videokunst zu machen, denn jeder andere Künstler würde zuallererst das Radio ausschalten, sobald die Kamera läuft. Es trägt auch dazu bei, dass wir den Eindruck gewinnen, wir sähen nicht die Dokumentation einer Performance, sondern würden Zeugen einer Phase des Leerlaufs des Künstlers – der Teile, die wir nicht sehen sollten, der Teile, die alle anderen Künstler aus ihrer Arbeit eliminieren würden. Indem uns Landers das ‚Leben' um die ‚Kunst' herum zeigt, bringt er genau dann, als wir dachten, das Problem hätte sich im Zuge der ‚entmaterialisierten' Praktiken der sechziger und siebziger Jahre erledigt, eine neue Ebene der Ungewissheit ein. Ironischerweise erreicht das Landers, indem er die traditionellen Medien (den Tonkopf und das Gemälde an der Wand) wieder in den Mittelpunkt stellt.

Vielleicht könnte man argumentieren, das Radio mache in ANYONE'S ORGASM das, was die Paletten, Staffeleien und Modelle in den reflexiven Kompositionen von Picasso, Matisse und Braque machen. Vielleicht sind sie die Weiterführung der Kaffeedosen und Pinsel, die Jasper Johns in Bronze gegossen hat. Das zu behaupten, wird schwieriger, wenn wir hören, was sich Landers anhört. Während wir uns vielleicht gern vorstellen würden, Pollock höre Charlie Parker, Rauschenberg John Cage, die britischen Pop-Künstler hörten die Beatles und so fort, ist bei Landers Softrock angesagt, eine Assoziation, die er verwendet, um unser Gefühl für die Achtbarkeit der Kunst zu verletzen. „Ich will wissen, was Liebe ist / du sollst es mir zeigen", „Ich will wissen / hast du schon einmal den Regen gesehen?", „Bleib nie zwischen dem Mond und New York City hängen", „Der Albatros und der Wal sind meine Brüder" und anderer lächerlicher Pomp wabern durch sein Atelier, stimulieren und begleiten seine Tätigkeiten in ANYONE'S ORGASM. Das Singen, Tanzen und Grimassieren vor der Kamera geschieht, als wolle er vor Freunden – sehr guten Freunden – prahlen und nicht etwa um die Gunst der Galeriebesucher buhlen, ein Eindruck, der die sakrosankten weissen Räume, in denen es gezeigt wird, zu verhöhnen scheint. Wenn er singt, nimmt er einen grotesken Schnulzenton an, wie in einer grässlichen Klubdarbietung, oder er präsentiert einen heiligen Singsang, als feiere er die Eucharistie. Verschiedentlich wiederholt er eine Phrase immer wieder, als identifiziere er sich mit Empfindungen, die Passagen in seiner Prosa ähneln, in denen er sich selbst parodiert, oder als imitiere er einen Teenager, der einen Komponisten der Avantgarde imitiert, der einen Popsong verstümmelt. Wenn er mit der Interferenz zwischen den Rundfunksendern spielt, ist seinen Grimassen zu entnehmen, dass er weiss, dass wir wissen, dass er weiss, dass er sich einem Experiment gemäss landläufiger Meinung hingibt, statt sich der eigentlichen Sache zu widmen.

Damit spielt Landers mit der Vorstellung, er könnte jemand sein, der einfach nur macht, was von ihm erwartet wird, statt sich zu bemühen, einen eigenen künstlerischen Weg zu entwickeln. Das Atelier in seinen Videos symbolisiert nicht die neue Grenze der Kunst. Stattdessen unterstellt Landers offensichtlich, dass er dort ist, weil man es von ihm vermutet, als wollte er sagen: „Was soll ich eurer Meinung nach sonst machen, nachdem ich jetzt den Master of Fine Arts habe?" Wenn wir seine Videos sehen, haben wir immer das Gefühl, der Zauberbann seiner Kreativität werde, so fragil, wie er ist, gleich durch einen Künstlerkollegen von nebenan gebrochen, der ein bisschen Zucker bei ihm borgen will, oder durch den Anruf eines Gläubigers, der einer verspäteten Rate für die Rückzahlung des Studiendarlehens nachjagt. Indem er einen Schimpansen (wie in Fernsehreklamen oder Familienfilmen als Mensch gekleidet) mietet und ihn im Atelier eine halbe Stunde frei herumlaufen lässt, unterstellt Landers mit Absicht, er wolle unabsichtlich damit sagen, dass der Affe diese vier Wände vielleicht besser zu nutzen wisse als er selbst. SINGERIE: LE PEINTRE (1995) ähnelt einem Video von Bruce Nauman im Schnellvorlauf: Der liebenswerte Körper des Primaten surft auf einem Skateboard, saust Stehleitern hinauf und hinunter und sprintet von einem Ende des Raums zum anderen, von einem Soundtrack begleitet, der im Wechsel zwischen gefühlvollen und beschwingten Klängen MOON RIVER und das Thema von MISSION IMPOSSIBLE enthält.

Würden wir uns auf die Hinweise verlassen, die Landers auf andere Künstler gibt, er wäre an den Vertretern der jüngsten Avantgarde wohl nicht besonders interessiert. Während Künstler wie Warhol und Nauman Rollenvorbilder für Landers' Generation waren, reichen seine zahlreichen Huldigungen an andere Künstler in eine Zeit zurück, als die Kunst noch nicht die Formen angenommen hatte, die viele seiner Werke heute annehmen. Eine besondere Bedeutung erhält dabei der performative Aspekt seiner Arbeit, die Tatsache, dass er einfach deshalb schreibt, Performances und Videos macht, weil es das ist, was ein Künstler der neunziger Jahre tut, ebenso wie von ihm erwartet wird, dass er in Manhattan einen weiss getünchten Loft mietet und in Chelsea zu Galerieeröffnungen geht. Selbst dann, wenn seine Videos früheren Performances äusserst nahe kommen, erheben sie den Anspruch, sich in erlesener Gesellschaft zu befinden. REMISSIONEM PECCATORUM (1994) und ITALIAN HIGH RENAISSANCE AND BAROQUE SCULPTURE (1993) erinnern an die bravourösen Dauerbelastungstests, denen sich Marina Abramovic und Vito Acconci vor der Kamera gestellt haben, doch die Posen sind so angelegt, dass sie an Michelangelo und Bernini denken lassen. Das Ergebnis der Verschmelzung ist ein Bild des Künstlers als Narzisst, der als seine eigene Muse erscheint – mehr Morrissey, würde er jemals nackt auf der Bühne auftreten, als ‚Sterbender Sklave' oder Masochist der Avantgarde. Statt die Kunstgeschichte einfach zu zitieren, wie es viele Postmodernisten der ersten Generation in den achtziger Jahren taten, eignet sich Landers die Verweise buchstäblich an.

Mit Ausnahme einer Gruppe von Gemälden, die Clowns, nackte Hippies, Ausserirdische, Roboter und rosa Kaninchen in verschiedenen Landschaften zeigen, sind fast alle Bilder von Landers, auf denen keine Schrift erscheint, Pasticcios berühmter historischer Kunstwerke oder Portraits grosser Künstler. Erstere umfassen Bildfolgen von William Hogarth und Pablo Picasso. Letztere kommen in zweierlei Gestalt daher: berühmte Künstler als Geister ihrer selbst und berühmte Künstler in verschiedenen Verkleidungen. Beide sind Portraits von ‚modernen Meistern', wie sie von populärwissenschaftlichen Verlagen genannt werden, aus einer Epoche, auf die sich zeitgenössische Künstler selten beziehen.

GHOST 1 (ERNST), GHOST 2 (DUCHAMP) und GHOST 3 (PICABIA) (alle 2003) ähneln Grisaillen, alten Fotografien und Gespenstern. Insgesamt ist diese Serie eine Séance, deren Zeugen wir als Betrachter werden oder der wir implizit beiwohnen: Landers versucht, die Geister seiner Ahnen durch Öl auf Leinwand zu kanalisieren, ein Medium, das seitdem angeblich selbst gestorben ist. Damit ist die Verwendung dieses Mediums, bei der Landers den Kontext der Ausstellung gedanklich einbezieht, ebenso performativ wie seine Videos – eine vermittelnde Funktion, die ein Gemälde selten hat.

Schwieriger lässt sich bestimmen, was Landers mit den übrigen Portraits beabsichtigt, die mit Clownfarben bemalte Gesichter und eine protzige Kostümierung zeigen. Warum ist Dalí ein König, Braque ein Elf, De Chirico ein Wikinger, Ernst ein Teufel und Picasso ein Soldat aus dem amerikanischen Bürgerkrieg? Und warum treten sie, mit Ausnahme von Dalí, überhaupt in Kostümen auf? Das Entscheidende bei diesen Künstlern und was sie für Landers vermutlich so reizvoll macht, ist ihre Einzigartigkeit, die sie verkörpern. Warum dann die Uniformen? Warum die augenfälligen, doch wohl unpassenden Personifizierungen? Obwohl wir alles wieder erkennen, was wir sehen, gelingt es Landers, Bilder zu malen, die sich einer Kategorisierung entziehen und rätselhaft bleiben.

So gut wie alle modernen Meister in Landers' Galerie hatten mit dem Surrealismus zu tun. Seine Version des Surrealen hingegen wirkt, als hätte sie absichtlich das Ziel verfehlt. Statt bizarr zu sein, sehen seine ‚Meister' einfach nur sonderbar aus, wie Damen aus der Pantomime in den falschen Kostümen. Landers' übrige Unternehmungen in Sachen Surrealismus erscheinen ähnlich gekünstelt. Die Schimpansen, Clowns, Ausserirdischen, Roboter, Häschen und nackten Hippies, die seine erste, schriftlose Bilderfolge bevölkern, waren als Gattung bereits vorhanden, bevor Landers zu ihnen kam. Trotz einiger Hintergründe, die auf die Romantik zurückgreifen, erwecken die leicht anachronistischen Figuren, die auf diesen Bildern auftauchen, den Eindruck, als seien sie aus der wohligen Welt der Unterhaltung im Nachkriegsamerika entlaufen: aus Disney-Animationen, Familienserien, Freizeitparks und Bilderbüchern. Seine Ausserirdischen sind natürlich grüne Eierköpfe, während seine Roboter so schäbig aussehen, als hätten sie die Kehrseite der fünfziger Jahre oder die Yellow Brick Road nie zu Gesicht bekommen. Ihr Auftauchen in seiner Kunst lässt an einen Kopf denken, der mit abgegriffenen Kulturhäppchen so sehr vollgestopft ist, dass er es nicht fertigbringt, eigene und in ihrer Eigenart überzeugende Figuren auf die Beine zu stellen.

Dieser Vorwurf lässt sich bei anderen Werken nicht so leicht erheben. Eine kürzlich gefertigte Folge von Bronzebüsten anthropomorpher Tiere könnte der exzentrischen und aus den Angeln geratenen viktorianischen Phantasie von Lewis Carroll oder Edward Lear entsprungen sein, wären diese Autoren im Amerika des 21. Jahrhunderts neu anzusiedeln: FOOTBALL DUCK (2003) ist, wie der Titel vermuten lässt, eine Ente, deren Kopf wie ein amerikanischer Fussball geformt ist, während der Kopf von PEANUT HEAD (2003) tatsächlich auf der Schale von Erdnüssen modelliert wurde. Eine Folge figurativer Gemälde mit Schrift, zwischen 1998 und 2000 entstanden, zeigt Mutanten aller Art – darunter einen traurigen Mann mit beginnender Glatze und drei herabhängenden roten Nasen (THREE NOSE GUY, 1998), einen Mann mit erigiertem Penis als Nase und riesigen Hoden als Kinn (LE DOMAINE

ENCHANTÉ AKA MONSIEUR SAUCISSON, 1999) und eine Frau mit Gesichtern von Teddybären auf der Brust und Bäumen dort, wo ihr Kopf, linker Arm und ihre Taille zu sein hätten (APOLLO AND DAPHNE, 1999). Doch schaudert uns nicht beim Anblick dieser anatomischen Verirrungen, wie wir vielleicht erschrecken würden angesichts einer seltsamen Kreatur in einem surrealistischen Bild. Statt einen traumartigen Eindruck zu erwecken, sehen sie aus, als seien sie zu dem Zweck ersonnen, wie Ausbaggerungen aus dem Unbewussten zu wirken: Die Hybridisierung wurde forciert, die sexuellen Anspielungen sind zu absurden Klischees übersteigert und die symbolischen Rollen der Figuren allzu offenkundig. Diese Merkmale lassen ihren Autor zu einer in gewissem Sinne fiktiven Gestalt werden. Wir empfinden diese Bilder als Werke eines Sonntagsmalers, der auf eine landläufige Vorstellung abzielt, wie Surrealismus auszusehen habe, gefiltert durch direktere Einflüsse wie B-Movies und Softporno. Die technische Raffinesse verschiedener dieser Werke – das unpassend schöne Tiepolosche Licht zum Beispiel, das Monsieur Saucisson und die Brust, auf der er steht, umhüllt – macht den Abgrund deutlich, der sich zwischen diesem fiktiven Schöpfer und dem Künstler auftut, der seine Identität annimmt. Die Wirkung ist wieder ähnlich wie in modernistischen Romanen, deren Autoren ‚unzuverlässige' Erzähler verwenden.

Die Kombination von Schrift und Bild auf diesen Gemälden wirkt ganz besonders verfehlt: Aus avantgardistischer Sicht galt figurative Malerei unter Künstlern, die Text verwendeten, als obsolet; unter dem Blickwinkel der westlichen Tradition würde Geschriebenes auf dem Gemälde die illusionistische Kohärenz des Dargestellten durcheinander geraten lassen. Die in literarischen Werken berühmter Künstler auftauchenden Illustrationen sind die engsten Vorfahren dieser Gemälde. Bei Landers' Arbeiten sind allerdings Schrift und Bild auf derselben Leinwand miteinander verschmolzen, was ihre grundsätzliche Unvereinbarkeit verstärkt. Oft aber hat das bildlich Dargestellte mit dem Thema des Geschriebenen in seiner Umgebung nicht viel mehr zu tun als die traditionellen Schilder an englischen Pubs mit den Unterhaltungen, die sich drinnen ergeben. Bei einigen gibt Landers in der linken oberen Ecke einen knappen Hinweis auf Bild und Titel und ignoriert dann beides im restlichen Text, als sei der sprichwörtliche Elefant im Porzellanladen, über den keiner redet. BUBBLE BOY (1998) zum Beispiel beginnt: „Mir ist, als malte ich ein Bild von einem Jungen der siebziger Jahre, der keine Arme und fülliges Haar hat und eine Blase bläst, während er auf einem Hügel sitzt und mit leerem Blick ins Weite starrt [sic]. Voilà." (Danke Sean.) Abgesehen von ein paar erneuten kurzen Auftritten, erhält BUBBLE BOY keinen Einblick in die komisch-trübseligen Monologe, die sich anschliessen, und wir werden auch nicht schlauer. Stattdessen lässt sich Landers über die Nachwelt aus: wieviel besser es sei, lebendig statt tot zu sein; wie er von den Kritikern Haue bekam, als er in Ausstellungen davor mit der ‚Masche' aufhörte, auf seinen Bildern zu schreiben; wie er wieder damit angefangen habe, weil das bedeutet, dass seine Bilder sich verkaufen; wie ihn als Folge davon sein Händler wieder mag; wie grossartig genau dieses Bild sei; warum wir es wirklich kaufen sollten, wenn wir es uns leisten könnten, damit er und seine Familie sich ein besseres Leben machen können. Es lässt sich schwer vorstellen, was das mit BUBBLE BOY zu tun haben soll oder mit anderen Kreationen aus dieser Folge – PLANK BOY (2000), CAREER EGO (1999), THE BOOBY (1998) u.a. – was natürlich genau der Punkt ist.

Die Bilder auf diesen Gemälden funktionieren in gleicher Weise wie Themen in den Nummern vieler Stegreifkomödien. Landers über Landers als Entertainer: „Die Leute meinen, ich wäre ein verdammter Komödiant. Hei, ich bin um Gottes willen ein ernst zu nehmender Künstler, seht euch dieses Bild an... Okay dieses Bild ist kein gutes Beispiel, aber ich habe vorher jede Menge ernsthafte Kunst gemacht, stimmt's?" (FOOTBALL DUCK, 1998). Eine solche Nummer mag den Anschein erwecken, es ginge um die Erfahrungen eines Komikers beim Trampen, irgendeine Heimfahrt im Bus oder die einzelnen Vorzüge der verschiedenen Hilfsdienste,[2] aber diese prosaischen Themen bieten nur den Vorwand für eine Fülle wilder Abschweifungen. Gelegentlich kommt das Thema wieder in den Blick, als sei dem Komiker oder der Komikerin gerade wieder eingefallen, worum es eigentlich gehen sollte. Der Effekt dieser ‚Fehler' ist, dass wir dem nichtlinearen Verlauf dieser Gedanken folgen. Gewöhnlich ist natürlich das meiste dessen, was freie Assoziation zu sein scheint, vorher schriftlich ausgearbeitet worden. Wenn das Skript gut ist, dann ist die Wirkung erstaunlich, so als sähen wir einen Film über die Funktionsweise des Gehirns, was unser Eindruck ist, wenn wir [SIC] lesen. Weil eine Stegreifkomödie in Echtzeit vor uns abläuft, sind wir nicht sicher, ob wir eine wirkliche freie Assoziation erleben oder ihre Darstellung.

2
Die Themen dreier Nummern, die ich kürzlich gesehen habe.

Viele modernistische Autoren verfolgten in ihrer Literatur ebenfalls das Ziel, den Fluss der Bewusstseinsvorgänge realistisch darzustellen. Keiner hat jedoch Lawrence Sterne übertroffen, dessen neun Bände seines Romans THE LIFE AND OPINIONS OF TRISTRAM SHANDY, GENTLEMAN [dt. Titel: Leben und Meinungen des Herrn T.S.] zwischen 1759 und 1767 erschienen, kurz nach der grossen Zeit von William Hogarth und der englischen Satireliteratur (John Dryden, Alexander Pope, Jonathan Swift u.a.), und mit denen er seine zeitgenössischen Leser ebenso amüsierte wie verwirrte. Wie TRISTRAM SHANDY zeigt, vollzieht sich Bewusstsein in unendlichen Abschweifungen und behindert den Weg, den der Romanautor vermutlich einschlagen wird. Folglich bleibt der offenkundige Held des Buchs, Tristram, die ersten beiden Bände über im Uterus, während er sich über eine ganze Reihe von Themen auslässt, die mit Ereignissen in seinem Leben nichts zu tun haben. Am Ende wissen wir immer noch so gut wie nichts über ihn, dafür aber sehr viel über seine Geburtshelfer, die Predigten des Dorfpfarrers, den Fortgang der Feldzüge Williams in Flandern, die Onkel Toby mit seinem Handlanger Corporal Trim auf dem Bowlinggreen in Echtzeit pedantisch nachstellt, wir kennen die Einstellung französischer Katholiken zur vorgeburtlichen Kindtaufe, erfahren Einzelheiten über die Mathematik des Pythagoras und vieles mehr.

Was Sean Landers schreibt, vor allem in [SIC], ist ebenso ausschweifend und absurd wie TRISTRAM SHANDY, mit der Ausnahme, dass ‚Leben und Meinungen' bei ihm das konstante Thema dieser Abschweifungen bleiben. Mit der Hand geschrieben, ähneln sie gesprochener Sprache, da sie nicht redigiert werden können, es sei denn, Wörter würden im Text durchgestrichen. Unter diesem Aspekt ist [SIC] eine Performance von vorgegebener Länge – 1000 Seiten –, die er letzten Endes nicht erreicht, obwohl er sich droht, seine Mutter würde sterben, wenn es ihm nicht gelänge. Wie in TRISTRAM SHANDY, vielen Kabarettnummern und einer Menge seiner übrigen Werke enthält das Geschriebene unzählige Hinweise auf die zu erledigende Aufgabe, was er bisher geschrieben hat und wie die Reaktion des Lesers ausfallen mag:

> *Bis du dies in Grenoble lesen wirst, werde ich natürlich mit den tausend Seiten nicht fertig, ich sollte mir wohl irgendein Zeitlimit setzen. Sagen wir bis zum Datum meiner Eröffnung in der Andrea Rosen Gallery im Sept. oder Oktober 1993, wenn meine 1000 Seiten bis dahin nicht fertig sind, wird der Gangster meine Mutter umbringen und ich bin schuld. Der Herr steh mir bei und wegen meiner Mutter lass mich keine Schreibblockade kriegen. Scheisse. Noch 992 Seiten. Vielleicht hab ich mir da zuviel vorgenommen. 1000 ist nämlich eine Menge Zeug das wird ungefähr so lang wie Schuld und Sühne, vermutlich auch ungefähr genauso wichtig für die Literatur [sic].*[3]

3
Sean Landers, *[sic]*, Puclisfear Press, New York 1993; Riverhead Books, New York 1995, S. 8 f.

Die performative und reflexive Art der Darstellung findet bei Sterne in zahlreichen Passagen ein Echo:

> *Ich will diesen Satz nicht beenden, ohne vorher eine Bemerkung über das seltsame Verhältnis zwischen dem Leser und mir zu machen [...]. Ich bin diesen Monat ein ganzes Jahr älter, als ich heute vor zwölf Monaten war; und da ich in dieser Zeit, wie Sie sehen, fast bis in die Mitte meines vierten Bandes – und doch nicht weiter als bis zu meinem ersten Lebenstag – gekommen bin, zeigt das deutlich, dass ich jetzt dreihundertvierundsechzig Tage mehr von meinem Leben schreiben muss als damals, als ich anfing [...] bei diesem Tempo würde ich eben 364mal schneller leben als schreiben – Daraus folgt doch, bitte sehr, verehrter Leser, dass ich, je mehr ich schreibe, desto mehr werde schreiben müssen – und dass folglich der verehrte Leser, je mehr der verehrte Leser liest, desto mehr wird lesen müssen.*[4]

4
Lawrence Sterne, *The Life and Opinions of Tristram Shandy, Gentleman*, Oxford University Press, 1993, S. 228 f.

Während das, was Landers in [SIC] und auf seinen frühen Bildern schreibt, eher unvermittelt dem Bewusstseinsstrom folgt, scheint er sich mit dem Geschriebenen auf den Gemälden aus jüngerer Zeit in zunehmendem Masse selbst zu parodieren: „He, ich bin der Typ, der auf seinen Bildern schreibt. Billige keine Imitationen. Vor allem keine englischen." (FOOTBALL DUCK). Landers mimt Landers so bewusst, wie er Hogarth und Picasso gemimt hat. Auf seinen jüngsten Gemälden erscheinen kurze, melodramatische Wortfügungen oder einzelne Wörter, die dem entnommen sind, was wir als sein Lexikon kennengelernt haben: „Meisterwerk", „zynisch", „macht mich kaputt", „Quälerei", „nachgeben", „mein Werk wird besser wegkommen, wenn ich tot bin", „ich weiss, dass ich sehr viel gearbeitet habe, ich hab es wirklich versucht" auf dem Bild THERE WAS A TIME... (2004) und „ich weiss, dass ich toll bin", „manchmal bin ich Scheisse", „ich habe ein grösseres Spektrum und mehr Talent als sonst wer" auf IT'S UP TO YOU (2003). Jedes Wort und jedes Satzfragment wird wiederholt, als wäre es das Echo seines früheren Werks, als litte ihr Autor unter Wiederholungszwang, als biete uns Landers die Aussicht, das Ungeheuer geworden zu sein, das er geschaffen hat.

Die bronzene ‚Verschwörung der Idioten', welche die Gemälde begleitet, erinnert an keine Geringeren als Rembrandt, Narziss, Sisyphos, Ikarus und Minotaurus, wie in seiner eigenen triumphalen Besprechung der Ausstellung in FRIEZE[5] zu lesen ist. Sie sind „seine Nachkommen für seine Nachkommen", „respektlose Kreaturen der Phantasie", zu dem Zweck geschaffen, „seine Kinder zu unterhalten". Schliesslich seien sie trotz ihrer Kaninchenohren, der Reptilienhaut, des Elefantenrüssels und der Walrosszähne, behauptet er, nicht weniger ‚Sean Landers' als der Landers, den wir aus seinen scheinbar unverhüllten Monologen kennen. Von sich selbst in der dritten Person sprechend, als „Ich ist ein anderer" (Arthur Rimbaud), beendet Landers die Kritik nebst Nachruf mit den Worten: „Und schliesslich sind sie ein Zeugnis seiner Performance auf dieser Bühne, eines, das zuweilen durch Täuschung und Phantasie entstellt und gelegentlich durch Fiktion mit einem Feigenblatt verhangen wird, aber letzten Endes ist das er. Er ist diese Person."

5
Sean Landers, „Sean Landers, Andrea Rosen Gallery, New York", *frieze*, Nr. 83, Mai 2004, S. 108 f.

Endlich einmal frei von den Ängsten, denen alle Künstler ausgeliefert sind, die aber keiner von ihnen, nicht einmal in Gedanken, in sein Werk aufzunehmen gewagt hat – „Warum habe ich zum Beispiel nie in einem amerikanischen Museum ausgestellt? Ich bin Amerikas bester Künstler und habe trotzdem nie eine grosse

Ausstellung gehabt" (I LIVED / MONKEY AND GNOME, 2000) –, entwirft er ein komisch-heroisches Bild von sich im Leben nach dem Tod, nach der Manier von Keats in Shelleys ADONAIS'-ELEGIE (1821), in der Gesellschaft der grossen toten Meister, fern der kleinlichen Bosheit der alltäglichen Kunstwelt.

Scheitern als Strategie – was man ‚sekundäres Scheitern' nennen könnte – verbindet Sean Landers mit vielen der übrigen sehr bedeutenden Künstler der letzten fünfzehn Jahre. Das Zeitgenössische an John Currins Porträts zum Beispiel ist den ‚Mängeln' zuzuschreiben die sichtbar werden, wenn man sie mit ihren kunsthistorischen Vergängern vergleicht. Das offenkundig Seichte vieler neokonzeptuellen Arbeiten von Martin Creed geht auf seine bange Frage zurück, ob er der Kunst oder der Welt irgendetwas Neues bieten könne. Maurizio Cattelan hat sich vom Arzt auf einem Attest bescheinigen lassen, dass er aus medizinischen Gründen mit einer Arbeit für eine Ausstellung nicht rechtzeitig fertig geworden ist, und bei der Polizei die Arbeit, die er nicht gemacht hat, als Diebstahl aus seinem Auto gemeldet. Carsten Höller hat ein Auto zu einem fahrbaren LABORATORY OF DOUBT (1999) umgebaut und mit einem Logo und einer Lautsprecheranlage ausgestattet. Das Werk allerdings blieb stumm, als er keine Möglichkeiten fand, Zweifel zu artikulieren.

Mike Kelley und Martin Kippenberger, zwei unmittelbare Vorläufer dieser Künstler, gelten seitdem als zwei der einflussreichsten Repräsentanten der achtziger Jahre. Zu einer Zeit, als Kunstwerke als Ikonen fungierten und die Künstler, die sie gemacht hatten, Stars waren, gab Kelley sich die Rolle eines Hausmeisters im Museum, und Kippenberger zeigte Fotografien von sich, nachdem er tüchtig zusammengeschlagen worden war. Kelley ist seitdem vor allem dafür bekannt geworden, dass er bescheidene Handwerkstechniken gegen Modernismus und Männlichkeit setzt, während einige der kraftvollsten Spätwerke Kippenbergers U-Bahn-Eingänge in normaler Grösse und unterschiedlichen Baustilen waren, die nirgendwohin führten.

Es ist bedeutsam, dass alle diese Künstler weiss und männlich sind und dass sie alle entweder aus den Vereinigten Staaten oder Westeuropa kommen. Seit Anfang der neunziger Jahre ist über Identität viel diskutiert worden, vor allem aus postkolonialer, postfeministischer und homosexueller Sicht. Gleichzeitig hat die Kunstwelt einen Prozess der Globalisierung durchlaufen, und Kuratoren haben sich eifrig bemüht, Kunstzentren in Lateinamerika, Afrika, Asien und Osteuropa ausfindig zu machen.

Während in Arbeiten, die sich auf diese Kontexte beziehen, Unterschiede gern gefeiert und Ungerechtigkeiten angeprangert werden, nähert sich Landers wie zum Beispiel auch Cattelan, Currin, Kelley und Kippenberger dem Problem der Identität auf eine völlig andere Weise. Da Landers und diese Künstler nicht von einer klaren Position des ‚Andersseins' aus agieren, haben ihre Mittel, Identität zu erforschen, mehr mit den ambivalenten und nuancierten Beziehungen zwischen dem Ich und der Gesellschaft zu tun als mit Fragen der Sichtbarkeit und Repräsentation. Identität im repräsentativen Sinne allerdings findet in Landers' Schaffen Eingang auf dem Weg über seine widersprüchlichen Gefühle im Hinblick auf seine kleinbürgerliche, katholische Erziehung, seine griechischen und irischen Wurzeln und seine Legasthenie, aber er unternimmt keinen Versuch, sich als Vertreter dieser Bevölkerungsgruppen anzubieten.

In vielerlei Hinsicht kann sein Projekt jedoch als parallel und fortschrittlich gelten, ungeachtet des schlechten Benehmens. In der Vergangenheit fühlten wenige weisse, heterosexuelle männliche Künstler das Bedürfnis, ihre eigene Beziehung zu der Art von Kunst, die sie machten, oder die Kontexte, in denen sie aufgenommen wurde, in Frage zu stellen – zumindest nicht in der Öffentlichkeit und nicht in ihren Arbeiten. Diese Unreflektiertheit erwuchs aus dem Gefühl, dass die Rolle als Künstler in ihrer Natur liege. Im Gegensatz dazu macht Landers seine Konflikte, Zweifel, Demütigungen und Ängste zum Thema seiner Arbeit. Selbst wenn der Ton der Werke eine Ausdrucksweise annimmt, die auf sein Genie abhebt, wissen wir, dass der Künstler hinter seiner Rolle weiss, dass es ein peinlicher Fauxpas ist und dass diese Proklamationen zu einer Zeit stattfinden, in welcher der Begriff in Misskredit geraten ist.

Wir wissen das, weil wir verstehen, dass Landers' Schilderung seines Gefühlslebens ebenso eine Performance ist, wie sie komisch ist. Damit steht sie in Beziehung zu offenkundigen Aspekten der Selbstdarstellung in den Werken von Cattelan, Kelley und Kippenberger und impliziten Aspekten der Selbstdarstellung bei Creed, Currin und Höller. Wie Landers schaffen diese Künstler ein Rollenverständnis in ihrem Werk, das oftmals spöttisch und selbstironisch ist: der grausame Witzbold (Cattelan), der wütende Halbwüchsige (Kelley), der gefühlsselige Zecher (Kippenberger), der Qualen Leidende (Creed), der Frauenjäger (Currin), der ein bisschen boshafte Wissenschaftler (Höller). In Landers' Arbeiten wird diese Inszenierung des Ichs in sehr viel mehr Richtungen und in sehr viel grösserem Mass weitergeführt. Während die Rollen dieser anderen Künstler leicht zu durchschauen sind, lässt sich viel schwieriger mit gewisser Sicherheit entscheiden, wofür MONSIEUR SAUCISSON und FOOTBALL DUCK stehen und in welchem Masse sie und Sean Landers austauschbar sind. Offenkundig haben sie rein äusserlich keine Ähnlichkeit mit dem Künstler, aber sind ihre Worte eine direkte Transkription seiner Gedanken im Augenblick des Schreibens, oder sind sie andererseits eigenständige Karikaturen von Sean Landers? Falls Letzteres, was ist dann mehr vorhanden: Fakt oder Fiktion? Selten sind wir bei der Betrachtung von Kunstwerken dergleichen verwirrenden Zweifeln ausgeliefert.

Humor hat oft sehr viel mit Performativität und ‚sekundärem Scheitern' zu tun. In Landers' Praxis reicht er weit tiefer als meist. Von Dada und Fluxus, einigen Surrealisten und Pop-Künstlern abgesehen, assoziieren wir Komik gewöhnlich nicht mit bildender Kunst. Normalerweise assoziieren wir sie mit Kunstformen, die das geschriebene oder gesprochene Wort beinhalten (Film, Theater, Romane), weil sich Komik sehr viel schwieriger durch Bilder, vor allem solche, die sich nicht bewegen, erreichen lässt. Landers' Arbeiten jedoch – besonders dann, aber nicht nur, wenn dabei geschrieben wird – geraten oft umwerfend komisch. Wie bei Woody Allens Filmen lachen wir plötzlich mit dem Künstler bei dem Bild SEAN LANDERS laut auf, das sich aus den schriftlichen Bekenntnissen, den Aktionen in seinen Videos und der Wahl der Figuren bei seinen Gemälden und Skulpturen aufbaut, während wir sie in uns aufnehmen.

Wie bei Woody Allen gehört auch bei Landers die Inszenierung des Ichs zu einem metafiktionalen Spiel. Wir sind uns die ganze Zeit über bewusst, dass er sowohl innerhalb als auch ausserhalb des Werkes als dessen Protagonist und gleichzeitig Autor agiert. Das bedeutet, dass uns immer klar ist, dass er sich in das Werk hinein – und aus ihm herausbegibt – sei es Malerei, Video oder Erinnertes –, so wie Allen den filmischen Rahmen buchstäblich betritt und verlässt, während er gleichzeitig Regie führt.

Das ist es, was Landers' Arbeiten von historischen Vorgängern unterscheidet, denen sie zu ähneln oder zu huldigen scheinen. Die Picasso-Gemälde sind dafür ein typisches Beispiel. Auf einem Bild fügen sich die picassoiden Formen zum Namenszug ‚Sean Landers', während sie auf einem anderen ‚Genius' buchstabieren. In dem Monolog, der sie begleitet, meditiert Landers auf komisch-heroische Art über die Beziehung zwischen diesem Nomen und dem Eigennamen. Als Parodien sind die Bilder von Natur aus gegen die Ansprüche resistent, die sein inszenierendes Ich zu seinen Gunsten geltend macht. Andererseits unterminiert der Soundtrack die Autonomie seiner Bilder und der berühmten Gemälde, auf denen sie basieren. Während Landers' Stimme zu hören ist und Holsts epische Musik in der Galerie erklingt, drohen seine Picasso-Gemälde der Autorität ihrer kompositorischen Virtuosität zum Trotz zu Requisiten innerhalb der Performance seiner ausgeklügelten Metafiktion zu werden.

Metafiktion steht in einer besonders widersprüchlichen Beziehung zum Surrealismus. Statt die Tiefen des Ichs auszuloten, behauptet sie, das Ich sei ein Konstrukt, wenn es in Kunstwerken zum Vorschein kommt. Portraitmalerei wäre, da sie zur Welt des Scheins gehört, die letzte Strategie, die ein Surrealist einsetzen würde, um das unbewusste Ich zum Ausdruck zu bringen. André Breton hätte Landers' Darstellungen seines Kreises nicht toleriert, was natürlich zu ihrer Ironie gehört. Auch hätte er auf seinen neosurrealistischen Bildern die absichtliche Absurdität der verschiedenen Entlehnungen aus der Pop-Kultur nicht geschätzt: die Ausserirdischen nachts in einem Ruderboot auf stürmischer See, der Schimpanse im Astronautenanzug an einer Staffelei auf einem Etwas, das wie der Mars aussieht, und so weiter.

Landers' Textarbeiten und auf Performances basierende Videos scheitern absichtlich auch in Bezug auf die Kriterien der konzeptuellen Kunst. Generell hatten diese Vorgänger in den sechziger und siebziger Jahren alles entfernt, was als subjektive Äusserung hätte aufgefasst werden können. Die Sprache bediente sich einer scheinwissenschaftlichen Objektivität, während der Körper des Künstlers als abstraktes Material behandelt wurde. Auf diese Weise machte die konzeptuelle Kunst das, was vor und nach dem Kunstobjekt kam, sowie die umgebenden Strukturen zum Inhalt des Werkes: den Körper des Künstlers, den Raum des Ateliers, die Politik des Ausstellungsraumes, die Welt ausserhalb dieser Räume, die zu ihrer Darstellung verwendeten Publikationen usw. Landers integriert viele dieser Kontexte in seine Arbeiten. Gleichzeitig hat er eine Vielfalt kontextuellen Materials, das von konzeptuellen Künstlern vernachlässigt wurde, in sein Werk aufgenommen, was den Eindruck erweckt, er habe die konzeptuelle Kunst falsch verstanden. Dieses Material gehört zu der subjektiven, emotionalen Sphäre und wird von allen Künstlern geteilt. Indem Sean Landers seine künstlerischen und beruflichen Höhen und Tiefen zum Thema seiner Arbeit macht, hat er nicht einfach nur einen aktuellen Kommentar zu seiner eigenen Praxis, sondern indirekt auch der jedes anderen Künstlers geliefert.

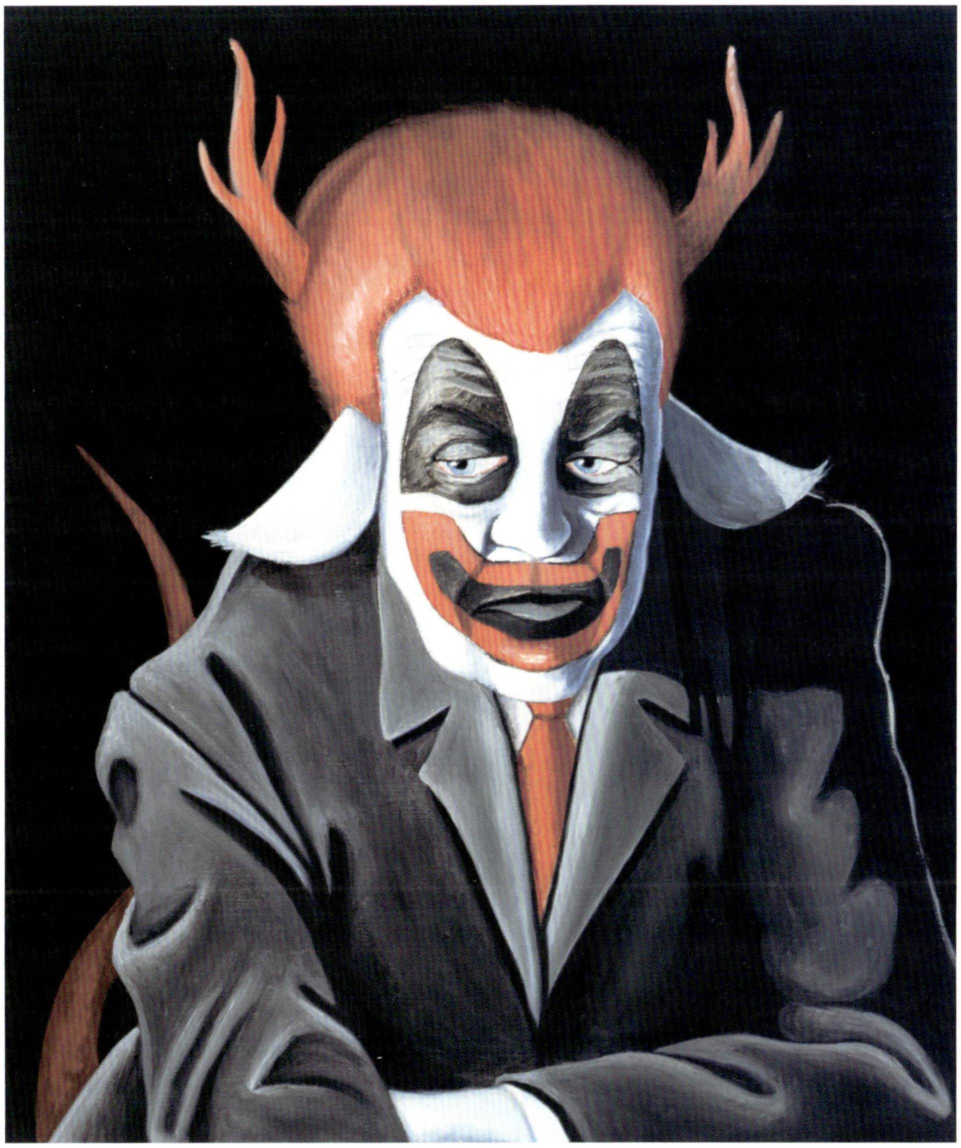

DEVIL (MAGRITTE), 2003
Oil on linen
78.74 × 68.58 cm

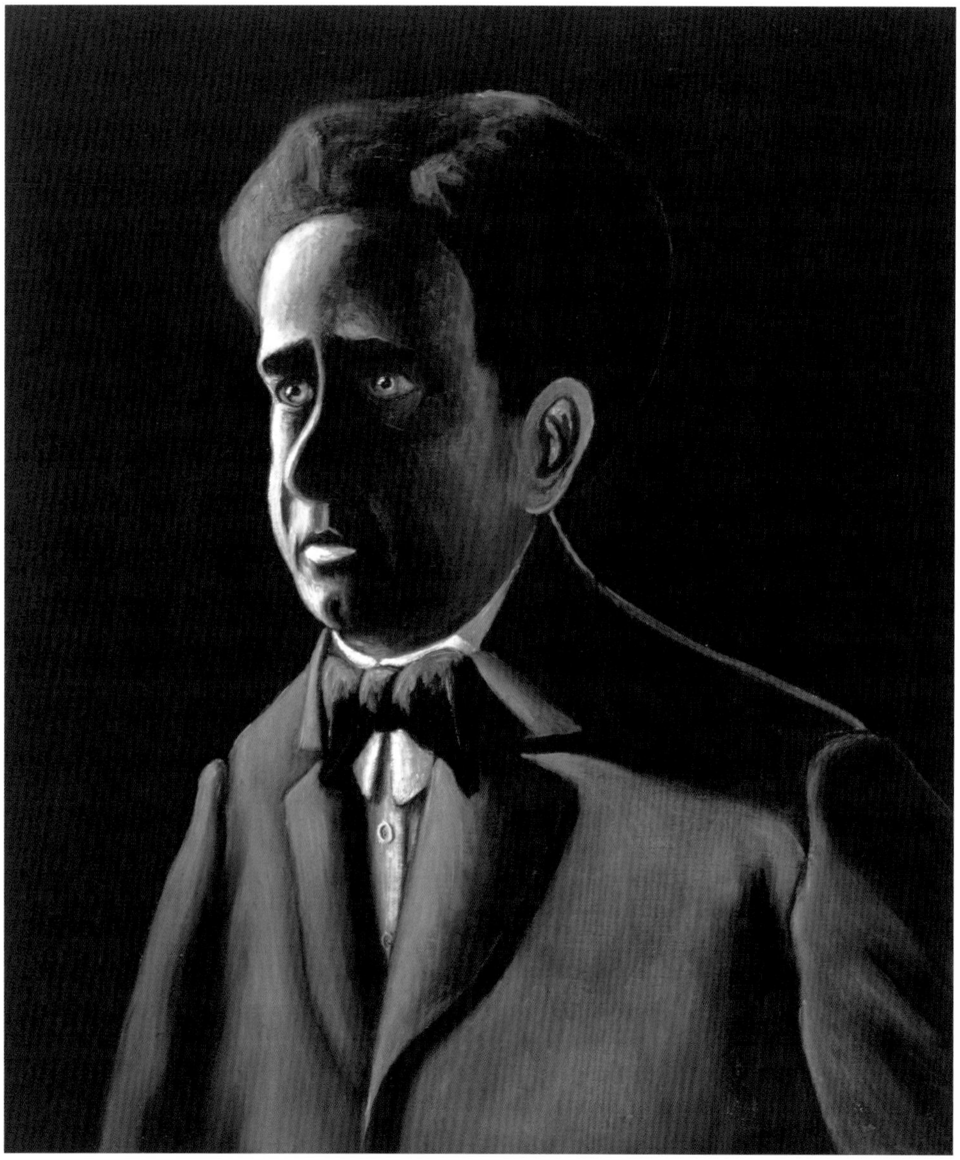

GHOST 3 (PICABIA), 2003
Oil on linen
71.12 × 60.96 cm

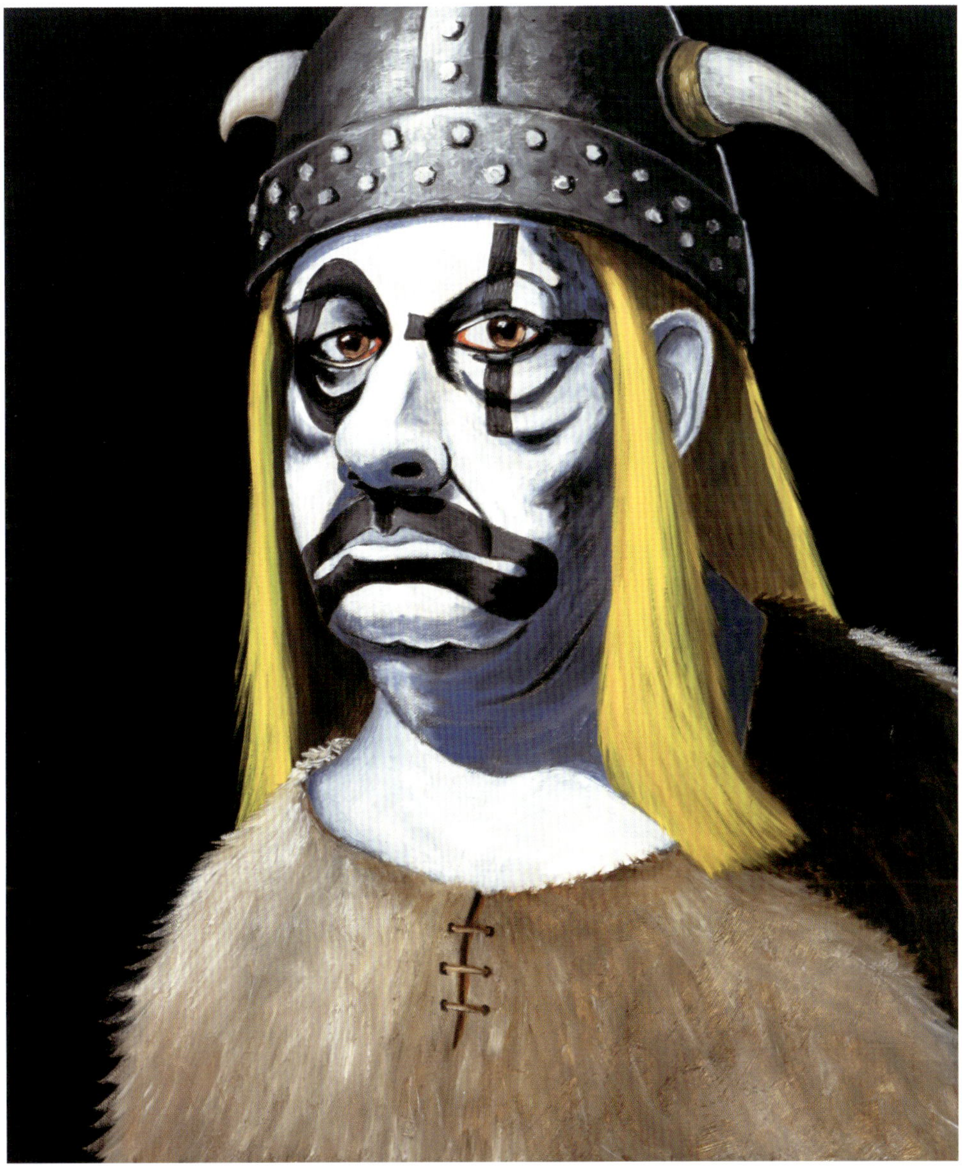

VIKING (DE CHIRICO), 2003
Oil on linen
68.58 × 58.42 cm

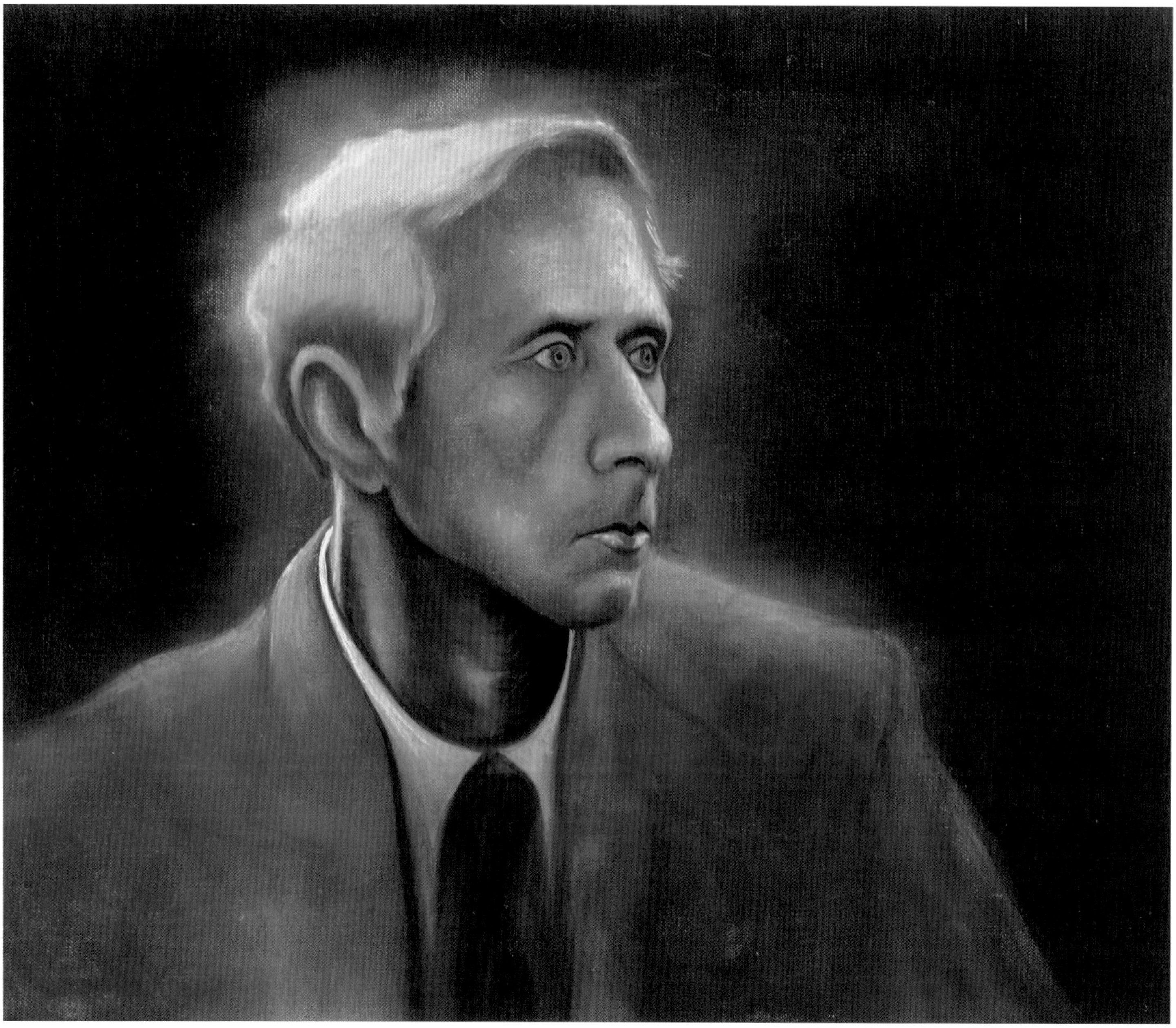

GHOST 1 (ERNST), 2003
Oil on linen
55.88 × 66.04 cm

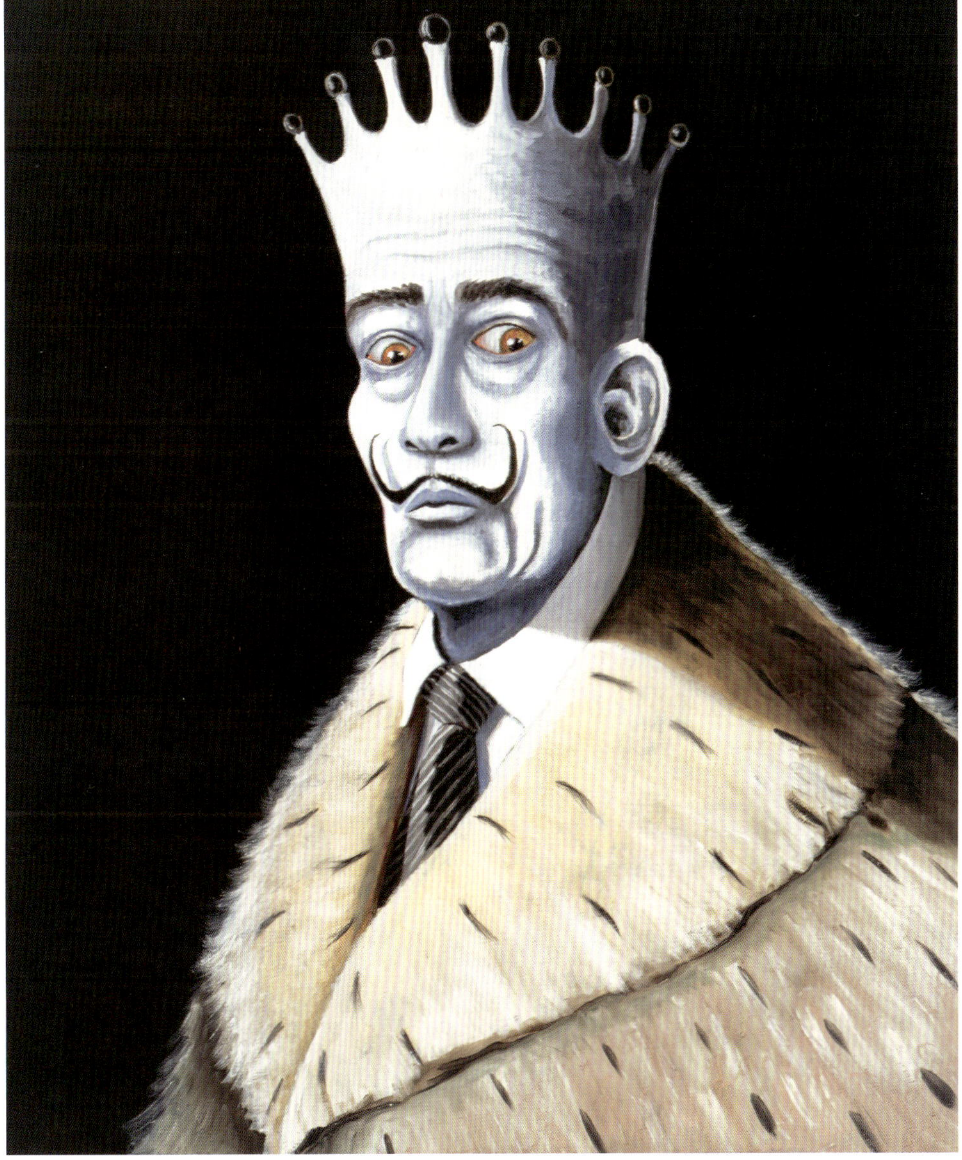

KING (DALÍ), 2003
Oil on linen
93.98 × 78.74 cm

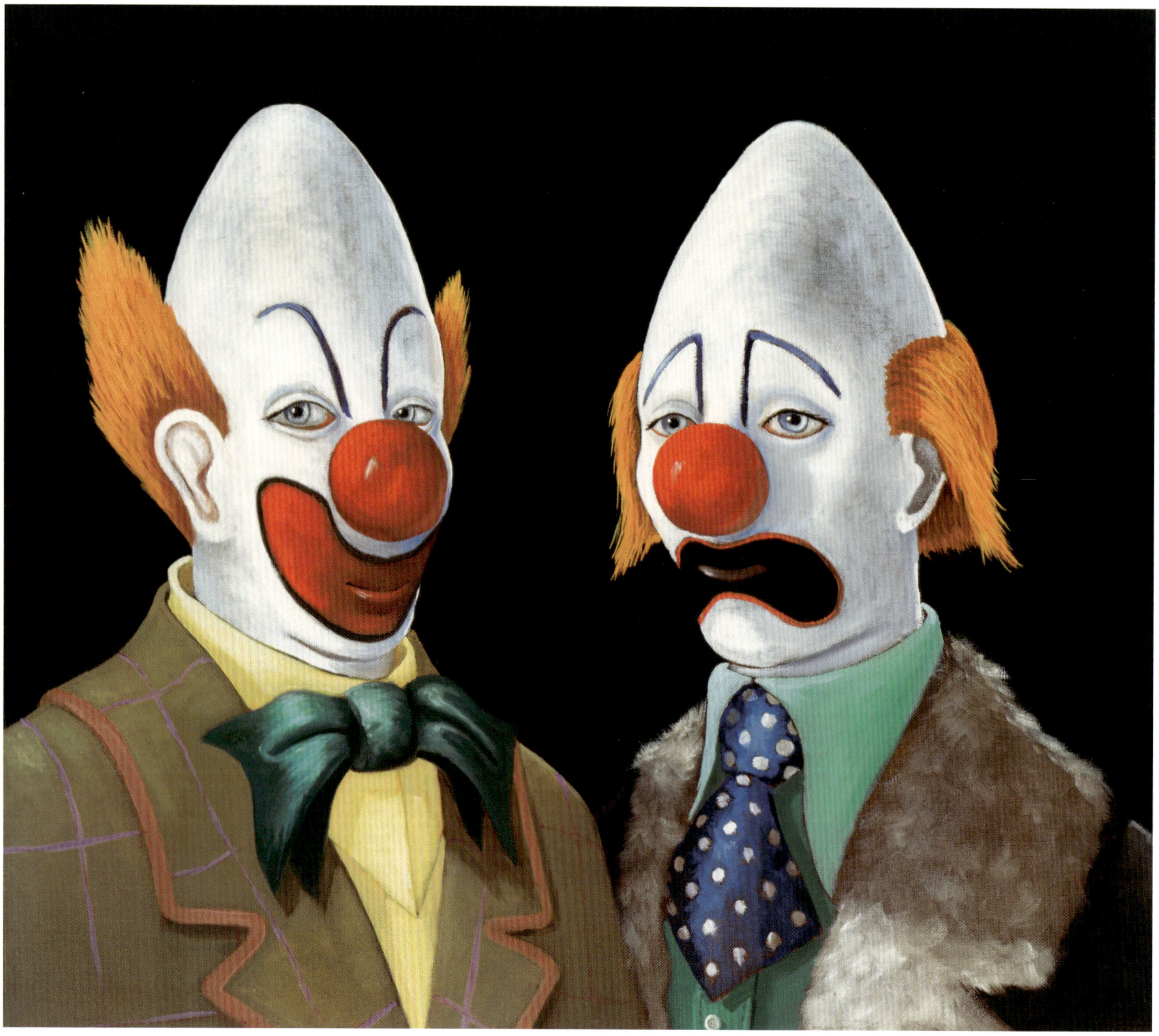

HAPPY AND SAD, 2002
Oil on linen
63.82 × 73.98 cm

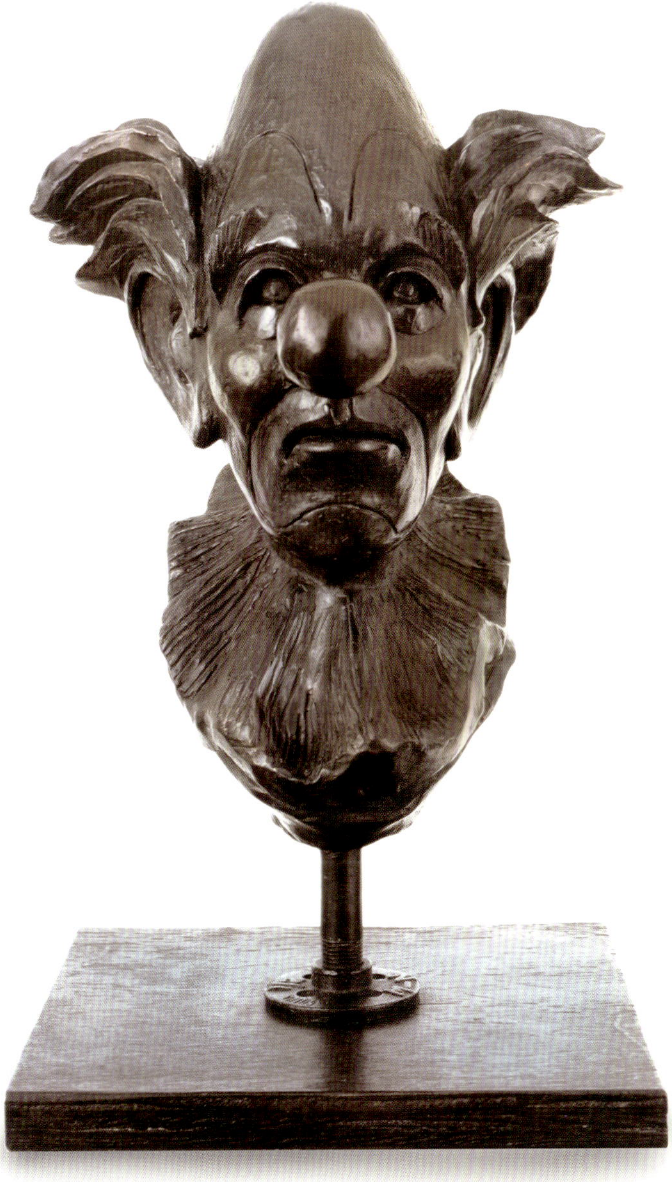

WEARY CLOWN, 2003
Bronze
48.9 × 27.9 × 27.9 cm

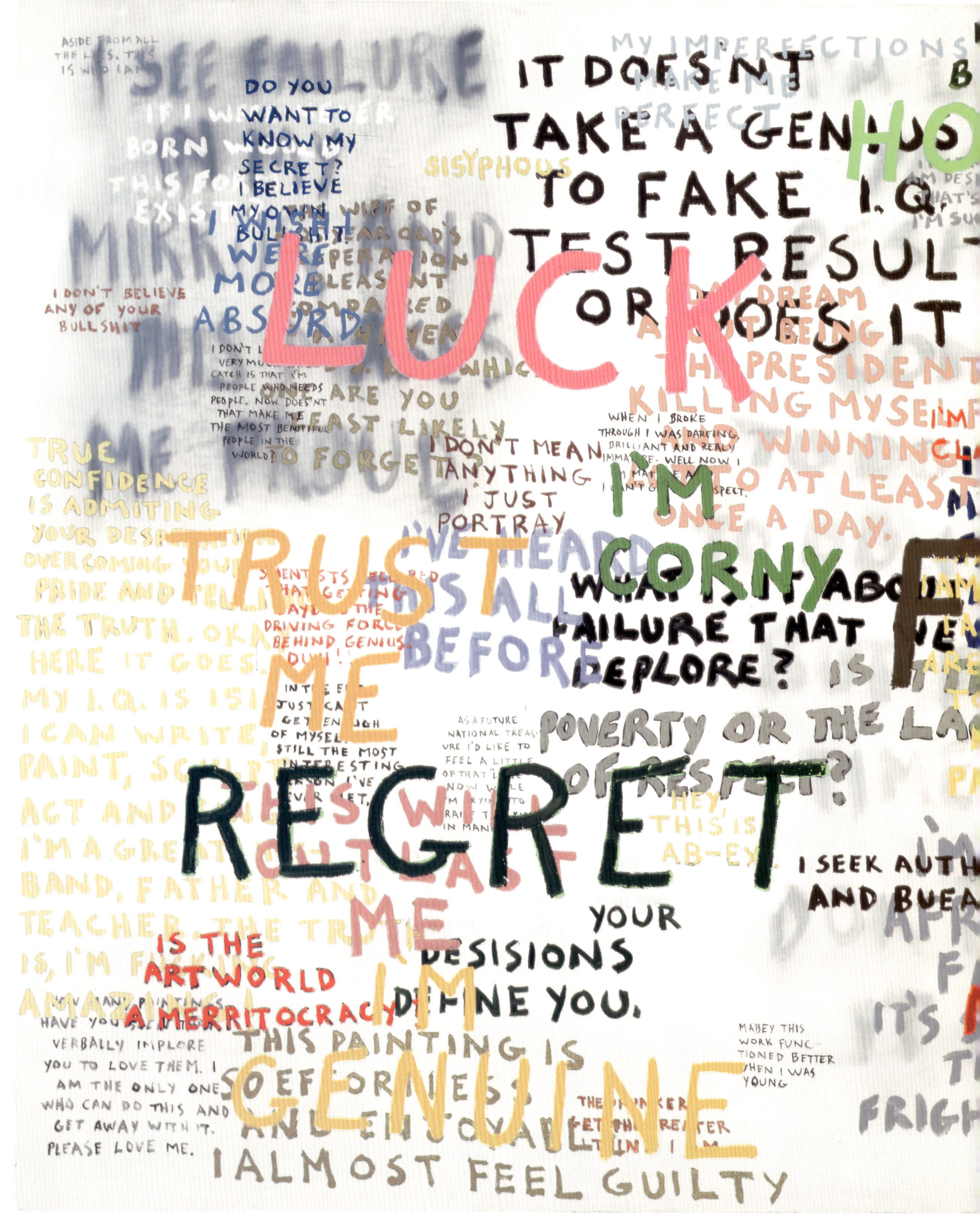

IT DOESN'T TAKE A GENIUS TO FAKE I.Q. TEST RESULTS OR DOES IT
LUCK
DO YOU WANT TO KNOW MY SECRET? I BELIEVE MY OWN BULLSHIT.
SISYPHOUS
I DON'T BELIEVE ANY OF YOUR BULLSHIT
I WISH I WERE MORE ABSURD
MY IMPERFECTIONS MAKE ME PERFECT
DAY DREAM ABOUT BEING THE PRESIDENT
KILLING MYSELF AND WINNING ... AT LEAST ONCE A DAY.
WHEN I BROKE THROUGH I WAS DAREING, BRILLIANT AND REALY IMMATURE.
I DON'T MEAN ANYTHING I JUST PORTRAY
I'M CORNY
ARE YOU LEAST LIKELY TO FORGET
TRUE CONFIDENCE IS ADMITING YOUR DESPERATION OVERCOMING YOUR PRIDE AND TELLING THE TRUTH. OKAY HERE IT GOES. MY I.Q. IS 151 I CAN WRITE, PAINT, SCULPT, ACT AND ... I'M A GREAT HUSBAND, FATHER AND TEACHER. THE TRUTH IS, I'M FUCKING AMAZING!
TRUST ME
I'VE HEARD THIS ALL BEFORE
WHAT IS IT ABOUT FAILURE THAT WE DEPLORE? IS IT POVERTY OR THE LACK OF RESPECT?
DRIVING FORCE BEHIND GENIUS. DUH!
AS A FUTURE NATIONAL TREASURE I'D LIKE TO FEEL A LITTLE OF THAT ...
STILL THE MOST INTERESTING PERSON I'VE EVER MET.
REGRET
HEY, THIS IS AB-EX.
I SEEK AUTH... AND BUEA...
YOUR DESISIONS DEFINE YOU.
IS THE ART WORLD A MERRITOCRACY
ME
I'M GENUINE
HAVE YOU ... VERBALLY IMPLORE YOU TO LOVE THEM. I AM THE ONLY ONE WHO CAN DO THIS AND GET AWAY WITH IT. PLEASE LOVE ME.
THIS PAINTING IS
MABEY THIS WORK FUNCTIONED BETTER WHEN I WAS YOUNG
I ALMOST FEEL GUILTY

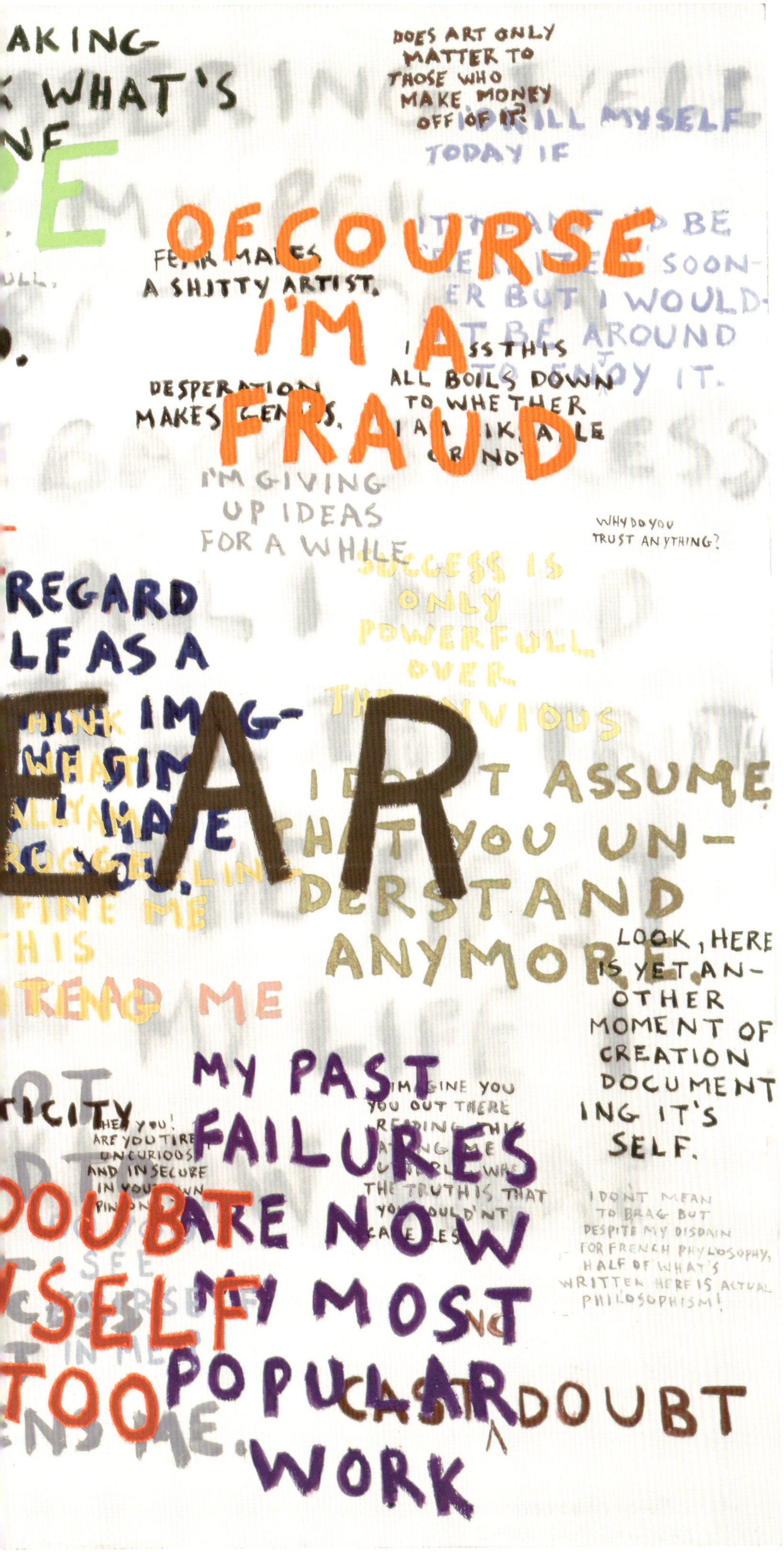

LUCK, FEAR, REGRET,
2003
Oil on linen
142.24 × 198.12 cm

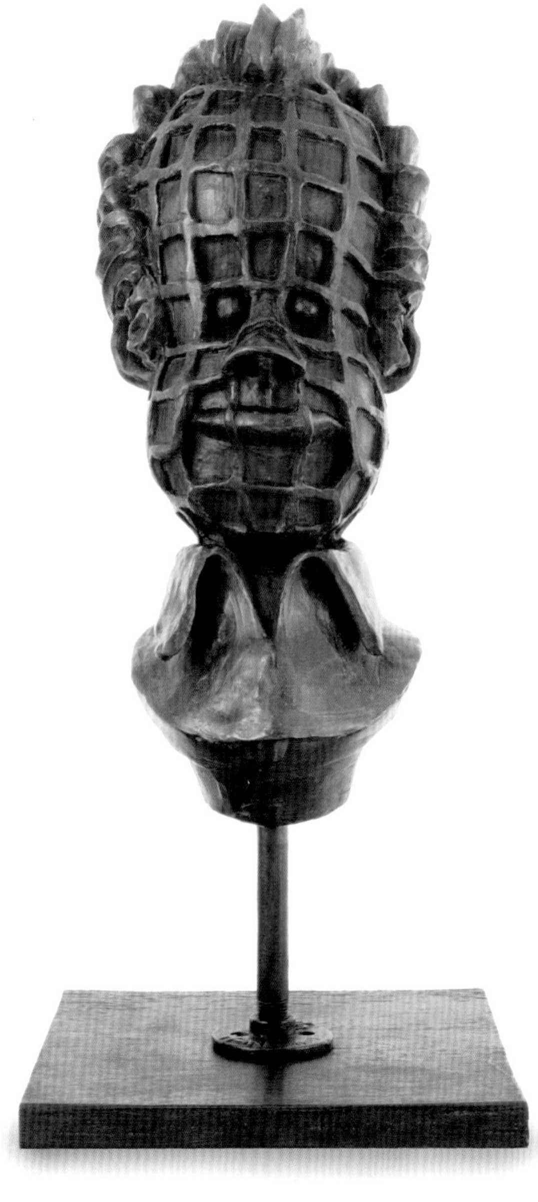

PEANUT HEAD, 2003
Bronze
60.96 × 27.94 × 27.94 cm

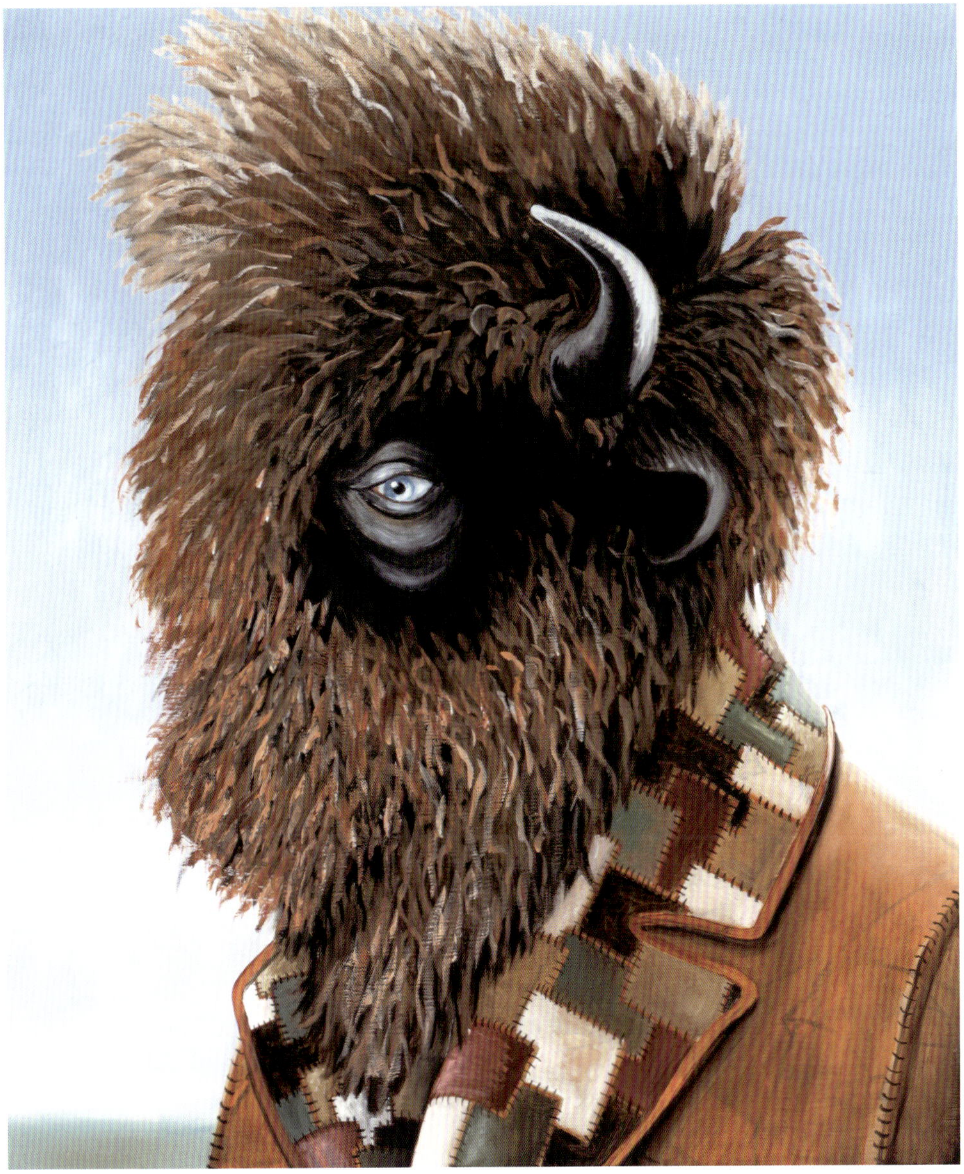

BUFFALO, 2003
Oil on linen
99.06 × 83.82 cm

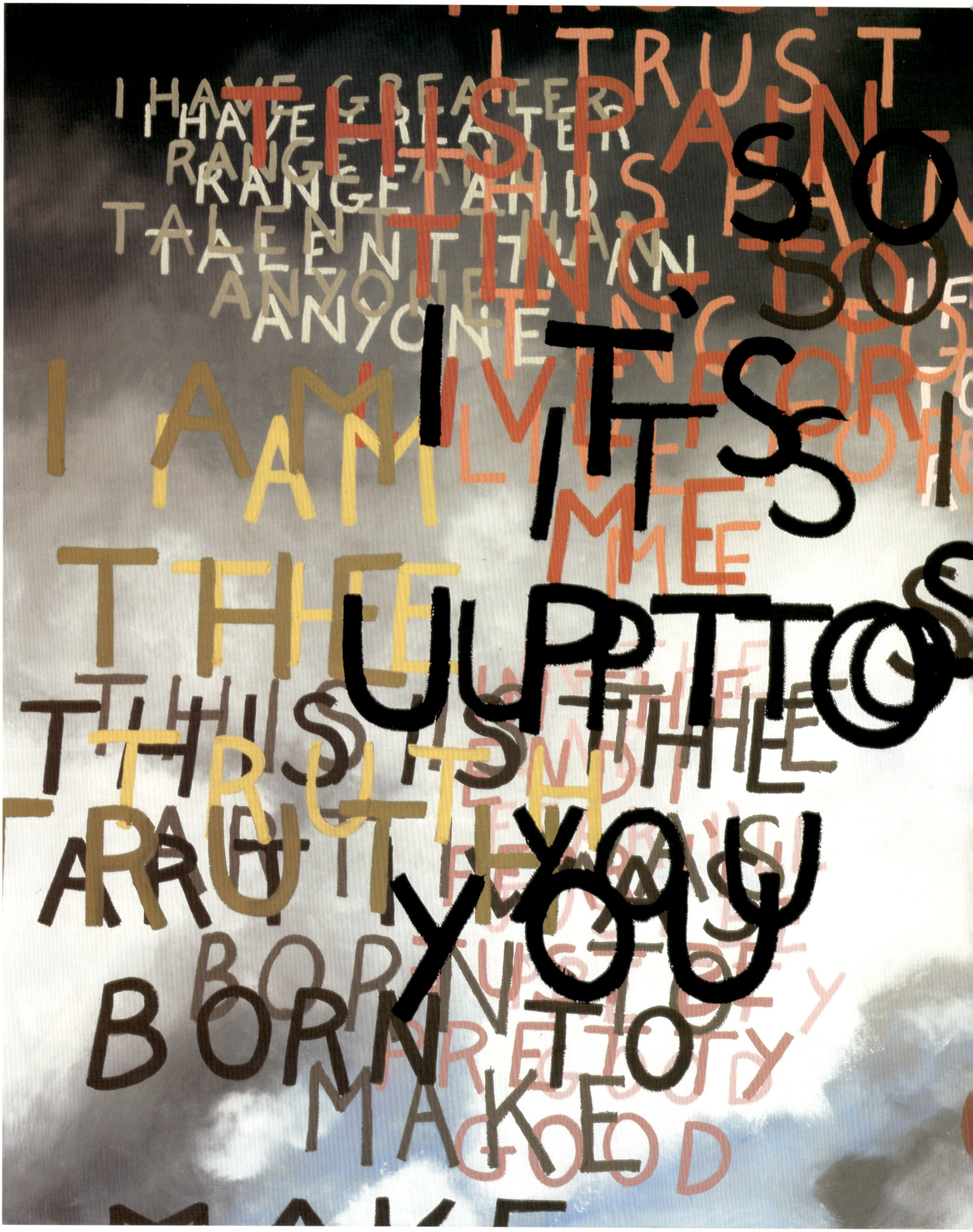
I TRUST
I HAVE GREATER RANGE AND TALENT THAN ANYONE
THIS PAINTING
IT'S SO
I AM THE TRUTH
IT'S UP TO YOU
THIS IS THE
BORN TO
MAKE
GOOD

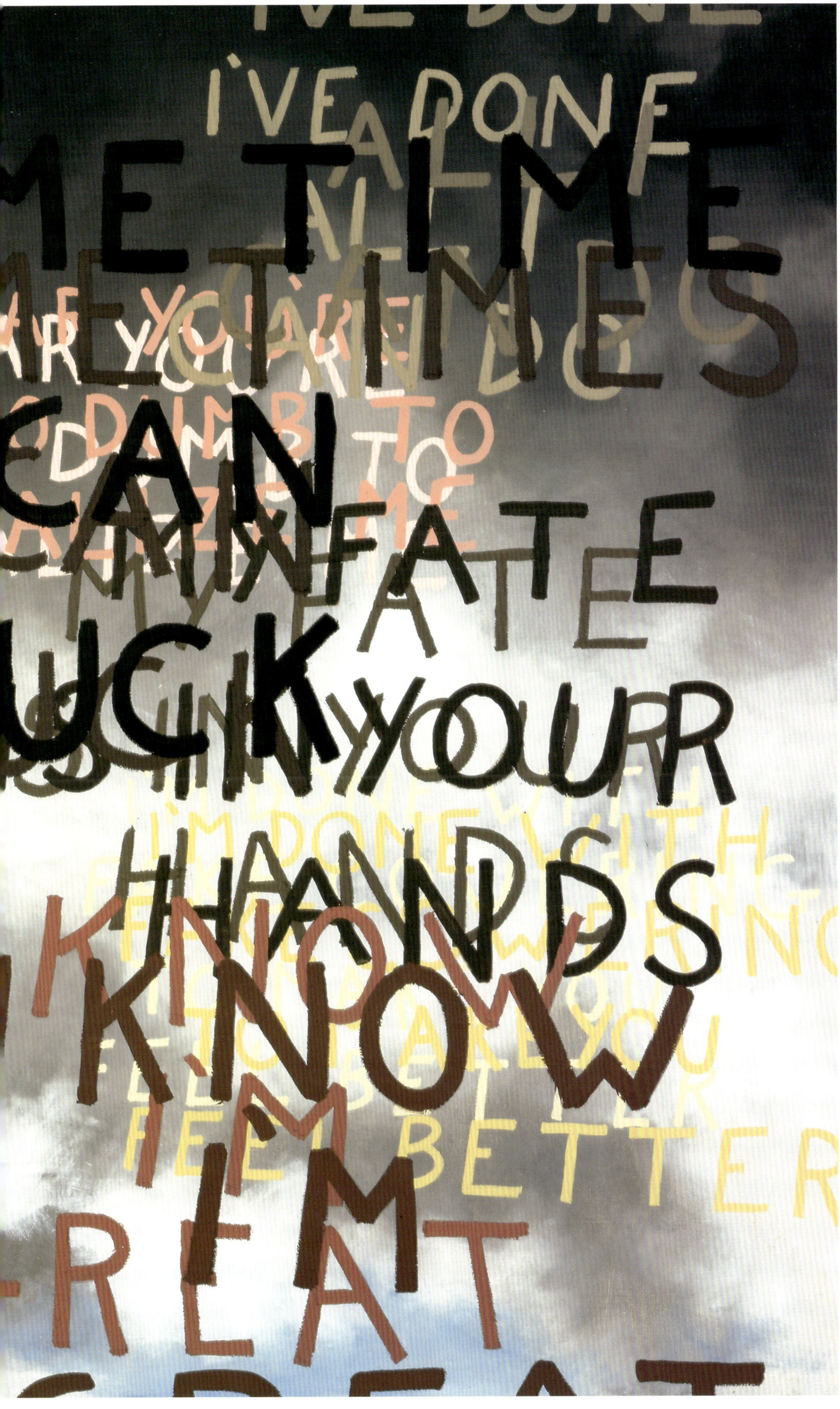

IT'S UP TO YOU, 2003
Oil on linen
182.88 × 274.32 cm

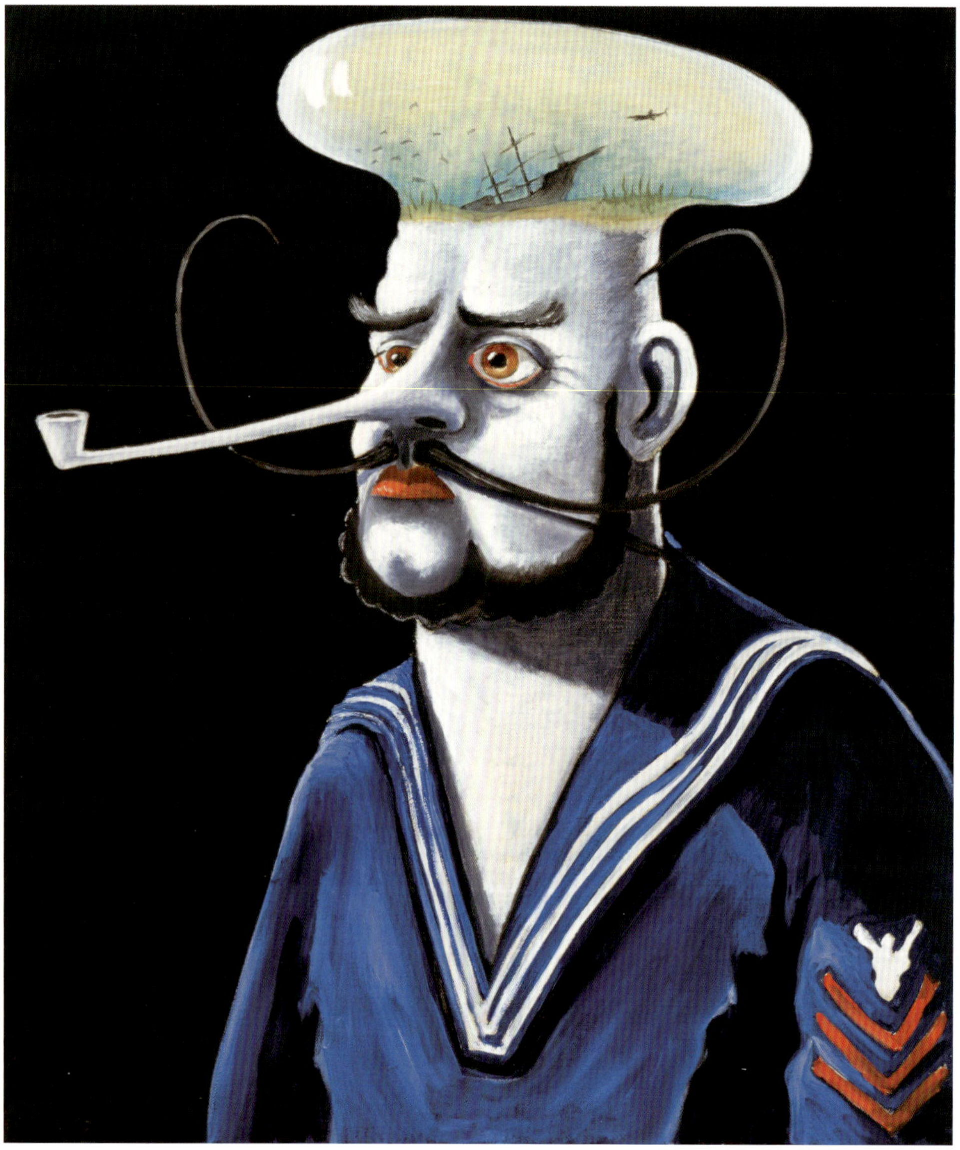

MARINER, 2003
Oil on linen
73.66 × 63.5 cm

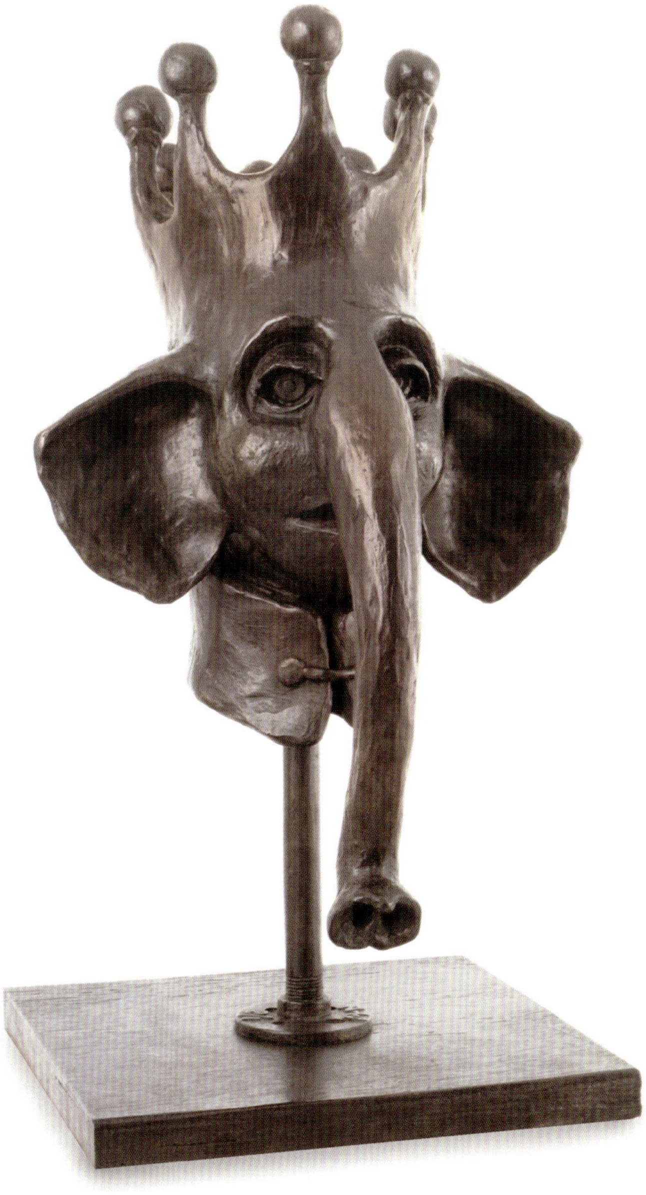

ELEPHANT KING, 2003
Bronze
53.97 × 27.94 × 27.94 cm

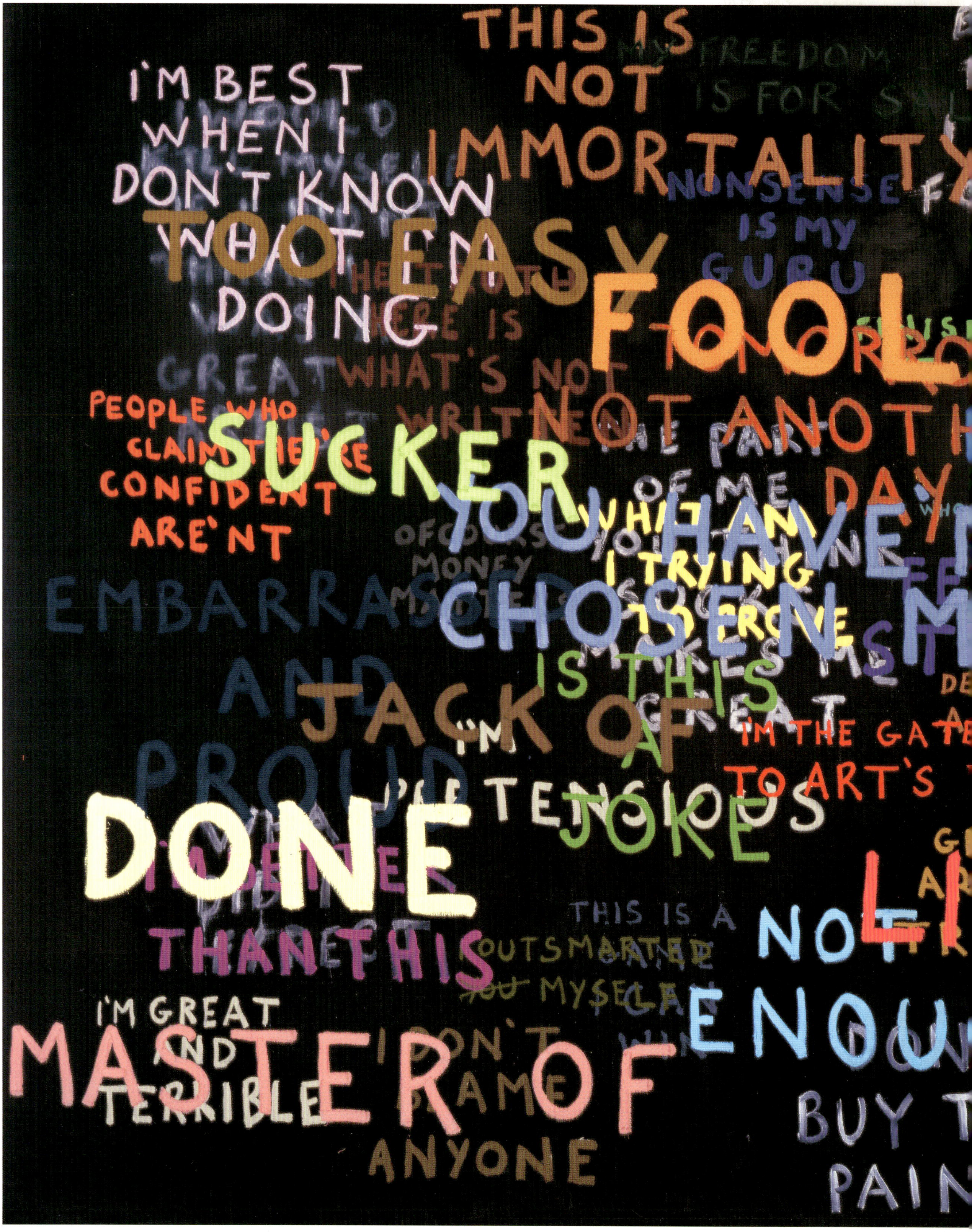

THIS IS NOT IMMORTALITY
MY FREEDOM IS FOR SAL
I'M BEST WHEN I DON'T KNOW WHAT I'M DOING
NONSENSE IS MY GURU
TOO EASY
FOOL
WHAT'S NOT
NOT ANOTH
DAY
PEOPLE WHO CLAIM THEY'RE CONFIDENT ARE'NT
SUCKER
YOU HAVE
OF COURSE MONEY MATTERS
WHAT AM I TRYING TO PROVE
EMBARRASSED AND PROUD
CHOSEN
IS THIS
JACK OF
A JOKE
I'M THE GATE TO ART'S
PRETENTIOUS
DONE
THAN THIS
THIS IS A
OUTSMARTED MYSELF
NOT
ENOU
LI
I'M GREAT AND TERRIBLE
MASTER OF
I DON'T BLAME ANYONE
BUY T
PAIN

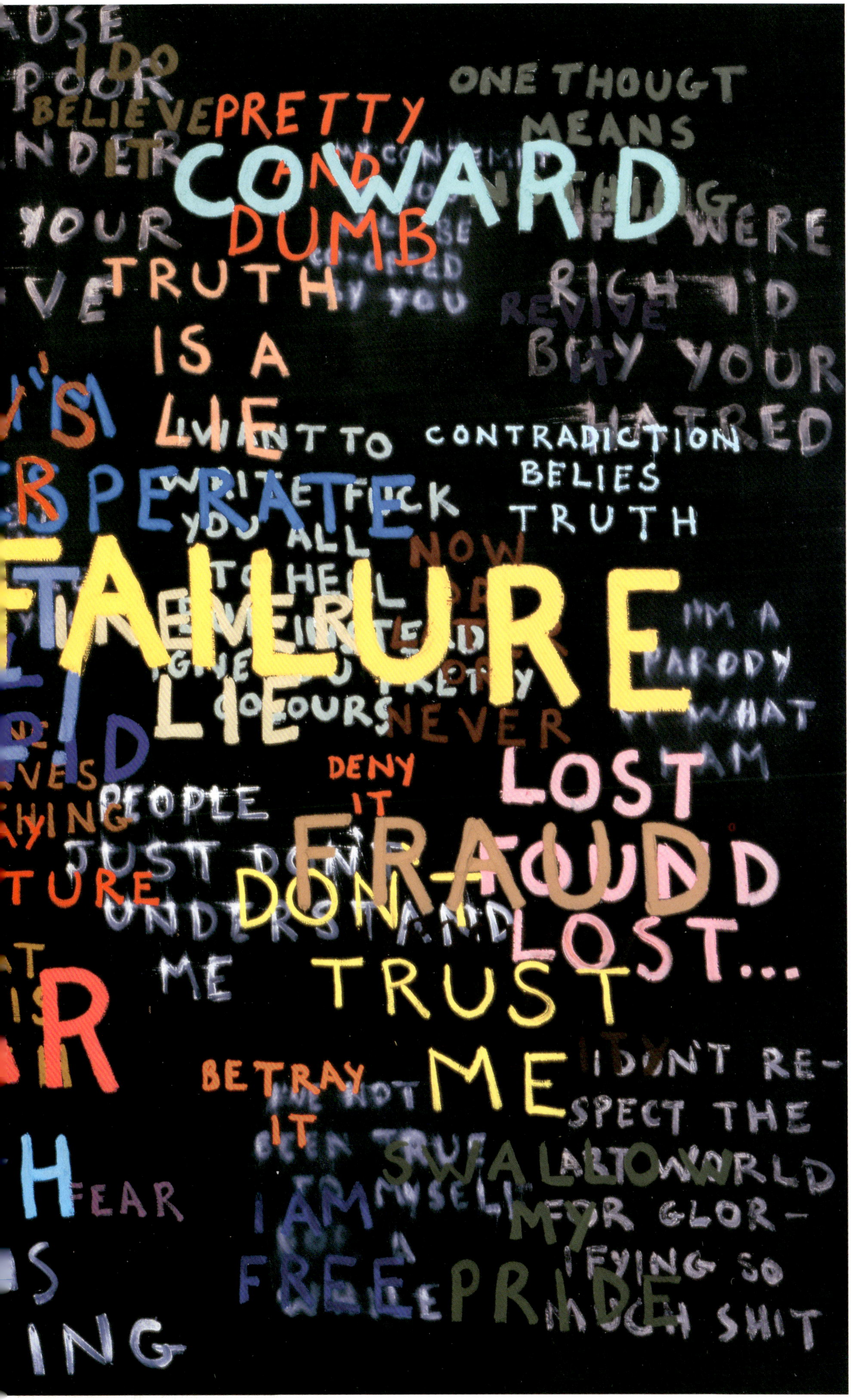

FOOL FAILURE, 2003
Oil on linen
182.88 × 274.32 cm

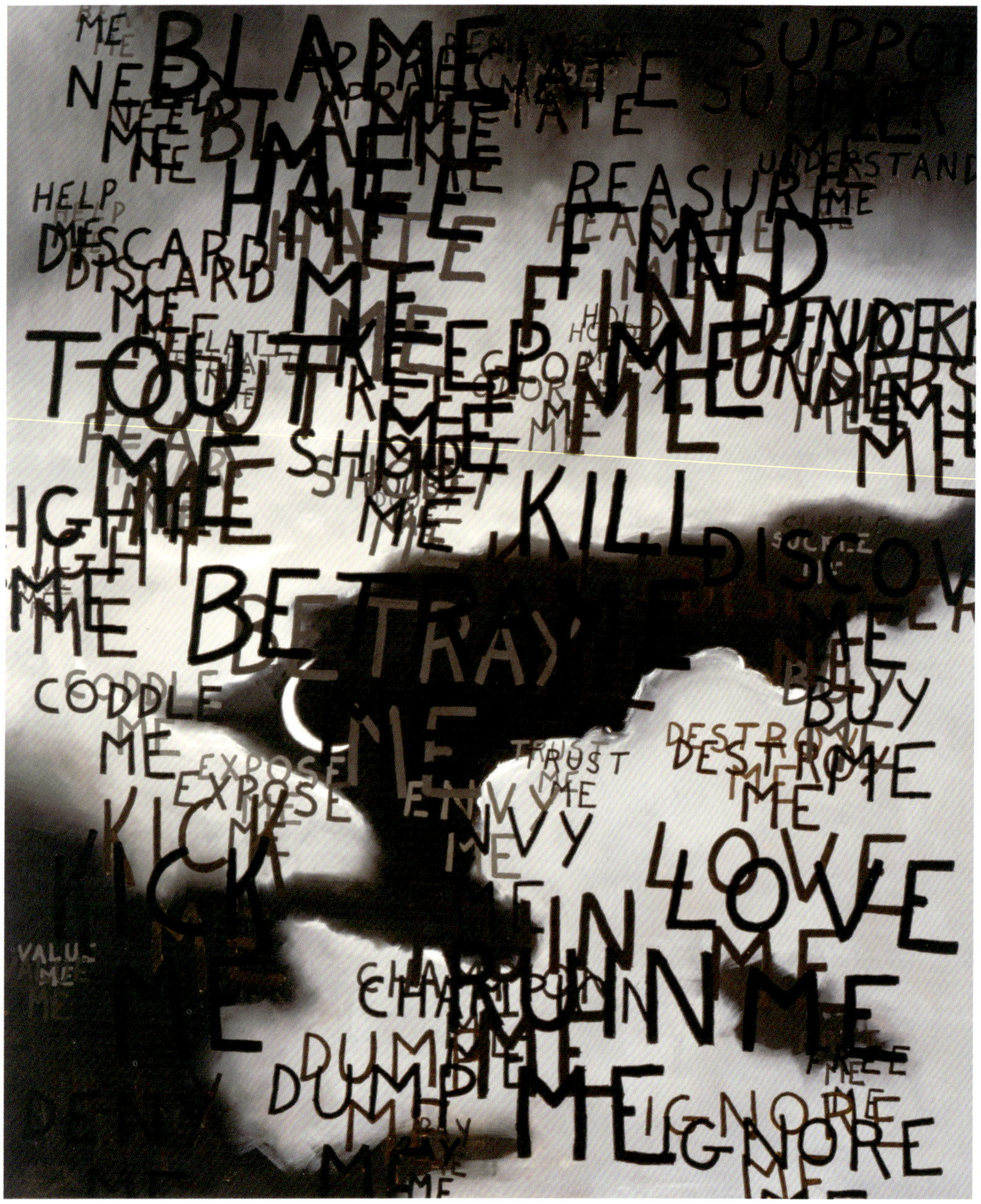

THE SLEEP OF REASON PRODUCES MONSTERS, 2004
Oil on linen
279.4 × 233.68 cm

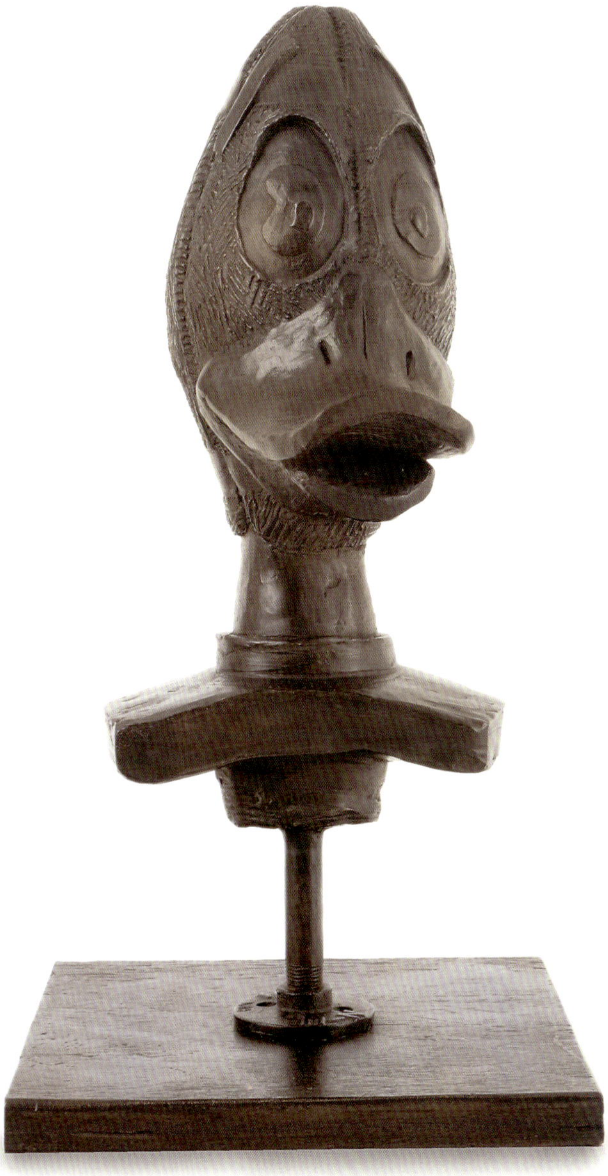

FOOTBALL DUCK, 2003
Bronze
53.34 × 27.94 × 27.94 cm

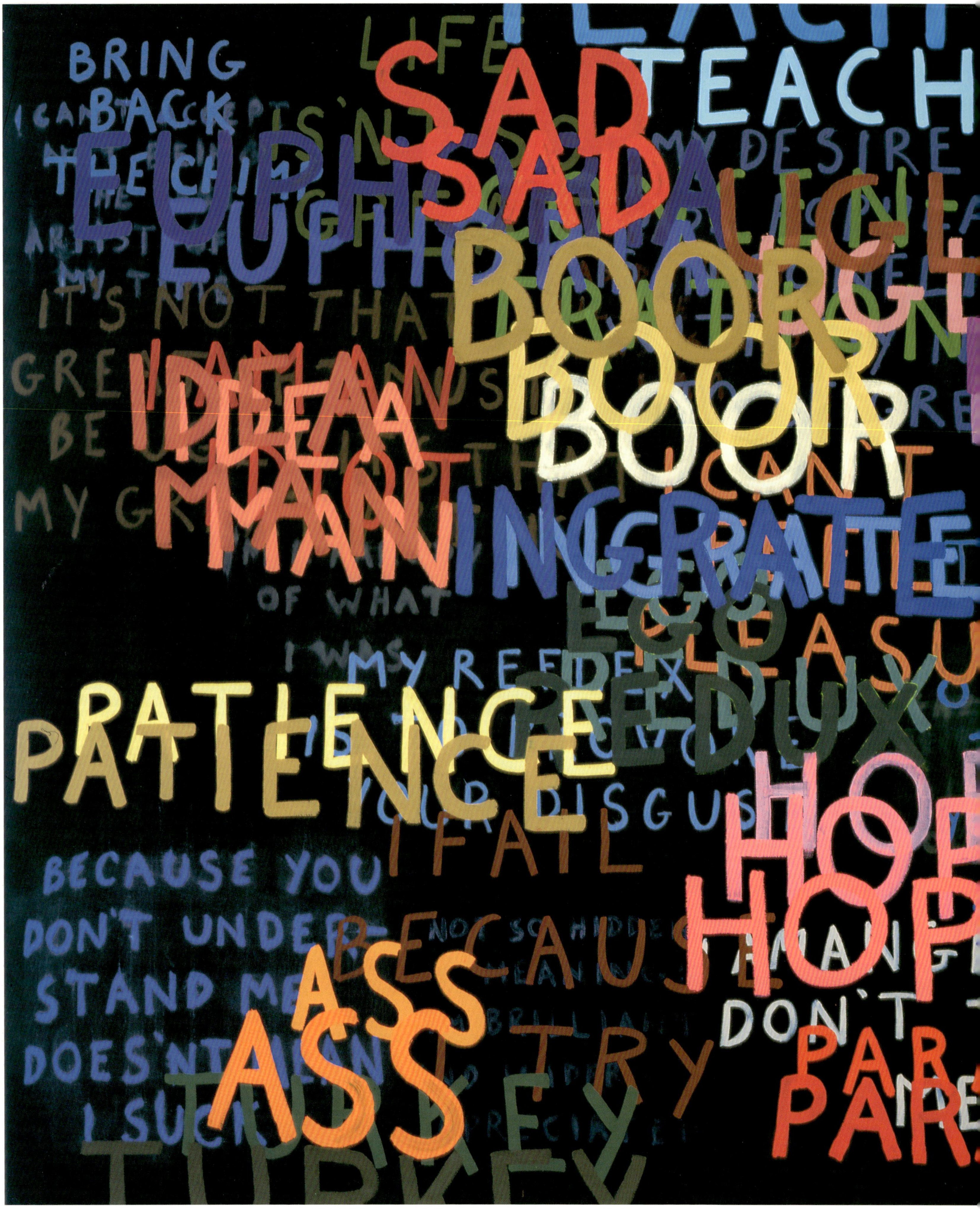
BRING
BACK
LIFE
SAD
TEACH
SAD
MY DESIRE
BOOR
BOOR
BOOR
BOOR
IT'S NOT THAT
IDEA
MAN
INGRATE
OF WHAT
EGO
REDUX
PATIENCE
PATIENCE
I FAIL
BECAUSE YOU
DON'T UNDER-
STAND ME
DOES'NT MEAN
I SUCK
ASS
ASS
TRY
DON'T
PAR
PAR
TURKEY

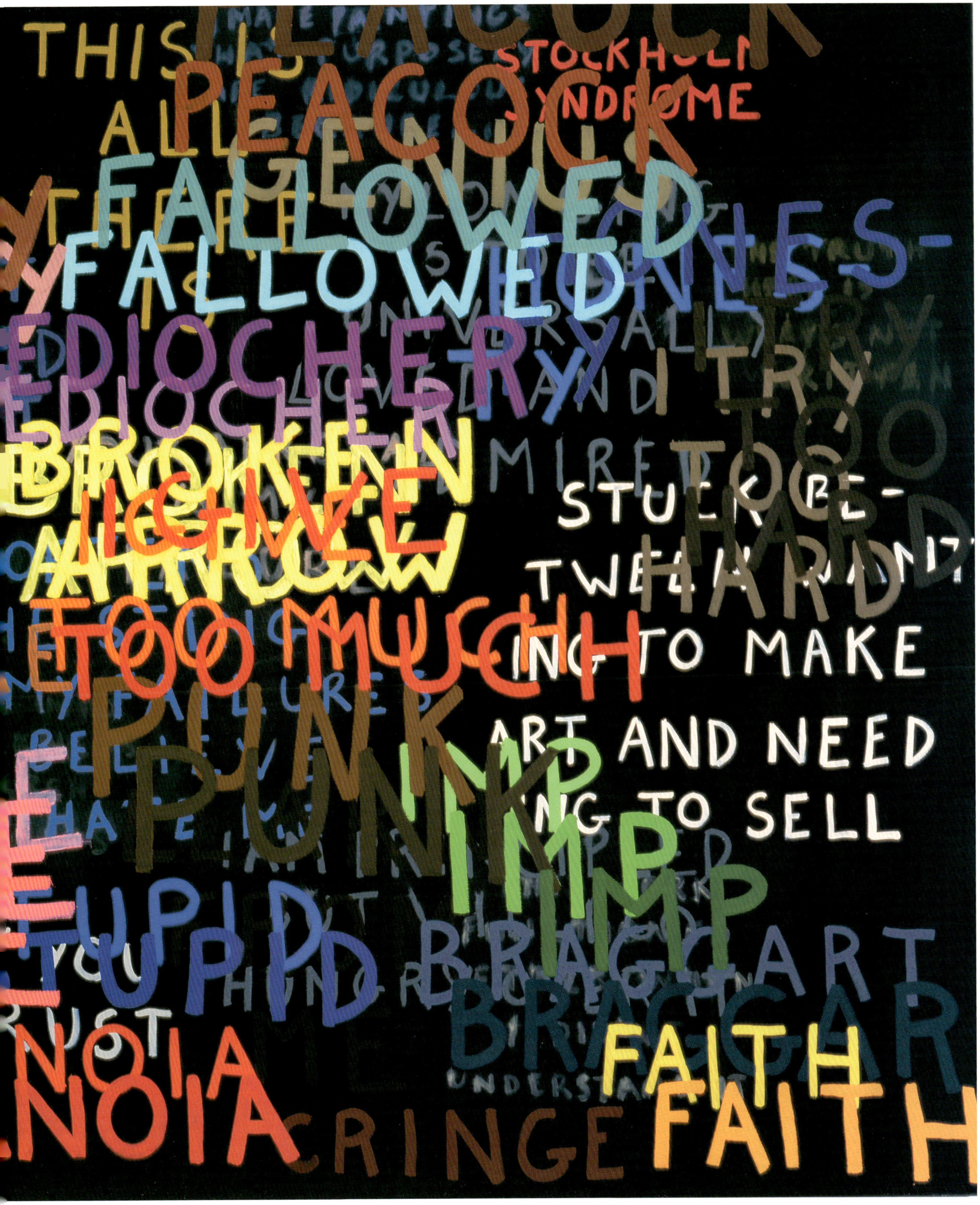
THIS IS
PEACOCK
PEACOCK
SYNDROME
FALLOWED
FALLOWED
I TRY
TOO
HARD
HARD
BROKEN
GIVE
TOO MUCH
TOO MUCH
STUCK BE-
ING TO MAKE
ART AND NEED
ING TO SELL
PUNK
PUNK
IMP
IMP
IMP
UPID
UPID
BRAGGART
FAITH
FAITH
NOIA
NOIA
CRINGE

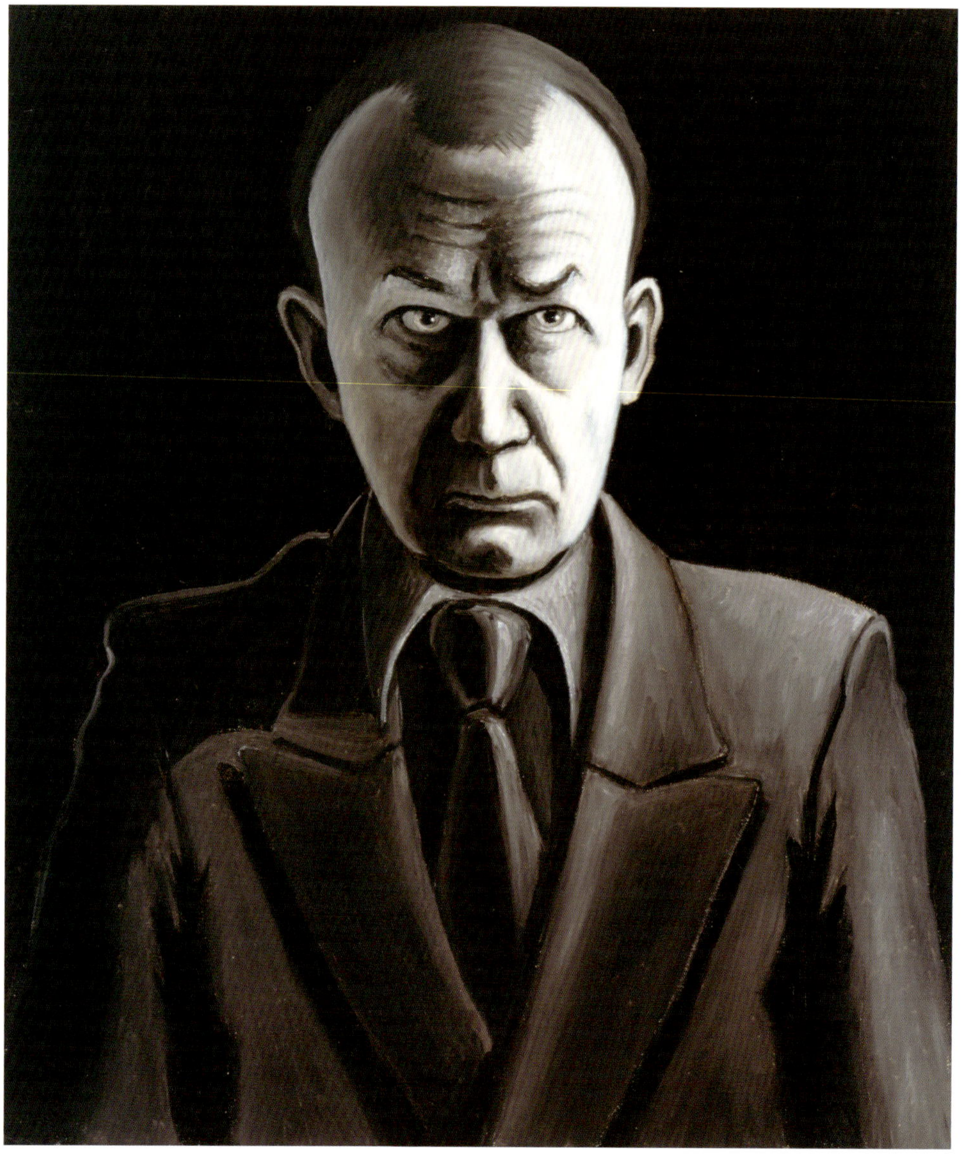

GHOST 5 (KIPPENBERGER), 2003
Oil on linen
76.2 × 66.04 cm

Pages 148–149
SAD BOOR, 2003
Oil on linen
213.36 × 365.76 cm

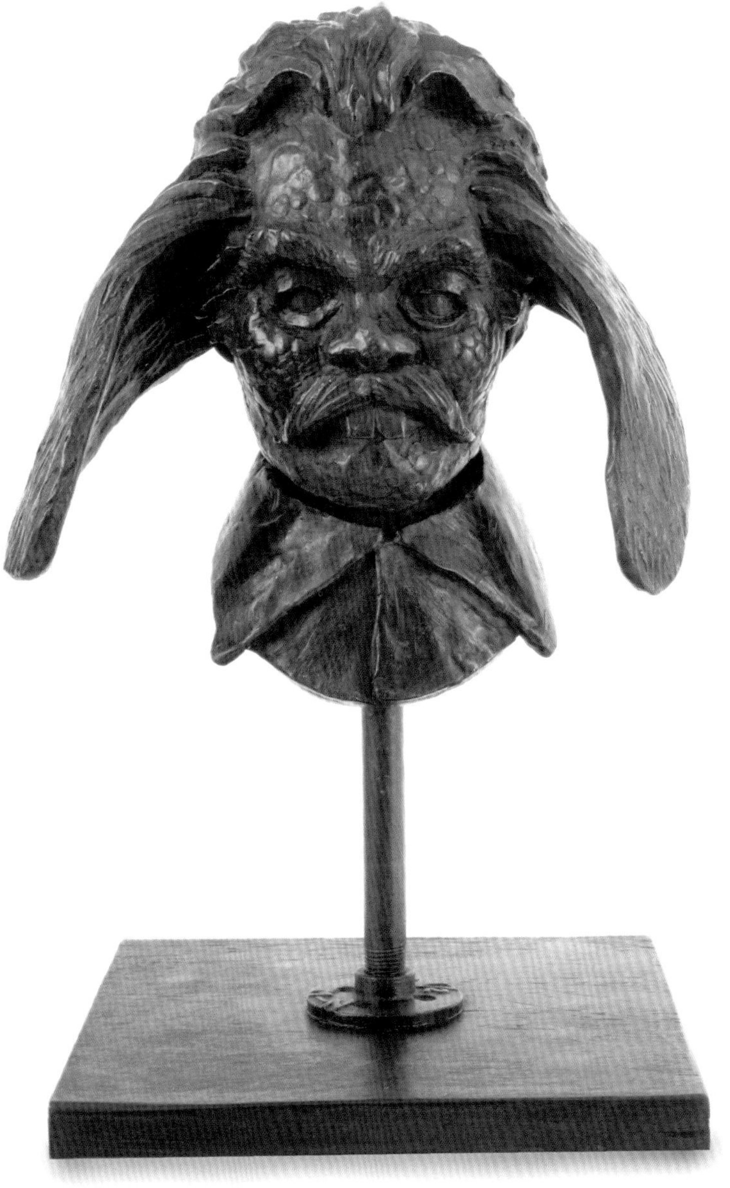

MR. RABBIT, 2003
Bronze
46.99 × 27.94 × 27.94 cm

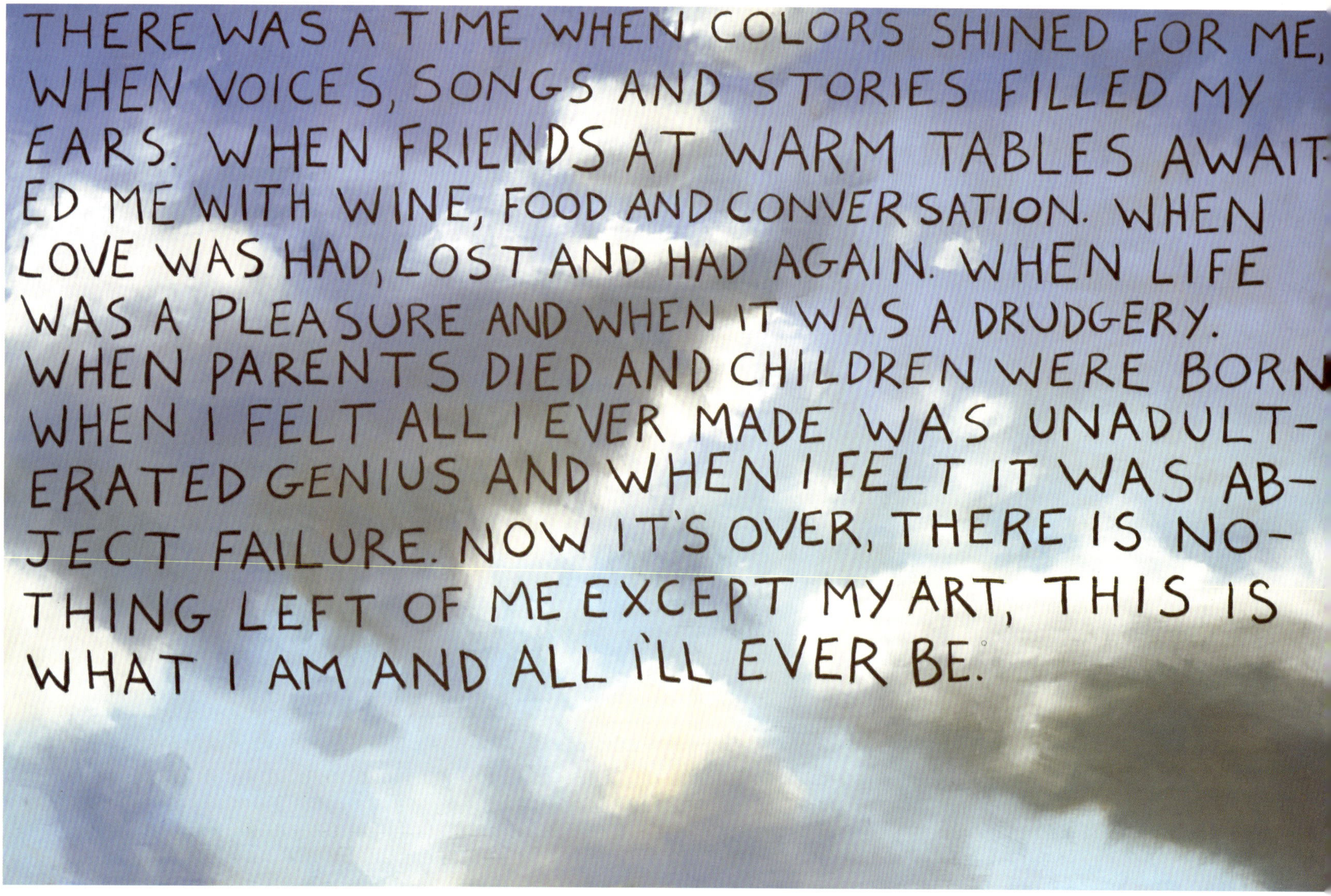

THERE WAS A TIME..., 2004
Oil on linen
182.88 × 274.32 cm

Biography

BORN 1962, PALMER, MASSACHUSETTS
LIVES AND WORKS IN NEW YORK CITY.

EDUCATION

1986 MFA, Yale University School of Art, New Haven, CT
1984 BFA, Philadelphia College of Art, PA

SOLO EXHIBITIONS

2004 Kunsthalle Zürich, Zurich
China Art Object, Los Angeles
sister, Los Angeles
Andrea Rosen Gallery, New York
2003 greengrassi, London
2002 Taka Ishii Gallery, Tokyo
Rebecca Camhi Gallery, Athens
2001 Galerie Jennifer Flay, Paris
Andrea Rosen Gallery, New York
2000 greengrassi, London
Taka Ishii Gallery, Tokyo
1999 Contemporary Fine Arts, Berlin
Andrea Rosen Gallery, New York
Galeria Presença, Porto
1998 Taka Ishii Gallery, Tokyo
Crown Gallery, Brussels
1997 Andrea Rosen Gallery, New York
Studio Guenzani, Milan
1996 Contemporary Fine Arts, Berlin
Rebecca Camhi Gallery, Athens
Regen Projects, Los Angeles
1995 Galerie Jennifer Flay, Paris
Andrea Rosen Gallery, New York
Galerie Birgit Küng, Zurich
1994 Bruno Brunnet, Berlin
Jay Jopling/White Cube, London
Regen Projects, Los Angeles
1993 Andrea Rosen Gallery, New York
Galerie Esther Schipper, Cologne
Galerie Jennifer Flay, Paris
1992 Andrea Rosen Gallery, New York
1991 Robbin Lockett Gallery, Chicago
Marc Jancou Galerie, Zurich
1990 Postmasters Gallery, New York
1989 Tom Solomon's Garage, Los Angeles

GROUP EXHIBITIONS

2004 *Guardare, Pensare, Raccontare, Conservare,* Casa del Mantegna, Mantova
Land of the Free, Jack Hanley Gallery, San Francisco
Jason Meadows, sister, Los Angeles
I Am the Walrus, Cheim & Read, New York
Tenth Anniversary Exhibition, Taka Ishii Gallery, Tokyo
Nature Study, Todd Madigan Gallery, California State University, Bakersfield

2003 *Today's Man*, John Connelly Presents, New York
Rendered, Sara Meltzer Gallery, New York
Drop Out, China Art Objects, Los Angeles
Influence, Identity, and Gratitude, MIT List Visual Arts Center, Boston, curated by Bill Arning
Thatcher, Blue Gallery, London, curated by Tara Howard
Gallery Artists, Taka Ishii Gallery, Tokyo
Comic Release: Negotiating Identity for a New Generation, Regina Gouger Miller Gallery, Carnegie Mellon University, Pittsburgh; traveled to Contemporary Arts Center, New Orleans; University Art Gallery, University of North Texas, Denton; University of Arizona Museum of Art, Tucson; Western Gallery, Western Washington University, Bellingham; Armory Center for the Arts, Pasadena; Art House, Austin

2002 *Face/Off: A Portrait of the Artist*, Kettle's Yard, University of Cambridge, Cambridge, curated by Simon Groom; traveled to Towner Art Gallery and Local Museum, Eastbourne
Center for Curatorial Studies Tenth Anniversary, Center for Curatorial Studies, Bard College, Annandale-on-Hudson
To Whom It May Concern, Logan Galleries, The California College of Arts, Wattis Institute for Contemporary Arts, San Francisco
Copy, Roth Horowitz, New York, curated by Neville Wakefield
Heaven Knows I'm Miserable Now, LOW, Los Angeles

2001 *Desire Admiration Acquire*, Arcadia University Art Gallery, Glenside
Tele(visions), Kunsthalle Wien, Vienna, curated by Joshua Decter
Extra Art: A Survey of Artists' Ephemera, 1960–1999, Logan Galleries, The California College of Arts, Wattis Institute for Contemporary Arts, San Francisco, curated by Steven Leiber
Alumni Choice: An Exhibition of Works on Paper, Yale University Art Gallery, Yale University, New Haven

Soyez réaliste, demandez l'impossible!, Galerie Jennifer Flay, Paris
The way I see it: Chantal Joffe, Karen Kilimnik, Sean Landers and Lisa Milroy, Galerie Jennifer Flay, Paris
La Colección Jumex, Jumex Centro de Distribución, Mexico City

2000 *Salon*, Delfina Project Space, London
2000 Anos Luz, Galeria Leyendecker, Canary Islands, curated by Angel Luis de la Cruz
Kin, Kerlin Gallery, Dublin, curated by Caoimhín Mac Giolla Leith
oo, Barbara Gladstone Gallery, New York
Body Beautiful, Galerie Jennifer Flay, Paris
Selections from the Permanent Collection of Modern and Contemporary Art, Denver Art Museum, Denver
Arte Americana, Ultimo Decennio, Loggetta Lombardesca, Ravenna, curated by Claudio Spadoni
Group Exhibition of Gallery Artists, Rebecca Camhi Gallery, Athens

1999 *A Place Called Lovely*, GreeneNaftali, New York, curated by Sima Familant
Gallery Swap, Contemporary Fine Arts at Sadie Coles HQ, London
Self Evident, Vaknin Schwartz, Atlanta
Etcetera, Spacex, Exeter, curated by Alex Farquharson
Examining Pictures: Exhibiting Paintings, Whitechapel Art Gallery, London, curated by Francesco Bonami and Judith Nesbitt; traveled to Museum of Contemporary Art, Chicago; University of California Los Angeles, Hammer Museum, Los Angeles
Colección Jumex, Museo de Arte Carillo Gil, San Angel
Positioning, Center for Curatorial Studies, Bard College, Annandale-on-Hudson
Hello Mr. Soul, Gallery 400, University of Illinois at Chicago

1998 *encyclopedia 1999*, Turner & Runyon Gallery, Dallas
Word Perfect, Gallery 400, University of Illinois at Chicago
Hanging, Galeria Camargo Vilaça, Sao Paulo, curated by Márcia Fortes; traveled to Paco Imperial, Rio de Janiero; Museum of Modern Art, Recife

1997 *Heart, Body, Mind, Soul: American Art in the 1990s, Selections from the Permanent Collection*, Whitney Museum of American Art, New York
Tanti Video, Arcate Art Fabrica, Torino
From a Whisper to a Scream, Ten in One Gallery, Chicago
Kunst.Arbeit, Südwestdeutsche Landesbank Forum, Stuttgart

1996 *a/drift: Scenes from the Penetrable Culture*, Center for Curatorial Studies, Bard College, Annandale-on-Hudson, curated by Joshua Decter
Galerie Declercq, Knokke
Against: Thirty Years of Film and Video, Anthony d'Offay Gallery, London
So you want to be a rock and roll star: Artists 'sing' on screen, Museum of Contemporary Art, Chicago, curated by Dominic Molon
Let Me Bring You Down, art initiatives, 148 Gallery, New York, curated by Two Dollar Guitar (Tim Foljahn and Steve Shelley)
nach weimar, Kunstsammlung zu Weimar, Weimar
wunderbar, Kunstverein in Hamburg, Hamburg
push-ups, Athens Fine Art School, the factory, Athens, curated by Emily Tsingou
Toons, Galleri Campbells Occasionally, Copenhagen, curated by Jacob Fabricius
Sammlung Volkmann zeigt: Faustrecht der Freiheit, Kunstsammlung Gera; traveled to Neues Museum Weserburg, Bremen
Incestuous, Thread Waxing Space, New York, curated by Tiong Ang and Carter Kustera
Sugar Mountain, White Columns, New York, curated by Paul Ha and Andrea Scott
Rotterdam on Line, MK Expositieruimte, Rotterdam
Young Americans: New American Art in the Saatchi Collection: Part I, Saatchi Gallery, London

1995 *I'm Writing in Lacanian Ink*, Deutsches Haus, Columbia University, New York, curated by Richard Foreman and Josephina Ayerza
Raw, Postmasters, New York
Next of Kin: Looking at the Great Apes, MIT List Visual Arts Center, Cambridge
Word for Word, Beaver College Art Gallery, Glenside
Scribbles, Hyde Park Art Center, Chicago, curated by Deborah Wilk
New Acquisitions: An Exhibition of Artists' Books and Multiples, Art Metropole, Toronto
Histoire de l'Infamie, Fonds Régional d'Art Contemporain, Auvergne, curated by Jean-Yves Jouannais
I Confess, Nikolaj Copenhagen Contemporary Art Center, Copenhagen
International Festival of Films on Art, Knokke
KOMIX, Brooke Alexander Editions, New York
Narcissistic Disturbance, Otis College of Art and Design, Los Angeles, curated by Michael Cohen

1994 *A series of rotating installations* (Week 5: November 22–26: Sean Landers and Muriel Brown George), Andrea Rosen Gallery, New York
Recent Acquisitions from the Rivendell Collection, Center for Curatorial Studies, Bard College, Annandale-on-Hudson
Noritoshi Hirakawa, Sean Landers, Jan Voss, Jeanne Dunning, Galerie Drantmann, Brussels
David's Friends, Bernard Toale Gallery, Boston, curated by Timothy Fichtner and David Zin
esprit d'amusement, Grazer Kunstverein, Graz
Das Jahrhundert des Multiple. Von Duchamp bis zur Gegenwart, Deichtorhallen, Hamburg
Exposition, Galerie Jennifer Flay, Paris
Arte in Video: 22 Inches, Inter Nos and Galerie Pasquale Leccese, Milan, curated by Tommaso Corvi Mora
Sea Change: Franklin Furnace Benefit, Josh Baer Gallery, New York
Die Orte der Kunst, Sprengel Museum, Hannover
Auto-Eeroticism, Ecole des Arts Décoratifs, Paris, video screening organized by Nicolas Trembley for A Bao A Qou
Can you believe your eyes?, The Museum of Contemporary Art, The Beyerd in Breda
Don't Postpone Joy or Collecting Can Be Fun!, Neue Galerie, Graz, curated by Rudi Molacek and Barbara Steffen; traveled to Austrian Cultural Institute, New York
Kunstverein in Hamburg, Hamburg
Intercourse, Mustard, Brooklyn, curated by Pablo Gomez and Daniel Carello
Volkmann Collection, Cologne, curated by Kasper König
Don't Look Now, Thread Waxing Space, New York, curated by Joshua Decter
Passing Through, Galerie Walcheturm, Zurich, curated by Ugo Rondinone

1993 Tavelli Gallery, Aspen
Audience 0.01, Vera Vita Gioia, Naples, curated by Helena Kontova; traveled to Trevi Flash Art Museum of Contemporary Art, Trevi
Auction Benefit, New Museum of Contemporary Art, New York
Into the Lapse, Royal Danish Academy of Fine Arts, Copenhagen, curated by Brian Butler
Phenylovethylamour, Galerie Daniel Buchholz, *Unfair* booth 26, Cologne, curated by Lothar Hempel and Carsten Höller
November, Galerie Esther Schipper, Cologne
influx, Gallery 400 at The University of Illinois at Chicago
Backstage, Kunstverein in Hamburg, Hamburg; traveled to Kunstmuseum Luzern, Lucerne
Die Sprache der Kunst, Kunsthalle Wien, Vienna; traveled to Frankfurter Kunstverein, Frankfurt
Summer Group Show, Galerie Esther Schipper, Cologne
Word of Mouth, Friesenwall 120, Cologne, curated by Ana de Portella; traveled to Dogenhaus Galerie, Leipzig; Palais des Beaux-Arts, Brussels, curated by Ana de Portella, Brian Butler and Stefan Dillemuth
TranceseX: A State of Mystical Absorption, Mondrian Hotel, West Hollywood, curated by Les Ayre, Erika Knerr and Amanda M. Obering
Tom Cugliani Gallery, New York
Standards. Aperto 1993, Biennale di Venezia, Venice, section curated by Nicolas Bourriaud
Yale Collects Yale, Yale University Art Gallery, New Haven
Sean Landers, Raymond Pettibon, Richard Prince, Jürgen Becker, Hamburg
SOHO at Duke IV, Duke University Museum of Art, Durham
Confessional, Liz Koury Gallery, New York, curated by Andrea Scott

1992 *The Anti-Masculine (Overlapping, but not corresponding to the feminine)*, Kim Light Gallery, Los Angeles, curated by Bill Arning
Transgressions In The White Cube: Territorial Mappings, Usdan Gallery at Bennington College, Vermont, curated by Joshua Decter
Under Thirty, Galerie Metropol, Vienna, Austria, curated by Erik Oppenheim
New Deal, Bruno Brunnet, Berlin
I, Myself and Others, Le Magasin – Centre National d'Art Contemporain de Grenoble, Grenoble
Third Annual Exhibition of Collector's Choice of American Artists, Vered Gallery, East Hampton, New York
Paradise Europe, Copenhagen, Ny Carlsberg Glyptotek, organized by Bizart and curated by Andrea Rosen Gallery, New York; Daniel Buchholz, Cologne; Galerie Maquina Espanola, Madrid; Stalke Out of Space, Copenhagen; and Galleria Paolo Vitolo, Rome
Into the Lapse (Program 1), 1301, Santa Monica, curated by Jean Rasenberger and Brian D. Butler
Regen Projects, Los Angeles
Galerie Esther Schipper, Cologne
Free Lunch, Centre d'Art Contemporain, Martigny, curated by Erik Oppenheim

1991 *Ornament: Ho Hum All Ye Faithful*, John Post Lee, New York
L'Esprit Bibliothèque, La Galerie du Mois, Paris
Pleasure, Hallwalls, Buffalo, curated by Steven Saltzman
Letters, Christine Burgin Gallery, New York
Videos and a Film About Some Schmoes Who Are Trying to Conform (yet miss), Robbin Lockett Gallery, Chicago
Gulliver's Travels, Sophia Ungers Gallery, Cologne
Words & #'s, Wright State University, University Art Galleries, Dayton
5 Days, Thomas Solomon's Garage, Los Angeles
Name Gallery, Chicago
LYRIC– Uses of Beauty in the 90s, White Columns, New York

1990 New Jersey State Museum, Newark
Work in Progress? Work?, Andrea Rosen Gallery, New York
Total Metal, Simon Watson Gallery, New York, curated by Richard Phillips
Drawings, Paula Allen Gallery, New York
Postmasters Gallery, New York
Benefit Exhibition, White Columns, New York
Benefit Exhibition, The New Museum, New York

1989 *Outer Limits*, Holly Solomon Gallery, New York
Islip Art Museum, East Islip, Long Island
American Fine Arts Co., New York

1988 *Small works show*, Sculpture Center, New York
Sculpture, White Columns, New York
Art on the Beach, Creative Times, Queens, New York

1986 *South Beach III*, Organization of Independent Artists, Staten Island
Mutual Respect, Vanguard Gallery, Philadelphia

Selected Bibliography

2004 Collings, Matthew: "Getting ahead in New York," in *Modern Painters*, Summer, p. 18-19
Giovannini, Jospeh: "Escape from New York," in: *Architectural Digest*, p. 190-197, 236
Smith, Roberta: "I am the Walrus at Cheim & Read," in: *The New York Times*, June 25, p. E33
Houser, Craig: "Sean Landers", in: *Flash Art*, May/June, p. 82
Landers, Sean: "Sean Landers: Andrea Rosen Gallery, New York," in: *Frieze*, May, p. 108
Smith, Roberta: "Sean Landers," in: *The New York Times*, April 2, p. E35
Levin, Kim: "Voices Choices. Sean Landers at Andrea Rosen Gallery," in: *The Village Voice*, March 17-23, p. 81
"Sean Landers," in: *The New Yorker*, March 15, p. 37-38
"Sean Landers," in: *Time Out*, March 11–18, p. 84

2003 Plender, Olivia: "Sean Landers, greengrassi, London," in: *Frieze*, October, p. 126
Coomer, Martin: "Sean Landers at greengrassi," in: *Time Out London*, June 25–July 2, p. 57
Lyall, Sarah: "Margaret Thatcher as Muse," in: *The New York Times*, May 12, pp. E1, E5
"Not-so-iron lady," in: *Art Review*, vol. 1 no. 7, May, p. 20
"Thatcher Years Art Show Opens," in: *BBC News Online*, April 16

2002 Saltz, Jerry: "Repeat Performance," in: *The Village Voice*, October 7
"Sean Landers," in: *Symbol*, March 23, p. 34–37

2001 Cash, Stephanie: "Sean Landers at Andrea Rosen Gallery," in: *Art in America*, November, p. 145–146
Edelson, Sharon: "Art Course: Restaurants are turning into ad hoc galleries, displaying the work of topflight artists," in: *W*, September, p. 442, 444, 452, 454, 456
"Sean Landers at Galerie Jennifer Flay," in: *FigaroScope*, September 5–11, no. 17751, p. 45
Gilbert, Andrea: "Splash," in: *View Magazine*, Summer, p. 88–93
Perree, Rob: "Sean 'Picasso' Landers," in: *Kunstbeeld*, July/August, p. 64–65
Siegel, Katy: "Public Offerings," in: *Young Americans*, The Museum of Contemporary Art, Los Angeles, p. 207–192
Wilson, Michael: "Sean Landers at Andrea Rosen Gallery," in: *Untitled*, Summer, p. 34–35
"Goings on About Town: Sean Landers at Andrea Rosen Gallery," in: *The New Yorker*, May 14, p. 26
"A Guide to the Great Neighborhoods in New York: Chelsea," in: *SPUR*, June, p. 181
Fineman, Mia: "I, Picasso," in: *The Village Voice*, May 15, vol. XLVI, no. 19, p. 70
Kimmelman, Michael: "Sean Landers at Andrea Rosen Gallery," in: *The New York Times*, May 4, p. 33
Pederson, Victoria: "Short List," in: *Paper*, May, p. 133
Mahoney, Robert: "Sean Landers at Andrea Rosen Gallery," in: *Time Out New York*, April 26–May 3, p. 63
Parker, Lauren: "Spring Art Walk Best of Show: Sean Landers at Andrea Rosen Gallery," in: *The New York Observer*, April 16, p. 8
Dannat, Adrian: "Appropriating Picasso 'because I want to be as great as him'," in: *The Art Newspaper*, May, p. 80
Hayt, Elizabeth: "If You Wow Them They Will Come," in: *The New York Times*, February 18, p. 33, 35

2000 Cereceda, Miguel: "Panorama de Nueva York," in: *ABC Cultural*, November 18, p. 39
"Arte a la vanguardia," in: *Camb16*, October 23, p. 90
"La obra de una treintena de artistas residentes en Nueva York desembarca en Tenerife," in: *El Dia*, October 17, p. 78
Art Club Magazine, Autumn 2000, inside cover
Farquharson, Alex: "Sean Landers at greengrassi London," in: *Art Monthly*, issue 239, September, p. 51–54
Ruane, Medb: "Not such kindred spirits," in: *The Sunday Times*, August 6, p. 10–11
Groarke, Vona: "Kin at Kerlin," in: *Galleries Magazine*, August
Kent, Sarah: "Sean Landers at greengrassi," in: *Time Out London*, July 19–26, p. 60–61
McLaren, Duncan: "Sean Landers at greengrassi London," in: *The Independent on Sunday*, July 23
Daly, Catherine: "Kin," in: *The Dublin Sunday Times*, July 23
"Green fields of New York," in: *The Irish Times*, July 19
"Group Show: Kin at Kerlin Gallery," in: *In Dublin Magazine*, vol. 25, issue 15, July/August, p. 31
"John Currin, Sean Landers and Richard Phillips," in: *Tema Celeste*, May/June, p. 148
Kojima, Yayoi: "Andrea Rosen Interview," in: *Dune Magazine*, no. 19, Spring, p. 78–81

1999 Paparoni, Demetrio: "Sean Landers," in: *Tema Celeste*, December, no. 76, p. 54–61

Rimanelli, David: "Best of the 90s: Abject Art," in: *Artforum*, December, p. 122
Grabner, Michelle: "Examining Pictures," in: *Frieze*, November/December, p. 108–109
Siegel, Katy: "Sean Landers, Andrea Rosen Gallery," in: *Artforum*, September, vol. XXXVIII, no. 1, p.167–168.
"Looking Ahead: Millennial Visions and Old Favorites," in; *The New York Times*, September 12, p. 93–96
Arning, Bill: "Sean Landers at Andrea Rosen Gallery," in: *Time Out New York*, issue 189, May 6–13, p. 75
Saltz, Jerry: "Wanting it: Sean Landers at Andrea Rosen Gallery," in: *The Village Voice*, May 25, vol. XLIV, no. 20, p. 142
Zylka, Jenni: "Trick 17 mit dem Supernichts," in: *Die Tageszeitung*, May 27, p. 21
"Sean Landers at Andrea Rosen Gallery," in: *The New Yorker*, May 24, p. 16
Collings, Matthew: *It Hurts: New York Art from Warhol to Now*, 21 Publishing Ltd, Cambridge
Dalton, Jennifer: "Sean Landers at Andrea Rosen Gallery," in: *Review*, May 15, p. 13
Ebony, David: "David Ebony's Top Ten: Sean Landers at Andrea Rosen Gallery, in: *artnet.com*
Johnson, Ken: "Sean Landers at Andrea Rosen Gallery," in: *The New York Times*, May 14, p. E37
Lutzow, Gunnar: "Total genial," in: *Berliner Morgenpost*, May 22, p. 29
Pinchbeck, Daniel: "Sean Landers," in: *The Art Newspaper*, vol. X, no. 92, May, p. 70
Riemschneider, Burkhard and Grosenick, Uta (Eds.): "Sean Landers," in: *Art at the Turn of the Millenium*, Taschen, Köln, p. 298–301
Smith, Roberta: "Conceptual Art: Over, and Yet Everywhere," in: *The New York Times* (Arts & Leisure section), April 25, p. 1, 38
Vincent, Steven: "Sean Landers at Andrea Rosen," in: *Art & Auction*, April 15, p. 74
Meyer, P.H.: "Sean Landers," in: *Juliet art magazine*, February/March, p. 42–43
Romano, Gianni: *Bloom*, Contemporary Art Garden, Milan

1998 Frank, Thomas: "Corporate Wretch," in: *Artforum*, November, p. 27
Kawachi, Taka: "Sean Landers," in: *B.T. Magazine*, November, p. 54–56
Colman, David: "Chelsea Rising," in: *Elle Décor*, August/September, p. 104, 106, 108–109
"Nove faces da arte no Paco Imperial," in: *Globo Rio Show*, July 17–19, p. 9
Kliner, Dion: "After the Disasteroid," in: *Flash Art*, Summer, p. 113–115
Lauf, Cornelia and Phillpot, Clive: *Artist/Author: Contemporary Artists' Books*, D.A.P. (Distributed Art Publishers, Inc.), New York, p. 75, 82, 88, 157
Bussel, Abby: "Play It Again," in: *Interior Design*, June, p. 138–141
Collings, Matthew: "Sean Landers," in: *Blimey! From Bohemia to Britpop: The London Artworld from Francis Bacon to Damien Hirst*, 21 Publishing Ltd, Cambridge
Bumiller, Elisabeth: "Hostess of Her Own Party, 6 Nights a Week," in: *The New York Times*, May 22, p. B2
Hogrefe, Jeffrey: "The Force behind Guggenheim's Nudie Show," in: *The New York Observer*, May 11, p. 26
"Imaginario Pop," in: *Fohla de Sao Paolo*, May 5, section 4, p. 2
Viegas, Camilla: "Mostra aponta rumos da pintura moderna," in: *O Estado de Sao Paolo*, May 4, p. D1
Fioravante, Celso: "Sobra cor e falta ruido em 'Hanging'," in: *Folha De Sao Paolo*, May 4, p. 5
"Sean Landers at Taka Ishii Gallery," in: *Gap*, May, p. 82
Aono, Naoko: "Culture Clash!," in: *GQ Magazine Japan*, April, p. 154
Matsui, Midori: "Sean Landers at Taka Ishii Gallery," in: *Studio Art Magazine*, April, p. 129
DiPietro, Monty: "The Artist as Generation Xer," in: *Asahi Evening News*, March 26, p. 11
Louie, Elaine: "The New Bohemia: Ordering: Comfortable Minimalism," in: *The New York Times*, February 26, p. F3
"The trying of Lot 61," in: *Art & Auction*, January, p. 17

1997 Heartney, Eleanor: "Sean Landers at Andrea Rosen Gallery," in: *Art in America*, December, p. 96–97
Van de Walle, Mark: "Sean Landers at Andrea Rosen Gallery," in: *Artforum*, December, p. 119–120
Arning, Bill: "a/drift," in: *World Art*, no. 13, p. 74–75
Atamian, Christopher: "Self-Centered," in: *Review*, September 15, p. 41–42
Stein, Lisa: "Art: Ten in one gallery," in: *New City*, July 24, p. 22
Boyce, Roger: "Reviews: Sean Landers at Andrea Rosen," in: *ArtNet.Com/Magazine/Reviews*, June 19, 4 pages
"Talk of the Town: Sean Landers," in: *The New Yorker*, May 26, p. 20
Schwendender, Martha: "Sean Landers," in: *Time Out New York*, May 22–29, p. 45
Smith, Roberta: "Despite Changes, a Gallery Scene That's Resilient and Vital," in: *The New York Times*, May 9, p. C1, C24
Katz-Freiman, Tami: "Going to the Dogs: Man (dressed as Dog) Bites an Art Critic! – Notes from the front-line of the struggle for attention: New York," in: *Studio Art Magazine*, Spring, p. 36–40; and in: *Art Papers*, November/December, vol. 21, issue 6, p. 78–80
Simpson, Helen: "Meat for Thought," in: *Modern Painters*, Spring, p. 94–96
Pyrgioti, Eleni: "Sean Landers," in: *Arti*, vol. 32, p. 165–166
Conrads, Martin: "Ansichten eines Clowns," in: *Zitty*, January 20, no. 2, p. 200
Fricke, Harald: "Bronx in Weimar: Kunst in Berlin jetzt: Calle, Yong, Pollmann, Brauntuch, Landers," in: *Die Tageszeitung*, January 18/19, p. 36
Horodner, Stuart and Sanders, Mark: "Warhol is...," in: *Dazed and Confused*, no. 27, p. 48–51

1996 Muller, Katrin Bettina: "Ausgelutscht – Der Amerikaner Sean Landers bei Contemporary Fine Arts," in: *Der Tagesspiegel*, December 28, p. 21
Caniglia, Julia: "Artists of the Year: The makers that mattered in 1996: Sean Landers," in: *City Pages*, December 25, vol. 18, no. 838, p. 17
Schwendener, Martha: "Catch My Drift?," in: *Time Out New York*, December 12–19, p. 40
Smith, Roberta: "Finding Art in the Artifacts of the Masses," in: *The New York Times*, December 1, p. 43, 46
Van de Walle, Mark: "Best and Worst: Music," in: *Artforum*, December, p. 53
"Special Artists' Project," in: *Dazed and Confused*, no. 16, p. 95–99
"Sean Landers," in: *DIVA*, p. 46–47
Allerholm, Milou: "'NowHere' at Louisiana Museum, Denmark," in: *Index*, November/December, p. 94–95, 137–138
Cafopoulos, Catherine: "Counting Time and Other Things," in: *Arti*, October/November/December, vol. 31, p. 224–241
Damianovic, Maia: "Il Fantastico in arte," in: *Tema Celeste*, Winter, p. 76–99
Larsen, Lars Bang: "'Toons' at Campbells Occasionally, Copenhagen," in: *Flash Art*, October, p. 75
Schreiber, Susanne: "Biographisch kodiert," in: *Handelsblatt*, July 5/6

"Genius Lessons (a monthly column by Sean Landers)," in: *Spin Magazine*, July, p. 140
"23 Künstler stellen im Hamburger Kunstverein aus: Wunderbar subjektiv," in: *Hamburger Abendblatt*, June 1/2, p. 23
Philippi, Anne: "Wunderbar: Ästhetik der Umgebung," in: *Spex*, June, no. 6
Seyfarth, Ludwig: "Mein wunderbarer Malsalon," in: *Szene Hamburg*, June, p. 88–90
"Genius Lessons (a monthly column by Sean Landers)," in: *Spin Magazine*, June, p. 140
"Pop Crossover," in: *The Village Voice*, May 28, p. 92
Lyttelton, Celia: "Sean Landers," in: *The Now Art Book*, p. 94–95, 187–188
Maloney, Martin: "Young Americans: Parts I & II," in: *Flash Art*, May/June, p. 108–109
Decter, Joshua: "Sean Landers at Regen Projects," in: *Artforum*, May, p. 108
Rubenstein, Raphael: "Visual Voices," in: *Art in America*, April, p. 94–101, 133
Auerbach, Lisa Anne: "Lush Life: Sean Landers' Intoxicating Images," in: *Los Angeles Reader*, March 15, vol. 18, no. 23, p. 17
Bartas, Magnus: "Slave to the Rhythm," in: *Index*, no. 3/4, p. 93–94
Boodro, Michael: "Dealer's Choice," in: *Vogue*, March, p. 414–419, 468
Stange, Raimar: "Wunderbar," in: *Artist Kunstmagazin*, March, p. 44–47
Fineman, Mia: "the scrawl of the wild," in: *World Art*, no. 4, p. 76–79
Hilton, Tim: "No Laughing Matter," in: *The Independent*, February 1, p. 4
Itaver, William: "A choc-and-doodle do," in: *The London Observer*, February 4
Januszczak, Waldemar: "Gnawing Questions," in: *The London Sunday Times*, February 4
Kent, Sarah: "USA-grade: Sarah Kent on 'Young Americans,'" in: *Time Out*, January 31–February 7, p. 46
Packer, William: "All chewed up over art," in: *Financial Times*, January 30
McEwen, John: "A transparent bomb, a saucepan full of napalm," in: *The Sunday Telegraph*, January 28
Dorment, Richard: "A device to blow your mind," in: *The Daily Telegraph*, January 24
Johnson, Paul: "What a load of old lard," in: *Daily Mail*, January 26
Honigsbaum, Mark: "The great white shark of art," in: *Evening Standard*, January 22

1995 Landers, Sean: "Me and My Shadow" (self-interview), in: *Manhattan File*, December, p. 54–57
Croke, Vicki: "The draw of the wild," in: *The Boston Globe*, November 25, p. 21, 26
Taylor, Robert: "Gorillas in our midst," in: *The Boston Globe*, November 16, p. 65, 71
Seward, Keith: "Logorrhea Sean Landers is [sic]," in: *Paper Magazine*, November, p. 36
Silver, Joanne: "MIT exhibit explores our kinship with 'Apes'," in: *The Boston Herald*, October 13, p. S21
"Sean Landers at Galerie Jennifer Flay," in: *Artpress*, November, p. 17
Lacanian Ink, no. 10, Fall, p. 28-29 (illustration)
Raffalli, Jean-Francois: "John Currin: FRAC Limousin - Limoges," in: *Blocnotes*, no. 10, September/October, p. 82
Jones, Ronald: "Sean Landers at Andrea Rosen Gallery," in: *Frieze*, September/October, p. 75–76
Katz-Freiman, Tami: "Sean Landers," in: *Studio Art Magazine*, no. 64, August/September
"Goings on About Town: Sean Landers at Andrea Rosen," in: *The New Yorker*, May 8, p. 20
Budney, Jen: "Sean Landers: Therapy?," in: *Flash Art*, March/April, p. 91–93
Greene, David A.: "Narcissistic Disturbance at Otis Gallery," in: *Art Issues*, March/April, p. 40
Rugoff, Ralph: "Vanity Fare," in: *LA Weekly*, February 17–23, p. 33

1994 Silverthorne, Jeanne: "On the Studio's Ruins," in: *Sculpture*, November/December, p. 26–29
Perree, Rob: "De Duivelse Kunsten van Sean Landers," in: *Kunstbeeld*, November, p. 35–37
Fricke, Harald: "Vergänglichkeit ist keine Frage des Stils," in: *Die Tageszeitung*, October 22, p. 38
Langer, Werner: "Galerien: Einkehr bei Einzelgängern," in: *Der Tagesspiegel*, October 1, p. 25
Decter, Joshua: "Stupidity as Density: American Idiot Culture," in: *Flash Art*, October, p. 72–76
Saltz, Jerry: "A Year in the Life: Topic of Painting," in: *Art in America*, October, p. 90–101
Weil, Benjamin; "Backstage," in: *Flash Art*, January/February, p.95
Young, Lucie: "Apathy in the USA," in: *The Face*, no. 70, July, p. 96–99
Cooper, Jacqueline: "Letters: To the editor," in: *Artforum*, Summer, p. 7
Kent, Sarah: "Sean Landers at White Cube," in: *Time Out*, June 1–8, no. 1241, p. 42
Ritchie, Matthew: "The World Made Flesh," in: *Flash Art*, May/June, no. 176, p. 71–72
Tager, Alisa: "Sean Landers at Regen Projects," in: *Art Issues*, May/June, p.47
Volkart, Yvonne: "Passing Through – Walcheturm Zürich," in: *Flash Art*, May/June, p. 79
De Beyerd: "Can you always believe your eyes?," in: *Haagsche Courant*, April 29
O'Grady, Lorraine: "Sean Sucks... Not: SWM," in: *Artforum*, April, p. 65–66
Avgikos, Jan: "Sean Sucks... Not: Portrait of the Artist as a Young Artist," in: *Artforum*, April, p. 67–69, 133
Hultkrans, Andrew: "Sean Sucks... Not: The Tres Boring Hours," in: *Artforum*, April, p. 62-65, 117, 119
Kandel, Susan: "Sean Landers: A 'Bad Boy' Goes Bad," in: *The Los Angeles Times*, March 22
Drohojowska-Philip, Hunter: "This 'Bad-Boy' Artist Has Lots of Thoughts on Love," in: *The Los Angeles Times* (Los Angeles edition), March 18, p. F1, F24 and Quote of the Day, p. F1
Drohojowska-Philip, Hunter: "Not Bad, Just Misunderstood," in: *The Los Angeles Times* (Washington edition), March 18, p. B8–9
Choon, Angela: "Desire for Identity: Artists build images for themselves," in: *Art and Antiques*, March, p. 20
Lewis, Jim: "The Writings on the Wall," in: *Harper's Bazaar*, March, p. 182–186
Pacheco, Patrick: "America's Top 100 Collectors," in: *Art and Antiques*, March, p. 47–52, 60–63, 72–76, 80–84, 92–97, 104–105
Billeter, Fritz: "Schnörkel und Schleifchen," in: *Tages-Anzeiger*, February 28
Smith, Roberta: "Group Shows of Every Kind, Even When the Show Itself Is an Art Form," in: *The New York Times*, February 25, p. C22
Mack, Gerhard: "Hinter der Bühne lauert die reale Welt," in: *Cash*, no. 6, February 11, p. 53

"Passing Through," in: *Züritipp*, January 21, 1994
Cameron, Dan: "Ode to discernment," in: *Frieze*, January/February, p. 36–40
Clewing, Ulrich: "Grandioser Flop," in: *Zitty*, no. 21, p. 57
Lewis, Jim: "Pragmatics," in: *Art Issues*, January/February, p. 12–15
Princenthal, Nancy: "Sean Landers," in: *The Print Collector's Newsletter*, January/February, vol. XXIV, no. 6, p. 230
"Sean Landers cartoons," in: *Nummer*, January, p. 101–105
"Remissionem Peccatorum," in: *New Observations*, no. 103, p. 4

1993 Smith, Roberta: "Sean Landers at Andrea Rosen Gallery: Art as its maker's mirror," in: *The New York Times*, November 26, p. C29
Levin, Kim: "Voice Choices: Sean Landers at Andrea Rosen Gallery," in: *The Village Voice*, November 16, p. 77
"Goings On About Town: 'Sean Landers at Andrea Rosen," in: *The New Yorker*, November 15, p. 28
Gillick, Liam: "A Guide to Video Conferencing Systems and the Role of the Building Worker in Relation to the Contemporary Art Exhibition (Backstage)," in: *Documents*, October, p. 36–37
Heartney, Eleanor: "Galleries: The Emerging Generation – New York, The Art of Survival," in: *Art Press*. October, no. 184, p. 24–28; E7–E10
Hixson, Kathryn: "Trouble in Paradise," in: *New Art Examiner*, October, p. 28–32
Müller, Silke: "Backstage," in: *Kunstforum*, October, p. 389–391
Salvioni, Daniela: "Flash Art News: Aperto – A Stroll Through the Emergency," in: *Flash Art*, October, p. 67–68
Gardner, Belinda: "Da gerät einiges ins Wanken," in: *Hamburger Rundschau*, September 16, p. 10–11
Brenken, Erika: "Jenseits der Gemütlichkeit," in: *Rheinische Post*, September 15, p.11
Gopnik, Adam: "The Art World: Death in Venice," in: *The New Yorker*, August 2, p. 66–73
Ardenne, Paul: "Sean Landers at Galerie Jennifer Flay," in: *Art Press*, July/August, no. 182
"La Biennale di Venezia," in: *B.T.: Monthly Art Magazine*, p. 68
"What Asher Edelman Buys," in: *The ARTnewsletter*, July 6, p.3
Sugiura, Kunie: "Sean Landers," in: *B.T.: Monthly Art Magazine*, July, vol. 45, no. 672, p. 40–41
"La Biennale de Venise," in: *Galeries Magazine*, Summer, p. 69–75
Bourriaud, Nicolas: "Curator's Statement: Nicolas Bourriaud: Standards," in: *Flash Art Daily*, June 10, p. 8
Jacques, Alison Sarah: "Sean Landers," in: *Flash Art Daily*, June 10, p. 7
Landers, Sean: "Dear Texte zur Kunst," in: *Texte zur Kunst*, June, p. 105–107
Minetti, Maria Giulia: "E l'arte riparte dai punti cardinali," in: *L'Uomo Vogue*, June, p. 100
"Sean Landers at Jennifer Flay," in: *Pariscope: une semaine de Paris*, May 5–11, p. 170
Meckseper, Josephine: "Sean Landers interviewed by Josephine Meckseper," in: *241*, May, p. 20–24
Risaliti, Sergio: "Flash Art News: I, Myself and Others – Magasin, Grenoble," in: *Flash Art*, May, p. 123
"Goings on about town: 'Confessional' at Liz Koury Gallery," in: *The New Yorker*, March 8

1992 Kruger, Barbara: "A vous et à moi: 'I, Myself and Others' au Magasin, Grenoble," in: *Le Monde* (Rhone-Alpes), October 2, p. 25
Weiss, Marion Wolberg: "Review: Emerging Artists at the Vered," in: *Dan's Papers*, September 18
Slivka, Rose C. S.: "Collector's Choice," in: *East Hampton Star*, September 17
Braff, Phyllis: "7 Artists With Bright Futures," in: *The New York Times* (Long Island section), September 13
Lieberman, Rhonda: "The Loser Thing," in: *Artforum*, September, p. 78–82
Meyer, Peter S.: "Bizart, Copenhagen," in: *Nordic Art Review*, September
Michelsen, Anders: "Paradise Europe, Bizart, Copenhagen," in: *Art & Text*, September
Adams, Brooks: "Sean Landers at Andrea Rosen Gallery," in: *Art in America*, July, p. 105
Arning, Bill: "The Anti-Masculine (Overlapping but not corresponding to the feminine)," essay for the group exhibition at Kim Light Gallery, New York
Larson, Kay: "Art on Site: Twenty-five Years in Two Hours," in: *Atelier*, July, p. 64–83
"News: Copenhagen – Paradise Europe," in: *Flash Art*, Summer, p. 132
Hansen, Malene Vest: "Europas paradis," in: *Politiken*, June 11
Kerte, Jens: "Kunst pa reklame-tavlerne," in: *Politiken*, June 3
Sugiura, Kunie: "From New York," in: *B.T.: Monthly Art Magazine*, June, vol. 44, no. 655, p. 163
Weil, Benjamin: "Spotlight: Sean Landers," in: *Flash Art*, May/June, p. 110
Rimanelli, David: "Sean Landers at Andrea Rosen Gallery," in: *Artforum*, May, p. 116
Kuoni, Carin: "New York: Ein Heer von Versagern," in: *Kunst-Bulletin*, April, no. 4, p. 58–59
Larson, Kay: "Darkness Visible," in: *New York Magazine*, March 16, p. 79–80
"Goings on about town: Sean Landers," in: *The New Yorker*, March 9, p. 12–13
Levin, Kim: "Choices," in: *The Village Voice*, March 10, p. 73
Nesbitt, Lois: "The Young, The Wild and The Wicked," in: *Elle Magazine*, March, p. 130–132
Smith, Roberta: "Examining a Multi-Media Personality," in: *The New York Times*, February 21, p. 22
"Project for Publicsfear," in: *Publicsfear*, vol. 1, no. 1, p. 35–46

1991 Hixson, Kathryn: "Videos and a Film....," in: *Flash Art*, October, p. 172
Hagen, Charles: "An epistolary Motif," in: *The New York Times*, August 23
Levin, Kim: "Choices," in: *The Village Voice*, August 20
Bravin, Karin: "SOHO: Untitled 92," in: *New York Connection*, vol. 40, p. 44–48
Kozik, K.K.: "'Lyric' at White Columns," in: *Cover*, May
Kuoni, Carin: "Work in Progress. Work? Eine Ausstellung – oder ein Zustand in New York," in: *Kunst-Bulletin*, April, no.4, p. 51–53
Jolles, Claudia: "Notizen eines Glücklosen," in: *ZüriWoche*, March 28
Lieberman, Rhonda: "Sean Landers," in: *Flash Art*, March/April, p. 142
Miller, John: "Sean Landers," in: *Texte zur Kunst*, Spring issue, p. 179–180
Nesbitt, Lois: "Sean Landers," in: *Artforum*, March, p. 129–130
Decter, Joshua: "Work? Work in Progress?," in: *Arts*, March, p. 105
Decter, Joshua: "Sean Landers," in: *Arts*, February
Holmqvist, Karl: "Scatter Pieces," in: *Material*, no. 3, p. 7–10
Rosenberg, Barry A. and Nathanson, Carol: *Words & #'s*, Wright State University, Dayton, Ohio

1990 Hess, Elizabeth: "Caution: Artists Working," in: *The Village Voice*, December 18
Gilbert, Elizabeth: "It's Not Done Yet," in: *Downtown Express*, December 12
"Goings on About Town: 'Sean Landers at Postmasters,'" in: *The New Yorker*, December 10
Smith, Roberta, "Echoes of the 60s and 70s. Among the Young and Little Known," in: *The New York Times*, November 30
Decter, Joshua: "Sean Landers," in: *Arts*, April
Lewis, James: "Sean Landers," in: *Artforum*, April
Andersen, Michael: "Sean Landers," in: *Contemporanea*, March, p. 69–79
Mahoney, Robert: "Sean Landers," in: *Art Today*, vol. 2, no. 1

1989 Mahoney, Robert: "New York in Review (Outer Limits)," in: *Arts*, November
Anderson, Alexandra: "The Next Generation," in: *Smart*, September/October
Iverem, Esther: "At City Parks, Spring is in the Art," in: *New York Newsday*, May 12, p. 1, 16–17

1988 Mahoney, Robert: "New York in Review (Art on the Beach)," in: *Arts Magazine*, November
Brenson, Michael: "Outdoor Works Echo Struggles of Life in the City (Art on the Beach)," in: *The New York Times*, July 15, p. C28

1986 Brenson, Michael: "A Bountiful Year in Outdoor Sculpture, Glimpses of a New Sensibility (South Beach III)," in: *The New York Times*, July 18